ESSAYS IN POLITICAL THEORY

Presented to George H. Sabine

Geo. H. Sabine

Essays in
Political Theory

Presented to George H. Sabine

EDITED BY

Milton R. Konvitz

Arthur E. Murphy

CORNELL UNIVERSITY PRESS

ITHACA, NEW YORK, 1948

Cornell University Press

London: Geoffrey Cumberlege

Oxford University Press

PRINTED IN THE UNITED STATES OF AMERICA BY THE

VAIL-BALLOU PRESS, INC., BINGHAMTON, NEW YORK

11-22-83
kmm

Preface

IN DISCUSSING the danger to civilization in the lag of the social sciences behind the physical, Raymond B. Fosdick, President of the Rockefeller Foundation, has pointed out that recent years have afforded proof that "the objective investigation of problems of human relations can produce results of incalculable practical value, when properly trained research workers, imbued with scientific detachment and integrity, are given an opportunity to carry on their activities with adequate resources." As part of this proof Mr. Fosdick cited the work of George H. Sabine in political philosophy (article in the *New York Times Magazine*, November 24, 1946).

On the occasion of the retirement of Professor Sabine from teaching at Cornell University, at the end of forty-one years as a teacher successively at Stanford, University of Missouri, Ohio State University, and Cornell (including four years as Dean of the Graduate School and three years as Vice President at Cornell), a group of colleagues and former students have considered it appropriate to express their intellectual indebtedness to him by preparing this *Festschrift*. The contributors to this volume are acting in a representative capacity, for the influence of Professor Sabine on students and colleagues has been widespread and deep; but for space limitations, many more contributions could be published.

In his essay on Carl Becker, Professor Sabine has stated that there was in Becker "the sense that he was dealing with life itself and yet with the detachment that gives to all purely intellectual activity something of the nature of play." All who have had the privilege of close association with Professor Sabine will detect in this characterization unconscious self-portraiture; for Professor Sabine has always taken it as his duty as a scholar "to guide men," as Emerson said, "by showing them facts amidst appearances," and to do so without attachment to the facts. The "scientific detachment and integrity" that Mr. Fosdick found in the published writings of Professor Sabine, his colleagues and students found even more in the seminar and conference room. Some of the papers in this *Festschrift* are concerned directly with Professor Sabine's philosophy. But his influence has been felt by all the contributors and by a generation of his students and friends, on whose behalf this tribute to a revered teacher is made.

THE EDITORS

Cornell University
Ithaca, New York
December 9, 1947

Acknowledgments

THE KINDNESS of the following publishers in granting permission to quote from their publications as listed is appreciated: Oxford University Press, *Poems,* by Gerard Manley Hopkins; J. M. Dent & Sons, Ltd., *The Laws of Plato,* translated by A. E. Taylor; Harvard University Press, Plato's *Euthyphro, Apology, Crito, Phaedo, and Phaedrus,* translated by H. N. Fowler, in the Loeb Classical Library edition, and Hesiod's *The Homeric Hymns and Homerica,* translated by H. G. Evelyn-White, in the Loeb Classical Library edition; The Macmillan Company, *The Meeting of East and West,* by F. S. C. Northrop; and Henry Holt and Company, Inc., *A History of Political Theory,* by George H. Sabine.

Contents

CONTENTS

viii

ESSAYS IN POLITICAL THEORY

Cleisthenes and the Development of the

Theory of Democracy at Athens

J. A. O. LARSEN

THE GREEK word *demokratia* is the name of a form of government—government by the people. It is the purpose of this paper to try to determine when the word was first adopted and to what particular form of government it was applied. It was developed in the city-state and, as such, was the government of a small community with a limited citizen body excluding slaves and usually foreign residents. To be sure, there were degrees even in this exclusiveness but, and this is more important, there were great differences in the internal structure of states that claimed to be democratic. Some elected officials by vote, others by lot; some opened offices to all, others limited them to people with property. In the more extreme democracies with numerous officials, huge juries, and pay for participation in the government, there was an intensity of political activity and an extent of participation in government by the average citizen unheard of today. Is this democracy or have more conservative governments an equal right to the name?

Neither the ancients nor the moderns are in agreement on the point. In attempting to answer the question it is necessary to center our attention on Athens, the only state for which we have adequate evidence. The practical question then becomes whether Solon or some later statesman was regarded as the founder of democracy. Statements to the effect that Solon was so regarded have been made by several scholars.[1] Since

---

[1] G. Busolt, *Griechische Staatskunde* (1920–1926; Vol. II [i.e., pp. 633 ff.] ed. by H. Swoboda), p. 858; Werner Jaeger, *Paideia*, I (Eng. ed., 1939), 223; J. Penrose

Periclean democracy cannot be excluded, this would include a considerable variety in forms of government. The theory is plausible enough in itself. Democracy is a name so easily coined that it would be understood the first time it was used. It would thus be natural that the earliest group that felt itself championing the government of the people should adopt this name, and that the meaning of the name should continue to evolve with the progressive liberalization of the government. It would also be natural enough for such a group to claim a predecessor as the founder of democracy, and Solon would be a not unlikely candidate for such a position. The only trouble is that the weight of the evidence is against the conclusion. In opposition to it, this paper will attempt to show that the name was adopted in the fifth century and that the democrats of that century looked upon Cleisthenes as the founder of democracy. This still leaves some time for development, but it limits the period and practically means that the extreme democracy of the Periclean age has a special right to the name. The origin of the name will be discussed first and next the evidence for the position of Solon and Cleisthenes in democratic thought.

It will be necessary to consider a number of Greek words. Fortunately many, such as monarchy, oligarchy, democracy, and aristocracy, are almost the same in English as in Greek. In such cases the English word will frequently be used and discussed as though it were Greek. Where transliteration in italics is used, the Attic form will be cited even for Herodotus, who wrote in Ionic, e.g., *monarchia* not *mounarchie*. In checking the usage of various authors dictionaries and indexes have proved very helpful.[2]

Apparently the earliest examples of the word democracy are to be found in Herodotus, Pseudo-Xenophon,[3] and Aristophanes. Of these,

---

Harland in *The Greek Political Experience: Studies in Honor of William Kelly Prentice* (Princeton, 1941), p. 27; Robert Cohen, *Athènes, une démocratie de sa naissance à sa mort* (Paris, 1936), p. 58.

[2] In addition to the Liddell-Scott-Jones *Greek-English Lexicon* the following works have proved particularly useful: M. C. Lane, *Index to the Fragments of the Greek Elegiac and Iambic Poets* (Cornell University, 1908); J. Enoch Powell, *A Lexicon to Herodotus* (Cambridge, 1938), cited as "Powell"; C. D. Buck and W. Peterson, *A Reverse Index of Greek Nouns and Adjectives* (Chicago, 1944), cited as "Buck."

[3] The reference is to the *Constitution of the Athenians* preserved among the works of Xenophon but now recognized as the work of an earlier author, who probably wrote during the first half of the Peloponnesian War. He frequently has been dubbed the "Old Oligarch."

2

only Herodotus, the oldest of the three, will require any detailed attention. Though the other two do not use the word so very often, it is clear that both the name and the institution are well known. Pseudo-Xenophon delivers a bitter attack on democracy but forgives the *demos* itself for democracy since anyone is to be pardoned for doing good to himself.[4] Here democracy is used with the connotation often given it by enemies, the rule of the lower classes in their own interest. Aristophanes not only makes several statements about democracy but can apostrophize it.[5] In Thucydides, of course, such expressions as to establish democracy, change the government to democracy, and overthrow democracy are common.[6] For Herodotus, Powell lists two examples of the noun and two of the related verb. It will be necessary to study these examples, the usage of some other words connected with forms of government, and a debate on the three forms of government, democracy, oligarchy, and monarchy, which Herodotus attributes to a group of Persian nobles. This debate cannot possibly be historical as given, and the word democracy does not occur in it. Nevertheless, it is extremely important as representing Greek political thought relatively early in the fifth century.

Herodotus' use of the word can be surveyed rapidly. In the account of the debate among the Greek tyrants guarding the bridge over the Danube for Darius during his Scythian expedition, Miltiades is reported to have argued for destroying the bridge, while Histiaeus of Miletus countered with the argument that each of them owed his position as tyrant to Darius and, if the power of the latter was broken, would be unable to maintain himself; every city preferred to be governed democratically, rather than tyrannically.[7] In 492 Mardonius is reported to have dismissed the tyrants of the Ionians and to have established democracies in their cities. This, Herodotus remarks, will be a surprise to those who do not believe that Otanes expressed the opinion that the Persians ought to be governed democratically.[8] Thus we have here in the same passage both the noun and the verb. The

---

[4] Ps.-Xen. 2. 20.

[5] *Acharnians* 618, *Birds* 1570; cf. *Acharnians* 642, *Frogs* 952, *Ecclesiazusae* 945, *Plutus* 949.

[6] E.g., i. 115. 3; iv. 76. 2; viii. 47. 2, 63. 3, 75. 2, 90. 1.

[7] Herod. iv. 137. 2.

[8] Herod. vi. 43. 3.

noun is not abstract but is used concretely in the plural referring to several democracies. Otanes is the spokesman of democracy in the debate already mentioned. The insistence that this debate is historical is a bit surprising, but more of that later. Finally, at the end of the delightful story of the wooing of Agariste, the daughter of Cleisthenes the tyrant of Sicyon, Herodotus identifies the son of Agariste and the successful suitor, Megacles, as the Cleisthenes who organized the tribes and established democracy at Athens.[9]

The language of these passages is that of Herodotus and, even when he claims to report a debate, cannot be taken as evidence for the usage of the time of the incident reported. Though, as already remarked, democracy is a word which would be understood the first time it was used, it seems safe to conclude from Herodotus that he did not invent the word. This is particularly true of the reference to Cleisthenes, which takes for granted that he is well known as the founder of democracy, and thus proves that he was so regarded by the contemporaries of Pericles and Herodotus.

The debate between the Persian nobles,[10] in contrast to the passages discussed, may throw light on the thought and language of an earlier period. Herodotus undoubtedly derived it from some predecessor. The very fact that he includes it at all, shows that the Greeks had begun their long controversy concerning the relative merits of the three forms of government. It is self-evident that the arguments recorded are arguments which already had been used by others. It is tempting to go farther and conjecture that a predecessor had combined them in a single work.[11] If Herodotus actually believed, as he says, that the debate took place,[12] then he must have taken it from an earlier work which described such a debate between Persian nobles. This suggests derivation from an early Ionic historian, and, though it is hard to believe that Herodotus was quite so naïve, an Ionic source is possible.

A brief summary of the debate will be given. In this an effort will be made to use the same type of noun as Herodotus does and to render *monarchos* by "monarch" and the like instead of speaking loosely about

---

[9] Herod. vi. 131. 1.
[10] Herod. iii. 80–82.
[11] For earlier theories see W. W. How and J. Wells, *A Commentary on Herodotus* (Oxford, 1912) on iii. 80.
[12] iii. 80. 1; vi. 43. 3.

monarchy. Similarly *plethos* will be rendered "mass" and *demos,* "people."

Otanes opens the debate urging that the management of affairs be entrusted to the Persians as a whole. He begins by saying that no one should be monarch and devotes most of his speech to an attack on monarchy—obviously an attack aimed at Greek tyranny rather than Persian kingship. In fact, the monarch is once referred to as tyrant. Then, when he comes to the positive side of his argument, the speaker refers to the mass as ruling and states that it has the fairest of all names, *isonomia,* or equality.[13] Democracy is not mentioned by name, but a later cross reference [14] makes it clear that Herodotus considers Otanes the spokesman of democracy. Next Megabyzus speaks in favor of entrusting the government to an oligarchy. He begins by stating his agreement with what Otanes has said against tyranny but disapproving of turning the power over to the mass. "For nothing is more stupid or insolent than a useless mob. That men should seek to flee from the insolence of a tyrant and fall under the insolence of an unbridled people is not at all to be endured." Then, after branding the incompetence of the mob, the speaker advocates selecting a group of the best men and entrusting power to them. Darius, the future king, speaks last. He expresses agreement with what Megabyzus has said against the mass but not with what he has said about oligarchy. He opens his own argument with the statement that with three kinds of rulers or ruling bodies available, if, for argument's sake, we grant that each of the three is the best of its kind, the best people, the best oligarchy, and the best monarch, then the last far outranks the others. Under an oligarchy, with many practicing virtues and competing in public service, quarrels are engendered leading to strife and ultimately to monarchy—another proof that this form of government is best. When the people rules, there is bound to be corruption, but the corrupt put their heads together and avoid quarrels. This goes on until a leader of the people appears and

---

[13] There is still disagreement concerning the etymology of ἰσονομία and on the question whether it means "equality" in general or specifically "equality before the law." The second part of the compound is derived from a root meaning to "distribute or divide," but the question is whether it is formed directly from some noun with this primary meaning or from the later noun νόμος meaning "law." See particularly Victor Ehrenberg, "Isonomia," in Pauly-Wissowa, *Real-Encyclopädie,* Supplementband VII, 293–301.

[14] Herod. vi. 43. 3.

puts an end to corruption. As a result he is admired by the people and becomes a monarch or is regarded as a monarch,[15] and thus he too demonstrates that monarchy is best.

Of the many observations that can be made concerning this debate three are of special importance for the present study. In the first place, the advocate of democracy does not use this word and applies no name to the form of government he favors except *isonomia*.[16] This suggests that *isonomia* is an earlier name for what was later called democracy and that Herodotus' source belongs to the period when this was the preferred term.

In the second place, tyranny and monarchy are noticeably prominent and, in fact, monopolize more than half of the debate. To be sure, the speech advocating democracy is about as long as the one advocating monarchy, but the greater part of it is devoted to an attack on tyranny. So far as time is concerned, this prominence of one-man rule supports the conclusion suggested by the use of *isonomia*. It harks back to a time when one-man rule was the chief issue in politics and political debates. For the early part of this period we have no contemporary prose records, but the controversy is reflected in the fragments of the poetry of the time. Thus Alcaeus reflects the strife and controversy of that period at Mytilene in which tyrant followed tyrant until Pittacus

---

[15] The usual interpretation is that he actually is made monarch but the meaning may be merely that he *de facto* has the dignity and power of a king. To put it concretely, it is uncertain whether the author has a Peisistratus or a Pericles in mind. Cf. the judgment of Thucydides (ii. 65. 9) on Pericles that the government was in name a democracy but in fact rule by the first citizens.

[16] This statement may be questioned by some who may hold that *demos* in certain cases means democracy. This meaning is recognized by Liddell-Scott-Jones, and Powell lists three examples of it in the debate, namely, iii. 81. 3, 82. 1 and 5. This interpretation is clearly wrong for two of the three examples. The mistake is due to the fact that Greek uses concrete expressions much more frequently than we do. This often is—and often must be—obscured in translations, but this should not be carried over into lexicons. In 82. 1, in the reference to the three forms of government, we have δήμου τε ἀρίστου καὶ ὀλιγαρχίης καὶ μουνάρχου. The key to the meaning is the use of monarch and not monarchy. Thus "oligarchy" here must mean the group of ruling men rather than the form of government, and *demos*, too, must refer to the ruler, that is, the people as the ruling body. The meaning is even more clear in 82. 5 where Darius asks whether the freedom of the Persians was "a gift of the people or of an oligarchy or of a monarch" (Macaulay's translation). The interpretation "democracy" can be defended for 81. 3, where Megabyzus wishes that those hostile to the Persians may make use of democracy, but even here I believe that δήμῳ . . . χράσθων means "let them make use of the demos (as ruler)."

6

was chosen with dictatorial powers to end the strife.[17] At Athens Solon had occasion both to answer the criticism of those who took him to task for failing to establish himself as a tyrant and to warn his fellow citizens of the coming tyranny of Peisistratus.[18] Thus the period goes back as far as to Alcaeus and Solon. It must have continued to the Persian War and probably a little beyond. In 492 Mardonius is said to have substituted democracies for tyranny in the cities of Ionia, and yet as late as 490, the year of Marathon, the Persians brought Hippias along to Greece, obviously with the intention of restoring him as tyrant at Athens. Herodotus' source is likely to be connected with the latter part of this period rather than the earlier.

In the third place, some of the arguments used in the debate repeat thoughts current about the time of the Persian War. In favor of government by the mass it is stated that it fills offices by lot, holds offices subject to account, and submits all plans to the general assembly. The reference to the use of lot would be natural for Athens any time after 487 B.C., when lot was introduced for the selection of archons. However, it is the accountability of magistrates that is specially emphasized by contrast with the irresponsibility of monarch or tyrant. The same contrast between the accountability of magistrates and the irresponsibility of monarchs appears in Aeschylus' *Persians,* performed in 472 B.C., in which Atossa remarks about her son that, even if he meets with calamity, he is not subject to account to the city but is still lord over the land. The idea is repeated in *Prometheus Bound* when Oceanus advises Prometheus not to kick against the pricks but to recognize that a harsh monarch not subject to account is ruling.[19] Thus the debate seems to point back to the time of the Persian War or soon after when the incipient democracy probably did not yet use that name but called itself *isonomia.*

Other evidence tends to confirm the conclusion that *isonomia* preceded democracy as the name for a form of government. Herodotus himself practically uses the two words as synonyms. After the death of Polycrates (ca. 525 B.C.), Maeandrius is reported to have offered to establish *isonomia* at Samos. Again, when Aristagoras began the Ionian

---

[17] Alcaeus, Frags. 39 and 87 and *passim* in E. Diehl, *Anthologia lyrica Graeca,* I ².
[18] Solon, Frags. 23 and 10 in Diehl, I².
[19] Aeschylus, *Persians* 213–14; *Prometheus Bound* 323–24.

Revolt, his first act is said to have been to renounce tyranny and establish *isonomia* at Miletus. However, when Mardonius a few years later made a similar change in the government of Ionic cities, he is reported to have deposed the tyrants and to have established democracies.[20] It is probably mere chance that causes Herodotus to use *isonomia* in his account of the two earlier events and *demokratia* in that of the last of the three. What is important is that the word was used before Herodotus. Probably the earliest example is the use of the adjective applied to Athens in two versions of a drinking song honoring the tyrannicides, Harmodius and Aristogeiton, who thus are represented as establishing *isonomia* in the city.[21] The song obviously belongs to the period after 510 B.C., when Hippias was expelled from Athens. To about the same period belongs the use of the noun by the physician, Alcmaeon of Croton, who defines health as "equality (*isonomia*) of the powers." [22] Since he goes on and describes the monarchy of one power as a cause of illness, it is clear that he has borrowed the entire figure from political thought.[23] One may even venture farther and say that the meaning given to the word in the political thought on which Alcmaeon drew was that of an equality or balance of elements within the state. By this time *isonomia* must have been a well-known term and the contrast between it and monarchy (or tyranny) a commonplace. The contrast is present also in the drinking song in which the government set up after the expulsion of the tyrant is *isonomia*. This is probably the approximate time of the origin of the name. Since the equality implied might be either absolute or proportional, there is no particular reason why the word could not have been used by Solon, but it is unlikely that it was. In a poem in which he expresses the idea of equality before the law, his vocabulary is different [24] and he speaks of similarity rather than equality. Hence, it is likely that the word originated in connection with the expulsion of the tyrant in 510. It may have been used some time before that date by the opponents of tyranny or it

---

[20] Herod. iii. 142. 3; v. 37. 2; vi. 43. 3.

[21] "Scolia anonyma," Nos. 10 and 13 in Diehl, II, 184 f.

[22] Alcmaeon, Frag. 4 in H. Diels, *Die Fragmente der Vorsokratiker,* 5th ed. by W. Kranz (Berlin, 1934–38); cf. G. Vlastos, *Class. Phil.,* XLII (1947), 156 f.

[23] V. Ehrenberg, *Aspects of the Ancient World* (New York, 1946), pp. 88 ff.

[24] Frag. 24. 18–20. In another poem he rejects *isomoivia* (equality of shares) while opposing the demand for redistribution of the land (Frag. 23. 21).

8

may have been adopted after the expulsion as a name for the new form of government. Whether the word was used first by the partisans of Cleisthenes or by his opponents is uncertain, though, as Ehrenberg has pointed out, the drinking song obviously originated in aristocratic circles. Whatever the origin of the term, it was soon appropriated by the popular party which, though it probably never had a complete monopoly on it,[25] employed it as a watchword until it was replaced by democracy.

What is the particular point on which *isonomia* is contrasted with tyranny? If this question can be answered at all, it will have to be done by an examination of the manner in which the word itself is used. *Isonomia* might refer to an equality or balance between several elements in society, that is, a balanced state, or to an equal share in the state or government, or to equality before the law in the sense that no one is above the law. This meaning—on the face of it the least likely—seems to be the one that was most emphasized in the period after the overthrow of the tyrants and that prevailed when *isonomia* was used as a popular watchword. In other words, the same idea was expressed by *isonomia* and in the emphasis on the contrast between the irresponsible tyrant and the responsibility of the republican magistrates, though this probably was neither the earliest nor the only meaning connected with it.

Several passages in which *isonomia* occurs teach us little concerning the meaning of the word except insofar as they indicate the contrast between it and tyranny. This is true of the drinking song honoring Harmodius and Aristogeiton and of the reports in Herodotus concerning the offer of *isonomia* by Maeandrius to the Samians and the establishment of *isonomia* at Miletus by Aristagoras. More is to be learned from Alcmaeon's use of the word. He contrasts an equality of powers with the monarchy of one power and makes health a balance of qualities. Clearly, in the political thought from which Alcmaeon borrows, *isonomia* meant a balanced state. Since the source of our evidence is a Pythagorean from Croton in Italy, we cannot assert for sure that the idea prevailed in contemporary Athens. Yet the ideal would be natural enough for those who favored a Solonian type of government and may well have been adopted by some of the more conservative opponents of tyranny,

---

[25] The related adjective is applied to oligarchy in Thuc. iii. 62. 3.

9

the forerunners of the moderate oligarchs of the fifth and fourth centuries. Nevertheless, it seems to have been much less widespread in the early fifth century than the emphasis on responsible government.

This emphasis on the responsibility of magistrates is seen clearly in the speech for popular government in the debate of the Persian nobles. This points out that monarchy can do what it wishes without being held to account. Even the best man, if placed in this position, degenerates and becomes guilty of excesses. Contrast the following: "The mass as ruler, in the first place, has the fairest name of all, *isonomia;* in the second place, it does none of those things which a monarch does. It fills offices by lot, it holds office subject to rendering account, and it submits all policies to the general assembly." Here there really is not merely one but three points on which the responsibility of *isonomia* is contrasted with the irresponsibility of monarchy: 1. A monarch can arbitrarily put into power whom he wishes; under *isonomia,* no one can select magistrates arbitrarily, but they are chosen by lot. 2. A monarch cannot be held to account; under *isonomia,* magistrates must give account of their stewardship. 3. A monarch can determine policies arbitrarily; under *isonomia,* no individual or small group of individuals can do this, but policies are subject to action by the general assembly open to all voters.

The same contrast between responsible and arbitrary government is found in Thucydides when *isonomia* is compared with *dynasteia,* the latter term meaning practically the same as tyranny except insofar as it means arbitrary rule by a small group of men instead of a single individual. The contrast probably is clearest in a passage in which the related adjective is applied to oligarchy and, in my opinion, also to democracy. The Thebans excuse their conduct during the Persian War on the ground that their city was ruled neither by an oligarchy under the principle of *isonomia* nor by a democracy, but a *dynasteia* of a few men held power—a form of government which is most fully opposed to law and to the rule of moderation and is closest to the rule of a tyrant.[26] The contrast between the two appears again in the account of the march of Brasidas through Thessaly. Since the majority of the Thessalians were friendly to the Athenians, he would never have been able to cross the country if it had not been the custom of the Thes-

---

[26] Thuc. iii. 62. 3; for the meaning of *dynasteia* cf. vi, 38. 3 and 89. 4.

salians to have a *dynasteia* rather than an *isonomia* as their form of government.[27] Here *dynasteia* refers to government by a small group that can ignore the will of the majority, though *isonomia* may also imply an equal share in government for every citizen. If all had shared in determining the policies of the state, Brasidas would not have been permitted to cross. The idea of equality seems even clearer when political equality of the mass is used as a watchword in civil strife and when, on another occasion, a democratic leader addressing young oligarchs remarks: "And so you would rather not be on an equality with the many?" [28] In the last passage, however, in addition to equality, the idea of irresponsibility or disregard of law is also present, for the young men addressed wish to hold office illegally.

Thus, though other ideas too are present, the evidence of Thucydides supports the conclusion that the concepts of responsibility and accountability were closely associated with *isonomia* and contrasted with the irresponsibility of the tyrant. However, in order to realize the importance of these ideas in Greek thought, at least from Aeschylus to Aristotle, it is necessary to remember that they can be used without any mention of *isonomia*, particularly by referring to the irresponsibility of tyrant or monarch. Two such references in Aeschylus have already been noticed. Both Aeschylus and Herodotus—Aeschylus in these two passages and Herodotus in the debate on the forms of government—use adjectives which imply the Athenian procedure known as *euthyna*. Thus the very language used implies a contrast with the manner in which republican magistrates were regularly held to account at the end of their terms of office. The same contrast is implied in Aristotle's definition of a species of tyranny par excellence as the monarchy which rules, without being subject to account, over equals and betters in the interest of the ruler and not of the ruled.[29] To be sure, the argument from irresponsibility and accountability was one which could, and was, turned against democracy, for, though all magistrates were held to account, the people itself was not. This began to be pointed out before the end of the fifth century. In the *Wasps* of Aristophanes produced in 422 a speaker bragging of what the dicasts can do concludes: "And this

[27] Thuc. iv. 78. 2–3.
[28] Thuc. iii. 82. 8; vi. 38. 5.
[29] *Politics* 1295a 17–22.

we do without being subject to account. None of the other magistrates does"—that is, does act without being subject to *euthyna*. Thucydides, too, represents a speaker addressing the Athenian assembly as saying that advice given in the assembly is subject to account, the hearers are not.[30] These passages seem to suggest that the people, the *demos,* is the tyrant who acts arbitrarily and cannot be held to account, but, though the argument is here turned against democracy, it is the same old argument.

It is now time to turn to the position of Solon and Cleisthenes in Greek democratic thought. To begin with Solon, as already noted, several modern scholars have asserted that he was regarded as the founder of democracy. This is, undoubtedly, in part because it seems natural for such a term to be applied first to a more conservative form of government and then later to a more extreme democracy. In fact, Aristotle states that there was such a development in the use of names.[31] Moreover, Isocrates in one speech calls Solon the founder of democracy, and Aristotle tells us that some think he was a good lawgiver and established the ancestral or old-fashioned democracy.[32] Moreover it is easy to be misled by the adjective *demotikos,* frequently translated "democratic," and so to see more evidence than there is. This adjective can be applied to an act or policy that favors the people or the lower classes without in any way implying that a democratic form of government is involved. Thus a sentence in Aristotle's *Constitution of the Athenians* has been translated: "There are three points in the constitution of Solon which appear to be its most democratic features." [33] This merely means that the three points appear to be the features most favorable to the people or the lower classes.

Actually the evidence indicating that the Greeks regarded Solon as the founder of democracy is weak and late. What little evidence we have from the fifth century favors Cleisthenes. Of those bearing witness to Solon, Isocrates in two other speeches gives the honors to

---

[30] Aristophanes, *Wasps* 587; Thuc. iii. 43. 4.

[31] *Politics* 1297b 24; cf. 1273b 35–1274a 21.

[32] Isocrates, *Areopagiticus* 16; Arist., *Pol.* 1273b 35. These are specific statements. On the other hand, when the orator Aeschines (*Against Ctesiphon* 257) speaks of Solon as "adorning democracy with excellent laws," the language is too rhetorical and loose to have much value as evidence except for the high regard in which Solon's laws were held.

[33] 9. 1, tr. by F. G. Kenyon.

Cleisthenes, while Aristotle does not say that he himself considered Solon the founder of ancestral democracy but that "some" do and points out that the government they had in mind was a mixed or balanced constitution. Thereby he practically tells us that those who made these claims for Solon were those who wished to modify the later democracy on conservative lines. Aristotle also mentions other critics who blamed Solon for giving too much power to the people. The answer is that he is not to be held responsible for later developments; he himself gave the people only the most necessary power.[34] Hence Aristotle seems to have regarded Solon as the founder of a balanced state. He does, however, point out that some of his measures furthered the later democratic development, but this is another matter. Thus, in his list of changes in the government of Athens, he correctly states that democracy took its rise or beginning from the work of Solon.[35]

Turning to Cleisthenes, it is clear that he himself did not call his government a democracy and, in addition, that the word was not in use at the time. The earliest name or watchword known for that form of government which was the lineal ancestor of democracy is *isonomia,* and even that word in the days of Cleisthenes, that is, in the period of the drinking song and Alcmaeon, was not exclusively democratic in its connotation and use. When it first was used extensively by the popular party, the connotation connected with it emphasized the responsibility of the magistrates to the law and their liability to be held to account. The use of a name emphasizing government of or by the people came later. It is not unlikely that, as some have maintained,[36] the word was first created by the opponents of this form of government and only later taken over by its advocates. It is noticeable that it is used only once in Pericles' funeral oration as reported by Thucydides,[37] and then the speaker appears to be on the defensive. It is true, he remarks, that the state is called a democracy because the government is in the hands, not of the few, but of the many. Yet, though in private disputes all are equal before the law, in public affairs each man is advanced according to his reputation more on account of merit than on account of his

---

[34] *Politics* 1273b 35–1274a 21, especially 1274a 15.

[35] *Constitution of the Athenians* 41. 2.

[36] R. Hirzel, *Themis, Dike und Verwandtes* (Leipzig, 1907), p. 263 n. 8 (on p. 264); Ehrenberg, "Isonomia," col. 297.

[37] Thuc. ii. 37. 1; cf. *Scholia* (ed. Hude).

station in life. As the scholiast remarks, the speaker insists that Athens is a democracy in name but actually an aristocracy. Undoubtedly he has in mind a form of government sometimes recognized as aristocratic under which magistrates are chosen by the vote of all the citizens. Obviously he is stretching his point, giving too much consideration to the generals and the few other officials elected by vote and ignoring the fact that most magistrates were chosen by lot. This defensive attitude suggests that democracy was a name used by its enemies. However, when it was taken over by the champions of democracy, they, so to speak, fixed the upper limits of this form of government by claiming Cleisthenes as its founder.

As already noted, Herodotus refers to Cleisthenes as the founder of democracy when, at the end of the story of the wooing of Agariste, he refers to the son of Agariste and her successful suitor as the Cleisthenes who organized the tribes and established democracy at Athens. Obviously Herodotus wishes to honor Pericles, for he proceeds to trace his descent from Cleisthenes through the second Agariste, who, when pregnant, dreamt that she had given birth to a lion and a few days later bore Pericles.[38] But this is only one side of the question. Cleisthenes is honored in his great-grandson, as is Pericles in his ancestor, but what is most important is that Herodotus takes for granted that Cleisthenes is well known as the founder of democracy. In other words, he was so regarded by the contemporaries of Herodotus and Pericles. In fact, this may well be the official view of Periclean democracy. Apparently it did not at first go unchallenged. It is reported that Cimon, Pericles' more conservative opponent, after the overthrow of the Areopagus, sought to restore the aristocracy of the time of Cleisthenes.[39] Our source is late, but the implication that one party claimed Cleisthenes as an aristocrat, the other, as the founder of democracy, is plausible.

If, however, this was a matter of dispute at an earlier date, it had been settled by 411 B.C. In that year, when a motion was passed authorizing a commission to bring in proposals for the safety of the state—a measure which paved the way for the oligarchy of the Four Hundred—Cleitophon, a moderate oligarch associated with Theramenes, secured

---

[38] Herod. vi. 131; cf. V. Ehrenberg, *Neugründer des Staates* (Munich, 1925), p. 58.

[39] Plutarch, *Cimon* 15. 3.

14

the addition of an amendment to the effect that the commissioners be instructed to examine the laws which Cleisthenes drew up when he established democracy. This was done, adds Aristotle, on the grounds that the constitution of Cleisthenes was not democratic but similar to that of Solon.[40] Here the statement about Cleisthenes embodied in Cleitophon's amendment must represent the normal view of the times. Yet the fact that he proposed this amendment, as well as Aristotle's explanatory remarks, indicates that already by 411 some of the oligarchs were aware that Cleisthenes really was not too democratic. Thus, by that year, not only was Cleisthenes fully established as the official founder of democracy, but also the oligarchs had begun to realize that they here possessed a weapon which could be used for undermining democracy. It is interesting to note that Isocrates also, who belongs to a similar group of the next century, though he once calls Solon the founder of democracy, in two other speeches gives the credit to Cleisthenes.[41] Thus the weight of the evidence even of Isocrates favors the latter. If this is taken as evidence for the point of view of the time, it strengthens the impression that the consensus of Greek opinion regarded Cleisthenes as the founder of Athenian democracy.

The conclusion just reached means that Periclean democracy has a special right to the name and that other Greek forms of government have a right to it only in proportion to how closely they approach Periclean democracy or carry out its ideals. A good case could be made for this even if Cleisthenes had called his government democratic, for, though it differed greatly from the democracy of Pericles, Cleisthenes' reforms set off a chain of reactions that caused the government to evolve rapidly. However, it seems that the word was not used in the days of Cleisthenes, that it was invented later, and that it was the Periclean age which dubbed Cleisthenes the founder of Greek democracy. This makes the claim of Periclean democracy infinitely stronger. For the student of the Greek state this means that, while he may think what he will of Periclean democracy, he should recognize its special claim to the name. He should also recognize that of the many varieties of democracy mentioned by Aristotle, only the more extreme—call it debased or per-

---

[40] *Constitution of the Athenians* 29. 3.

[41] Isocrates, *Areopagiticus* 16; *Antidosis* 231–232 and 306; *Concerning the Team of Horses* 26–27.

verted, if you will—has a real right to the name. The others, in fact, are perversions which claim a name which really does not belong to them.

How did this state of affairs come about? This can be suggested only in the very briefest way. The fifth century was one of open conflict between oligarchy and democracy. This is reflected in the literature of the period in Aeschylus, in the debate on the forms of government in Herodotus, in Pseudo-Xenophon, in the funeral oration attributed to Pericles, and in the forged constitution of Draco, which actually found its way into Aristotle's *Constitution of Athens*. On the political side, we have ostracisms, the assassination of Ephialtes, and the oligarchic revolutions of 411 and 404. However, after the restoration of democracy in 403 this changed. Undoubtedly there were a few outspoken extremists, but the moderate oligarchs joined the democrats in the support of the government, though in so doing they did not change their general attitude towards democracy. Hence, though democracy was the accepted ideal of government, the former moderate oligarchs continued to advocate the same changes which they had advocated before, but they no longer spoke of them as oligarchic but as contributing to a better democracy. A part of this procedure was to appeal to the past. This was done already during the Peloponnesian War and continued in the fourth century, when the tendency is represented particularly by Isocrates. The more of the past the conservative champions could claim as democratic, the stronger their case would be. The democrats had already, so to speak, presented them with Cleisthenes. At times they tried to appropriate also Solon. Undoubtedly when Aristotle ranks various kinds of more conservative institutions as democratic, this is in part a result of the same movement.

Plato and the Law of Nature

GLENN R. MORROW

IT IS PLAUSIBLE to suppose that Plato's philosophy was an important factor in the formulation of the Stoic doctrine of the Law of Nature. The Stoics were notoriously dependent upon their predecessors, and it is in fact generally believed that the Law of Nature, like so many other parts of their philosophical system, was developed by the appropriation and adaptation of ideas that had originated earlier. Historians have seldom failed to cite, as an anticipation of the Stoic doctrine, the fragment of Heraclitus affirming that "all human laws are nourished by the one divine law." After Heraclitus the conception of a "higher law" meets us with increasing frequency, in the dramatists, orators, and philosophers of the fifth and fourth centuries. In Antisthenes and the Cynics the protest against convention and law is coupled with an appeal to nature, which unmistakably suggests the Stoic ethics. But what distinguishes the Stoic utterances on the higher law from those that are ordinarily cited from their predecessors is the elaborate philosophical basis on which they rest. For the Stoics the Law of Nature is the law of "right reason" (ὀρθὸς λόγος, *recta ratio*), deriving its authority from the divine reason in the cosmos, and making its claim upon men by virtue of the fact that human reason is itself derived from the divine reason and constitutes man's true nature. Behind the Stoic doctrine, therefore, lies a developed and distinctive cosmology, and an equally distinctive anthropology. These philosophical foundations give its peculiar stability and character to the Stoic doctrine of a higher law. It is no longer simply an expression of moral protest against positive law, nor a pious declaration of religious faith, but a rationally grounded and firmly

17

maintained philosophy of law. If we attempt to trace the ancestry of this doctrine, we can hardly be content to derive it from the sources just mentioned. There is nothing in the extant remains of these thinkers to lead us to suppose that they held such a conception of nature and of human nature as this doctrine implies. On the other hand, we can hardly avoid supposing that the idealism of Plato is somehow involved in the parentage of the Stoic doctrine, either directly or through Aristotle's version of that idealism.[1]

The external evidence, it is well to note, establishes a strong presumption in favor of this supposition. When the Stoic tradition emerges from the tantalizing obscurity of the fragments into the full light of Cicero's expositions, we find the Law of Nature set forth most completely and systematically in Cicero's *Laws,* a work which, by its title, its form, and its contents, shows clearly its author's intense admiration for Plato and his dependence upon him. The doctrine that *lex* is *ratio summa insita in natura* is declared to be the opinion of "the most learned men," and though Cicero does not here name these learned men, Plato is mentioned so often in this treatise, and in such reverential terms, that we must suppose him to be included in the group.[2] Again Cicero relies very heavily upon the Stoic Panaetius, and Panaetius is known to have been himself a devoted admirer and consistent follower of the teachings of Plato.[3] Furthermore the fragments of the early Stoics, unsatisfactory as they are, show that this doctrine was formulated by Zeno, and that the influence of Plato upon the Stoic school at its very beginning was considerable.[4] It seems therefore that Cicero was able to

---

[1] Plato's contribution has usually been overlooked. Friedrich Solmsen is the first, so far as I know, to have insisted upon it. See his *Plato's Theology*, 1942, Ch. x, especially p. 167. After this article had been submitted to the Editors of this volume, my attention was called to two very recent studies on the same theme: "Plato's Theory of Natural Law," by Joseph P. Maguire, in the *Yale Classical Studies*, X (1947); and Werner Jaeger's article, "Praise of Law: The Origin of Legal Philosophy and the Greeks," in *Interpretations of Modern Legal Philosophies*, ed. by Paul Sayre (New York, 1947).

[2] *De Legibus* I. 18. For Cicero's admiration of Plato see *De Leg.* I. 15; II. 14; III. 1, 5, 32.

[3] A. Schmekel, *Die Philosophie der mittleren Stoa* (1892), pp. 18 ff.; 47–85; Sabine and Smith, *Cicero On the Commonwealth* (1929), p. 29; Cicero, *Tusculan Disputations* I. xxxii, 79.

[4] Diogenes Laertius VII. 88; Cicero, *De Natura Deorum* I. 36; II. 21; II. 57–58. For Chrysippus, see von Arnim, *Stoicorum Veterum Fragmenta* (1938), III, no. 314; Diog. Laert. VII. 128; Cicero, *De Nat. Deor.* I. 39.

find such impressive agreement between his favorite author, Plato, and the Stoic sources from which he drew, because Plato's influence had been continuous upon the Stoic school from Zeno to Panaetius. But enough of this; our concern is not with the external evidence, but with Plato's thought itself.

A striking fact, too little noted, about the Stoic Law of Nature is that it involves the union of two concepts which in the fifth century were regarded as antithetical—*nomos* and *physis*. The Stoic phrase, νόμος φύσεως, would probably have sounded strange and even paradoxical to the cultivated Athenian of the Socratic Age. Neither this phrase, nor any other that implies a connection between *nomos* and *physis*, is clearly attested in the extant literature of the fifth and early fourth centuries, outside the writings of Plato.[5] This can hardly be an accident, since the remains of the dramatists, orators, and historians are considerable in bulk and contain frequent references to both *nomos* and *physis*. These terms are uniformly treated, with the exception above mentioned, as if they referred to incompatible things—*nomos* standing for something peculiarly characteristic of human life, something variable, contingent, and often arbitrary; *physis* standing for an order of occurrences or a disposition of forces independent of human contrivance, something primal, unchanging, and universal. With such connotations it is hardly to be expected that these two terms would be found in harmonious conjunction in our texts. It is even difficult to find the idea of justice associated with *physis*, at least in the literature of this period.[6]

---

[5] The only plausible instance I have found is Thucydides V. 105, which is discussed later in this article. The νόμιμον [πέφυκε] of Euripides' *Bacchae* 895 is probably a corruption of μόνιμον, as in *Phoenissae* 538 (cf. Plutarch, *De Fraterno Amore*, p. 481A). The Pindar fragment (νόμος ὁ πάντων βασιλεύς) comes from Plato's *Gorgias* 484; the κατὰ φύσιν sometimes read with this fragment seems to be an addition suggested by *Gorgias* 488b and *Laws* 690b and 715a. Callicles' doctrine that might makes right is put forward in Plato's *Gorgias* 483e as representing the law of nature. But was Callicles a historical person, and if so did he express himself in this fashion? This point is discussed later. Hirzel's statement (*Themis, Dike und Verwandtes* [1907], p. 388) that there are numerous references in fifth-century literature to a φύσεως νόμος is not only unsubstantiated by any examples in his text, but is actually contradicted by his own later statements that none of these advocates of the law of nature regarded νόμος as a cosmic principle (p. 390), and that none of them was able to bridge the gap between νόμος and φύσις (pp. 391–392).

[6] The idea of cosmic justice was of course a notable feature of the cosmologies of Anaximander, Heraclitus, Parmenides, and Empedocles, and seems to have served an important function in helping to establish the idea of the orderliness of nature.

Justice was identified with law, and the very distinction between the just and the unjust was regarded as a matter of convention, or *nomos*. When the partisans of *physis* in this controversy desired to set up a standard by which positive law was to be judged, they seldom, if ever, made use of their adversaries' concept, the δίκαιον; instead they relied upon the useful (συμφέρον), or the noble (καλόν), or more vaguely "the things of nature" (τὰ τῆς φύσεως).[7] It is evident, therefore, that between the close of the fifth century and the end of the fourth a notable transformation took place in the meaning of one or both of these concepts, so as to permit their union in the Stoic doctrine.

The word *nomos* is as old as the epic poets, and seems originally to have been used to denote the ways of behavior characteristic of any group of living beings, whether men or wild beasts. Thus Hesiod uses it in *Works and Days*:

The Son of Cronos has ordained this *nomos* for men. Fishes and beasts and winged fowl devour one another, for right (δίκη) is not in them; but to mankind he gave right, which proves far the best (ll. 276–280; Evelyn-White's translation).

In later days *nomos* was applied only to human ways of behavior; but it never lost its original meaning of custom, nor its association with justice. Whenever a later writer speaks of νόμοι, he tends to imply not merely strict law, the law contained in published statutes, but also customary law. Likewise the δίκη which characterizes *nomos*, as used by Hesiod, remains throughout all later history an inseparable part of the concept. Law is primarily an embodiment of justice, and conversely the just man is he who obeys the laws. But two other elements later came

---

But once the orderliness of nature had been accepted, the physiologers could dispense with justice. See Gregory Vlastos, "Equality and Justice in Early Greek Cosmologies," *Classical Philology*, XLII (1947), 156–178.—It is not safe to use Plato's text as evidence of fifth-century usage, since the evidence is highly ambiguous. *Cratylus* 412–413 would suggest that justice was thought of as a cosmic principle by some contemporaries of Socrates. *Gorgias* 484 (see note 5 above) and *Laws* 690b and 715a suggest that might was regarded as natural justice. On the other hand *Laws* 889e says the νέοι σοφοί denied absolutely the existence of natural justice; and with this the account of Protagoras' views of justice agrees (*Theaetetus* 167c, 172a, 177c). The doctrine that justice is the interest of the sovereign (τὸ συμφέρον τοῦ κρείττονος) is put forward by Thrasymachus (*Rep.* 338e) without any reference to nature; whereas in *Laws* 714c the exponents of this doctrine seem to regard it as the "natural definition" (φύσει ὅρος) of justice.

[7] In addition to the evidence given in the following pages, see Aristotle, *Soph. El.* 173a 7–18.

to be associated with the idea of *nomos:* the element of constraint, and the element of enactment.[8] Customary law in its early stages is usually felt by a people as only vaguely compelling; conformity results without the machinery of courts and penalties. Similarly these customs are usually regarded as owing little to human contrivance; they are the gift of the gods, or a part of the unchanging order of things. For the Greeks this state of innocence was ended by the process of political unification and of colonization. When two or more communities found it expedient to join forces for mutual protection and benefit, their tribal and local customs had to be harmonized, and something like a common law, the law of the city, had to be set up, in some respects overriding the earlier and more familiar customs. Such a common law of the city was felt to have, and would need to have, more explicit power of constraining than the earlier customs; and furthermore it was seen to have arisen from something like explicit legislation or enactment, by the deliberate choice of "the best." The effects of colonization were obviously similar. A group of colonists might consist of persons from various cities (though ordinarily that was not the case), and always there would be the need of explicitly affirming in a new environment the laws that were to govern the new community, and of providing for their enforcement. Stresses and strains within a community, as in Athens prior to the time of Draco, often led to the demand for changes in the law, or at least for its codification and enforcement. Draco's legislation was an attempt to meet this demand and his laws have ever since been a notorious example of the element of constraint inherent in law, though it is probable that he endeavored to do no more than systematize and set down the existing practices. Solon's law, by contrast, involved a vast reform of existing institutions, and it is to Solon that later Athenians nearly always looked as the founder of their law. It is significant that both Draco's and Solon's prescriptions were first put forward as θεσμοί—i.e., positive enactments or declarations of right. We hear of many other legislators of the seventh and sixth centuries—Zaleucus of Locri, Charondas of Catana, Lycurgus of Sparta, and other even more shadowy figures—all of whom are credited with having made widespread revisions in the laws of their respective cities. The term universally ap-

---

[8] For the development here described see Hirzel, *Themis, Dike und Verwandtes,* pp. 376 ff.

plied to these ancient legislators—νομοθέτης—shows a clear recognition of the positive element in their legislation. By the beginning of the fifth century the Greeks were well aware of this element of human judgment and positive enactment in the laws under which they lived. The course of political events in the fifth century only deepened this awareness. At Athens, for example, the successive changes in the constitution, the increasing resort to legislation, the growth of litigation, the widespread contacts with other peoples and other laws, and the heightened sense of individual interests distinct from those of the community, all converged in their influence to give the Athenian citizen the conviction that his laws were to a great extent the result of legislation or enactment, and derived much of their authority from the sanctions explicitly attached to them.

Yet, so strong was the traditional association of law with justice, it appeared inconceivable that there should be justice apart from law. The relations of the two concepts had to a great extent been reversed. Whereas in the beginning law was regarded as finding its norm in justice, in the fifth century justice came to be defined in terms of law.[9] Under these circumstances the only recourse open to one who felt the injustice of his city's law was to appeal to a higher law. Sometimes the appeal was made on religious grounds, as in the moving chorus of Sophocles' *Oedipus the King*, to

the laws born of Olympus, that pace on high the heavenly ether, not begotten of mortal human nature (ll. 865–870).

Sometimes the appeal was made to πάτριοι νόμοι, ancestral customs, as more authoritative than the innovations of later times. Again an appeal was often made to universal νόμιμα, common to all mankind, or to the common laws of all Greeks. Finally, more vaguely, an appeal could be made to the "unwritten law," by which might be meant any one of the above-mentioned higher laws.[10] These various protests testify to the uncertain moral foundations of positive law, but they provided no clearly defined alternative. The πάτριοι νόμοι, and the universal νόμιμα,

---

[9] *Ibid.*, p. 384.

[10] It is to be noted that none of these is an appeal to the Law of Nature, though they are frequently cited as such. The universal νόμιμα and the common Hellenic law can be regarded as precursors of the *jus gentium*, but this is different from the Law of Nature, even though Cicero and the Roman jurists frequently drew upon it to supply content to the Law of Nature.

were different in content, but not in formal character, from the νόμοι
from which appeal was made. To critical reflection they would reveal
the same defects. The divine law was presumably free from the defects
of human judgment, but the appeal to such a divine law could be (and
was) effectively countered by the observation that belief in the gods
is itself a convention supported by the sanctions of the city's laws. As
Euripides' Hecuba declares:

By law (νόμῳ) we learn that there are gods, and mark out the bounds of justice
and injustice (*Hecuba* 799 f.).

In short, there seemed no escape from the "tyranny of *nomos*." The
dilemma of the fifth-century thinker is nicely exemplified in the attitude of Socrates. Before the Athenian court he declares firmly that he
must "obey God rather than men." Yet he was a loyal subject of the laws
of Athens, and according to Xenophon he fully concurred in the current
opinion that justice means conformity to the laws.[11]

The notion of *physis* belongs to an entirely different context. The idea
of *nomos* is the product of reflection on political and moral experience;
the conception of *physis* was worked out by the early Greek scientists—
those men of Miletus, Ephesus, Clazomenae, and Abdera, of Sicily and
southern Italy, who attempted to explain, in terms of familiar elements
and processes, the phenomena of the heavens and all the other varied
occurrences in the cosmos that surrounds human life. The speculations
of these early thinkers were universally designated, from the fifth century onward and perhaps even earlier, as inquiries into *physis* (περὶ
φύσεως).[12] These inquiries were introduced into Athens in the fifth century by Anaxagoras, and the shock they gave to the older beliefs of the
Athenians is one of the major events of that century. The meaning of
the term *physis*, universally used to designate the object of these inquiries, varied somewhat with the thinker and with the context in
which the term was used.[13] Sometimes it referred to the primary stuff,
or kinds of stuff, of which the ordered cosmos is constituted; sometimes it denoted that ordered cosmos itself, *rerum natura;* sometimes

[11] Xenophon, *Memorabilia* IV. iv. 12; vi. 6. For the identification of νόμιμα and
δίκαια in the fifth and fourth centuries see Hirzel, *op. cit.*, p. 384 n. 4.
[12] Cf. Plato's *Phaedo* 96ab.
[13] The literature on this subject is extensive. It is conveniently and competently
reviewed in Mansion, *Introduction à la Physique Aristotélicienne*, 2nd ed. (1946),
pp. 59–65.

23

the form or constitution of any person or thing within that cosmos; and sometimes the originating power or agency through which this order came about, whether in the cosmos as a whole, or in its separate parts—the *natura naturans* of Spinoza. But these varied meanings had a common core. Underlying all these investigations into *physis* was the assumption that there are certain enduring primary characters or elemental forces which, if understood, would explain the origin and behavior of the cosmos and all its parts.

The contrast between *nomos* and *physis* is therefore unmistakable. *Nomos* varies from place to place and from time to time, whereas *physis* has the character of necessity (ἀνάγκη) and is therefore invariable. *Nomos* is transitory, while *physis* is "ageless and deathless." *Nomos* is the product of human contriving; but the forces at work in nature, and the order they bring about, are independent of human agency. Furthermore *physis* is primary, not merely in the order of being, but also in time; for *nomos,* together with all other human institutions, is a late occurrence in cosmic history. A fragment of Archelaus, a pupil of Anaxagoras, tells us that living beings arose "where the warm and the cold were first mingled together in the earth; men were then separated off from the other animals, and set up kings and laws and the arts and cities and all the rest." [14] For all these reasons *physis* came inevitably to be identified with the real and the true, whereas *nomos* is merely convention, what is accepted or acknowledged, whether rightly or wrongly. The culminating import of this antithesis between *physis* and *nomos* is revealed to us best in the famous fragment of Democritus: "By convention (νόμῳ) there is sweet, by convention there is bitter; by convention there is hot, by convention there is cold; by convention there is color, but in truth (ἐτεῇ) there are atoms and the void." [15] Thus *nomos* comes to stand for the whole complex of human opinions, beliefs, and traditions; and the contrast between *nomos* and *physis* is generalized into a distinction between popular belief and what we would call scientific understanding. The former is relative, transitory, and unstable, whereas the latter is sure and abiding, since it rests upon the real nature of things. This distinction meets us later in Plato's well-known contrast between opinion and knowledge, and still later, in a

---

[14] Diels, *Die Fragmente der Vorsokratiker,* 5th ed. (1935), II, 46.
[15] *Ibid.,* p. 139.

fashion which shows clearly its origin, in the contrast Aristotle draws between discussions that are "logical" (λογικοί) and those that are "physical" (φυσικοί). The former, proceeding by the use of conceptions (λόγοι), are essentially dialectical and lead only to probable conclusions, while the latter are based on the *physis* of the matter in question and are, as we would say, scientific.

It was only natural that this generalized distinction between *nomos* and *physis* should have been used as a tool for the analysis of human institutions themselves. But here the partisans of *physis* seem to have confronted an unpleasant dilemma. Strictly interpreted, the distinction between the just and the unjust should have been denied any standing in the order of nature, just as the distinction between the hot and the cold was regarded as merely a matter of convention. Archelaus followed this course, so it seems, and declared roundly that "the just and the shameful exist not by nature but by law." [16] A similar doctrine is implied by Thrasymachus, as he is represented in the first book of Plato's *Republic*. From this point of view all possible moral and political rules would be merely institutions, in the literal sense of the word, existing θέσει, not φύσει. But to drop the inquiry here was to leave unsatisfied one important purpose widely cherished by the partisans of nature. A large part of the appeal of this concept lay in the prospect it afforded of finding a standard of judgment more reliable than inherited opinions and traditions. If nature is the criterion of truth, can we not also find in nature a standard of justice? The traditional opinion was that law is somehow the embodiment of a justice beyond the law. What then could be more logical than to attempt to do, by means of the concept of *physis*, what had been impossible with *nomos*, i.e., to distinguish between real justice, a justice that exists by nature, and the more or less imperfect embodiments of justice found in the law?

This is precisely the problem that Plato set himself to solve; but apart from the writings of Plato there is little evidence that the thinkers of the fifth century thought in terms of "natural justice," still less that they succeeded in formulating an explicit theory of it. The identification of justice with law was too thoroughly fixed in the minds of careful

---

[16] *Ibid.*, p. 45. This may have been the view of Protagoras also. Hirzel, *op. cit.*, p. 382; Burnet, *Greek Philosophy* (1920), pp. 114 ff. Cf. Plato, *Theaetetus* 172a, 177c.

thinkers. When justice was identified with law, and when law was regarded as the antithesis of nature, then it was obviously not easy to bring nature and justice together. Nevertheless the attempt was made in various ways to find in nature some standard of conduct, if not a principle of justice. The investigators of nature recognized a *physis* of man, as well as of the other parts of nature. What man does by nature was contrasted with what he is and does by law. The former springs from what is primordial in him, from the structure and constitution provided by *physis*, independent of human agency. The latter represents what he is and does as the result of human art and human institutions. Since *physis* stands for the real, the former is the real man, the latter a kind of artifice, an addition to nature, if not an imposition upon nature. Thus the Athenian envoys, in Thucydides' memorable account,[17] appeal to nature to support their demands upon the Melians, pointing out that a compulsion of nature ($φύσις ἀναγκαία$) drives both gods and men to seek to rule wherever they can. The Athenian envoys do not pretend, however, that their actions are just or right; they rebuke the Melians for bringing in such irrelevant considerations; the question to be discussed is not one of right, but one of expediency. This is certainly not a doctrine of natural justice; and though Thucydides seems to regard their behavior as conforming to a law that is eternal and inescapable, it is a *nomos* that has lost all its familiar associations with justice and is but another name for necessity ($ἀνάγκη$).

A more reasoned interpretation of nature's standard was put forward by the Sophist Antiphon, in a work entitled appropriately *On Truth*.[18] Antiphon accepted without question the current identification of justice with law. Justice, he says, consists in not transgressing any of the laws of the city to which one belongs. He then draws a sharp contrast between "the ways of the law ($τὰ τῶν νόμων$)" and "the ways of nature ($τὰ τῆς φύσεως$)." "The ways of the law are adventitious ($ἐπίθετα$); the ways of nature are necessary ($ἀναγκαῖα$); and in most cases the ways of the law are in conflict with nature." But what are the ways of nature? Antiphon finds the answer to this question in the impulse to self-preservation, or the pursuit of one's vital interests. "We all, whether Greeks or barbarians, take in air through the mouth and nostrils. . . .

---

[17] V, 86–111, esp. 89, 90, 105.
[18] Diels, *op. cit.*, II, 346 ff.

To live and to die are a part of the order of nature. Men live when they get what is useful (τὰ συμφέροντα), and die from the opposite." Sometimes, he seems to admit, the laws further the interests of those who are supposed to obey them, but usually not. Hence "he who transgresses the rules of law, and does so unobserved, is none the worse for his transgression; but if, what is impossible in fact, a man acts contrary to nature, then he is truly harmed (δι' ἀλήθειαν βλάπτεται), whether or not men know of his action." The clear import of Antiphon's doctrine is to replace justice by utility; or, if justice has any authority at all, this authority is derivative from its utility. The way of nature is for each man to pursue what is useful to himself; this is the principle by which men not only should act, but inevitably do act. Thus Antiphon's concept of the useful provides a philosophical basis for such declarations as those of the Athenian envoys, and for any other assertion of private interest against traditional rules of justice, provided only that the interest can really be pursued to advantage.

Thus the partisans of *physis*, in the age preceding Plato's philosophical activity, had largely succeeded in discrediting *nomos*, and with it the idea of justice. The standard suggested by nature was not indeed always conceived in the ruthless form in which it is presented by the Athenian envoys. There is a pronounced vein of cosmopolitanism and even humanitarianism in some of the surviving fragments of this controversy. Antiphon himself denies that nature makes any distinction between Greeks and barbarians. The Sophist Hippias, as reported by Plato, argues that men are alike by nature and therefore are all kinsmen and fellow-citizens.[19] Unfortunately, neither Plato nor any other source informs us concerning the philosophical grounds, if any, on which Hippias based his cosmopolitan sentiments. But the idea of a common humanity transcending the distinctions of law and custom meets us often in Euripides, which is good evidence of its interest, if not its appeal, to the men of the fifth century. It is often said that these thinkers advocated a doctrine of natural justice, which they set above the justice embodied in law. But there is little evidence to support this interpretation. The distinction between natural and legal justice appears in Plato and Aristotle, but that is not sufficient evidence that it had been formulated by their predecessors. So far as the fifth century is concerned,

---

[19] *Protagoras* 337cd.

what we clearly know is that justice was identified with law and law was recognized to be a product of human contriving, not a part of the order of nature.[20] Yet the sentiment of a kinship between man and nature undoubtedly persisted from a former age. It shows itself in the poets,[21] and in the philosophers too, on occasion. Anaxagoras' assumption of *nous* as a cosmic principle is a conspicuous example; so also is the cosmic teleology of Socrates, as expounded by Xenophon. Yet Anaxagoras' *nous* seems to have been little more than a poetic designation for ἀνάγκη, and Socrates' cosmic piety, as reported by Xenophon, has very fragile logical foundations. If justice and law were to be vindicated, it would have to be shown that they belonged to the order of nature, or could claim in some way a foundation in nature.

Two different solutions to this problem were worked out in the fourth century, leading to two distinct conceptions of "natural justice," based respectively upon what later came to be called the Law of Nature and the Social Contract. The former conception of natural justice was arrived at by a transformation of the concept of *physis*, so as to permit the incorporation of the peculiarly human conception of law, as an intelligent ordering of events for the achievement of an end, into the very structure of the cosmos. This is the conception of natural justice that is familiar to us from the Stoics, and for which, as I think it can be shown, Plato provided the indispensable philosophical foundation. The other conception of natural justice is quite different. It takes over without essential modification the impersonal and indifferent cosmos of the fifth-century physiologers, and founds justice upon an agreement made by human beings to abstain from injuring one another. This is the doctrine we find in Epicurus. "Natural justice," he says, "is a contract of mutual expediency, to prevent one man from harming or being harmed by another." [22] With the origins of this doctrine we are not here concerned,[23] but it is fairly certain that it had its advocates in the fourth

---

[20] Cf. Euripides, Frag. 920 (Nauck):

ἡ φύσις ἐβούλεθ,᾽ ᾗ νόμων οὐδὲν μέλει.

[21] Cf. the appeal to nature in Jocasta's argument for equality, in Euripides' *Phoenissae* 543–548.

[22] Diogenes Laertius X. 150.

[23] The doctrine may have its origin in Antiphon, who said that all laws are "agreements" (Diels, *op. cit.*, II. 347). If such agreements protect the interests of

century before Epicurus espoused it.[24] The important thing for us to note is its divergence from the doctrine of Natural Law. It bases justice on a contract between human beings, a contract springing presumably from man's natural impulse to protect his vital interests; the other finds justice in the cosmos, and its authority is independent of any agreement between human beings. These two views were universally regarded in antiquity as antithetical; the partisans of the one were sharply opposed to those who espoused the other. As in later days the Stoics were arrayed against the Epicureans on this issue, so in the fourth century we find Plato and Aristotle on the one side, and the "sophists" on the other.[25]

We are ready now to see how Plato laid the foundations for the Stoic conception of natural justice. The logical starting point of Plato's thought is found in his attempt to define justice, not as it is embodied in and identified with law, but "justice itself," αὐτὸ τὸ δίκαιον. We can readily understand why the problem of justice is central in the *Republic*, and why law plays such a minor role in the argument and in the construction of the ideal state. Plato saw, as clearly as the thinkers whom he combated, the provincialism, the capriciousness, and the tyranny of *nomos*. Plato's Socrates is never portrayed as asking "What is law?" Instead he goes directly to the examination of the concept which had traditionally been the measure and norm of law. In this examination the Platonic Socrates employs the method and presuppositions of the theory of Ideas. For Justice is a universal and therefore is an Idea, a reality truly existing (ὄντως ὄν); and the task of dialectic is to bring to light those reminiscences by means

---

those who enter into them, justice and law would have a foundation in nature, since the protection of one's interests is a dictate of nature.

[24] Aristotle mentions a certain Lycophron, "the Sophist," who held the view that law rests on a contract (*Politics* 1280b 10). Cf. Demosthenes XXV. 16: νόμος . . . πόλεως συνθήκη κοινή; Aristotle, *Rhet. ad Alex.* 1422a 2: νόμος . . . ὁμολόγημα πόλεως κοινόν. Glaucon, in Plato's *Republic*, is pictured as expounding a common opinion when he declares that law and justice are based on a contract entered into by self-seeking men for mutual protection against injury (359a).

[25] See Kaerst, *Geschichte des Hellenismus*, 3rd ed. (1927), I. 514 f., for some apt remarks on the failure to realize that the theories of Natural Law and the Social Contract, which appeared together in modern times, were originally (and rightfully) regarded as antithetical conceptions. But Kaerst seems to be mistaken in interpreting Antiphon as an exponent of *Naturrecht*. The principle that Antiphon derives from nature is τὸ συμφέρον, not τὸ δίκαιον: the latter term he always uses with reference to positive law. But his theory does seem to provide a foundation for the opposing view, the *Vertragslehre*.

of which the mind may clearly apprehend the object of its search. Once this Idea has been accurately determined, there can be knowledge about justice, a science of morals and politics, consisting of the true principles of social order. Such principles will represent genuine justice, with correspondingly higher authority than current traditions; they will be knowledge, true, enduring, authoritative, as contrasted with varying and transitory opinions.

The first stage of this search for the meaning of justice involved the critical examination of current theories, both those that denied the reality of justice and those that endeavored to replace justice and law, in the traditional sense, by a standard derived from nature. The latter type of theory is dramatically presented by Callicles in the *Gorgias*, who declares that laws are made by the weak to protect themselves against the strong, and that by nature the superior or the strong man is entitled to override these laws and to get what he can. Callicles is described as setting this forth as a doctrine of natural justice, and as corresponding to a law of nature. If Callicles was a real person and actually expressed himself in these terms, we have an instance of an attempt prior to Plato to unite the concepts of nature and justice; but we know nothing about this Callicles other than what Plato's dialogue contains. It may well be that he is a dramatic fiction, and that Plato has chosen to show, in his own terminology, how the partisans of might would have to defend their doctrine if it was to withstand philosophical criticism. In any case, this principle of conduct cannot stand, for Callicles will not admit some of its necessary implications, which shows that it does not belong to the order of intelligible Ideas. In the *Republic* a similar refutation is given of Thrasymachus' doctrine that justice represents simply the interests of the ruler, or the dominant class in the state; for the concept of ruling, strictly considered, does not imply the idea of ruling for one's own interest, in fact is incompatible with it. Thus Plato disposes of both aspects of the doctrine that private or special interest is the real standard by which law and justice are to be judged. Plato's own formula is well known. When a state is so ordered that all essential social functions are performed, and performed by the individuals or classes most fitted to perform them, then justice is present. This is "justice itself," and whoever has grasped it has the pattern by which human life is to be regulated. It is irrelevant to our purpose here to examine the validity of the reasoning by which

30

this view is supported. Its central element is the idea of unity, or concord. This was of course an old ideal; it had been one of the main motives of Solon's legislation, and it was to become a watchword of the Stoics in later times. What Plato contributed was the doctrine that this human ideal, when it is realized, is the embodiment of an Idea whose being belongs beyond time and space and all human affairs to an intelligible order that "really is."

The next step in our examination is to note that this order of intelligible entities, the ὄντως ὄντα, is described by Plato as existing "by nature" (φύσει), or "in nature" (ἐν τῇ φύσει).²⁶ In the *Parmenides*, when Socrates is being asked to defend the doctrine of Ideas, he expresses his conviction that these forms of justice, beauty, goodness, considered in and by themselves, are established in nature (ἑστάναι ἐν τῇ φύσει) as paradigms which other things imitate (130b). The same thought and language are found in the *Republic*, where the inferiority of the imitative arts is based upon their being imitations of sense objects, which themselves are imitations of the intelligible world. The artist who paints a picture of a bed copies a bed made by a carpenter; the carpenter who makes a bed copies the bed that exists in nature (597b-d). There is only one such natural bed; it is bed itself, the Idea Bed. The illustration is a homely one, but the point is clear. Another significant example of this usage occurs in the *Republic*, when Socrates is describing how the perfect state might be established. We must have, of course, a philosopher-king; and how will he proceed? He will look constantly to his models, the "naturally just," "naturally noble" (φύσει δίκαιον, καλόν), and all the rest, endeavoring to create imitations of them in human society (501b). For Plato, in short, "justice itself" and "natural justice" mean the same thing; natural justice is the Idea Justice, the paradigm to be followed by the legislator and statesman. These passages should suffice to make it clear that Plato has identified the order of nature and the order of true being, which for him is the Ideas.²⁷

---

²⁶ This particular turn given to the doctrine of Ideas has been seldom noted and its significance has therefore usually been overlooked. Likewise Plato's conception of φύσις has not received the attention it deserves. Mansion (*op. cit.*, pp. 82–92) gives an interesting account of Plato's conception of nature, but in overlooking Plato's identification of the Ideas with the φύσει ὄντα, he regards Plato as replacing the older theory of *physis* by a theory of soul, whereas it would be truer to say that what Plato does is to set up a new conception of *physis*.

²⁷ Other apt examples could be given. *Phaedo* 103b distinguishes the ideal opposite (τὸ ἐναντίον . . . τὸ ἐν τῇ φύσει) from the concrete opposites discussed earlier

This identification must be kept in mind, if we would understand the numerous references in the dialogues to what is "according to nature" (κατὰ φύσιν) and what is "contrary to nature" (παρὰ φύσιν).[28] Only when legislation and institutions conform to the intelligible order can they be said to be in agreement with nature; and conversely, the disturbance of the ideal relations, whether of mind to body, or more generally of the ruling element and the subordinate elements in any whole, is contrary to nature.

Plato's identification of the world of Ideas with the natural order—of the ὄντως ὄντα with the φύσει ὄντα—was a momentous event in Greek philosophy. This identification of course follows directly from the status the Ideas occupy in Plato's system and from the accepted meaning of *physis*. Like the investigators of nature before him, he was searching for the first and basic principles of the visible world, the changeless beyond the flux of events, the one beyond the many. Where his predecessors had found water, air, fire, or the atoms, he finds the Ideas. As they had distinguished from the fluctuating opinions and actions of men a cosmic order of vaguely material forces independent of human contrivance, so Plato distinguishes the intelligible world of Ideas from the world of opinion and becoming. But the conception of *physis*, though remaining formally the same, has clearly undergone a momentous transformation in content, a transformation without which the Stoic appeal to nature could hardly be understood. Plato's *rerum natura* is not constituted of visible or material objects. Its permanent stuff is not any of the hard objects of sense, not

---

in the dialogue. Cf. Burnet's note on this passage in his edition of the *Phaedo:* "All Greek thinkers use the word φύσις of that which they regard as most real. The Ionians meant by it the primary substance; Socrates means by it the world of εἴδη." Cf. Adam's note on *Republic* 597b, in his edition of the *Republic:* "The φύσις or 'nature' of anything means its Idea, and the φύσις or nature of all things (*rerum natura*) becomes an expression for the World of Ideas." Perhaps it is thus that we should interpret the cryptic reference in Aristotle's *Metaphysics* 1070a 18: οὐ κακῶς ὁ Πλάτων ἔφη ὅτι εἴδη ἐστίν ὁπόσα φύσει. For other instances in Plato's text, see *Cratylus* 389b ff.; *Epistle VII,* 341d, 344d; and the passages cited in note 28.

[28] The expressions παρὰ φύσιν, κατὰ φύσιν occur with great frequency in Plato, though they are rare in other writers of the fifth and fourth centuries (Mansion, *op. cit.,* p. 109). Some instances: to make laws according to nature (*Rep.* 456c); the naturally constituted state (*Rep.* 428e); the genuine political art (*Statesman* 308c); the natural relations between concepts (*Statesman* 283d; *Sophist* 256c); the naturally desirable (*Philebus* 22b); natural states of the body (*Philebus* 32ab); the natural priority of ruling to ruled (*Rep.* 444d; *Phil.* 27a; *Timaeus* 45b; *Phaedo* 80a); unnatural vice (*Laws* 838e); genuine intelligence (*Laws* 875d).

even the hard atoms of Democritus' refined perception. It is an order of
Ideas, and in some sense akin to the mind of man. For not only is it intelligible, it is also purposive and beautiful, being united under the Idea
of the Good, and thus it satisfies our desires for meaning and value, as
well as truth. This is the *physis* which for Plato forms the setting for human life, and which by contrast shows up the impermanence, imperfec-
tion, and disorder in the world of becoming. The counterpart of this
transformation of the cosmic significance of *physis* is a similar transformation of the conception of human nature and of the nature of all other
things within the cosmos. The nature of man is not to be read off from the
behavior of this or that particular man or society of men—e.g., the Athenian envoys, or Callicles' "strong man"—but from the Idea Man; the
"natural man" is the ideal man, a being whose intelligence, spirit and appetites are functioning in harmonious concord. Whatever promotes this
supremacy of intelligence, and this co-operation of spirit and appetite
under the guidance of intelligence, is "according to nature," and whatever hinders or destroys this ideal ordering is "contrary to nature." Such
is the import of Plato's doctrine of Ideas.

It was hardly to be expected that of this revolutionary interpretation
of *physis* would be easily grasped by Plato's contemporaries. Perhaps he
himself was not at first aware of its implications. Whatever be the reason,
whether a development of Plato's own thought, or the need of making
explicit the contrast between his views and those of the cosmologists,
we find in the *Timaeus* and the *Laws* a deliberate effort to set forth this
new doctrine of *physis* in terms of the natural science of his predecessors. The contrast between his views and theirs is set forth most suc-
cinctly in the tenth book of the *Laws*, in a passage explicitly concerned
with the theories of "our modern men of enlightenment," i.e., the thinkers of the fifth and early fourth centuries, referred to as "modern" to distinguish them from the poets and cosmogonists of an earlier period.[29]
Here Plato gives us his version of that movement of scientific thought
traced briefly in an earlier part of this paper. These modern wise men, he
says, declare that everything is either the product of nature ($\phi \acute{v} \sigma \iota s$), or
of art ($\tau \acute{\epsilon} \chi \nu \eta$), or of chance ($\tau \acute{v} \chi \eta$), the "grandest and fairest of things"

---

[29] 886d. Vlastos, *Classical Philology*, XLII (1947), 176–177, gives a good dis-
cussion of the identity of these $\nu \acute{\epsilon} o\iota$ $\kappa \alpha \grave{\iota}$ $\sigma o\phi o \acute{\iota}$.

being the product of nature and chance, while art plays a secondary role and produces only insignificant results.

"Fire and water, earth and air—so they say—all owe their being to nature and chance, none of them to art; they, in turn, are the agents, and the absolutely soulless agents, in the production of the bodies of the next rank, the earth, sun, moon, and stars. They drifted casually, each in virtue of their several tendencies; as they came together in certain fitting and convenient dispositions—hot with cold, dry with moist, soft with hard, and so on in all the inevitable casual combinations which arise from blending of contraries—thus, and on this wise, they gave birth to the whole heavens and all their contents, and, in due course, to all animals and plants, when once all the seasons of the year had been produced from those same causes; not, so they say, by the agency of mind, or any god, or art, but, as I tell you, by nature and chance. Art ($\tau\acute{\epsilon}\chi\nu\eta$), the subsequent late-born product of these causes, herself as perishable as her creators, has since given birth to certain toys with little real substance in them, simulacra as shadowy as the arts themselves, such as those which spring from painting, music, and the other fellow crafts. Or if there are arts which really produce anything of genuine worth, they are those which lend their aid to nature, like medicine, husbandry, gymnastic. Statesmanship in especial, they say, is a thing which has little in common with nature, but is mainly a business of art; legislation, likewise, is altogether an affair not of nature, but of art, and its positions are unreal."

"Unreal—but how so?"

"Why, my dear sir, to begin with, this party assert that gods have no real and natural, but only an artificial being, in virtue of legal conventions, as they call them, and thus there are different gods for different places, conformably to the conventions made by each group among themselves when they drew up their legislation. Then they actually declare that the really and naturally laudable is one thing and the conventionally laudable quite another, while as for right, there is absolutely no such thing as a real and natural right, mankind are eternally disputing about rights and altering them, and every change thus made, once made, is from that moment valid, though it owes its being to artifice and legislation, not to anything you would call nature" (889b–890a; A. E. Taylor's translation).

What is novel in Plato's presentation is the generalization of the contrast between *physis* and *nomos* into a contrast between *physis* and *techne*. The latter term denotes all that belongs to planning intelligence, and law becomes only one of its manifestations. According to this view, *techne* does not belong to the order of nature; nature, strictly construed, is devoid of intelligence. This of course is contrary to Plato's conception of *physis*. Since *techne* implies knowledge, and since knowledge involves an apprehension of the world of Ideas, and since this ideal world is for Plato the order of nature, knowledge and art will certainly be closer to nature than the inanimate materials and processes regarded by the inquirers into nature as primary. As Clinias puts it, "We must with all our strength defend the claim that law and art exist by nature (ἐστὸν φύσει), or at least are not inferior to nature, since they are the offspring of mind (νοῦς), in accordance with right reason (ὀρθὸς λόγος), as I believe, and as I understand you to maintain" (890b).

In the argument that follows, Plato does not appeal to his doctrine of Ideas. Instead he meets the partisans of *physis* on their own ground, the processes of change in the visible world. The argument purports to show that in the explanation of these processes soul is prior to fire, water, earth, and air. The argument is a more elaborate version of the doctrine of the *Phaedrus* that soul is the source of change (ἀρχὴ κινήσεως), since soul is that which can move itself as well as impart motion to other things. Since the alleged primary realities of the physicists, water, air, and the other elements, are capable of motion only when acted on by something else, they are obviously secondary to the self-moving soul. Thus the advocates of nature "have argued their case fallaciously." Soul, the Athenian Stranger declares,

is among the primal things, elder-born than all bodies and prime source of all their changes and transformations. But if this is indeed so, must not all that is akin to soul needs be of earlier birth than all that is proper to bodies? And so judgment and foresight, wisdom, art and law, must be prior to hard and soft, heavy and light; ay, and the grand primal works and deeds, for the very reason that they are primal, will prove to be those of art; those of nature herself—wrongly so called—will be secondary and derivative from art and mind.

Clinias asks, "Why 'wrongly so called'?" and the answer of the Athenian Stranger makes the point to which we have been working.

Why, by nature they mean the production of things primary; but if we can show that soul came first—that it was not fire, nor air, but soul whose origin is earliest—it will be most accurate to say that the existence of soul is eminently natural.[30]

Here the argument stops, with the natural priority of soul and all its attributes, including *techne*. The completion is provided by the *Timaeus*, where the importance of *techne* in the nature of things is set

---

[30] 892a-c. φύσιν βούλονται λέγειν γένεσιν τὴν περὶ τὰ πρῶτα. The precise significance of this phrase has been much disputed, though its general meaning is clear. See the discussion in Mansion, *op. cit.*, p. 85 n. With Taylor's translation compare Veazie: "the first creative power" (*Archiv für Gesch. der Phil.*, XXXIII [1920], 15).

forth emphatically and in detail. This book belongs to the same order of inquiries as the various books "on nature" attributed to the Ionian and Sicilian scientists; its theme is "the gods and the generation of the universe (γένεσις τοῦ παντός)." Plato warns us on several occasions that what he has to say about the visible world and its genesis is only a "likely account." [31] It lacks the precision and consistency that belong to science, in his conception of the term, whose object is being (οὐσία). But there is no doubt he thinks it as properly science as the accounts given by his predecessors; it is "as likely an account as any." In explaining the generation of the visible world Plato departs radically from the tradition set by his predecessors. Instead of regarding the cosmos as the result of forces vaguely biological, such as love and strife, or of blind mechanical processes, such as condensation and rarefaction, or mingling and separation, Plato puts forward the view that the generation of the world is analogous to the planned production of a work of *techne*. The mythical figure who presides over its construction is the Craftsman, or Demiurge, who employs the subtlest resources of knowledge and skill to fashion the materials of the world into an order of beauty and goodness. Here the Ideas, the order of true being, appear again as the model or pattern to which the Demiurge constantly looks as he fashions the visible world. The question discussed in the *Laws*, whether *physis* or *techne* is prior, is nowhere raised in the *Timaeus*, for the whole point of the cosmic myth is to assert the primacy of the Demiurge, and his knowledge of the eternal pattern, over the visible cosmos and the materials employed in its construction. We may well ask whether the visible cosmos is itself *physis* or a copy of *physis*. Strictly speaking it is the latter, since it is constructed in the likeness of the eternal models, and these are true being. Yet being constructed by "the best of causes" it is "by nature the fairest and best of products." [32] The divine and invisible *nous*, which is truly primary, is nevertheless made manifest in the visible cosmos, the *physis* of ordinary discourse.

Thus in Plato's later dialogues we find fully worked out a conception of *physis*, including an idealization of the visible *physis* or cosmos, that could lend itself to the uses which the Stoics later were to make of the

---

[31] 29b-d, 48d, 68d, 72de.
[32] 30b; cf. 29a. For a fuller account, see Solmsen, *op. cit.*, pp. 131 ff.

term.[33] The order of nature, which is manifest in visible nature or the cosmos, is an order in which intelligence ($\nu o\hat{v}s$) is the essential ingredient—not merely intelligence as represented by the world of Ideas, but a planning intelligence, superior to, but also akin to, the highest intelligence in man. The cleavage so poignantly expressed by Euripides' Hecuba between the "necessity of nature" and the "mind of man" no longer existed for Plato's thought.[34] Necessity there is, but it is on the whole subordinate to the *nous* upon which the order of nature is dependent.

But we have not yet got the Law of Nature. Before Plato could arrive at this conception certain very grave difficulties had to be overcome. He had emancipated himself from the tyranny of *nomos;* he had found a point of moral support in the conception of natural justice, the justice based on insight into the intelligible order. But the first form which his emancipation took was a complete repudiation of law as being below the level of science. Law appeared to be all too human. The *Republic* not only makes no provision for legislation, but it also contains many disparaging remarks about courts of justice, litigation, and tinkering with the laws. In the *Statesman* it is explicitly said, what Plato doubtless believed all along, that the statesman equipped with the "royal science" ought not to be bound by laws. He should be free, like any competent technician, to disregard conventions, whenever his knowledge shows him that a departure from precedent will serve his ends more effectively. He will be guided by *techne*, rather than *nomos;* and between these two terms there seems to be a tension similar to the earlier opposition between *physis* and *nomos. Techne* represents com-

---

[33] The echoes of Plato's cosmology are unmistakable in Cicero's account of Zeno and Cleanthes, in *De Natura Deorum*. Zeno: *ratione mundus utitur* (ii. 21); *natura ignis artificiosa* (ii. 57); *natura non artificiosa solum sed plane artifex* (ii. 58). Cleanthes: *mens atque animus totius naturae* (i. 37); *nihil ratione censet divinius* (*ibid.*). Likewise from Plato's cosmology come the Stoic doctrine of the world soul, the doctrine of Providence, and (through Aristotle) the distinction between $\theta\epsilon\delta s$ and $\H{\upsilon}\lambda\eta$ ($\tau\delta$ $\pi o\iota o\hat{\upsilon}\nu$ and $\tau\delta$ $\pi\acute{a}\sigma\chi o\nu$). Plato's conception of $\phi\acute{\upsilon}\sigma\iota s$ also influenced Aristotle, it hardly needs to be said, not only in his doctrine that the $\phi\acute{\upsilon}\sigma\iota s$ of sensible things is the form, the $\epsilon\mathring{\iota}\delta o s$, but also in his conception of $\phi\acute{\upsilon}\sigma\iota s$ (i.e., *rerum natura*) as imbued with order and purpose.

[34] Euripides, *Troiades* 886–887:

$$Z\epsilon\acute{\upsilon}s, \ \epsilon\mathring{\iota}\tau' \ \mathring{a}\nu\acute{a}\gamma\kappa\eta \ \phi\acute{\upsilon}\sigma\epsilon os \ \epsilon\mathring{\iota}\tau\epsilon \ \nu o\hat{\upsilon}s \ \beta\rho o\tau\hat{\omega}\nu,$$
$$\pi\rho o\sigma\eta\upsilon\xi\acute{a}\mu\eta\nu \ \sigma\epsilon.$$

petent and sure intelligence, whereas *nomos* stands for what has seemed right or expedient, either to the popular assembly or to the rich,[35] and therefore is inevitably infected with ignorance or selfishness. Furthermore, *nomos,* being a general rule, cannot take account of the peculiarity of particular cases—a defect from which the competent technician would presumably be exempt. These are the two grounds on which Plato, in the *Statesman,* maintains that rule by laws is inferior to rule by a sovereign who possesses the political *techne.* Yet in this same dialogue, by an apparent *volte-face* which has always puzzled the commentators, Plato maintains that in the present state of human affairs it is better that rulers should be bound by law. And in the *Laws* he not only reaffirms this principle, setting up elaborate devices to ensure that all holders of public office can be called to account before courts of law, but engages himself in the painstaking task of formulating the details of legislation appropriate to a good community. This change of attitude is not merely a reluctant compromise with philosophical principle because of the intractability of human affairs. It can be shown, I think, that the conception of *nomos* underwent a change in Plato's thinking, giving rise to distinctions previously absent from his thought—distinctions that the Stoics were to make good use of later.

If we probe deeply into the tortuous argument of the *Statesman,* we can discern two distinct admissions to the credit of law. The first is Plato's declaration in favor of constitutional government, that is, a government in which law is supreme, even over the ruler. This concession to law is necessary in the "present age," Plato says, because our rulers do not possess the royal science and cannot be expected to acquire it. Law therefore is necessary as a protection against the selfishness and the ignorance of rulers. Plato goes so far as to suggest that any government of law, however faulty the law may be, is better than irresponsible rule. This doctrine has the appearance of a compromise between the ideal of *techne* and the political realities that Plato so earnestly wished to influence. But there is another admission made in the *Statesman* that amounts to a modification of the ideal itself. Even a ruler possessing political *techne,* says Plato, would find it necessary to rule by laws. He would, of course, as master of the political art, be free to

---

[35] 298cd; cf. 293a, 294b, 297a.

38

alter the general rules as changing circumstances demanded, just as a trainer of athletes will lay down certain rules governing diet and exercise, though reserving the right to modify these rules if his art requires it (294c–295b). Laws then would be necessary even in the state governed by the true and scientific statesman. This being so, law becomes a necessary ingredient in the ideal and not merely a makeshift substitute for it. The practical application is made two pages later. Plato has previously declared that there is only one right and genuine polity, the state in which the scientific statesman is supreme, and that all other so-called states and constitutions—the aristocracies, oligarchies, tyrannies, and democracies of our experience—are but more or less imperfect imitations of the ideal. Such states must of course be governed by law, recognized as having authority over rulers as well as subjects; but the only way in which these "imitation states" can be truly saved by the rule of law is by employing the written laws of the ideal state (297d). Here we have a clear recognition of a higher law. *Nomos,* as well as *techne,* belongs to the intelligible order and therefore exists by nature.

It will confirm this interpretation of Plato's thought if we note certain kindred ideas found in contemporary documents originating in the Academy. There is no definition of law in the dialogues that are known to have been written by Plato, but there is considerable evidence that the members of the Academy attacked the problem. Aristotle in the *Topics* (140a6) cites as an illustration of a bad definition, "Law is a measure or image of the naturally just." This shows very definitely the influence of Plato's theory of natural justice: the φύσει δίκαιον is the pattern; *nomos* is the likeness, or imitation, of this eternal pattern. A still more instructive attempt is found in the little dialogue *Minos.* Beginning with the formal definition of law as "a judgment of the city" (δόγμα πόλεως),[36] Socrates leads his companion to see that a δόγμα is an opinion (δόξα), and that an opinion may be either true or false; but law is good, therefore law must be a true δόγμα, or in other words, a discovery of what is (315a). At least that is what law means to be (βούλεται εἶναι). The variety of human law is then noted, and this leads to the conclusion that not all so-called laws succeed in discovering what is, and that when a law fails to do this it fails of being a law. A similar

---

[36] Cf. *Laws* 644d.

contention is put forward by Socrates in the *Hippias Major*, a dialogue that is more likely to have been written by Plato himself. Here the good is said to be the object of law, and when legislators fail to attain the good in their legislation they have failed to make laws (284de). In the *Rhetoric* (1375b2) Aristotle advises a litigant whose case cannot be supported by the written law to argue that the law in question is not really law, since it is neither true nor expedient, and therefore fails to realize the aim of law. All this points very definitely to a tendency in Academic circles to think of law, in the strict sense of the term, as identical with its ideal. A *nomos*, truly so called, is not merely a "judgment of the city," but a judgment that is what it purports to be, i.e., a means of attaining the good, or a discovery of reality. Doubtless these Academics continued to speak with the vulgar and to apply the term *nomos* also to the legal and moral rules that were currently regarded as binding, however defective they might be from the point of view of the ideal. Such a way of speaking would be confusing on occasion, but the very confusion would testify to a nascent distinction between ideal and positive law.

Now this confusion is present in Plato's *Laws*, obscuring but not concealing a very real distinction between two kinds of law. The whole composition seems at first reading to be a eulogy of law. Gone is the opposition between *nomos* and *techne;* instead they are named together as "the offspring of nous according to right reason" and therefore as most truly existing by nature (890d). The word *nomos* is said to be cognate with *nous* (957c); and again, *nomos* is "the appointment of nous," νοῦ διανομή (714a). There remains but one thing greater to be said of law and Plato says it; law is divine (θεῖος).[37] Now such language can only be taken as applying to an ideal law. Plato has much to say about the laws and institutions of existing states, such as Crete, Sparta, Athens, Persia; and some of his remarks are most critical. He is especially severe in his criticism of the laws of Sparta, devised as they are for the encouragement of the warlike virtues to the neglect of wisdom and temperance. They aim only at victory in war, whereas the true aim of legislation is peace and concord. He deals at some length with the contention that there are as many kinds of laws as there are types of constitutions, and that in every case the standard by which

---

[37] 716a, 957c; cf. 762e, 713a-e, and *Ep. VIII* 354e.

the law should be judged is its service to the party or group in power. According to this familiar doctrine, democratic law should serve the interests of the demos and oligarchic law that of the rich, there being no higher natural standard than the interest of the dominant class. Against this doctrine he contends that to interpret law as essentially partisan is to misunderstand its true nature and purpose. "When laws are not for the common interest of the whole community, they are not true laws (ὀρθοὶ νόμοι)." [38] Furthermore, Plato finds far too many defects in the particular chapters of existing law—the laws of slavery, for example, or marriage, or property, the laws governing the constitution of the courts and their procedure, the laws governing resident aliens, to mention only a few examples—for him to regard them as the offspring of *nous* in accordance with right reason, and obedience to them as obedience to God (762e).

But it would be a mistake to assume that Plato regarded the institutions which he himself sets up as embodying in all their detail the divine law whose praises he sings. There are too many references to the role of chance as affecting the work of a human legislator, there is too vivid a recognition of the need of divine providence (θεία μοῖρα), and there are too many admitted concessions to circumstances. [39] Besides, Plato says that every system of legislation must provide means for its own revision as experience shows the need of additions or alterations (769d ff.), and such means are provided in his own system of government. All this shows that we are not expected to identify Plato's divine law with the details of his own legislation. Where then are we to look for the content of this ideal law? The only other alternative, it would seem, is to look for it in the principles laid down for the guidance of legislators, in the norms of legislation, so to speak, with which the detailed prescriptions are frequently introduced. It is these norms which determine whether actual legislation has that "rightness" (ὀρθότης) which right reason requires. The aim of law, Plato says, is to make the citizens happy, by providing them with all the goods of life—first the divine goods, wisdom, temperance, justice, courage; and then the human goods, health, beauty, strength, and wealth. [40] Law aims at the

---

[38] 715b; cf. 714a–715a.
[39] 691e, 709ab, 798a, 875c.
[40] 631a-d; cf. 963a.

common good, not at the special interests of any individual or class.[41] This common good at which law aims consists of liberty, wisdom, and fraternity; [42] and the condition of them all is equality, without which men cannot be friends of one another, nor free.[43] These are the fundamental aims of all legislation that truly deserves the name, and we may infer that only laws that embody these purposes can be designated the product of *nous* in accordance with right reason. It is here, I think, in these norms of right law, that we find the real meaning of Plato's θεῖος νόμος, as the pattern which the legislator must follow in the varied and particular circumstances under which he frames his laws.

Although Plato's θεῖος νόμος is nowhere in his text called the law of nature, its right to be so called has, I think, been clearly established in the preceding pages. Once the conception of an ideal law had been attained, it was but a short step from the "natural justice" which occurs so often in Plato's pages to "natural law"; and thus the way was fully prepared for the Stoic phrase. Plato's own term, θεῖος νόμος, goes back to Heraclitus, and may have been deliberately chosen for that reason. If so, we may regard it as an indication that Plato considered himself to have vindicated Heraclitus' insight into the fundamental dependence of human law upon the logos in nature.[44] If Plato did in fact derive inspiration from Heraclitus, this would help to account for the favor which Heraclitus enjoyed with the Stoics. The extant fragments of Heraclitus are too few and too enigmatic to enable us to judge how much of his doctrine of *physis* Plato may have taken from Heraclitus, and it seems clearly misguided to try to read into these fragments detailed anticipations of Stoic doctrine.[45] So far as we know, it is Plato's doctrine the Stoics built upon. The ideal law that prescribes liberty, wisdom, friendship, equality, and concord has a content very similar to that of the Law of Nature as the Stoics conceived it. Its authority, like that of the Law of Nature, rests upon the divine reason in the cosmos and right reason (ὀρθός λόγος, *recta ratio*) in man. No

[41] 875a; 714b–715b; 628a-e.

[42] 693b; 701d; cf. 693d–699d.

[43] 744b, 757; cf. 684d, 694a, 695c, 697c.

[44] Hirzel, *op. cit.*, p. 377 n., has pointed out how frequently Plato connects νόμος with λόγος. *Rep.* 587a,c; 604a; 607a; *Laws* 802e, 816e, 835e; *Ep. VII* 327c, *Ep. VIII* 355a,c.

[45] As Hirzel does, *op. cit.*, pp. 393 f.

prior contract, nor any positive enactment, is required to make it valid. It existed before all positive law, and its authority overrides that of any positive laws that run counter to it.[46]

On one important point there might seem to be a marked difference between Plato's ideal law and the Stoic Law of Nature. The Stoics thought of their law as binding all rational beings into a world community, whereas Plato's thought was directed explicitly toward the self-enclosed state, the small city-state of Greek tradition. Yet it does not follow that, because Plato's positive legislation was designed for a city-state, his ideal law is equally limited in its range. Since the ideal law is the offspring of cosmic *nous*, its sphere of validity is as broad as the cosmos itself. Plato's introduction of this doctrine in the *Laws* probably shows that he was primarily concerned to establish law upon a firm basis in the Greek cities of his time. But the doctrine had an application far broader than his immediate intention. The conception of a divine ordering of the cosmos would tend to instill the sentiment of world citizenship as much as the sentiment of membership in the political community.[47] There are striking anticipations of the Stoic emotion of world loyalty in the admonition that follows Plato's demonstration of the providential ordering of the world.[48] To world loyalty there needs to be added the explicit recognition that all mankind participate in a sphere of rights and duties transcending political boundaries. This was explicitly affirmed by the Stoics, and there are many suggestions of it even in Plato's law. He affirms that law governs the relations between cities,[49] and makes it clear that metics and foreign visitors are "sharers in the law" as well as the citizens of the state.[50] In this respect he seems to have gone farther than even the relatively liberal law of Athens. Furthermore, as Kaerst has pointed out,[51] there breathes through

---

[46] To show the extent of the Stoics' dependence upon Plato's canons of right legislation would require a thorough comparison of the Stoic sources with Plato's *Laws*. This comparison obviously cannot be undertaken here, but I think it has been shown that such an inquiry would almost certainly be fruitful of results.

[47] Cf. Solmsen, *op. cit.*, p. 163.

[48] *Laws* 903b-d.

[49] 645b; cf. 628de.

[50] See my article, "The Status of the Alien in Plato's *Laws*," in *Scientia*, XXXV (1941), 38–43.

[51] Kaerst, *op. cit.*, I, 105.

all Plato's political theory a yearning for a higher kind of community, for which the earthly city is only an imperfect substitute. He was the prophet of another world, and as such he pointed beyond his own time, and beyond the limitations of Greek political life; and thus his thoughts became a ferment out of which a universal culture could emerge.

Aristotle on Law

FRANCIS D. WORMUTH

T HE RULE of law, it is argued, is preferable to that of any individual."[1] This sentence of Aristotle's has had an extraordinary
history. Harrington in his *Oceana* by the phrase "the empire of laws
and not of men" described the impartiality which he fancied would
result from bicameralism. John Adams detached "the government of
laws and not of men" from bicameralism and in the Massachusetts
Declaration of Rights in 1780 made it a consequence of the separation
of legislative, executive, and judicial powers. Roscoe Pound has identified the rule of law with judicial review of legislation;[2] the Supreme
Court has made it the ground for judicial review of administrative
action;[3] in 1937 the Senate Judiciary Committee reported that the
President's bill to enlarge the Supreme Court, although constitutional,
violated the rule of law;[4] to Walter Lippmann[5] and Friedrich von
Hayek[6] the rule of law means an economy which lacks central direction. The trial of the German leaders at Nuremberg by a law made
ex parte, ex post facto, and *ad hoc* has been hailed as a vindication of
the rule of law.

Aside from these specific applications, the phrase "the rule of law"
is widely used as a rhetorical expression. Law becomes the highest of
all values, or the indispensable medium in which values are set. Liberty,
equality, and justice are somehow subsumed under the rubric law. In

[1] *Politics* III, 16, 3 (Jowett translation).
[2] "Rule of Law," *Encyclopaedia of the Social Sciences.*
[3] St. Joseph Stockyards Co. v. United States, 298 U.S. 38 (1936).
[4] 75th Congress, 1st Session, Report No. 711, p. 15.
[5] *The Good Society* (Boston, 1937).
[6] *The Road to Serfdom* (Chicago, 1944).

this usage, law is a flexible term; it can mean either of two diametrically opposite things. It can stand for the idea of an austere and inflexible code, not to be mitigated by administrative discretion or other purposeful adaptation. There is no pretext here that law is other than positive law, yet by its invariability it somehow borrows the impressiveness of cosmic justice. On the other hand, the expression "the rule of law" is sometimes used in denouncing governmental actions which are indisputably legal in terms of positive law; here the appeal is to a higher law which overrides mere human fiat.

Both of these senses of the term are thought to have originated in Aristotle.[7] He did indeed write the sentence quoted above; and he also spoke of a natural justice superior to human laws. Yet he could hardly have believed both in the inflexible application of positive law, to the disregard of meliorative considerations, and in a superior morality which nullified positive law. The argument of this essay is that he believed in neither—or, rather, in the former not much, in the latter not at all.

Aristotle's views on law are not easily discovered. The relevant material is not confined to one branch of his system. Fortunately it is not in all cases necessary to describe the theoretical framework in which significant ideas are embedded. Even so, the approach must be slow, and the path leads through many of his works.

Politics deals with human action, and rests therefore on psychological considerations. "There are," said Aristotle in his treatise on psychology,[8] "two powers in the soul which appear to be moving forces—desire and reason, if one classifies imagination as a kind of reason." Voluntary action always involves desire (*orexis*); reason (*nous*) alone cannot originate activity. Moral action consists in the guidance of desire by reason. Moral choice is desire penetrated by reason (*orexis dianoëtike*) or reason prompted by desire (*nous orektikos*).[9]

There are three qualities of the *psyche,* faculty, passion, and habit. Since virtue is neither of the first two, it must be a habit.[10] Accordingly, moral virtue is acquired through habituation. One becomes virtuous

---

[7] See, for example, John Dickinson, *Administrative Justice and the Supremacy of Law* (Cambridge, Mass., 1927), pp. 80, 127 n.

[8] *De Anima* III, 10, 1.

[9] *Nicomachean Ethics* 1139b, 4.

[10] *Ibid.,* II, 5. Cf. *Categories,* 8.

through doing virtuous acts.[11] But such a habit is not enough to solve the problem of choice. An intellectual virtue, practical wisdom or *phronesis,* must also be present. "Virtue makes us aim at the right mark, and practical wisdom makes us take the right means." [12] The intellectual virtue of *phronesis* is therefore indispensable to all the moral virtues.[13]

Now the area of action and choice is the area of the variable and contingent, as opposed to the realm of scientific thought, which deals with the necessary and immutable.[14] Consequently ethics and politics— the latter embraces the former—must be content with rough and imprecise rules, which cannot solve particular cases with any exactness. At this point Aristotle has recourse to Plato's favorite examples of the physician and the pilot, who deal with the unique by their peculiar skills and not by general rules.[15] The man possessed of the moral skill suitable to the solution of particular cases is the *phronimos,*[16] for he has practical wisdom. Since practical wisdom deals with action, it involves particulars as well as universals. The *phronimos* has a grasp of both. The particulars are more important, and an empiric who has had experience with particulars but lacks knowledge of universals is a better guide than one who knows the universals only.[17]

Phronesis when applied to the affairs of the state is political wisdom.[18] It is the virtue of the ruler.[19] The controlling part of political wisdom is legislation. The *Ethics* is primarily directed to the legislator. According to Aristotle, the end of life is happiness; the happy man is virtuous; and virtues are habits inculcated by laws. A primary function of laws, indeed, is to educate the young in the habits of virtue.[20] It is

---

[11] *Ibid.,* II, 1.
[12] *Ibid.,* VI, 12, 6 (Ross translation).
[13] *Ibid.,* VI, 13, 6.
[14] *Ibid.,* VI, 1–4.
[15] *Ibid.,* I, 3; II, 2.
[16] *Ibid.,* 1107a, 1.
[17] *Ibid.,* VI, 7, 7.
[18] *Ibid.,* VI, 8.
[19] *Politics* III, 4, 17.
[20] *Nic. Eth.* X, 9; *Politics* VIII, 1. The father of the family has an advantage over the legislator because he can prescribe a regimen more immediately suited to particular needs, just as the physician in private practice can prescribe the treatment appropriate to the individual, and the boxer can train his pupil in a style of fighting peculiarly suited to him. *Nic. Eth., loc. cit.*

true that laws are also needed to prevent injustice,[21] for most people respond to punishment rather than persuasion.[22]

Since the laws achieve their effect through habit, they should not lightly be changed. "For the law has no power to command obedience except that of habit, which can only be given by time, so that a readiness to change from old to new laws enfeebles the power of the law." [23] This is the only deterrent Aristotle finds to change. Politics should advance as the arts do.[24] The ancient customs and laws were "exceedingly simple and barbarous," [25] and Aristotle has a very low opinion of contemporary laws. The cities reputed to be the best governed do not have constitutions framed with a regard to the best end; [26] and every city has failed in the elementary requirement of adapting its laws to the spirit of its constitution.[27] In most cities, "the laws may be said generally to be in a chaotic state," and "if they aim at anything, they aim at the maintenance of power: thus in Lacedaemon and Crete the system of education and the greater part of the laws are framed with a view to war." [28]

In addition to the question of the relation of the laws to the ruled, there is the question of the relation of laws to the ruler. Plato in his *Statesman* had asked whether it is better to be governed by the discretion of an absolute ruler or by the laws, and in the *Laws* had definitely concluded in favor of laws. He assumed, of course, that the laws would be good laws—the very laws, in fact, that he was laying down. In his discussion of the comparative virtues of monarchy and law in Book III of the *Politics*, Aristotle also assumes that the laws are good. But he does not come out with a complete indorsement of the rule of law.

His discussion takes the form of a canvass of the arguments on each side. The fifteenth chapter offers Plato's major argument in favor of monarchy, that "laws speak only in general terms, and cannot provide for circumstances; and that for any science to abide by written rules

---

[21] *Ibid.*, 1134a, 30.
[22] *Ibid.*, X, 9, 9.
[23] *Politics* II, 8, 24 (Jowett translation).
[24] *Ibid.*, II, 8, 18.
[25] *Ibid.*, II, 8, 20. And see *Metaphysics* II, 3.
[26] *Politics* VII, 14, 15.
[27] *Ibid.*, V, 9, 12.
[28] *Ibid.*, VII, 2, 9.

is absurd." To this Aristotle offers the current reply, also from Plato,[29] that the king is likely to be influenced by passion, whereas the law is impersonal. The rejoinder is made that discretion is needed in particular cases, to deal with what Plato in the *Statesman* called "the endless irregular movements of human things," which cannot adequately be anticipated in general laws. Aristotle disposes of the whole problem by proposing that the best man, he who possesses the statesman's art, establish general laws, but leave it open to determine particular cases to which the law is not well suited by discretion. The power of discretionary decision should be vested in a considerable number, rather than in the one wise man, for their aggregate wisdom will outweigh his, and they are less corruptible and less likely to be influenced by passion.

Turning now to the topic of law, Aristotle observes that the argument for equality, and a constitution in which the citizens govern and are governed in turn, is in a sense an argument for law, "for an order of succession implies law." And then he recurs to Plato's argument for law in the *Laws*, which Aristotle renders in the oft-quoted phrase, "The law is reason (*nous*) unaffected by desire (*orexis*)." Now this is perfectly good Platonic psychology, for to Plato reason was indeed a moral faculty which dominated but was unaffected by desire.[30] It is the point of view Aristotle attacked as Socratic: "Socrates, then, thought the virtues were rules or right principles (for he thought they were, all of them, forms of scientific knowledge), while we think they *involve* a rational principle." [31] For Aristotle, moral action was reason penetrated by desire, and law was the handmaid of morality: it existed in order to habituate men to virtue. Law must therefore share the appetitive and purposive element which is found in virtue itself. This is suggested in the only definition of law, unfortunately a casual one, that Aristotle has left us. In the *Ethics* he recognizes two features of law: it has coercive power, and it is a rule resulting from "a sort of *phronesis* and *nous*." [32] Since *phronesis* is linked to virtue,[33] this definition imports

---

[29] *Laws* 875.
[30] *Republic* 439–441.
[31] *Nic. Eth.* VI, 13, 5 (Ross translation).
[32] X, 9, 12. For a contrary gloss on the passage, see J. Cook Wilson, "On the Meaning of *Logos*," *Classical Review*, XXVII (1913), 113, 116.
[33] X, 8, 3.

49

desire into law. The language of the *Politics* must be taken as a para-
phrase of Plato rather than an encomium by Aristotle. This is made clear
when Aristotle concludes his weighing of rival arguments: "These are
the principal arguments concerning monarchy. But may not all this be
true in some cases and not in others?" And Aristotle goes on to say that
laws are suited to some peoples and polities, and not to others.

Aristotle's argument in favor of law and against discretionary decision is stated more fully in the *Rhetoric* than in the *Politics*. There he
gives three reasons for confining the jury to the application of pre-
established rules of law rather than permitting them to decide cases
as they arise. First, one or a few legislators will possess better judgment
than the jurymen called upon to decide particular cases. Moreover,
legislation is the result of long deliberation, whereas judgments in
suits are decided on the spur of the moment.

But what is most important of all is that the judgment of the legislator does
not apply to a particular case, but is universal and applies to the future,
whereas the member of the public assembly and the dicast have to decide
present and definite issues, and in their case love, hate, or personal interest is
often involved, so that they are no longer capable of discerning the truth
adequately, their judgment being obscured by their own pleasure or pain.[34]

The upshot is that Aristotle found two advantages in laws in relation
to the ruled: they trained some citizens in virtue; and they restrained
the others from evil. Leaving aside the makeweight arguments—the
superiority of the legislator to the jurymen, and the like—there is one
virtue in law in relation to the ruler or the dicast: it corrects the bias
which pleasure or pain may introduce into his uncontrolled judgment
in a case in which he is interested. This reminds one of the advice in
the *Ethics*: "Since to hit the mean is hard in the extreme, we must as a
second-best, as people say, take the least of the evils" by "drawing well
away from error, as people do in straightening sticks." [35] It would be
best to find the solution uniquely suited to the situation by *phronesis,*
but the fact that the case is individual raises the possibility of interest
on the part of the ruler. He should therefore lean backward into general
law, which although inaccurate is also dispassionate. This is all that
the rule of law meant to Aristotle.

It was clear enough to Aristotle that rules of law were inaccurate

---

[34] *Rhetoric* I, 1, 7 (J. H. Freese translation; Loeb Classical Library).
[35] II, 9.

tools for the solution of problems. The whole area of conduct was one of contingency, in which reasoning was only probable, and general rules fitted roughly a majority of the cases. Only the *phronimos*, making a particular decision, could hit the center of the target in a particular case. This appears, indeed, to have been the usual Greek view of human affairs in the fourth century. The true physician, says Plato, will cure a man by his proper skill, which is superior to written rules, and will even compel his patient for his own good against the written rules; [36] and the only objection Aristotle raises to this proposal is that the physician may be in league with the patient's enemies. [37] Isocrates, urging Philip of Macedon to lead the Greeks against the Persian king, said that he had singled out Philip "because I saw that all the other men of high repute were living under the control of polities and laws, with no power to do anything save what was prescribed"; Philip, on the other hand, had "untrammeled freedom" to consider all Hellas his fatherland. [38] It has been complained that Aristotle's *Ethics* is deficient in casuistry. Aristotle himself makes a point of the difficulty of prescribing formulas. [39] Circumstances alter cases; unique problems demand unique solutions.

It follows that legal justice is likely to fall short of complete justice. This is recognized in the *Ethics*, where Aristotle passes from the consideration of law to equity. [40] The law speaks generally, but about some subjects it is not possible to make a general statement which will be correct. Equity is a correction of legal justice where the law errs because of its generality. Equity says what the legislator himself would have said "if he had known." It is therefore better than legal justice, although not better than absolute justice. [41]

In fact this is the reason why all things are not determined by law, *viz.* that about some things it is impossible to lay down a law, so that a decree is needed. For when the thing is indefinite the rule also is indefinite, like the leaden rule

---

[36] *Statesman* 293–295.
[37] *Politics* III, 16, 7.
[38] *To Philip* 14, 127, in *Isocrates* (G. Norlin translation; Loeb Classical Library).
[39] *Nic. Eth.* IX, 2.
[40] *Ibid.*, V, 10. And see *Rhetoric* I, 13, 11–19.
[41] Since equity builds on the law, it will rest on the same moral base as the law itself. It is a more accurate implementation of the moral assumptions of the law; it corrects the law in its application rather than in its inception. See J. A. Stewart, *Notes on the Nicomachean Ethics* (Oxford, 1892), I, 529.

used in making the lesbian moulding; the rule adapts itself to the shape of the stone and is not rigid, and so too the decree is adapted to the facts.[42]

The reference to a decree needs explanation. There was at Athens a yearly scrutiny of the laws by a large jury of Nomothetai, which after hearing argument enacted new laws and repealed old. Decrees were a subordinate form of legislation passed by the citizenry assembled in the Ecclesia. One of the laws forbade the adoption of any legislation dealing with an individual, except in the extraordinary procedure of ostracism. Laws were thought of as necessarily general, as Aristotle testifies.[43] He defined decrees, on the other hand, as dealing only with particulars, and considered it a reproach to democracies that they resorted to government by decree.[44] But in the passage quoted above he concedes that decrees may be needed in order to introduce equity into the law.

Aristotle proposed two other corrections of law by equity. The generality of legislation makes exact definition impossible, and a literal application of the law may work injustice; here it is better to follow the intention of the legislator than the written law.[45] Moreover, arbitration should be preferred to the law courts, for the arbitrator looks to equity.[46]

Aristotle's views on the relation of law to justice are clear enough in the discussion of equity, but they are clouded by his importation of three other ideas from common speech: the unwritten law, universal law, and natural justice. These ideas should be carefully held apart, but Aristotle himself does not do so.

The expression *agraphoi nomoi*, unwritten laws, had a variety of uses. On one occasion Aristotle assimilated equity to the idea of unwritten law.[47] But what might be called the technical use of the term treats the unwritten laws as divine commands which enjoy an authority superior to human laws. Sophocles in *Oedipus the King* [48] speaks of

---

[42] *Nic. Eth.* 1137b, 27–32 (Ross translation).
[43] *Rhetoric* I, 1, 7.
[44] *Politics* 1292a.
[45] *Rhetoric* I, 13, 13–19.
[46] *Ibid.*, I, 13, 19.
[47] *Ibid.*, I, 13, 12.
[48] 863 ff., in *Sophocles* (F. Storr translation; Loeb Classical Library).

52

> those laws ordained on high,
> Whose birthplace is the bright ethereal sky.
> No mortal birth they own,
> Olympus their progenitor alone.

The same poet's Antigone defies human law in the name of

> The immutable unwritten laws of Heaven.
> They were not born today nor yesterday;
> They die not; and none knoweth whence they sprang.[49]

The speech *Against Andocides,*[50] wrongly attributed to Lysias, speaks of "the unwritten laws . . . whose very author is unknown." These and similar expressions refer, as Miss Macurdy has shown,[51] to religious customs inherited from the past and attributed to the gods. They were largely limited to the duty of piety to gods and parents, the incest taboo, and the requirement of burial of the dead.

The idea of the unwritten laws was broadened out in Xenophon's *Memorabilia*[52] to something like a *jus gentium*, for there they are said to be uniformly observed in every country. They are still derived from the gods. The *Rhetorica ad Alexandrum*[53] speaks of an "unwritten and universal law" practised by the whole or the greater part of mankind. Here there is no reference to the gods. Euripides considered the rules of morality to be universal: "In foreign land, as here, shame is but shame."[54] Aristotle in the *Rhetoric* speaks of a universal law, *koinos nomos*, unwritten and everywhere recognized, which he contrasts with particular or written law.[55] He then asserts that universal law exists by nature, for there is a common idea of natural right and wrong among men, even when there is no communication or agreement among them. As examples to be cited by the rhetorician who is obliged to appeal from the established laws to this higher law, he offers Antigone's defiance of Creon, Empedocles' "universal precept" against taking life, and Alcidamas' declaration that nature condemns slavery.[56] Probably

---

[49] *Antigone* 454 ff., *ibid.*

[50] § 10, in *Lysias* (W. R. M. Lamb translation; Loeb Classical Library).

[51] *The Quality of Mercy* (New Haven, 1940), pp. 111–112.

[52] IV, 4, 19.

[53] 1422a.

[54] *Andromache* 244. See R. B. Appleton, *Euripides the Idealist* (New York, 1927), p. 82.

[55] *Rhetoric* I, 10, 3.

[56] *Ibid.*, I, 13, 2.

53

these examples are to be considered merely as weapons of the rhetorician, and not the opinion of Aristotle, for he certainly thought that
some men are slaves by nature; and it is hard to believe that he supposed burial customs to be invariable.[57] He makes his purpose clear
enough:

> For it is evident that, if the written law is contrary to our case, we must have
> recourse to the general law and equity, as more in accordance with justice;
> and we must argue that, when the dicast takes an oath to decide to the best
> of his judgment, he means that he will not abide rigorously by the written
> laws; that equity is constant and never changes, even as the general law, which
> is based on nature, whereas the written laws often vary (this is why Antigone
> in Sophocles justifies herself for having buried Polynices contrary to the law of
> Creon, but not contrary to the unwritten law). . . .[58]

And he goes on to offer arguments to be used when the written law
favors the disputant: that the dicast's oath is not intended to emancipate him from the law; that universal law, like absolute good, is not
adapted to the peculiar needs of the community; that one might as
well not have laws if one does not use them; that disobedience to the
laws does a permanent harm which outweighs any immediate gain;
that the most approved laws forbid one to try to be wiser than the
laws.[59]

Still it is true that Aristotle in the *Rhetoric* does seem to recognize
a *koinos nomos* which exists by nature. And the *Nicomachean Ethics* [60]
declares that there is a natural justice which has the same force everywhere and does not depend upon opinion, in contrast to legal justice,
which specifies among things originally indifferent.

This is an astonishing evolution. The *agraphos nomos* had as its
background the ancestral customs and ritualistic practices of the
Greeks. It was a provincial idea, the creed of conservatives like
Sophocles.[61] The idea of *physis* or nature as a standard, on the other

---

[57] See *Nic. Eth.* V, 7. Cf. Herodotus III, 38: The Greeks burn their parents'
corpses, and the Indians eat theirs; each nation regards the other's practice as re-
volting. "*Nomos* is king of all."

[58] *Rhetoric* I, 15, 3–6 (J. H. Freese translation: Loeb Classical Library).

[59] *Ibid.*, I, 12.

[60] V, 7, 1. See V, 9, 12; VIII, 13, 5.

[61] Jacques Maritain is only the latest to say that the idea of natural law goes back
to "the great moralists of antiquity and its great poets, particularly Sophocles.
Antigone is the eternal heroine of natural law, which the Ancients called the *unwritten law*, and this is the name most befitting it" (*Les droits de l'homme et la loi
naturelle* [New York, 1942], p. 78). The unwritten law of Sophocles was the com-

hand, had been used by the sophists and "physical investigators," as Plato called them, to discredit *nomos,* local usage and custom. But the unwritten law passed into a universal law which was a kind of *jus gentium,* and ended, in the hands of Aristotle, as a sort of *jus naturale*—although Aristotle usually speaks of natural justice rather than natural law.

The idea of a natural justice superior to *nomos* is quite at variance with the method of the *Nicomachean Ethics,* which Stewart has accurately said undertakes to form common opinions into a system.[62] Marshall thought, "It is remarkable that Aristotle, who has traced quite correctly the genesis of moral conduct, should have been carried away by the fiction of a natural justice." [63] But at a superficial view, natural virtue and justice seem quite in harmony with one aspect of Aristotle's system, its teleology. If there is a function for which men exist,[64] if even the lower animals seek some good,[65] one would expect these to be called natural. So, by what may be a metaphorical use of the word *physis,*[66] Aristotle says that man is by nature political,[67] and that slavery, the family, the village, and the state are natural institutions.[68]

Some passages in Aristotle's discussion of *physis* are compatible with the idea of natural virtue. In speaking of the nature of a thing, we mean its entelechy, its completed realization.[69] Indeed, by nature we mean the goal or purpose for which everything exists.[70] Popular morality did not hesitate to declare virtue to be natural. Euripides thought that right action, which seeks the mean, is in accordance with *physis;* wrong action is a violation of *physis.*[71] And not only popular morality: the *Eudemian Ethics* says that by nature the good is an object of wish, and it is a contravention of nature when one wishes evil; [72] a wicked

---

plete opposite of M. Maritain's natural law. It was to Sophocles a conscious symbol of opposition to the new humane and rationalistic spirit represented by Euripides.

[62] *Op. cit.,* II, 120–121.
[63] *Aristotle's Theory of Conduct* (London, 1905), p. 304.
[64] *Nic. Eth.* I, 7, 10–12.
[65] *Ibid.,* X, 2, 4.
[66] See Octave Hamelin, *Le systeme d'Aristote* (Paris, 1931), p. 302.
[67] *Politics* 1278b, 20.
[68] *Ibid.,* I, 2.
[69] *Physics* 193b, 28.
[70] *Ibid.,* 194a, 28.
[71] Rhys Carpenter, *The Ethics of Euripides* (New York, 1916), p. 29.
[72] II, 10, 25; 10, 27.

man is contrary to nature.[73] It is not clear how these expressions are to be taken, for the *Eudemian Ethics* also recognizes that full-fledged virtue, the exercise of *phronesis,* is not natural; [74] but if the author did not intend to assimilate virtue to *physis,* his language is extremely incautious.

In any case, nothing is clearer than that the idea of natural virtue is inconsistent with the Aristotelian system. Aristotle expressly excluded the subject of ethics from the domain of *physis.* The *Physics* [75] recognizes as natural those things which have a principle of change or rest within themselves. Such are material forms, animate and inanimate. A change resulting from this innate principle of movement is natural; that produced by an outside agent is not natural. When the body "naturally" achieves health, this is the work of nature; a physician who cures himself achieves the result by art rather than nature, for it is not by the intrinsic principle of his being that he recovers. Art, and intelligence generally, lie outside the domain of nature.

The *Parts of Animals* [76] declares that it is the business of the science of nature to study the *psyche,* but only that part of it which man has in common with the other animals, the irrational part. If the intellect were included, all studies would be swallowed up in natural science, since when intellect was introduced all the objects of cognition would also be introduced. Moreover, it is evident that it is the irrational rather than the rational part of the *psyche* that is responsible for growth and movement, which are the preoccupation of natural science.

The *Metaphysics,*[77] like the *Physics,* limits natural science to the area of theoretical knowledge, to the exclusion of the arts and of practical studies—such as ethics. Moreover, it says that natural science is concerned exclusively with material substances, and with the *psyche* only to the extent that it is dependent upon matter. Marcel de Corte finds here a suggestion that intelligence, being incorporeal, is reserved for metaphysics.[78]

Another passage in the *Metaphysics* [79] has a bearing on the question.

---

[73] VII, 6, 13. Less striking are II, 8, 14–15; VIII, 3, 7–8.
[74] III, 7, 11.
[75] II, 1.
[76] 641a, 34-b, 10.
[77] VI, 1.
[78] *La Doctrine de l'intelligence chez Aristote* (Paris, 1934), p. 16.
[79] IX, 5.

Discussing potencies, Aristotle points out that nonrational potencies behave always in the same way, and produce the same effects; and this, we know from the *Physics,* is the hallmark of nature. Rational potencies, on the other hand, produce effects which depend upon the will or desire of the actor. The *Nicomachean Ethics* recognizes four "efficient causes" of motion: nature, necessity, chance, and "reason and everything that depends upon man." [80] This does not mean that man cannot be a natural cause—he is, for example, the efficient and natural cause of his offspring [81]—but insofar as he acts through reason and choice he is a cause outside nature.

It appears, then, that nature does not reach up to the rational element in the *psyche* of man. The practical studies—politics and ethics—and the productive studies—Aristotle has left us in this field only the *Poetics,* unless the *Rhetoric* be considered also to belong here—must develop their own principles. This the *Nicomachean Ethics* undertakes to do. Virtue is not natural, but acquired. If virtue were natural, it would be inevitable; all men would have been born good or bad. But we acquire good or bad characters by the activities in which we engage. "Neither by nature, then, nor contrary to nature do the virtues arise in us; rather we are adapted by nature to receive them, and are made perfect by habit." [82] It is true that Aristotle speaks of "natural virtues," [83] but what he seems to have in mind chiefly is that courage which is a passion rather than a virtue.[84] In the *Politics* he says that citizens should be by nature intelligent and courageous; i.e., they should be Hellenes.[85] To these natural capacities must be added habit and rational principle.[86]

Aristotle's explicit teachings on nature and ethics make it necessary to re-examine the passages in which he speaks of a universal law and a natural justice. It has always been assumed that these were intended to establish a Thomistic jurisprudence with natural law at its apex.[87]

---

[80] III, 3, 7.

[81] *Physics* 193b, 8.

[82] *Nic. Eth.* I, 1.

[83] *Ibid.,* VI, 13, 1; VII, 8, 4.

[84] *Ibid.,* III, 8, 12. L. H. C. Greenwood, *Aristotle: Nichomachean Ethics: Book VI* (Cambridge, 1909), p. 56, regards the natural virtues as states of desire preliminary to virtue. See Plato, *Republic* 375e, 530c; *Laws* 963e.

[85] VII, 7, 1–4.

[86] VII, 15, 7. See Plato, *Statesman* 309–310.

[87] St. Thomas thought so in his commentary on V, 7, of the *Nicomachean Ethics.* See also E. M. Cope, *An Introduction to Aristotle's Rhetoric* (London, 1867), pp.

But two considerations make the passages in the *Rhetoric* of doubtful value as evidence of Aristotle's opinions. To begin with, the book is intended to teach rhetoricians to plead cases; and Aristotle in fact offers arguments on both sides of the question. The discussion seems quite in the spirit of that in the *Sophistic Elenchi*,[88] where Aristotle says that the contrast between *physis* and *nomos* is a sophistical device for involving one's opponent in a paradox. We are not obliged to believe that the *Rhetoric* is doing anything more than reporting the stock phrases of current oratory; and indeed the huddling together of unwritten law, universal law, natural justice, and equity is unlike the careful analysis Aristotle bestows on ideas he takes seriously. Furthermore, we know that Aristotle was willing to accept popular premises which he considered imprecise if they led to conclusions he indorsed; the *Nicomachean Ethics,* for example, adopts for convenience the popular twofold analysis of the *psyche,* although it differs from that in the *De Anima.* Now the unwritten, universal, and natural laws are used in the *Rhetoric* to introduce equity, an idea which Aristotle did take seriously—and one which he subjects to careful analysis. It is not safe to build a jurisprudence on the basis of a few sentences in the *Rhetoric.*

The difficulties offered by the *Nicomachean Ethics* appear to be terminological rather than substantial. Book V, Chapter 7, where the account of "natural justice" occurs,[89] is concerned with political justice, which it divides into natural and legal. Political justice has been declared in the preceding chapter to exist by and under positive law, so we cannot really be confronted here by a conflict between *physis* and *nomos.* Nor does Chapter 7 suggest such a conflict. It deals with the area of the morally indifferent. Some things are intrinsically right and wrong; others require legal specification, as the amount of a prisoner's ransom and the size of measures in markets. Aristotle's natural justice is the division of law dealing with what we call *mala in se;* his legal justice is our *mala prohibita.* This distinction between the two kinds of wrong is found in every legal system; and it is found, as with Aristotle, within the system. *Malum in se* is *malum* at positive law; it is true that it was prohibited because of moral opinions, but its status as law does not

239 ff.; E. Zeller, *Aristotle and the Earlier Peripatetics* (London, 1897), II, 176; V. Johnson, "Aristotle on *Nomos,*" *Classical Journal,* XXXIII (1938), 351.

[88] 173a, 7–19.

[89] Cf. V, 9, 12, and VIII, 13, 5.

raise a question of natural law or of the invalidity of positive law. *Malum prohibitum* exists, as Aristotle says, where it is necessary to specify, because of expediency, among things originally indifferent. Aristotle's choice of terms was unfortunate, although not much more so than ours. Evidently he adopted the nomenclature of *physis* and *nomos* because the sophists had already made it familiar to his audience. Perhaps his division of positive law into natural and legal justice is the strongest evidence that he had no conception of a natural law which annuls positive law. He believed that laws were good or bad, but he never denied the name of law to bad laws.

To Aristotle virtue and justice were not natural, nor yet merely conventional. Ethics comes from *ethos* or habit; one becomes virtuous by habituation, which it is the function of laws to establish. But there are bad habits as well as good,[90] and bad laws as well as good.[91] There is a standard by which habits and laws are to be judged. Good habits implant this standard. The process of becoming virtuous seems not to be intellectual, and yet not unintellectual. Aristotle draws a parallel between the method of science and the method of ethics. Science proceeds by induction from particulars to universals, and then reasons downward from universals to particulars by the logical syllogism.[92] Morality has its universals also, but these are achieved by habituation rather than by induction; from the universals one proceeds to action by the practical syllogism, which it is the task of *phronesis* to apply.[93] Undoubtedly Aristotle believes that there are universals in ethics, but they seem less at home there than in the scientific studies. A happier term is his *orthos logos*. In a man with the proper natural endowments, good habits establish an *orthos logos*. This supplies a rule, or is a rule, for conduct; more than that, it seems to be a sort of mental character or disposition or personality.

The *orthos logos* of Aristotle has been variously translated—right reason, right plan, right thought, right rule, right disposition, ratio.[94]

---

[90] *Nic. Eth.* VII, 10, 4; 14, 4.

[91] *Ibid.*, VII, 10, 5.

[92] *Ibid.*, VI, 3; *Posterior Analytics* II, 19.

[93] *Nic. Eth.* I, 4, 5–7; 7, 21; VI, 7, 6–7; *Movement of Animals* 7.

[94] For discussions see Sir Alexander Grant, *The Ethics of Aristotle* (London, 1885), I, 487 n.; Stewart, *op. cit.*, I, 4, 17, 173, 174, 202, 206–7; II, 4–5, 24, 107; John Burnet, *The Ethics of Aristotle* (London, 1900), pp. 79 n., 80 n., 247, 252 n., 286 n.; Greenwood, *op. cit.*, pp. 167–8; J. Cook Wilson, "On the Meaning of *Logos*,"

The meaning is probably somewhat fluid. Plato had used the expression without fixed meaning.[95] It was in common use in the Academy.[96] With Aristotle not merely is *logos* right, but *orexis* is sometimes *orthe*.[97] But with all reservations, the *orthos logos* of Aristotle appears to represent a moral set which results from good habituation, and stands at an apex corresponding to the position of the universals in scientific thought. It supplies the point of departure, the end to be accomplished; *phronesis* discovers the means to the end, although it must be confessed that Aristotle runs this intellectual virtue over to some degree into the moral area, and confuses it with *orthos logos*.[98]

The Aristotelian *orthos logos* calls to mind at once the *orthos logos* and *recta ratio* of the Stoics. But the *orthos logos* of the earlier Stoics was not concerned with ethics at all; it was a concept in the field of epistomology.[99] The right reason of late Stoicism was an undifferentiated reason applied in the field of ethics; the Aristotelian *orthos logos*, on the other hand, is not an intellectual operation, although it has indefinite intellectual overtones.

This is a sufficiently unsatisfactory way to establish an ethics; but it is Aristotle's. He believed, as we have seen, in an intrinsic right and wrong. But he believed also in adaptation to purpose. This does not get him into any difficulties in the *Ethics*. Fixed ethical standards are not inconsistent with particularized applications in variable circumstances. But in the *Politics* the standards also become relative.

There is such a thing as the perfect state.[100] But there is also a state best suited to the particular circumstances,[101] and here the form of the perfect state would be inappropriate—in fact, bad. There is a form best suited to states in general.[102] And these demand different qualities

---

Classical Review, XXVII (1913), 113; J. L. Stocks, "On the Aristotelian Use of *Logos*," *Classical Quarterly*, VIII (1914), 9; Leon Robin, *Greek Thought* (New York, 1928), p. 264; H. W. B. Joseph, "Aristotle's Definition of Moral Virtue," *Philosophy*, IX (1934), 168, 176–177 n.

[95] Grant has collected instances, *loc. cit.*

[96] Burnet, *op. cit.*, p. 79 n.

[97] *Nic. Eth.* 1139a, 25, 31.

[98] *Ibid.*, VI, 13, 5.

[99] Rudolf Hirzel, *Untersuchungen zu Cicero's philosophischen Schriften* (Leipzig, 1877), II, 10 ff.; Emile Bréhier, *Chrysippe* (Paris, 1910), pp. 101 ff.

[100] *Politics* II, 1, 1; VII; VIII.

[101] *Ibid.*, IV, 1, 3; 11, 21.

[102] *Ibid.*, II, 6, 16; IV, 11, 1.

in their citizens. In the perfect state, the good man is the good citizen.[103] In other states, the bad man may be a good citizen.[104] The virtue of the citizen is relative to the constitution.[105] It is no longer possible to say, as Aristotle says in the *Ethics,* that the interests and ends of the individual and the state are the same.[106]

The laws, too, must be suited to the constitution.[107] If we remember the role of laws in forming character, it appears that all virtue is being sacrificed to expediency. To a degree this can be explained. Aristotle is describing how to maintain one of the three legitimate forms of government, and presumably the best the situation will permit, although they are all perversions in comparison with the perfect state.[108] But this is carrying the idea of the second-best pretty far. It means accepting a second-best virtue. Every state will have its own ethics, and virtue will become conventional after all.

This illustrates a strong bias in Aristotle's thought. He was convinced of the uniqueness of situations, and the appropriateness of unique solutions. As we have seen law prove inadequate because of its generality, so virtue itself fails to meet the demands of the variable. It is this bias that deserves emphasis in a study of Aristotle's conception of law. His attitude toward law was thoroughly pragmatic. Law was a means to an end, and not always the best means to that end. This is generally true of the pre-Hellenistic Greeks. Jowett has said that to the Greeks law was "a sacred name" and "the highest object of reverence." [109] If this were so, they would not deserve the respect they have received.

---

[103] *Ibid.,* III, 18; IV, 7, 2. Cf. III, 4, 4–5.
[104] *Ibid.,* III, 4, 4.
[105] *Ibid.,* III, 4, 3.
[106] *Nic. Eth.* I, 2, 8.
[107] *Politics* III, 11, 20–21; IV, 1, 9–10.
[108] *Ibid.,* IV, 8, 1.
[109] *The Dialogues of Plato* (London, 1892), IV, 441, 447.

Vico on Roman Law

MAX H. FISCH

THOUGH Vico was largely self-taught, he took the degree of "doctor in both the laws." And though he held the chair of rhetoric at the University of Naples from 1699 to 1741, he aspired to a chair of civil law, and it was only after his unsuccessful competition for such a chair in 1723 that he "despaired of ever holding a worthier position in his native city," [1] and devoted himself to the development of his New Science.

In his boyhood Vico spent two months under a private teacher of law, "attending lectures full of cases on the minutiae of the practice of both [civil and ecclesiastical] courts. The lad could not discern the principles of these cases as befitted one who had already begun to acquire the universal mind from metaphysics and to reason of particulars by axioms or maxims." Under such instruction "only the memory was exercised and the intellect suffered from lying idle." [2]

He proceeded to study by himself, using the texts of Vulteius and Canisius as guides respectively to Roman civil and to canon law. In the study of Roman law by the aid of Vulteius, he says that he "found a great pleasure in two things."

One was in seeing how, in their summaries of the laws, the scholastic interpreters had abstracted into general maxims of justice the particular considerations of equity which the jurisconsults and emperors had indicated for the just

---

[1] G. B. Vico, *Opere*, V (Bari: Laterza, 1911), 46; *The Autobiography of Giambattista Vico*, tr. by M. H. Fisch and T. G. Bergin (Ithaca: Cornell University Press, second printing, 1944), p. 164. All references to the *Opere* of Vico are to the edition in the series *Scrittori d'Italia* published by Laterza. The English translation of the *Autobiography* is hereafter cited as E.T.

[2] *Opere*, V, 6–7; E.T. 115–116.

disposition of cases. This attracted him to these medieval interpreters [Accursius, Bartolus], whom he later perceived and judged to be the philosophers of natural equity. The other was in observing with what great diligence the jurisconsults themselves examined the wording of the laws, senate decrees and praetors' edicts which they interpreted. This won him to the humanist interpreters [Alciati, Cujas], whom he later perceived and considered to be pure historians of the Roman civil law. Each of these pleasures was a sign: the one of all the study that he was to give to investigating the principles of universal law, the other of the profit he was to derive from the Latin language, especially from the usages of Roman jurisprudence, the most difficult part of which is knowing how to define the legal terms.[3]

It was a chance conversation "on the right method of teaching jurisprudence" [4] that led to Vico's employment as tutor to the Rocca family, and thus to the nine years of leisure and security during which his self-education was completed. From canon law he was led into dogmatic theology and scholastic philosophy, and from thence into a lifelong devotion to St. Augustine.[5] From Roman civil law he was led, by way of a passage in Horace, into the ethics of the Greeks, and particularly that of Aristotle, "to which, as he had observed in his reading, the authorities on the various principles of the civil institutes frequently referred."

And in this study he noticed that Roman jurisprudence was an art of equity conveyed by innumerable specific precepts of natural law which the jurists had extracted from the reasons of the laws and the intentions of the legislators. But the science of justice taught by moral philosophers proceeded from a few eternal truths dictated in metaphysics by an ideal justice, which in the work of cities plays the role of architect and commands the two particular justices, the commutative and the distributive, as it were two divine artisans, to measure utilities by two eternal measures, namely the two proportions demonstrated in mathematics, the arithmetical and the geometrical. Thus he began to realize how the legal discipline is less than half learned by the method of study which is commonly observed.[6]

As a result of like excursions in other directions, and of "constant reading of orators, historians and poets," [7] Vico became like his contemporary Leibniz a man of immense erudition. The only conspicuous deficiency in his learning was mathematics and mathematical physics.

---

[3] *Opere*, V, 7–8; E.T. 116 (mistranslated in first printing).
[4] *Opere*, V, 9; E.T. 118.
[5] *Opere*, V, 10; E.T. 119.
[6] *Opere*, V, 11; E.T. 120–121.
[7] *Opere*, V, 12; E.T. 123.

But the solid core of his self-education, as of the curriculum at the University of Naples, was Roman law.

The chief function of the propaedeutic chair of rhetoric, in which Vico spent almost his entire professional lifetime, was to prepare students for admission to the law course. The incumbent had also, however, the duty of delivering the annual inaugural oration or convocation address at the University. It was characteristic of Vico, as one of his biographers has remarked,[8] that, when he needed only to deliver an exhortation to study, expressed in exemplary Latin, he spent most of the allotted time in working out the philosophic rationale of his counsels.

Six of these inaugural orations, delivered from 1699 to 1706 or 1707, have survived in a manuscript copy. A seventh, delivered in 1708, was revised, amplified, and published by Vico in 1709 under the title "On the Method of the Studies of Our Time." It deserves translation into English as a classic of the general theory of education, but, as might have been expected, the longest section is that devoted to jurisprudence, and Vico later went so far as to say of this, his first published book, that its argument was "a first draft" of his *Universal Law*.

And because Vico always had the aim of winning distinction for himself and the University in the field of jurisprudence by other means than lecturing on it to youngsters, he discussed at length in this dissertation the secrecy of the laws of the ancient Roman jurisprudents and essayed a system of jurisprudence for interpreting even the private laws from the point of view of the constitution of the Roman government.[9]

What was here briefly sketched, and later worked out in greater detail in the *Universal Law* and the *New Science*, was a historical jurisprudence based on a history of Roman law in which the major changes in private law were explained in terms of the major changes in constitutional and public law.

We pass over Vico's *Ancient Wisdom of the Italians* (1710) and his *Life of Antonio Carafa* (1716), which do not bear directly on Roman

---

[8] H. P. Adams, *The Life and Writings of Giambattista Vico* (London, 1935), p. 72.

[9] *Opere*, V, 32; E.T. 147. Encouraged by the reception of this work, Vico appears to have contemplated republishing it along with the six preceding orations, revised to bring them into harmony with it, and to make of the seven a comprehensive treatise on the philosophy of education, under the title *De studiorum finibus naturae humanae convenientibus*. (*Autobiografia di Giambattista Vico* . . . a cura di Fausto Nicolini [Milan: Bompiani, 1947], p. 227.) The best analysis of the orations in relation to Vico's later works is in the book by Donati cited in note 38 below.

law. It is worth remarking, however, that the former won him the friendship of Gravina, whose work on the origin and development of Roman law [10] may have contributed to Vico's ideas on the subject, and that the preparation of the life of Carafa gave him occasion to study Grotius *On the Law of War and Peace,* with the result that Grotius became, after Plato, Tacitus, and Bacon, his favorite author. In 1717 he was asked to prepare a new edition of Grotius, and had annotated it as far as the middle of the second book (thus covering over two-fifths of the whole work) when he abandoned the enterprise because of a religious scruple.[11]

We come now to the *Universal Law,* which, next to the later *New Science,* was Vico's chief work. It was published in three volumes. The first (1720) was entitled "On the One Principle and the One End of Universal Law." The second (1721) bore the more curious title "On the Constancy of the Jurisprudent," and was divided into two parts: the first, quite short, "On the Constancy of Philosophy," and the second, quite long, "On the Constancy of Philology." The latter begins with a chapter entitled "A New Science Is Essayed." The new science turns out to be "philology" in the sense of history, which is to be made a science by being reduced to philosophic principles. The third volume (1722) consists of notes and supplementary essays. The *Universal Law* as a whole may be described as a philosophy of law founded on a historical jurisprudence, which in turn is founded on a new science of the history of human culture in general, or of what Vico often calls "the principles of humanity."

Vico hoped that the *Universal Law* would win him a chair of law in the University of Naples. When that hope was disappointed, he turned to the development of the "new science" on its own account, no longer with primary reference to its use as a foundation for the philosophy of law, though that use was never forgotten and Roman law continued to be the chief source of illustration. Two editions of the *New Science* appeared during his lifetime (1725, 1730), and a third, which he was seeing through the press at the time of his death, appeared a few months later (1744).

As early as 1731, Vico composed a set of "Corrections, Meliorations

---

[10] *De ortu et progressu iuris civilis* (Naples, 1701).
[11] *Opere,* V, 38–39; E.T. 154–155.

and Additions," called the "Third," with a view to the third edition. The manuscript, which has survived, includes a great deal of material which was not incorporated in the third edition when it finally appeared thirteen years later. This is true, for example, of an appendix containing two *Ragionamenti* or discourses, one on the Law of the Twelve Tables and the other on the *lex regia* or Royal Law "of Tribonian." Their omission is especially remarkable in view of the fact that in the same year, 1731, Vico composed a continuation of his Autobiography in which he referred to them in the following way:

In order that the *Universal Law* should not be missed, since Vico was much less satisfied with it than with the *First New Science*, of which it was but a sketch, and since he considered it necessary for two passages only—one on the fable that the Law of the Twelve Tables came from Athens, the other on Tribonian's fable of the "Royal Law"—he reworked these into two *Discourses*, composed with more unity and greater vigor.[12]

So much by way of prologue to indicate the extent of Vico's lifelong preoccupation with Roman law. We proceed now to give a summary account of some of his more striking views concerning it, beginning with the subjects of the two discourses just mentioned.

THE LAW OF THE TWELVE TABLES

The traditional story of the Law of the Twelve Tables may be pieced together from Livy, Dionysius of Halicarnassus, Pomponius, Pliny the Elder, Cicero, and a pseudepigraphic letter of Heraclitus.

In the course of the long struggle between the plebeians and patricians, a tribune of the plebs proposed in 462 B.C. that five men should be elected to draw up a code of law to bind the consuls in the exercise of their judicial powers. The patricians successfully opposed the project for eight years, and then achieved a further delay by sending an embassy to Greece in 454 B.C. to procure copies of the laws of Solon and other Greek codes, and to acquaint themselves generally with the institutions, customs, and laws of the various Greek states. The embassy returned in 452, and a commission of ten, the Decemvirs or Tenmen, was set up to take the place of the magistrates of the year and to draft the

---

[12] *Autobiografia* (ed. Nicolini, 1947), 111; E.T. 193. For the *Ragionamenti* see *Opere*, IV–2, 275–306.

proposed code. Plebeians were declared eligible, but only patricians were elected.

Assistance in interpreting the Greek laws collected by the embassy, and in drawing up the new code based upon them, was provided by Hermodorus, an Ephesian who chanced to be living in exile at Rome. This was the Hermodorus of whom Heraclitus had said: "All the Ephesians from the youths up would do well to hang themselves and leave their city to the boys. For they banished Hermodorus, the best man of them, saying, 'We would have none among us who is best; if there be such a one, let him be so elsewhere and among other people.' " [13]

The Tenmen brought their code before the assembly of the centuries for ratification, after which the laws were inscribed on ten bronze tablets and set up in the market place. The work was not considered complete, however, and a second commission of ten was elected for the following year (450). In spite of the fact that the second Tenmen included three or more plebeians, their rule was oppressive, and the two tablets of laws which they added to the previous ten included a prohibition of intermarriage between patricians and plebeians. When their work was done, the Tenmen refused to lay down their office, and their rule was brought to an end only by revolution.

The Twelve Tables, however, became the source of all public and private law. Near them, in front of the old rostra, was erected at public expense a statue of Hermodorus the Ephesian, "interpreter of the laws drawn up by the Tenmen." [14] So was fulfilled what Heraclitus had dreamed of Hermodorus before his departure for Rome: "In a dream I saw the diadems of all the earth come before your laws and prostrate themselves in the Persian fashion, while your laws stood in majesty over them." [15]

As late as 1712, Vico seems to have had no doubt concerning this traditional story. He thought of the first ten tables as being filled with laws brought from Greece, and of the other two as containing a few laws preserved from the regal period of Rome.[16]

---

[13] Frag. 114.
[14] Pliny, *Nat. Hist.* XXXIV, 21.
[15] Ep. VIII (ed. Bywater), p. 76.
[16] *Opere*, I, 243.

Nine years later, in the second volume of the *Universal Law,* he included two chapters on the questions "What was imported from Attic law into the Law of the Twelve Tables?" and "What was effected by the Law of the Twelve Tables?" In these, without as yet questioning that Heraclitus had written the famous letter to Hermodorus or that Hermodorus had drafted the laws and been honored by a statue, he rejected the story of the embassy to Greece, regarding it as invented by the patricians to put off the plebeians, and he denied that the laws were imported from abroad. They were native Roman laws, and the analogies some of them bore to certain Greek laws were evidence not of borrowing but of parallel development. The Roman patricians, however, had a practical not a scientific grasp of law, and they therefore employed Hermodorus, a man of wisdom from a more advanced culture, to advise them as to which of their laws should be communicated to the plebs and which withheld, and to reduce the former to a written code. What was effected by the code was the communication to the plebs, under severe limitations not at first apparent to the latter, of *patria potestas* and the rights depending upon it. The auspices were still withheld, along with those magistracies and that form of marriage (*conubium*) which depended upon the auspices.[17]

In the first edition of the *New Science* (1725), Vico rejects the entire story of the intervention of Hermodorus and argues that the letter of Heraclitus (dispatched "by the same post by which Pythagoras made his journeys to the far corners of the earth") was an "imposture" like the oracles of Zoroaster and the verses of Orpheus. The census of Servius Tullius had been an agrarian law by which the plebs had been granted bonitary ownership of land. The Law of the Twelve Tables in its original form was essentially a second agrarian law by which the plebs were granted quiritary ownership of the land. But in subsequent centuries, before they reached the writers to whom we owe our knowledge of them, "there were interpolated in the Twelve Tables a great many laws and rights communicated to the plebs by the nobles after a long time and many contests."[18]

From this to the position taken in the later editions of the *New Science* (1730, 1744) and in the "First Discourse" (1731) the step is

---

[17] *Opere,* II–2, 564–580.
[18] *Opere,* III, § 87, §§ 161 ff.

comparatively short. The Twelve Tables, he now says, never existed as an official code: there never was an official code divided into tables. What did happen at the time to which the code is traditionally assigned was the enactment of the agrarian law above referred to, and its inscription on a bronze tablet as the first written law of Rome. To this first "table" others were added from time to time, until there were so many that they were called "twelve," a poetic expression for a great number. The question when and by whom the (literally) Twelve Tables known to our later literary authorities were compiled is not explicitly answered or even raised by Vico, but the only view compatible with what he does say is that it was an unofficial anthology of laws compiled early in the first century B.C.

The development of Vico's conception of the Twelve Tables is parallel to that of his conception of Homer. In his inaugural orations, and particularly in the *Method* (1709), the poet is a man of philosophic wisdom, and his fictions have a didactic intent. What the philosopher teaches in severer fashion, the poet teaches by delighting. Homer is the chief of poets in this respect. It is not surprising, therefore, that the Stoics discovered their own doctrines in his poems and claimed him as the prince of their sect.[19] In the second volume of the *Universal Law* (1721) there is a chapter "On the Origin of Poetry" in which Vico denies that Homer had any philosophic wisdom and says that his pre-eminence as a poet was due to his having lived so near to the heroic age "when language was still ill-furnished, the senses still reigned, and reason was as yet comparatively feeble." [20] In the third volume (1722) there is a dissertation "On Homer and His Two Poems" in which it appears that what is to be found in Homer is not the natural theology or philosophy of later philosophers, but the social history of the heroic period narrated in the language of that period, namely "poetic characters" and myths. But these had already suffered corruption before reaching Homer. In the first edition of the *New Science* (1725) Homer is placed in the third of three ages of heroic poets and is said to have collected the "fables" inherited from the first through the second, and to have composed his poems of them.[21] His wisdom was not the esoteric

---

[19] *Opere*, I, 97.
[20] *Opere*, II–2, 377.
[21] *Opere*, III, § 288.

wisdom of the philosophers, who first arose in later ages, but the common or vulgar or "civic" wisdom of the heroic peoples. Shortly after the appearance of the first edition, however, shrewd readers suggested to Vico that the logical conclusion of his argument was that the Homer hitherto believed in never existed.[22] By 1728, accordingly, he had reached the position taken in the later editions of the *New Science:* that Homer was "an idea or a heroic character of Grecian men insofar as they told their history in song." [23]

Similarly, Vico at first accepted the traditional story of the Twelve Tables as compiled at Rome from the laws of the most advanced culture then existing, by the aid of philosophic wisdom in the person of Hermodorus, the friend of Heraclitus. Gradually he came to see in the fragments, except for later interpolations, the vestiges of the culture of a still barbarous people. He first rejected the story of the embassy to Greece and reduced the role of Hermodorus to that of advising the Roman patricians which of their laws to extend to the plebs, and of committing these laws to writing. Finally he denied that Hermodorus had ever come to Rome, reduced the decemviral legislation to an agrarian law, and the Tenmen themselves to poetic characters.

Because the law of quiritary ownership when it was extended by the nobles to the plebeians was the first law to be inscribed on a public tablet (the sole purpose for which the decemvirs were created), all the laws making for equal liberty which were later inscribed on public tablets were attributed to the decemvirs because of their aspect of popular liberty.[24]

Vico himself was quite conscious of the parallel between the case of Homer and that of the Twelve Tables, and brought his final views regarding the two into relation in the concluding paragraph of his "Discovery of the True Homer."

Wherefore Homer's poems should henceforth be highly prized as being two great treasure stores of the customs of early Greece. But the same fate has befallen the poems of Homer as the Law of the Twelve Tables; for, just as the latter, having been held to be the laws given by Solon to the Athenians and subsequently taken over by the Romans, has up to now concealed from us the history of the natural law of the heroic nations of Latium, so the Homeric

---

[22] *Opere,* IV–2, § 873. References to the English translation (*The New Science of Giambattista Vico,* tr. by T. G. Bergin and M. H. Fisch, Ithaca: Cornell University Press, 1948) will not be added, since it employs the same paragraph numbers.

[23] *Opere,* IV–2, § 873; 1730 ed., p. 377.

[24] *Opere,* IV–1, § 422; cf. 1730 ed., p. 210.

poems, having been regarded as works produced by a single supreme poet, have hitherto concealed from us the history of the natural law of the nations of Greece.[25]

The reconstruction of these hitherto concealed histories, and the elucidation of their common pattern, is the larger part of the burden of the *New Science*.

But how did the traditional conception of Homer and the traditional story of the Twelve Tables arise? By the two forms of vanity which Vico calls the conceit of the scholars and the conceit of the nations. In the later "human" age, the conceit of the scholars, who have lost the key to the poetic language of earlier ages, and will have it that whatever they know is as old as the world, leads them to read their recondite, individual, discursive wisdom (*sapienza riposta*) into the laws and the poetry of the "divine" and "heroic" ages, whose wisdom was in fact common, collective, and poetic (*sapienza volgare*). And the national vanity of Rome, with its short history and recent emergence from barbarism, ascribed its laws to an older and wiser people, an ascription which Greek national vanity readily seconded, if indeed it had not prompted it. Here, as in the legendary founding of Rome by Aeneas, the vanity of two nations converged from opposite sides upon the same result. As Vico puts it in the latter case: "Thus, by two different manifestations of the conceit of nations—that of the Greeks in making such a noise about the Trojan war, and that of the Romans in boasting an illustrious foreign origin—the Greeks foisted their Aeneas upon the Romans and the latter finally accepted him as their founder." [26]

THE ROYAL LAW OF TRIBONIAN

The following passage appears in the *Digest* of Justinian as an excerpt from Book I of Ulpian's *Institutes*, and it is incorporated in nearly the same words in the *Institutes* of Justinian: "What the Emperor has determined has the force of a statute; seeing that, by a Royal Law (*lex regia*) which was passed concerning his sovereignty, the people transfer to him and confer upon him the whole of their sovereignty and power." [27]

It has commonly been supposed that this "royal law" was a law

[25] *Opere*, IV–2, § 904; 1730 ed., pp. 381 f.
[26] *Opere*, IV–1, § 772; 1730 ed., p. 351.
[27] *D.* 1.4.1. pr.; *Inst.* 1.2.6.

passed for each emperor beginning with Augustus, corresponding to the *lex de imperio Vespasiani* or law conferring the sovereignty on Vespasian. The concluding clauses of this law, preserved on a bronze tablet discovered in the Middle Ages, confer certain specific powers on Vespasian, exempt him from all laws from which his predecessors were exempted, and authorize him to perform all acts which his predecessors were authorized to perform.[28] Cassius Dio says that the Senate freed Augustus "from all compulsion of the laws" and suggests that a similar provision was included in the acts conferring imperial power on his successors.[29]

In a chapter on the *lex regia* in his *Universal Law*, Vico begins by remarking that the whole point of the opening chapters of the *Annals* of Tacitus, devoted to Augustus and Tiberius, is to show his readers "by what arts free commonwealths are transformed into royal ones—arts of which neither Augustus nor Tiberius would have had any need if the Roman people in their supreme assembly had conferred kingship upon the one and the other." The Roman historians, he goes on, who record the most inconsequential laws on the merest minutiae, know nothing of any such law. The very name of king was odious to the Romans. The confused testimony of a single Greek author, Cassius Dio, is insufficient. And the *lex de imperio Vespasiani*, far from being a *lex regia*, is not properly speaking a *lex* at all; it "contains nothing but a *senatus-consultum* in which the Senate declares allegiance to the Roman princeps." [30]

In the second and third editions of the *New Science* and in the "Discourse concerning the Royal Law of Tribonian," Vico flatly asserts that the *lex regia* is an invention of Tribonian ("a Greekling more ignorant of things Roman than the first barbarian glossators were"), which he not only inserted in the *Institutes* but fastened on Ulpian in the *Digest*. And Vico develops at length the theory already hinted in the *Universal Law*, that the transition from republic to monarchy takes place not by human intent or design but by the force of circumstances (*rebus ipsis dictantibus* in the phrase he likes to quote from Pomponius), in virtue

---

[28] Bruns, *Fontes*, ed. 6, 192–194.

[29] LIII, 28.2, 18.1.

[30] *Opere*, II–1, 169–170. See the compromise view proposed by Mommsen, *Römisches Staatsrecht*, II³, 877–879, according to which it was a *senatusconsultum* incorporated in a *lex*.

of "an eternal royal law by which nations come to rest under monarchies."

This natural royal law is conceived under this natural formula of eternal utility: Since in the free commonwealths all look out for their own private interests, into the service of which they press their public arms at the risk of ruin to their nations, to preserve the latter from destruction a single man must arise, as Augustus did at Rome, and take all public concerns by force of arms into his own hands, leaving his subjects free to look after their private affairs and after just so much public business, and of just such kinds, as the monarch may entrust to them. Thus are the people saved when they would otherwise rush to their own destruction.[31]

The most interesting part of the "Second Discourse" is the chapter of corollaries in which Vico moves from this "eternal royal law" to the doctrine that international law is a law of force and that "unjust wars" are legitimized by victory, as are principates over free peoples. A few of the opening corollaries will indicate the drift of the argument.

1. The great common error of the learned writers, who reason of public law by the rules of private law, is confuted. 2. The authority of laws follows upon the authority of arms, not, as is commonly supposed, the reverse. . . . 4. Civil law is observed between citizens [of the same nation], because they are subject to a common supreme authority of arms, and they have therefore no recourse but to contend at law. 5. The natural law of nations is a law of public force which obtains between civil powers which have no common civil law.[32]

WRITTEN AND UNWRITTEN LAW

Apropos of a passage in the *New Science* on the natural priority of customary or oral law to written law, Vico drafted a paragraph in the "Third Corrections" which was not incorporated in the third edition, but which is worth translating as a further indication of Vico's attitude toward Tribonian and his associates in the codification ordered by Justinian.

And here we may be allowed to make a digression concerning Tribonian, who in the *Institutes* will have it that the division of Roman law into written and unwritten was received at Rome from Greece; that is, from Athens which as a popular commonwealth wrote its laws and from Sparta which as an aristocratic commonwealth adhered to custom. And whereas it was, is and will be the civil nature of all peoples to live finally by customs and by laws—because, before the invention of common script, divine providence had ordained that they

[31] *Opere*, IV–2, § 1008, 1730 ed., p. 432; cf. § 1455–§ 1459.
[32] *Opere*, IV–2, § 1460–§ 1472.

should live by customs, and later, when letters had been invented, that they should live also by laws . . . (whence natural law, which preceded civil law in all nations, is defined by the jurisconsults as "a law established by divine providence in the customs of men")—the Romans were obliged to learn this from the Greeks! This error, along with others as grave as they are numerous, arose out of another: that the law of the Twelve Tables had come from Greece to Rome. . . . Here we shall only observe that Tribonian, Theophilus and Dorotheus, who composed the *Institutes* and who must have been the most highly reputed of all Greek jurisconsults of those times, betrayed how deficient if not utterly lacking they were in philosophy by beginning their treatment of the principles of jurisprudence with such an absurd error. And we may add that they were extremely ignorant of matters Roman. And, to cap it all, they undertook to treat of laws framed in a tongue that was alien to them; in which connection the thing which is so necessary is regarded by Cujas . . . as the most difficult, namely the definition of the legal terms, which turns on the very interpretation of the words. From all these considerations it is evident *what an irreparable damage these men did to Roman jurisprudence when they broke up the writings of the Roman jurisconsults into minute fragments,* whereas if they had left the books intact while bringing them together into one corpus, the philologians would have had other testimonies than inscriptions, coins and medals for discovering the antiquities of Rome, and the philosophers would have had other lights for discovering the nature of this world of nations![33]

It may well be thought that, since Tribonian and his collaborators can scarcely be reproached for carrying out Justinian's orders, Vico's condemnation is excessive and requires to be explained. It is probably sufficient to say that, though he was apparently not directly acquainted with the *Antitribonianus* of François Hotman, his first guide to the study of Roman civil law was, as we have seen, the *Institutes* of Vulteius, who was one of Hotman's most faithful and enthusiastic disciples.

TESTAMENTARY SUCCESSION AND DISTRIBUTIVE JUSTICE

We have already observed how large a part in the development of his thinking Vico ascribed to his study of Greek ethics, and in particular of the Aristotelian theory of justice. We have also noted that, two or three years before writing his *Universal Law,* he studied and annotated

[33] *Opere,* IV–2, § 1259; italics mine. Cf. Pietro de Francisci, "L'antitribonianismo di G. B. Vico," *Rivista internazionale di filosofia del diritto,* V (1925), 428–436. The same number of the *Rivista* (also published as a separate under the title *Per il II centenario della "Scienza nuova" di G. B. Vico*) contains other articles on aspects of Vico's philosophy of law and interpretations of Roman law not here considered.

Grotius *On the Law of War and Peace.* In Grotius he encountered a simplification and criticism of Aristotle's theory and of a certain extension of it.

Grotius adopts Aristotle's distinction between "friendships" or social relationships of equality and those of inequality, and bases upon it a distinction between two types of law, rectorial and equatorial (*ius Rectorium, ius Aequatorium*). Passing on to Aristotle's theory of particular justice, which was then currently reduced to the distinction between distributive and commutative justice, Grotius substitutes for this distinction that between what he calls attributive justice and what he calls expletive justice (*iustitia expletrix*). He does not explicitly assign attributive justice to rectorial law, and expletive justice to equatorial law, and it is not clear whether such a connection is intended. The important points, however, are these: (1) Grotius rejects Aristotle's attempt to base the distinction between the two forms of particular justice on that between arithmetic and geometric proportion. (2) He also rejects a view held by unnamed persons, the effect of which would be to connect attributive justice with public law and expletive justice with private law.

Not more true, again, is that which some say, that attributive justice is concerned with public property, while expletive justice is concerned with private property. On the contrary, *if a man wishes to give a legacy from property belonging to him, he acts in comformity with attributive justice;* and the state which pays back, from public funds, what a citizen has advanced for the public interest, is discharging the function of expletive justice.[34]

In his *Universal Law,* Vico took occasion to defend Aristotle against Grotius' criticism. He says that Grotius failed to observe that the question whether a geometric or arithmetic proportion applies is determined by the question whether the persons concerned are taken as equal or unequal. Thus Vico identifies distributive justice (which he calls *rectrix*) with relations of inequality, commutative justice (which he calls *aequatrix*) with relations of equality. And, taking over the terms rectorial law and equatorial law from Grotius, Vico explicitly identifies distributive justice with the former and commutative justice with the

---

[34] *De jure belli ac pacis,* Bk. I, ch. 1, § VIII.3 (tr. by F. W. Kelsey in *Classics of International Law,* p. 37); italics mine. Grotius is mistaken in asserting that what he calls expletive justice was called synallagmatic or contractual justice by Aristotle, whose term was rectificatory or corrective.

latter. Matters but lightly touched by Grotius in these connections are developed in detail by Vico.

The main point for our present purpose, however, is that Vico goes on to defend the further view rejected by Grotius, that distributive justice applies to public and commutative justice to private affairs (*Justitia rectrix in publicis, aequatrix in privatis rebus obtinet*), and to discuss at length the example we italicized in the above quotation from Grotius.

Why Testaments Are a Part of Public Law

Nor is this principle disturbed by the fact that the paterfamilias in bequeathing has regard for merits. For, as we have said, it is by a superior right, indeed by a certain right of supreme power, that the father makes his testament, and the making of it has a certain aspect of public law. It is for this reason that in Roman statutes it is said to belong to public law; not, as is commonly thought, because it is approved by public authority. For all rights of private utility are for this reason rights of public authority. But a testament belongs to public law because the family is as it were a small commonwealth with the paterfamilias as its prince, as the commonwealth is as it were a great family with the prince as its father or lord. For this reason the paterfamilias in his testament bequeaths (*legat*) the family to his heir as the prince in his mandates bequeaths (*legat*) a state [i.e., a province to be administered by the "legate" as governor]. It is in this way that I interpret the article of the Law of the Twelve Tables: "The provisions of the will of a paterfamilias concerning his property or the guardianship of his family, shall be law." . . .

Likewise Guardianships, Adoptions, Families, Associations

And for these reasons, guardianship also in Roman statutes is said to belong to public law, because it is a case of rectorial law. For this reason in a free commonwealth every adoption is by a *lex curiata,* and now a formal adoption is accomplished by a rescript of the prince; and every family and association is a part of public law because it involves rule.

Why Wars Belong to Private Law

On the other hand, this principle is not contravened by the fact that civil powers in concluding treaties and in declaring and waging wars look to their own (*suum*), whence in fetial law the phrase for declaring war was "to demand satisfaction." For in that matter they are regarded as equals, and they confirm the fact by the name itself in calling their enemies equals.[35]

In a subsequent chapter Vico enlarges on the fact that the same verb *legare* is used both for the appointment of a provincial governor by the emperor and for the bequeathing of property by a testator. He em-

---

[35] *Opere,* II–1, 67–68.

phasizes again the analogy between the legislative power of the paterfamilias and that of the emperor: *Quod principi placuit legis habet
vigorem* is true of both. And he adds the remark that the heir represents the testator as the governor represents the emperor.[36]

In the second volume of the *Universal Law,* Vico returns to the theme
that "in his testament the paterfamilias is a sovereign prince," cites
the same article of the Twelve Tables, and adds:

Thus the testator in his testament legislates so that whatever he has appointed
(*legassit*) in it will be law, and, as a sovereign prince, bequeaths his estate as
a state (*legat hereditatem tanquam rempublicam*). Whence, as the legate [or
governor] in the state [or province] bequeathed (*legata*) to him represents the
sovereign prince by whom he is appointed (*legatur*), so the heir in the estate
represents the deceased paterfamilias.[37]

This conception of the primitive family as a political organism, of
the inheritance of its property as a consequence of the inheritance of
sovereignty over it, and of the testament of historical times as a survival
of the monarchic power of the primitive *patres,* became one of the
major themes of the *New Science.* The following is a representative
passage:

The heroes must have been so called in the sense of "lords of the families" in
distinction from the *famuli,* who were in effect slaves. *Heri* had this same
meaning in Latin, whence *hereditas* for inheritance, for which the native Latin
word had been *familia.* With such as origin, *hereditas* must have meant a
despotic sovereignty, and by the Law of the Twelve Tables there was reserved
to the family fathers a sovereign power of testamentary disposition in the
article *Uti paterfamilias super pecunia tutelave rei suae legassit, ita ius esto:*
"Whatever the paterfamilias has disposed concerning his property or the
guardianship of his family, shall be law." The disposing was generally called
legare, which is the prerogative of sovereigns; thus the heir becomes a "legate"
[or legatee] who in inheriting represents the defunct paterfamilias, and the
children no less than the slaves were included in the words *rei suae* and
pecunia. All of which proves only too conclusively the monarchic power that
the fathers had had over their families in the state of nature. This they were
bound to retain in the state of the heroic cities. These must in origin have been
aristocratic commonwealths, that is, commonwealths of lords, for the fathers
still retained their power even in the popular commonwealths. All these
matters will later be discussed at length.[38]

[36] *Opere,* II–1, 94–95.

[37] *Opere,* II–2, 430.

[38] *Opere,* IV–1, § 513. For a much fuller account to which I am greatly indebted,
see Benvenuto Donati, *Nuovi studi sulla filosofia civile di G. B. Vico* (Florence,
1936), pp. 373–407. Donati's book treats other topics relevant to the subject of my

And so they are in the sections on "Poetic Economy" and "Poetic Politics."

PLEBISCITES AS A SOURCE OF PRIVATE LAW

The sources of law at Rome in republican times were (1) statutes (*leges*), (2) plebiscites, (3) opinions of pontiffs and later of *prudentes*, (4) edicts of magistrates (especially the urban praetor and the curule aediles), and (5) custom. Strictly speaking, *leges* or statutes were enactments passed by the whole people meeting either in the assembly by centuries or in that by tribes. At least from the time of the Hortensian law in 287 B.C., however, plebiscites or enactments of the plebeian council were equally valid with *leges* and were frequently so called, as they will be in what follows here.

About eight hundred *leges* have come down to us. Of the five hundred whose proposers are identified, three hundred were plebiscites. There was thus a preponderance of tribunicial over consular initiative in general. It is not surprising that there was also a preponderance of public over private law, but it was greater than we should have expected. All but thirty of the eight hundred *leges* were concerned with matters of public law. The really striking fact, however, is that all thirty of those concerned with private law were plebiscites. Since the *concilium plebis* had no exclusive competence in matters of private law, it would appear that the plebeians had a special interest in the fixing of norms governing private relations. Now the main institutions of private law had their origins in custom and were developed by praetorian edict and by jurisprudence, both conservative and both bearing the mark of the patrician monopoly of law in earlier times. It was thus in the nature of the case that the plebiscites bearing on private law, in relation to the system of the civil law as a whole, should have an exceptional character. Yet they are the most typical expression of the struggle of the plebeians to wrest that system from patrician monopoly.[39]

---

essay which I have been obliged to omit. It is the best available guide for a student approaching Vico from the point of view of the philosophy of law.

[39] This paragraph is the briefest possible summary of the results reached by Giovanni Rotondi in a series of studies culminating in his *Leges publicae populi romani* (Milan, 1912). For a fuller account see Donati, *op. cit.*, pp. 343–372.

The ostensible intent of the *Universal Law* is to construct a general theory of law and of the state. In the course of his argument, Vico takes occasion to sketch in its principal outlines the history of Roman law, because of its exemplary value. What is most to our present purpose is the dependence of private law on constitutional and public law. The turning point of the struggle between patricians and plebeians was reached when plebiscites acquired the force of *leges* or statutes. This gave rise to tribunicial legislation in favor of popular liberty. The senate, the real power behind consular legislation, now turned its activity in the direction of public law. The patricians ceased to be the authors of private law and sought to become its guardians, jealously retaining the science of law and watching over the application of established law to the adjudication of private cases.

Hence in the free commonwealth tempered by survivals of patrician power (*ex optimatibus mixta*) all the decrees of the senate had to do with public law. They either authorized the enactment of public laws or lent the authority of the senate to public laws already enacted [in the *comitia*]. . . . None of them has a consul's name prefixed to it. Those decrees of the senate on the other hand which have to do with private law and which bear the name of one of the consuls, all belong to the time of the principate, such as those with which Justinian's *Corpus Juris* abounds. Therefore, when the time and author of a senate decree are in doubt, the following rule may boldly be applied. Those which have to do with public law other than penal belong to the free commonwealth; those on the other hand which have to do with private law belong to imperial times.

But whereas the fathers had to deal openly with the people in matters of public law, they kept private law and the science of it a closed secret, and no enactment of private law was ever proposed to the people by a consul, except the *lex Poetilia Papiria de nexu*. . . . For the rest, almost all the enactments of private law in the free commonwealth were tribunicial, and all . . . were in favor of liberty. For it is the custom of the weak to demand equal law (*ius aequum*) against the strong, and it is the common vow of strength that there shall be no laws enacted. For this reason it is a constant rule that the occasion for tribunicial laws has always been some injustice on the part of the strong, or some secret scheme of theirs against which measures had to be taken.[40]

When Rotondi's attention was called by Donati to Vico's earlier researches and anticipation of his main conclusion, Rotondi gladly paid tribute to his forerunner.

[40] *Opere*, II–1, 190–192. Cf. the axiom in the *New Science* (*Opere*, IV–1, § 283): "The weak want laws; the strong withhold them; the ambitious, in order to win a following, advocate them; princes, in order to equalize the strong with the weak, protect them." And cf. Plato, *Gorgias* 483b: "The makers of laws are the weak and the many, and they make laws and distribute praise and blame with a view to themselves and to their own interests. And they terrify the stronger and those who

Vico proceeds to establish his thesis by passing in review the private-law legislation of republican times, with a documentation which for his time was complete. He remarks in conclusion:

I would scarcely have enumerated these laws, but would only have given a general account of them in my usual way, if the understanding of them which is now current were not such as to lead one to think that I have proposed a false criterion in the matter.

THE CANULEIAN LAW

In the examples so far given of Vico's interpretations of Roman law, even the most conservative scholar will recognize some merit. In several of them, and in others not here considered, the most radical Italian and German historians of Roman law in the last generation might have found (as some of them did find) anticipations of their most cherished views, from which Roman-law scholarship has since receded. It is only fair that I should now add an example or two of interpretations in which Vico so far stands alone.

We have noted that the Twelve Tables included a prohibition of intermarriage between patricians and plebeians. According to the traditional story, this was abrogated a few years later by a plebiscite proposed by the tribune Gaius Canuleius.

Vico's view is that what was demanded in the Canuleian rogation was not that plebeians should be permitted to marry patricians, but that plebeian marriages should be endowed with the same legal status and consequences as patrician marriages—not *conubia cum patribus* but *conubia patrum*.

In the second volume of the *Universal Law* Vico says that the three institutions upon which Rome was founded were *conubium, patria potestas,* and *nexum. Conubium* depended on the auspices, which were the prerogative of the *patres,* and it was therefore not available to plebeians. Upon *conubium* depended *domus, familiae, gentes,* the right of testamentary disposition, the right of intestate succession by direct heirs (*heredes sui*), agnates, and gentiles in turn, and guardianships.

---

are able to get the better of them, in order that they may not get the better of them. They say it is shameful and unjust for one to have more than another, and define injustice as seeking to have more than others. For, knowing their own inferiority, they are only too glad, I suspect, if they can even things up."

By the Law of the Twelve Tables, the plebeians acquired the right of quiritary ownership, conveyed by *mancipatio,* and along with it the right of what Vico calls "private-law *conubium*" by *conventio in manum.* But of what avail was that? In order that they too might have a house, a family, and a *gens,* and all the rights thereto appertaining, what they needed to obtain was "public-law *conubium,*" the principal solemnity of which was the taking of auspices. This is what they obtained by the Canuleian law: *conubia patrum,* the right "to celebrate solemn nuptials with the public auspices with which the patricians themselves celebrated them." [41]

In the first edition of the *New Science,* Vico observes that the traditional view according to which the plebeians sought intermarriage with the patricians involved an inversion of the natural order of human desires, which is: "first riches, then honors and offices, and finally nobility." [42] In the later editions, he emphasizes more clearly than before the fact that it was the economic advantages of full citizenship which they sought. Down to the struggle over *conubium,* he says, the plebeians were simply laborers "without any rights of citizenship."

For when, by the second agrarian law, conceded to them by the nobles in the Law of the Twelve Tables, they had gained quiritary ownership of the fields, as we showed many years ago in our *Principles of Universal Law* (in one of the two passages on whose account we do not regret the publication of that book), yet, because by the law of nations strangers were not capable of civil ownership, and the plebeians were not yet citizens, they were still unable to leave their fields intestate to their kin, because they did not have *sui heredes,* agnates, or cognates, which relations were all dependent on solemn nuptials. Nor could they even dispose of their fields by testament, for they were not citizens. Hence the lands assigned to them soon returned to the nobles, from whom they had had the title to their ownership. When they had become aware of this, within three short years they demanded the right of *conubium.* In the condition of miserable slaves that Roman history clearly relates that of the plebeians to have been, they did not demand the right of intermarrying with the nobles, for in that case the Latin would have read *conubia cum patribus.* What they did ask was the right to contract solemn nuptials just as the fathers did, and so they demanded *conubia patrum,* the principal solemnity of which was the public auspices called by Varro and Messala major auspices, those meant by the fathers when they said the auspices were theirs. The plebeians, in making this demand, were in effect asking for Roman citizenship, whose natural principle was solemn nuptials, which were therefore defined by the juris-

---

[41] *Opere,* II–2, 550–555, 574–575.
[42] *Opere,* III, § 185.

consult Modestinus as the sharing of every divine and human right—*omnis divini et humani iuris communicatio*—than which no more proper definition can be given of citizenship itself.[43]

MONSTERS

Dionysius of Halicarnassus ascribes to Romulus himself the following limitation on the father's power of life and death over his children during the first three years of life, after which presumably his power was absolute.

[Romulus] obliged the inhabitants to bring up all their male children and the first born of the female, and forbade them to destroy any male children under three years of age unless they were maimed or monstrous from their very birth. These he did not forbid their parents to expose, provided they first showed them to their five nearest male neighbors and these also judged the offspring monstrous. Against those who disobeyed this law he fixed various penalties, including the confiscation of half their property.[44]

We learn from Cicero that the Twelve Tables permitted, if they did not enjoin, the killing at once of "terribly deformed" male children.[45] And Seneca, in his essay *On Anger*, says: "Unnatural progeny we destroy; we drown even male children who at birth are weaklings or monsters." [46]

Late Roman jurists interpreted the terms *monstrum, portentum, prodigium*, as used in this connection, to mean offspring so deformed physically as to be incapable of becoming healthy adult human beings. Modern scholars have on the whole adopted this interpretation. More recently, however, students of ethnology, folklore, primitive religion, and comparative jurisprudence have seen in *ablegatio* (putting away or out of sight) and related practices, not a concern for viability, or capacity for self-support and a role in community defense, but a concern to rid the family and the community of an omen, a portent, a menace to the social group. From this point of view, the consultation of the five nearest male neighbors required by the law of Romulus would represent the group interest in protecting itself from such evil omens. It has been conjectured that monsters included not merely the physically

---

[43] *Opere*, IV–1, § 598; 1730 ed., p. 282.
[44] *Ant. Rom.* II, 15; Bruns, *Fontes*, ed. 6, p. 7.
[45] *De leg.* III, 8, 19.
[46] *Dial.* III, 15, 2.

deformed, and not merely those who had some mystic defect such as being born with the feet foremost or cutting the upper teeth first, but bastards, offspring of adultery or of incest, and those borne by vestal virgins. It would follow that most monsters were physically normal and healthy.[47]

From this position there is still a considerable leap to Vico's, and I am not aware that any historian of Roman law has taken it. Vico's view first appears in the third volume of the *Universal Law* (1722), in a passage from which it may be conjectured that it was first suggested to him by an opinion of the Neapolitan advocate Domenico Caravita in which Caravita, citing Antoine Favre, asserted that in Roman law the children of unmarried mothers were called monsters.[48] The final version of Vico's interpretation appears in the second and third editions of the *New Science.*

In Roman law, as Antoine Favre observes in his *Iurisprudentiae papinianeae scientia,* children born of prostitutes are called monsters because they have the nature of men together with the bestial characteristic of having been born of vagabonds or of indeterminate copulations. Of such sort we shall find those monsters to have been (children born of noble women without benefit of solemn nuptials) whom the Law of the Twelve Tables commanded to be thrown into the Tiber. . . .[49]

It was the civil beauty [of heroic birth] and no other that was cherished by the Spartans, the heroes of Greece, who cast down from Mt. Taygetus the ugly and deformed offspring, that is, those born of noble women but without benefit of solemn nuptials. Such too must have been the monsters condemned by the Law of the Twelve Tables to be thrown into the Tiber. For it is not at all likely that the decemvirs, in that parsimony of laws proper to the first commonwealths, would have given any thought to natural monsters, because of whose extreme rarity anything rare in nature is called monstrous, when even in the superfluity of laws with which we are now afflicted, legislators leave to the discretion of judges those cases that seldom present themselves. . . .[50]

Vico goes on to connect this interpretation with the struggle over *conubium* and with the rogation of Canuleius, as he had already done in the *Universal Law.*

---

[47] Fulvio Maroi, "L'interpretazione dei 'monstra' nella legislazione decemvirale secondo G. B. Vico," *Rivista internazionale di filosofia del diritto,* V (1925), 453–465; Lucien Lévy-Bruhl, *La Mentalité primitive* (Paris, 1922), pp. 158, 169–170; Eng. tr., pp. 148, 157–158.

[48] *Opere,* II–3, 692.

[49] *Opere,* IV–1, § 410.

[50] *Opere,* IV–1, § 566; 1730 ed., p. 270.

This must be what Livy has in mind when, with as much good faith as ignorance of the Roman antiquities of which he writes, he says that if the nobles shared *conubium* with the plebeians the resulting offspring would be *secum ipsa discors*, which is as much as to say a monster of mixed and twofold nature, the one heroic, of the nobles, the other feral, of the plebeians who "practised marriages like those of wild animals"—*agitabant conubia more ferarum*. This phrase Livy took from some ancient writer of annals and used it ignorantly, for he quotes it as if it meant [that such bestial marriages would result] "if the nobles intermarried with the plebeians." But the plebeians in their miserable state of *quasi* slavery could not ask any such thing of the nobles. What they demanded was the right of contracting solemn nuptials (for such is the meaning of *conubium*), which right was at that time confined to the nobles. But among animals no species has intercourse with another. We must therefore say that [*more ferarum*] was a phrase of insult applied by the nobles to the plebeians in that heroic contest. For inasmuch as the latter did not possess the public auspices, whose solemnities were required to make marriages legitimate, none of them had a determinate father (by the well-known definition in Roman law that *nuptiae demonstrant patrem*—the marriage ceremony identifies the father), and with reference to this uncertainty the plebeians were said by the nobles to have intercourse with their mothers and daughters as beasts do.[51]

GREEK PHILOSOPHY AND ROMAN LAW

We turn now to two more general questions regarding the historical relations between philosophy and law: (1) the influence of Greek philosophy upon Roman law, and (2) the typical relation between philosophy and law in a single culture, as exemplified by that of Greece.

The still unsettled question of the influence of Greek philosophy upon Roman law [52] was already an old one in Vico's time. One of the widely held positive views was that the schools of Sabinus and Proculus, the former founded by Ateius Capito and the latter by Labeo, owed their divergences to Epicurean influence upon the former and Stoic influence upon the latter.

In the *Universal Law* Vico has a chapter on the "sects" of the jurisconsults in which he denies any such influence and shows how the alleged divergences would arise spontaneously within the Roman legal tradition itself. This is not to deny all acquaintance with Greek philoso-

---

[51] *Opere*, IV–1, § 567; 1730 ed., p. 271.

[52] There is a convenient brief summary, with references to some of the recent literature, in Fritz Schulz, *Principles of Roman Law* (Oxford, 1936), pp. 129–131. M. H. Fisch, *Stoicism and Roman Law* (typewritten dissertation, Cornell University Library, 1930), though amateurish and needing radical revision, has still some value for reference purposes.

phy on the part of the jurisconsults. But if Labeo, for example, was an adherent of Stoicism, that was the philosophy of the man, not of the jurisconsult.[53] Vico has another and earlier chapter: *Philosophia iuris-consultorum a sapientia heroica derivata*—"The Philosophy of the Jurisconsults was derived from Heroic Wisdom." That is, it was derived from the common or poetic wisdom of the Roman heroic period, which was essentially the same as that of all the heroic peoples, and not from the esoteric and discursive wisdom of the Greek philosophers of Hellenistic times. And he attempts to show this in the case of particular doctrines which had been ascribed to philosophic influence.[54]

In the *New Science* Vico developed the theory of a natural succession of "sects of the times," for which perhaps the nearest English equivalent is "climates of opinion." He distinguishes three and calls them religious, punctilious, and civil respectively.

The jurisconsults accordingly justify their views as to what is just by appealing to the sect of their times. . . . For these [three sects of times] are the proper sects of Roman jurisprudence, in which the Romans concurred with all other nations of the world; sects taught them by divine providence, which the Roman jurisconsults set up as the principle of the natural law of nations; and not the sects of the philosophers, which some learned interpreters of Roman law have forcibly intruded therein. . . . And the emperors, when they wish to give a reason for their laws or for other orders issued by them, say that they have been guided by the sect of their times. . . . For the customs of the age are the school of princes. . . .[55]

Elsewhere in the *New Science* he says that the Stoics and Epicureans were alike "monastic or solitary philosophers," and that their respective doctrines of chance and fate incapacitated them for "reasoning of commonwealth or laws," and must have made them uncongenial to Roman jurisprudence, which made divine providence its first principle. They are therefore "to be chased from the schools of jurisprudence" into which certain scholars have vainly intruded them.[56]

GREEK PHILOSOPHY AND GREEK LAW

On the relation between philosophy and law within a single culture, as exemplified by the Greek, there is a long passage in the *New Science*

---

[53] *Opere*, II–1, 246.
[54] *Opere*, II–1, 209–213.
[55] *Opere*, IV–2, § 979; cf. 1730 ed., p. 405.
[56] *Opere*, IV–1, § 130, § 335; IV–2, § 1404.

on Socrates, Plato, and Aristotle—"a fragment of the history of philosophy told philosophically"—to which I shall merely refer the reader, since it does not lend itself to quotation or summary. Vico maintains not merely that "laws come first and philosophies later" but that the Socratic and post-Socratic logic, metaphysics, and moral philosophy developed out of the disputations of the Athenian assembly and courts: first popular government; then laws; then philosophy.[57]

ANCIENT ROMAN LAW A SERIOUS POEM

The passage on Greek philosophy to which I have just referred occurs in one of the most brilliant and eloquent chapters of the *New Science*. It bears the title: "Corollary: That the Ancient Roman Law Was a Serious Poem, and the Ancient Jurisprudence a Severe Kind of Poetry, within which Are Found the First Outlines of Legal Metaphysics in the Rough; and How, among the Greeks, Philosophy Was Born of the Laws."

We have already remarked the parallel development of Vico's conceptions of Homer and of the Law of the Twelve Tables. We have also noted his view that the wisdom embodied in the early Roman law of which the Twelve Tables contain the chief vestiges was a common and poetic, not a recondite and reasoned wisdom. In this chapter, however, Vico argues at length that ancient Roman law was itself a kind of dramatic poetry, whose fictions and personifications stand to the "real" things and persons of earlier heroic law in a relation analogous to that in which the fictitious types or masks of the New Comedy of Menander stand to the "real" persons of the Old Comedy of Aristophanes.

Ancient jurisprudence was throughout poetic. By its fictions what had happened was taken as not having happened, and what had not happened as having happened; those not yet born as already born; the living as dead; and the dead as still living in their estates pending acceptance. It introduced so many empty masks without subjects, *iura imaginaria*, rights invented by imagination. It rested its entire reputation on inventing such fables as might preserve the gravity of the laws and do justice to the facts. Thus all the fictions of ancient jurisprudence were truths under masks, and the formulae in which the

---

[57] *Opere,* IV–2, § 1040–§ 1043. A somewhat similar view of the relation between law and pragmatism is suggested in M. H. Fisch, "Justice Holmes, the Prediction Theory of Law, and Pragmatism," *Journal of Philosophy*, XXXIX (1942), 85–97; see p. 94 and note 22.

laws were expressed, because of their strict measures of such and so many words—admitting neither addition, subtraction, nor alteration—were called *carmina* or songs. . . .

Thus all ancient Roman law was a serious poem, represented by the Romans in the forum, and ancient jurisprudence was a severe poetry. . . . And from the masks called *personae* which were used in these dramatic fables, so true and severe, derive the first origins of the doctrine of the law of persons—*De iure personarum.*[58]

CONCLUDING REMARKS

The intention of this essay has been to bring Vico to the attention of students of Roman law and of the philosophy of law, and to provide for those with little Latin and less Italian some initial help over the language barriers. My selection from the topics treated by Vico, though representative, has been too small and my account of each too slight to warrant any formal conclusions. It has not been possible within the limits of the essay to give adequate indications of the extent to which Vico's views coincide with or deviate from those now prevalent among historians of Roman law, and I have given almost no indication of the extent to which they were anticipated by still earlier thinkers. The following remarks are offered therefore as opinions, not as conclusions from the evidence adduced.

1. The major philosophic requirement of our time is an adequate social philosophy.

2. Law is a more promising base and proving ground for such a philosophy than any of the existing social sciences or any synthesis of them that has so far been conceived.

3. The philosophy of law needs to be nourished by the kind of acquaintance with law that historians seek as well as by the kinds that policemen, lawyers, judges, litigants, legislators, and voters have.

4. Among past thinkers, none abler than Vico has united the philosopher's interest with the historian's, brought them to bear upon a concrete system of law in the successive stages of its development, recorded the results of a lifetime's intense and sustained study, and developed a social philosophy in the process.

5. If a thinker now undertaking to construct a social philosophy grounded in law is capable of profiting from the insights and mistakes

---

[58] *Opere*, IV–2, § 1036–§ 1037; 1730 ed., pp. 422 f.

of past attempters, he will find a serious study of Vico worth his while.

6. Taken simply as an interpreter of Roman law itself, Vico has had no equal in originality or audacity. He makes blunders, is guilty of oversights, and neglects to check his references or his memory. He is far from proportioning his beliefs to the objective evidence for them. Many of his conjectures are quite fantastic. But any student of Roman law above the crib and cram level will find him worth reading alongside some sober and dependable guide. And even the seasoned scholar who wants to freshen his eyes for a review of the sources may find what he wants in the *Universal Law* and *New Science*.

7. In spite of Vico's willingness to allow the *Universal Law* to be forgotten except for the two passages he later reworked into the *Ragionamenti*, it contains a great deal more that is of permanent interest to students of Roman law and of legal philosophy, and that was not incorporated in or superseded by the *New Science*. It deserves an English translation with an introduction and notes designed to show, among other things, its relations to the *New Science*, to earlier and later interpretations of Roman law, and to present-day scholarship.

Mr. Northrop and Mr. Locke

ARTHUR E. MURPHY

JOHN LOCKE died nearly 250 years ago and ought, on a strictly chrono-logical estimate, to be now a little deader than Queen Anne. That it should be morally and politically important today to keep the record straight on what he taught is striking evidence of the continuing vital-ity of his ideas. And it is important. For the teachings of Locke are woven pervasively into the fabric of the ideology to which, in Britain and America, we still appeal when we are called on to interpret and justify our political purposes and behavior. What we make of his doc-trine is therefore a factor in what, in the present confusion and con-flict of ideologies, we make of ourselves and our freedom. Fairly under-stood and wisely used it can continue to be a spiritual resource of great value. Unintelligently perpetuated or arbitrarily misunderstood it will block the path of progress toward national and world understanding. In the long run what we think about and, more fundamentally, how we think with the political ideals that received their classical formula-tion in Locke's philosophy may well be more decisive for the political future of America than what we think of President Truman or Governor Dewey or Senator Taft.

Yet it is extraordinarily difficult to make a just contemporary assess-ment of this philosophy. The documents are readily available, the per-tinent facts of Locke's life and work are for the most part known, and of commentators and interpreters there seems to be no end. The diffi-culty lies in a different area. It is one of the commonplaces of criticism in the history of ideas that we no longer share the preconceptions of the great thinkers of the Enlightenment. Our climate of opinion has altered since the late seventeenth and eighteenth centuries, and much that could plausibly be held to be self-evident in the days of the Glorious Revolution is so no longer. This observation is usually offered as evidence of the historically determined limitations of the thinkers of the past. They did their thinking in terms of an "outmoded" science. They had never heard of Einstein or Darwin or Freud. And they had not lived through the disillusioning social conflicts which are the most patent facts of twentieth-century experience. Through no fault of their own, they simply could not see what we can see today, and their theories must, in consequence, be qualified and corrected from the standpoint of our larger wisdom. Mr. Northrop's recent and widely influential *Meeting of East and West* [1] provides a characteristic example of such reinterpretation as applied to the philosophy of Locke.

It is not less true, however, though perhaps less obvious, that this limitation of perspective can work both ways. We are indeed in a position to take account of facts that Locke knew nothing of. But it may equally be the case that he was in a position to see clearly much that his critics, in the confused sophistication of their contemporary anxieties and enthusiasms, are no longer able so justly to discern. To understand Locke by cutting his ideas to the measure of our current preconceptions and preoccupations would then be not only to misunderstand him but to cut ourselves off in the process from a source of insight and sound judgment which we can ill afford to lose. I believe that this is in fact what has happened in many of the recent revaluations of Locke's philosophy and notably in that of Mr. Northrop. Since this reinterpretation is far more widely read than the original and more congenial to our dominant habits of thought, it is likely to pass current before long, except in a small circle of professional scholars, as all of Locke that is intelligible to a "modern" mind or relevant to our present problems.

If this should happen, the loss would be a grave one. For it is precisely the aspect of Locke's political philosophy which challenges our current preconceptions and affirms an ideal no longer widely honored or understood among us which has contributed most to our freedom in the past and has most to teach us in the present if our minds are not already closed to it. In the belief that they are not yet closed and, if we are to preserve our freedom, must not become so, I have undertaken in

---

[1] *The Meeting of East and West,* New York: Macmillan, 1946.

90

this paper to set the Northropian version of Locke's philosophy by the side of the original and to indicate the discrepancy between them. My purpose is not polemical but constructive—to indicate not, save incidentally, what is wrong in Northrop but what is abidingly right in Locke and what, in a sound philosophy, we cannot do without. At a time when the recovery, defense, and perpetuation of the ideals of our tradition are matters of concern in orthodox and even in official circles, this would seem to be a task to which a philosopher may well, and with propriety, direct his efforts.

I

Mr. Northrop's account of Locke occurs in the context of his own ambitious synthesis of ideologies as a basis for world understanding, where it serves a threefold function. (*a*) It illustrates and verifies his general thesis that ideologies are based on and derive their cogency from accepted theories of natural science and the theories of knowledge implied in them. Mr. Northrop claims that Newton's physics had epistemological consequences which his friend Locke made explicit in a theory of the human self or person as a mental substance. It was on the foundation thus laid that Locke developed the moral and political philosophy of "atomistic" individualism which is perpetuated in the Declaration of Independence and the "free culture of the United States." "In short, the traditional culture of the United States is an applied Utopia in which the philosophy of John Locke defines the idea of the good." [2]

(*b*) The major peculiarities and limitations of our traditional ideals are held to be directly referable to the inadequacies of this philosophy. Because no understandable relation can be discovered between mental substances, the good for man must be "defined in terms of free, equal and independent mental substances." [3] And, in consequence, "there are no social laws given by nature or divine right; there are only laws in so far as they are made and entered into with the consent of the governed." [4] Because Locke's epistemology reduces the immediately given content of experience to the status of a mere appearance unequally yoked in a three-term relation to unperceived material substances and

---

[2] *Meeting*, p. 71.
[3] *Meeting*, p. 121.
[4] *Meeting*, p. 75.

to these blank mental substances or observers, our culture has over-valued the theoretical component of reality and undervalued the aesthetic. Hence our "blankish Protestant souls" [5] and our emotional deficiency in comparison with the Mexicans and the Chinese. And because Locke, as a result of his egocentric individualism, gave primacy to property rights over human, social, and economic needs, we have lamentably failed to institute needed political reforms and to come to a just understanding with other nations.[6]

(c) The recognition that this philosophy rests upon a now outmoded science and is without a theoretical leg to stand on can be expected to free our minds from the dogmatic limitations of our traditional ideology and open them to those positive insights of other cultures that are needed to correct the one-sidedness of our own, and to provide a new basis for world understanding. In this happy consummation a two-term relation of epistemic correlation, in harmony with the latest developments in physical science, supersedes the discredited three-term relation of appearance in Locke's epistemology. The aesthetic component of reality, to which only the East has done substantial justice, can then be mated with the theoretical knowledge of the West. And the individualism of American culture, emancipated from Lockean errors, can come to terms with the "organic, hierarchical, communal conception of the good individual and the good state" [7] of Aristotle and the Catholic Church, and with the "Marxian thermodynamic concept of a person" [8] as well.

Essentially, therefore, the understanding of John Locke and the liberal tradition, as Mr. Northrop presents it, is the exposure of past errors and cultural limitations from which we must now free ourselves if we are to go forward on the path of scientific enlightenment, aesthetic appreciation, and a global synthesis of ideologies. He does not blame Locke for the errors of his epistemology, which were the natural outcome of the up-to-date physics of his day, and he gives him "everlasting credit" for his contributions to the cause of tolerance. But he leaves no doubt that, in his judgment, this philosophy, in the ideological form in which we have inherited it, is a liability rather than an asset to

[5] *Meeting*, p. 160.
[6] *Meeting*, pp. 45 ff.
[7] *Meeting*, p. 174.
[8] *Meeting*, p. 241.

our culture, an impediment to the better understanding that we seek. And most of his readers, if they are not also readers of Locke, are likely to agree with him.

As against this, I shall undertake to show that the central factor in Locke's moral and political individualism is not at all the denial, on epistemological grounds, of any essential or "organic" relation between mental substances, but rather the affirmation, on moral grounds, of a quite distinctive relation between free and rational men, in terms of which the nature of legitimate political authority can be defined. To determine the ground and limits of such authority as against that arbitrary exercise of power which is "force without right" was the primary aim of Locke's political philosophizing. What he had to say made practical sense in just that context, and still makes excellent sense today. But Mr. Northrop cannot make that kind of sense of it because there is no place at all in *his* philosophy for the essential moral ideas with which Locke worked throughout. Instead, he is compelled to attribute to Locke views which that judicious philosopher explicitly rejected and to ignore the plainest and most emphatic statements of his actual intent. The result is a remarkable triumph of the constructive imagination over intractable materials, but it is not Locke. The trouble is that it is alleged to be Locke, and that Mr. Northrop, by uttering epistemological maledictions and sticking critical pins into the effigy he has constructed, may be supposed by his more incautious readers to have disposed effectively of the original. Since the original is the root and basis of our liberal ideals, which can retain their vitality only so long as they are understood and honored by those who profess them, this operation may in fact be unhappily successful. To vary the metaphor, we are in danger here of selling our birthright of freedom for a mess of global ideology because we no longer see that birthright for what it is or value it at its authentic worth. That would be a bad bargain not only for America, but for world unity as well. We do not understand the ideals of other cultures better by misunderstanding our own, or adequately enrich an intercultural synthesis by offering to it anything less than the best we have. That best is the theory and practice of intellectual, moral, and political freedom in a form and at a level which neither medieval, Mexican, Manchu, nor Muscovite culture has so far equaled. In the understanding and use of that freedom we still have much to learn from John Locke.

So much by way of allegation. Now let us look at the record.

II

Mr. Northrop's analysis has its essential middle term in Locke's alleged identification of the human person with the "mental substance" entailed by his epistemology. Such a mental substance is presented as what comes out of the Newtonian physics, and our traditional ideology in turn, with all its atomistic and egocentric consequences, is what comes out of the attempt to find the political good for man in the relation, or lack of relation, between such substances. Not only is this held to be the way that Locke actually did reason but, under the circumstances, the only way in which he could have reasoned. For, in the "Lockean articulation of Newton's science,"

the whole of reality is nothing but material substances in public space and time acting upon mental substances to cause the latter to project sensed qualities in sensed space and time as appearances. Consequently, no alternative remains but to identify the soul of man and the political person with the mental substance, since these are the only substances which have consciousness.[9]

For Locke, "the person is, as we have noted, an independent, atomic mental substance, knowable only in one's own self by subjective introspection, and having no conceivable or specified relations to other mental substances or persons."[10] "The modern Lockean scientific and philosophical theory," Mr. Northrop insists,

specifies no relation between the many mental substances.—This point is tremendously important. It is, in fact, the basis for the entire modern Lockean democratic theory of social organization, whether it be ecclesiastical or civil. Because Locke's philosophical theory of a person as a mental substance prescribes no relation between the persons, or mental substances, making up society, there are no social laws prescribed, either by God or by nature. Hence, no alternative remains but to regard the laws of ecclesiastical or civil government as mere conventions, having their sole authority in the private, introspectively given opinions of the atomic individuals and their joint majority consent.[11]

---

[9] *Meeting*, p. 83.
[10] *Meeting*, p. 88.
[11] *Meeting*, pp. 86–87.

This theory, further, is held to have a specific relation to Locke's characteristic views both of toleration and of property rights.

Locke's modern concept of the soul as a supposedly introspected mental substance gave a new, revolutionary, and exclusively ego-centric form to the emphasis upon the individual conscience, previously fostered by both Catholic and Protestants, and laid the philosophical basis for the doctrine of complete religious toleration as a positive good which we now take so much for granted in democratic societies.[12]

And

For Locke, as we have noted, man, as a legal person, was identified fundamentally not with the material substances of his body but only with the mental substance.

It was left for Feuerbach and Marx to "treat man as a creature with a body" and thus to bring a "naturalistic realism" into our economic and political thinking.[13]

These passages are worth quoting at length because they indicate clearly the main line of Mr. Northrop's interpretation of Locke. The striking thing about them is that they all assert as established fact something which is simply not the case, namely, that Locke identified the human person, as the subject of legal and political rights, with an "introspectively given mental substance" which was the novel outcome of Newton's physics. This identification is offered as a particularly striking instance of the way in which theories of natural science determine, by way of an epistemological specification of the idea of the good for man, the structure of moral thought and political ideology.

In fact, however, Locke did not identify "person" and "mental substance" at all, but was at pains to distinguish them. In the *Second Essay on Civil Government*, where his discussion of the true function and limits of political society occurs, there is no reference to "mental substances," to Newton, or to a three-term relation of appearance. And in the *Essay Concerning Human Understanding*, where he does deal at length with epistemological issues, he is quite explicit. "Self," he tells us,

is that conscious thinking thing (whatever substance made up of, whether spiritual or material, simple or compound, it matters not) which is sensible,

---

[12] *Meeting*, p. 84.
[13] *Meeting*, p. 250.

or conscious of pleasure and pain, capable of happiness or misery, and so is concerned for itself, as far as that consciousness extends. Thus everyone finds, that whilst comprehended under that consciousness, the little finger is as much a part of itself as what is most so.[14]

And

Person, as I take it, is the name for this self. Wherever a man finds what he calls *himself*, there, I think, another may say is the same person. It is a forensic term appropriating actions and their merit; and so belongs only to intelligent agents capable of a law, and happiness and misery.[15]

The ideas of "person" and of immaterial or mental substance are quite distinct, personal identity being compatible with diversity of substances and material substance (e.g., "the little finger") being included in the idea of the person as well as mental. And this is important precisely because, as Locke remarks, "person" is a forensic or moral term, belonging only to agents capable of a law. There may be no "conceivable" relation between mental substances, as Mr. Northrop claims, but there is a very clearly conceivable relation between persons, which is essential to the very idea of personality, that of merit and accountability under a law. Personal identity is the "sameness of a rational being," and it is on the idea of man as a rational being, capable of a law, and accountable under it, not on that of blank, atomic mental substance that Locke bases his moral and political philosophy.

This might be surprising if "mental substance" was the new, Newtonian cornerstone on which Locke built his theory of knowledge and society. In fact, however, the whole notion of substance, material or immaterial, is a scholastic and Cartesian heritage about which he is obviously uneasy and which his emphasis on ideas as the source of all our knowledge puts in a dubious, not a preferred and central position, in his theory of knowledge. "*Substance and accidents of little use in philosophy*" is the summary heading of a characteristic passage,[16] and the idea of spiritual substance is said to be as clear as that of material only because "our idea of substance is equally obscure, or none at all, in both; it is but a supposed I know not what, to support those ideas we call accidents." [17] And while we are held to be intuitively aware of

---

[14] *Essay Concerning Human Understanding*, Pringle-Pattison edition, p. 194.
[15] *Human Understanding*, p. 198.
[16] *Human Understanding*, p. 102.
[17] *Human Understanding*, p. 165.

our own existence as selves, this carries with it no direct access to mental substance.[18] On the contrary, "the substance of spirit is unknown to us; and so is the substance of body equally unknown to us." [19] If the doctrine of religious toleration were based in fact on "Locke's modern concept of the soul as a supposedly introspected mental substance," it would have not so much a dubious as a nonexistent foundation.

Fortunately, however, it is more justly and securely based. Locke's political philosophy is the expression not of epistemological confusion but of moral insight and practical wisdom. From the idea of man as mental substance nothing but chaos can be deduced as the natural basis of political society. With man as a rational creature or moral person, which is in fact Locke's starting point, the case is different. Mr. Northrop says, as we have seen, that on Locke's philosophical theory "there are no social laws prescribed, either by God or by nature." But Locke says that men, by their very nature independently of their status in particular political groups, have a law to govern them, which is at once the law of nature and of God. For reason is "the common rule and measure **God** hath given to mankind" [20] and

it is certain there is such a law, and that too as intelligible and plain to a rational creature and a studier of that law as the positive laws of commonwealths, nay, possibly plainer; as much as reason is easier to be understood than the fancies and intricate contrivances of men, following contrary and hidden interests put into words; for truly so are a great part of the municipal laws of countries, which are only so far right as they are founded on the law of Nature, by which they are to be regulated and interpreted.[21]

Not only is this a law prescribed by God and nature. It defines a community and a moral order to which men belong intrinsically and in virtue of their nature as men. Mr. Northrop says:

Thus, in the essential nature of the Lockean person, there is no scientifically and philosophically grounded social relation joining him to other persons, with a content sufficient to provide a new law of nature, independent of the

---

[18] Mr. Northrop seems to recognize this at times, since he tells us in another place (*Meeting*, p. 449) that "In the Cartesian and Lockean foundations of traditional modern Western culture both the material substances and the mental substances are theoretically inferred rather than immediately apprehended factors." How this is supposed to be reconciled with the repeated reference to Locke's "doctrine of the soul as a supposedly introspected mental substance" is not made clear.

[19] *Human Understanding*, p. 171.

[20] *Second Essay on Civil Government*, Everyman edition, p. 122.

[21] *Civil Government*, p. 123.

private opinions of individual men, for the grounding of ecclesiastic or civil law. Consequently, nothing remains but to regard all laws as mere conventions, having their authority solely in the free consent of the majority.[22]

But Locke says that quite independently of such conventions every man, in virtue of his nature as a rational and morally responsible being, lives with others under the common ties of the law of Nature,

by which law, common to them all, he and all the rest of mankind are one community, make up one society distinct from all other creatures, and were it not for the corruption and viciousness of degenerate men, there would be no need of any other, no necessity that men should separate from this great and natural community, and associate into lesser combinations.[23]

The reason that Mr. Northrop is unable to take such assertions seriously is that the relation thus specified is moral, arising from the nature of man as a rational creature, not epistemological, deducible from the supposed implications of Newton's physics. It is no wonder that Locke's theory makes but little sense in the pattern thus imposed upon it. Yet Mr. Northrop cannot wholly ignore the emphatic assertions of Locke on just this point. The passage in which he attempts to deal with them is enlightening.

Locke did, to be sure, speak of all people in the state of nature as subject to the law of reason. But this law of reason must not be interpreted as the organic social principle of Hooker and Aristotle. What reason led men to, in the case of Locke, was nature conceived as mechanistically determined material substances and men in the state of nature as individual observers who are mental substances, whose interrelation cannot even be clearly conceived. These mental substances were, however, conscious and hence sensitive to persons and things other than themselves; also their reason did take them to the theory of mental substances, according to which all individuals are absolutely free and independent.[24]

This, if true, would be important. For it is on the idea of freedom thus conceived—the freedom of men as dubiously related mental substances—that Mr. Northrop holds the Declaration of Independence to be based. This is elsewhere elaborated. "Locke, having defined the good for the individual in terms of nothing but freedom of the mental substances, quite apart from any determinate content of their consciousness, has no alternative but to define the good for the state in terms of

---

[22] *Meeting*, p. 88.
[23] *Civil Government*, p. 181.
[24] *Meeting*, p. 87.

98

nothing but the 'consent' of a majority of such individuals." [25] Thus have we come by the idea that government derives its just powers from the consent of the governed.

But Locke, so far from defining the good for men as the freedom of their mental substances "quite apart from any determinate content of their consciousness," defines freedom itself in terms of a very special sort of consciousness, and the behavior based upon it. "The freedom then of man, and liberty of acting according to his own will, is grounded in his having reason, which is able to instruct him in that law he is to govern himself by, and make him know how far he is left to the freedom of his own will." [26] So the parental power, about which Locke has a good deal to say,

is nothing but what parents have over their children to govern them, for the children's good, until they come to the use of reason, or a state of knowledge, wherein they may be supposed capable to understand that rule, whether it be the law of Nature or the municipal law of their country, they are to govern themselves by—capable, I say, to know it, as well as several others, who live as free men under that law. [27]

To live as free men under the law—that would make no sense for men as material substances determined by the laws of Newton's physics, or as mental substances brooding blankly over their private mental states, and conscious of each other as equally blank and brooding. It made sense for Locke because the freedom he valued was that of men born free "as they are born rational" and capable therefore, in the mature development of their powers, of distinguishing between just and arbitrary governmental claims and obeying the one as freely as they were prepared to resist the other.

So again for equality. In speaking of the Declaration of Independence Mr. Northrop remarks: "This document said that *all* men, not merely Anglo-Saxon white men, were by nature free and equal. Certainly, each was a mental substance." [28] And this insight, again, is attributed to Locke and his Newtonian philosophy. But it was not as mental substances that Locke held all men to be equal. "Though I have said above 'That all men by nature are equal,' I cannot be supposed to understand

---

[25] *Meeting*, p. 122.
[26] *Civil Government*, p. 146.
[27] *Civil Government*, p. 204.
[28] *Meeting*, p. 110.

all sorts of 'equality.'" [29] What sort then? Why, "the equality I there spoke of as proper to the business in hand, being that equal right that every man hath to his natural freedom, without being subjected to the will or authority of any other man." [30] What rights mental substances have under the laws of Newton and epistemology I leave it for Mr. Northrop to make clear. What Locke wanted to make clear was the equal right that men have under the law of God and right reason, a law which governments are obligated in moral right and justice, not mechanism nor yet epistemology, to respect.

The idea that the political state has its final authority in the consent of the governed also takes on a different meaning as we pass from Mr. Northrop's Locke to the original. For the former, this doctrine affirms the lack of any objectively grounded social or organic relation between mental substances. Hence the laws of ecclesiastical or civil government are "mere conventions, having their sole authority in the private, introspectively given opinions of the independent atomic individuals and their joint majority consent." [31] Mr. Northrop contrasts this with the philosophy of Hooker, for whom man is

by his very nature "a political animal." He is not, as with Descartes or Locke, a purely self-sufficient, independent mental substance. Consequently, for Hooker, neither the basis for religious doctrine nor the source of the sovereignty of the state is in the subjective private opinion of the individual or in a mere convention into which a majority of the many private individuals enter. Instead, it has its source both religiously and politically in the objective, organic, hierarchical principle joining individuals to each other in the community and themselves to nature in the universe.[32]

"Mere" consent is something arbitrary, subjective, and private, a poor basis indeed for social order of any kind. It is no wonder Mr. Northrop hankers, by contrast, for the "organic, hierarchical, communal conception of the good" which he finds in Aristotle and the medieval philosophy of the Catholic church.

In Locke's philosophy, however, the contrast is not quite so simple as this. Men living under government are properly to be thought of as "a society of rational creatures, entered into a community

---

[29] *Civil Government*, p. 142.
[30] *Civil Government*, p. 142.
[31] *Meeting*, p. 87.
[32] *Meeting*, p. 173.

100

for their mutual good, such as have set rulers over themselves, to guard and promote that good," [33] and their consent to the authority of such rulers is grounded on their judgment that this good is in fact being justly served, within the limits of its proper powers, by the government set up for that purpose. "Mere" private opinion would indeed be arbitrary, but it is the essence of rational judgment, on Locke's theory, that it is not. Such judgment is, on the contrary, the only means we have by which the arbitrary can be distinguished from the just, or objectively valid truth from a merely egocentric bias. That men should seek the truth in this objective way and guide their lives by it is perhaps the most basic of all Locke's philosophical teachings. To maintain an "indifference" toward all preconceived opinions and a willingness to be guided only by the evidence, he tells us, is essential to the proper conduct of the understanding. "This I own is no easy thing to do, but I am not enquiring the easy way to opinion, but the right way to truth; which they must follow who will deal fairly with their own understandings and their own souls." [34] This is the effective freedom of the understanding and this the "care of his own soul" which Locke held belongs to each man—to make up his own mind on the merits of the issues that confront him, and to give his consent where and as his own uncoerced judgment dictates. "It is conceit, fancy, extravagance, anything rather than understanding, if [the mind] must be under the constraint of receiving and holding opinions by the authority of anything but their own, not fancied, but perceived, evidence. This is rightly called imposition, and is of all other the worst and most dangerous sort of it." [35] And that truth, as capable of demonstration to "rational, understanding being" as the propositions of Euclidean geometry, can be attained in morals Locke explicitly affirmed.[36] So much for the claim that Locke's appeal to consent based on individual judgment as the basis for governmental authority was or was meant to be an appeal to "mere subjective private opinion."

Yet there remains an important difference between Locke's theory and the "organic" alternative with which Mr. Northrop contrasts it. It is

---

[33] *Civil Government*, p. 201.
[34] *The Conduct of the Understanding*, Oxford Press edition, p. 80.
[35] *Conduct*, p. 34.
[36] *Human Understanding*, p. 277.

not that Locke denies that man is a social and even a political animal. "God, having made man such a creature that, in His own judgment, it was not good for him to be alone, put him under strong obligations of necessity, convenience, and inclination, to drive him into society, as well as fitted him with understanding and language to continue and enjoy it." [37] It is rather that Locke maintains that the presence of such "objective" relations is not enough to define the *just* powers of a free government, or to provide an answer to the question as to why and where it *ought* to be obeyed. The consent of the governed is the final locus of political authority because a government exists, under the natural law, to further a mutual good, and it is in the minds of free and rational men that its claims on their loyalty must be judged. An arbitrary or tyrannical government, on the other hand, is one under which a man "as if he were degraded from the common state of rational creatures, is denied a liberty to judge of, or defend his right," and is thus worse off than in "the unrestrained state of Nature." [38] Political force without right is tyranny, and of the true character of such tyranny free men who have "the sense of rational creatures" [39] will finally judge for themselves.

That is what Locke was talking about when he wrote his justification of the revolution of 1688 and Jefferson when he framed the Declaration of Independence. The embattled farmers of Lexington and Concord did not take up arms in defense of their inalienable and, indeed, inviolable status as unrelated mental substances, but of their rights, and not least of their right to a government under which their responsible judgment as to what was right would be the final basis of public order and of civil law. The relation of consent thus established between free men and their government is not something less than an "organic" relation, but something more, a "more" which Mr. Northrop's analysis has not been able to discern, perhaps because it is grounded in a moral, not a physical or epistemological relation.

It remains only to consider two specific rights which, on Mr. Northrop's interpretation, are supposed to follow from Locke's theory of the person as a mental substance, and to see what can be made of them in

---

[37] *Civil Government,* pp. 154–155.
[38] *Civil Government,* p. 162.
[39] *Civil Government,* p. 234.

terms of Locke's own theory. The first is the right of private property or, as the critic states it, "the Lockean principle of the primacy of property rights over human, social and economic needs," [40] or "the Lockean democratic thesis that the sole justification for the existence of government is the preservation of private property," which "makes it self-contradictory and hence unconstitutional for even a vote of the majority to place human rights above property rights in any issue between the two." [41] Mr. Northrop believes that the costs of this doctrine have been tragic, and that unless we can rid ourselves of it "there is grave danger that neither the debacle of 1932 nor even Pearl Harbor and Corregidor, will be able to teach us." [42]

But how does the matter stand with Locke? He did maintain, of course, that the chief end of civil society is the preservation of property,[43] and that this sets a limit to the powers and functions of government, whose proper business it is to serve the ends for which it was set up. It is well to remember, however, as the modern reader may not, that Locke meant by property the "life, liberty and estate" [44] of all citizens, not merely the corporate privileges of large-scale industry, and that he based the right to it on the "property" every man has in his own "person" and in "the 'labor' of his body and the 'work' of his hands" which are "properly his." [45] It is a long way from such a view to the proprietary claims of American and British oil companies in Mexico which Mr. Northrop offers as its appropriate twentieth-century development.[46]

The striking fact is, however, that *any* emphasis on the "primacy of property rights" would be a curious anomaly in Locke's philosophy if Mr. Northrop's reinterpretation of it were correct. For it is precisely a right growing out of man's *bodily* life and effort, and expressed in his public relations to other persons in the material world. If Locke, as alleged, had identified man as a legal person, "fundamentally not with the material substances of his body but only with the mental substance," [47] and had thought of mental substances as concerned primarily

---

[40] *Meeting*, p. 45.
[41] *Meeting*, p. 97.
[42] *Meeting*, p. 147.
[43] *Civil Government*, p. 158.
[44] *Civil Government*, p. 159.
[45] *Civil Government*, p. 130.
[46] *Meeting*, pp. 42 ff.
[47] *Meeting*, p. 250.

with the introspective awareness of their own blank souls and private mental states, this would indeed be a curious emphasis in his thought. And how he could hold that the right to property made it unconstitutional for even the vote of a majority to place human rights above property rights if he also taught that there are *no* social laws transcending "the private introspectively given opinions of the independent atomic individuals and their joint majority consent," [48] it is difficult to see.

In fact, however, Locke held *both* that "any part of our bodies vitally united to that which is conscious in us, makes a part of ourselves" [49] or persons, and that there is a law, the law of Nature, which defines primary social rights and with which no government, with or without majority consent, can justly tamper. *The law of Nature ceaseth not in society.* Hence his theory does make sense. But it does not make sense, in terms of it, to oppose "property rights" to "human rights" in the New Deal manner. For property rights in Locke's philosophy *are* human rights; they define the goods whose secure enjoyment a man is entitled to because he has worked for them and because it is just and proper that he reap where he has sown. The doctrine is moral, and the limit it sets on governmental powers is a moral not a physical or epistemological limit. It may properly be criticized on moral grounds and by reference to the claim that there are other no less human rights than those of "life, liberty and estates" with which a free government ought justly to concern itself. To denounce it, however, because it makes property, not "human rights," the exclusive concern of a democratic government is to attack a caricature and not the doctrine itself.

It is well to remember, also, that the major reason why Locke was inclined to restrict the concern of a just government to "property" rights was not his high regard for property but his relatively low regard for government. Property is precisely the sort of thing a government can protect through the police power—the pursuit of truth needs and can profit by no such intervention. This is not because it is not important what men think but because it is extremely important that they think for themselves. Thus

the business of laws is not to provide for the truth of opinions, but for the safety and security of the commonwealth, and of every particular man's goods

---

[48] *Meeting,* p. 87.
[49] *Human Understanding,* p. 198.

and person. And so it ought to be. For the truth certainly would do well enough if she were once left to shift for herself. She seldom has received, and I fear never will receive, much assistance from the power of great men, to whom she is but rarely known, and more rarely welcome. She is not taught by laws, nor has she any need of force to procure her entrance into the minds of men.[50]

In these days of thought control and congressional inquisition there is a truth in this, I think, that not even the Einsteinian modifications of Newton's physics have altogether outmoded.

The notion that whatever is socially desirable is a proper object of governmental action and control, and that, in consequence, if a theory restricts the scope of such control it thereby circumscribes the area of common good is Mr. Northrop's notion, not Locke's. "But idolatry, some say, is a sin, and therefore not to be tolerated. If they said it were therefore to be avoided, the inference were good. But it does not follow that because it is a sin it ought therefore to be punished by the magistrate."[51]

This brings us directly to Locke's defense of toleration and its place in his moral and political philosophy. Mr. Northrop expresses great admiration for this doctrine, not once but repeatedly. Yet it is difficult to see how, in his version of Locke's philosophy, this admiration could possibly be warranted. The defense of toleration rests, of course, on Locke's great saying that "the care, therefore, of every man's soul belongs unto himself, and is to be left unto himself." And here is Mr. Northrop's explanation of it.

Upon this basis the individual alone, consulting his own mental substance introspectively, is the sole criterion of the correctness of his religion, and the religion of one man cannot be shown to be incorrect by appeal to any other man's doctrine, whether it be that of the Roman Catholic St. Thomas or the Protestant Calvin.—This Lockean idea that the individual man alone, consulting his own private, introspectively given mental substance or soul, even before the 'correct doctrine' had affected that soul, or even before the soul has been 'born anew,' is the only judge of the religious man, is a very novel thesis in the history of the Western world.[52]

Since Locke specifically held that the substance of mind or spirit is unknown to us,[53] it is hard to see what information his introspective

---

[50] *A Letter Concerning Toleration*, Cassell edition, p. 176.
[51] *Toleration*, p. 172.
[52] *Meeting*, p. 84.
[53] *Human Understanding*, p. 171.

consultation of it could supply him, about either God or man, or what warrant it could give for that freedom of the understanding, which is a freedom not in the introspection of private opinions but in the judgment of public truth, that John Locke was interested in defending. Locke's own version is quite different. He does indeed hold that "true and saving religion consists in the inward persuasion of the mind, without which nothing can be acceptable to God." But he goes on at once to explain this. "And such is the nature of the understanding, that it cannot be compelled to the belief in anything by outward force. Confiscation of estate, imprisonment, torments, nothing of that nature can have any such efficacy as to make men change the inward judgment that they have framed of things." [54] The limitation of the magistrate's power in such matters is grounded not in the introspective autonomy of private mental content, which in any case would be inviolable, but on the impertinence of force as a ground for judgment or rational belief *about anything.* "For laws are of no force at all without penalties, and penalties in this case are absolutely impertinent, because they are not proper to convince the mind." [55] And thus it is that "no religion that I believe not to be true can be either true or profitable unto me." [56]

To base the claim that a man has a right to judge for himself the truth of those doctrines by which he guides his life on the dubious theory that he has a privileged means of access to his own blank mental substance is to trivialize it beyond all reasonable recognition. It is good to know that this is Mr. Northrop's reading of the liberal theory, not that of John Locke. But it is, again, not surprising that he should have so understood it. If the freedom of the mind were indeed the freedom of Lockean mental substance "as a completely local, independent thing having nothing in common with all other persons and things," [57] this is about what it would amount to. Considered as the freedom of the understanding of a rational creature, sharing common laws of reason with all other men and concerned to arrive at the objective truth as, on the evidence, he discovers it to be, the case is somewhat altered. But it is, once more, a case which Mr. Northrop, on the basis of his own preconceptions, cannot even state.

---

[54] *Toleration,* p. 148.
[55] *Toleration,* p. 149.
[56] *Toleration,* p. 164.
[57] *Meeting,* p. 461.

In summary, then, the "Lockean-democratic ideology" as *The Meeting of East and West* portrays it, is the socially indefensible and aesthetically barren outcome of a mistake in epistemology, itself the consequence of a long since outmoded stage of physical theory. That we should have garnered from it the good fruit of freedom would be, if it actually had happened, the most amazing harvest of grapes from thorns on record. Fortunately, the past is secure against our current misunderstanding. But the liberal faith that has come to us from that past is not. It can maintain its hold in the minds of men who have "the sense of rational creatures" only so long as they can make sense of it and, through it, of their own political purposes and ideals. It is a matter of importance therefore that we do make sense of it, and that we turn in consequence from Mr. Northrop to Mr. Locke for a just and accurate estimate of its rational grounds and its abiding value.

III

The serious and central question which a re-examination of Locke's political theory raises for us today is not whether we can still base our philosophy of freedom on the notion of man as a Newtonian mental substance, for it never was so based, but whether we can still base it on the notion of man as a rational creature, capable of discerning and governing himself by moral laws, and of judging the limits of political authority in terms of them. Professor Sabine has stated this issue with admirable clarity.

Anyone who now reflects upon the beginnings of democratic social philosophy, and upon the types of political reform to which it originally led, will see that at its root lay a fundamental act of faith. This was the belief in the essential reasonableness of human nature and of human action.—It was at once an appeal to individual judgment and a sublime confidence in the moral rightness of individual judgment, when this is allowed to follow its nature.—From this confidence, intellectual and moral, in the reliability of rational judgment were derived the typical democratic reforms.[58]

That this is specifically true of Locke's contributions to such philosophy and such reforms, our preceding analysis will, I hope, have made abundantly clear.

---

[58] *Democracy and Preconceived Ideas* (Columbus, Ohio: The Walter J. Shepard Foundation, 1945), pp. 4–5.

Professor Sabine goes on to show that more recent interpretations of human nature, borrowing their content from biology and their animus from the voluntaristic philosophies of the later nineteenth century, do little to support this faith. As an ideology expressing a moral preference and commitment we now see that it does not follow from any purely scientific reading of the facts of man's being and behavior. But then, of course, it never did. It rested rather on the values affirmed in the political habits and discipline, the tangible interest, and the moral tradition and aspiration of the English-speaking peoples, raised in the minds of their intellectual leaders to the level of a self-evident truth to which right-thinking men everywhere ought to agree. Men could plausibly be claimed, by reference to it, to be worthy of political freedom because in good measure these men had shown themselves to be so. But the claim that they had a *right* to such freedom was more than a report of their past behavior; it was a projection of their future purpose, a selection of the values on which they were prepared to stake their lives, their fortunes, and their sacred honor, as they would hardly have been prepared to do if they had really supposed it was the epistemological implications of Newton's physics that they were defending.

They were by no means impractical idealists. Their claims were in the line of what they took to be their own substantial interests, and they made no secret of this. But neither were they mere opportunists and propagandists, employing a received ideology to manipulate the responses of the masses for ends that would not bear inspection. Their philosophy helped them to believe that the freedom to pursue these interests for a mutual good was a right to which in reason and justice they were entitled. The generalization of such rights in a theory of what man "by nature" is and, under decent political conditions, will prove himself to be, was a courageous universalization of this claim. The community to which it was addressed was in principle world-wide, and men "as men" were held to be capable of recognizing its claims and sharing in its values. As a moral basis for political authority, this doctrine is by no means outmoded. No moral philosophy that professes a lower ideal or limits its goods on principle to a narrower society can, in the long run, command the consciences of free men, or give order and justice to their aspirations.

But while Locke's political philosophy was universal and rational in its intent, it was, like all human constructions, local and limited in its content and articulation. The "reasonableness" he took for granted was the sort he found exemplified in the social behavior of the prosperous Englishmen of his own time, and the "great and natural community" of mankind in which under the law of Nature all men participate was an overoptimistic extrapolation which only an inherited theology could render credible. We should have learned but little from hard experience if we did not recognize today that a universal moral community is not a gift of nature but a precarious social achievement toward which we must work if we are to justify our ideals, but which we dare not presuppose as an accomplished actuality at the basis of existing social relations. Our ideals are reasonable and relevant only if they appeal to capacities in actual human nature which can be developed in the direction they define and which are supremely worth developing. If the established facts of scientific inquiry proved the nonexistence of such capacities or the impossibility of such development, then indeed would our faith be vain. In fact, however, it is not by facts as such that our rational ideals are contradicted, but by competing ideologies, in which a selection of such facts, taken out of context, is used to document the philosophical confusion and dignify the moral inadequacy of a "scientifically" enlightened age. There is much that John Locke did not see that we now must take account of, and much he took for granted that needs questioning and qualification today. But when it comes to the formulation of the ideals in terms of which moral judgment can be brought to bear on political practice in the interest of human freedom, we may still go further than Locke and fare worse.

On this point again, and finally, we may profitably refer to Mr. Northrop's proposed synthesis of ideologies for confirmation. Having failed to find a sound theoretical "foundation" for political freedom in the "Lockean" mental substances, he proceeds to seek it elsewhere, and comes up with quite a supply of contributions. The major one, perhaps, is found in the all-pervasive, undifferentiated aesthetic continuum to which the wisdom of the East can point us.

The realization of the ultimacy and irreducibility of this undifferentiated aesthetic continuum has one other consequence. A genuine basis for human freedom is provided. It is not by a spurious invention of a so-called practical reason, which places the supposed demands of the earthly, temporary, local human being above all factually grounded, scientifically verified or positivistically given principles that a meaning for freedom in human nature is to be found. Instead, as the Orient noted long ago, freedom has its basis in that part of the nature of man and things which is indeterminate and thus a potentiality for a determinateness that is not yet.[59]

And again:

Man is in part free because he, in his essential nature, is in part indeterminate. At any time man can withdraw into the indeterminate aesthetic component of his nature, giving up any commitment to determinate, transitory, aesthetic qualities, or to determinate, inferred theoretical theses, thereby in part escaping the determinism which attaches to all determinate things; and, because of this capacity, he may also *freely* accept the determinate, taking all its causal consequences, as Orozco and the Spanish have so truly seen.[60]

It is not in withdrawal into the indeterminacy of the undifferentiated, however, that the distinctive sort of freedom which we value as a moral and political heritage is manifest. For this is a freedom not of withdrawal but of affirmation, and of a peculiar sort. Indeterminacy may in some sense be its condition, though even that is highly questionable, but it is certainly not what constitutes it as a positive achievement. We must look farther. And Mr. Northrop tells us where to look. For "a person, like everything else in the universe, is the aesthetic component of the nature of things joined to the theoretic component of the nature of things by the two-termed relation of epistemic correlation." [61] What is lacking in the aesthetic component may thus be made good in the theoretic, and "the theoretic component of anything is that thing precisely as it is known by the natural scientists' postulationally designated, indirectly and experimentally confirmed theory." [62] "This means, in the case of man, that in the theoretic component of his nature he is precisely what experimental physicists, chemists, biologists, and psychologists find him to be." [63] On this level we get the Marxian "thermodynamic concept of a person and the nature of his rights," [64] "the individual physiological freedom to be oneself," [65] and, taking account also of the determinate elements in the aesthetic continuum, the "psychological freedom of the

---

[59] *Meeting*, p. 343.
[60] *Meeting*, p. 471.
[61] *Meeting*, p. 466.
[62] *Meeting*, p. 465.
[63] *Meeting*, p. 464.
[64] *Meeting*, p. 241.
[65] *Meeting*, p. 475.

110

emotions and the sentiments" [66] as well. There seems to be here almost an embarrassment of riches.

One kind of freedom, however, is lacking, and that is what has traditionally been known as moral freedom—the freedom of man that is manifest in his responsible acceptance of a law he gives to himself because he recognizes it as right. Now Mr. Northrop does speak of man, in virtue of his aesthetic indeterminacy, as having the capacity to "freely accept the determinate, taking all its causal consequences." [67] But the determinate which he thus "freely" accepts is, on this view, simply what the latest scientific theories tell him about the nature of the world and himself. If this means that he accepts the *de facto* causal uniformities of things as canons of physical, chemical, biological, and psychological behavior we need only remark with Carlyle, "Gad, he'd better." If it means that he accepts the latest *account* of nature which the scientists of the moment are offering, we may suggest respectfully that he include several grains of indeterminacy in his acceptance since they will almost certainly be different shortly. But by no ideological alchemy can such "acceptance" of the scientifically determined order of things by the aesthetically indeterminate individual be construed as a substitute for the acceptance of moral principles by a rational person as a basis for responsible choice and action. The claim that, without the idea of man as a moral person, Mr. Northrop's exotic, intercultural mélange provides a synthesis in which "justice is done to the independence, integrity and freedom of the individual, which it is to the everlasting credit of Descartes, Locke, Hume, Bentham and Mill and traditional modern Protestantism and democracy to have fostered" [68] is palpably illegitimate.

For the individualism of Locke, at least, and of traditional Protestantism and democracy, was a moral individualism, a faith in man as, in Bishop Butler's words, "in the strictest and most proper sense a law unto himself." On this his right to judge for himself was based, and it was to such judgment, in turn, that claimants to political and ecclesiastical authority were expected to submit their case. If our zeal to keep up with the latest thing in physics or physiology, or to mate the cultures of East and West in an epistemologically solemnized global union, leads

---

[66] *Meeting*, p. 476.
[67] *Meeting*, p. 471.
[68] *Meeting*, p. 475.

us to a philosophy in which we can no longer even make sense of this great insight, we shall be spiritually poorer than our ancestors, for all our borrowed "wisdom." Insofar as Mr. Northrop's analysis serves, in the sustained thoroughness of its misconception of liberal ideas, to make this clear, there is something of permanent importance to be learned from it.

The Substance of the Social Contract

BERTRAM MORRIS

"My intention here is not to exclude the consent of the people from being one foundation of government where it has place. It is surely the best and most sacred of any. I only pretend, that it has very seldom had place in any degree, and never almost in its full extent. And therefore some other foundation of government must also be admitted."—DAVID HUME

THE social contract is an inchoate moral prescription. It is not a historical event by which man somehow miraculously rises from the state of nature to the civil state; nor is it a justification of blind allegiance to historical states, past or present. It is a loose formulation of a principle which a state must embody if it is to be justified morally, and that justification is, in essence, the consent of the governed in the affairs of state. Governments do exercise powers, sometimes legitimately, and sometimes not. Jefferson was not amiss in insisting that the legitimate exercise of power derives from those who are governed. But consent is of necessity limited to the extent to which a people form a community. It becomes a reality only as they develop common interests which they pursue together. The compact is socially significant when a people participate intelligently and willingly in public affairs.

In his classic conception of the contract, Hobbes perceives clearly the need for a community of interests before the civil state can come into existence. He fixes, however, upon what may be considered to be the least cohesive of conditions for the formation of the state—the overweening desire for self-protection, such that a people gives up its "rights" in order that a sovereign power can be established. If the resulting sovereignty is not quite absolute, this is only because self-preservation is thought to be more important than the state itself. Hobbes seizes

113

upon the least social of human interests as the nerve of the social structure. He has an abundance of critics who have exercised their skill in
portraying how fantastic it is to develop a social structure out of the
blind urgency of self-preservation, on the one hand, and enlightened
prudence, on the other. It may well be a cause for wonder that a giant
intellect which can create the social contract out of chaos could discover
no more sound basis for peace than that of merely prolonging creature
existence.

I would suggest that, regardless of the strain put upon our imagination to see how society can come into being out of enlightened self-
interest, nevertheless what gives moral force to Hobbes' theory of the
contract is the agreement that derives from a mutuality of interests. Because of this agreement, which in his theory is unquestionably attenuated, he is able to derive principles of social justice, which are, of course,
equally attenuated. He tells us clearly that "Justice and Injustice are
none of the Faculties, neither of the Body, nor Mind. If they were, they
might be in a man that were alone in the world, as well as his Senses,
and Passions. They are Qualities, that relate to men in Society, not in
Solitude." [1] Insofar as a man is a social being, there are social virtues
that constitute the moral fiber of his life. Throughout the *Leviathan*,
Hobbes is desperately trying to establish laws of justice in the civil
state—so much so that he is compelled to assert that the sovereign cannot commit "injustices," but only "inequities." That he is unconvincing
in his attempts to establish justice in the state is clearly traceable to his
thwarted attempt to derive social relationships out of self-interest. Professor Sabine has tersely expressed the difficulty as follows: "Since the
'right' resigned is merely the use of natural strength and 'covenants
without the sword are but words,' this is a contract only in a manner of
speaking. Properly it is a logical fiction to offset the anti-social fiction of
his psychology." [2] Because Hobbes' view of the social contract is neither
a historical account of the origin of the state nor a sufficient basis for
establishing political obligation, its moral content approaches zero. He
provides no practical framework in which citizens can participate in the
continuing decisions of social life, but only an alleged ground (and even
this is qualified) for the obedience of subjects to their sovereign. Hobbes

---

[1] *Leviathan*, Pt. I, ch. 13.
[2] *A History of Political Theory*, p. 468.

114

makes use of the contract in order to prevent the governed, once they have committed themselves to the state, from having any authority in the organization of political life.

Those who carry forth the development of the theory discover a basis for the contract in the ends of social life. In spite of his attempt to limit the sphere in which the contract is enforceable, Locke recognizes the need for explicit institutional organizations to overcome "the inconveniences" of the state of nature. There exist *social* relationships— that is, natural laws—in the state of nature, for man is morally bound "as much as he can, to preserve the rest of mankind"; but the inherent limitations of the natural state are such as fall short of that agreement by which men "mutually enter one community and make one body politic." In the *Second Treatise of Civil Government* Locke's unquestioned commitment to private property, spelled out as life, liberty, and estate, alone prevents him from establishing the interests of the community as superior to that of the individual. In the *Letter Concerning Toleration,* however, he suggests at least in a negative way that the public good may override private interests. He asserts: "The public good is the rule and measure of all law-making. If a thing be not useful to the commonwealth, though it be never so indifferent, it may not be established by law." [3] If Locke does not push the theory of the compact though to its extreme conclusions, and no doubt he had good pragmatic reasons for not doing so, Rousseau nevertheless does.

In setting up the general will as the sovereign power, indivisible and inalienable, Rousseau establishes the political pattern by which alone the individual comes to find his true interests expressed in the paramountcy of the public good. Certainly, the Citizen of Geneva has to use sleight of hand to discover that the general will manifests itself in a curious process of canceling out particular wills; [4] but he leaves us in no doubt that community interests are morally prior and superior to any private interest. And interestingly enough, although both Hobbes and Rousseau wish to establish an authoritarian state, the one seeks to do it by imposing the authority on its people externally, whereas the other seeks to do it by disclosing that that authority is the true expression of the people. In the one case, sovereignty is suffered as the lesser of two

---

[3] Appleton-Century, 1937, p. 194.
[4] *Social Contract,* Bk. II, ch. iii.

evils; in the other, it is the positive community of interest which has come to fulfillment.

These brief historical comments are intended merely to focus attention upon the social contract as constituting foundations of political obligation that are peculiarly relevant to our own times. In view, however, of Hume's scorching criticism of the social compact, justification of these foundations is all the more necessary. Hume was unquestionably right in distinguishing between promises and the social contract, and in pointing to the separate derivations of each. And he was doubly right in asking whether men do in fact have the opportunity to leave the state if they find it not to their liking. Finally, even if the contract were once made, he is sensible in raising the question as to why one should be bound by a contract that no longer pleases him and that he does not care to abide by. In the light of his analysis, we may address ourselves to the following questions: What may the contract significantly mean? How can it be known? In what sense should it exercise compulsion over men? And, finally, what possible relevance can it have to contemporary political life? Although it is not quite clear that Hume actually rejected the contract, satisfactory answers to these questions are called for. I conceive that our task is to determine what kind of answers will meet these questions.

A FUNCTIONAL MEANING OF THE SOCIAL CONTRACT

If "the social contract" as a phrase has outlived its usefulness, the substance of its meaning has not. From Althusius on, with the possible exception of Hobbes, the theory of the contract was motivated by a liberal impulse. If this was only "mild" in Althusius, it became more militant in those who were justifying the liberal revolutions. But unless the tradition of liberalism can be reinterpreted in terms significant for the conditions of contemporary life, it had better be relegated to the rubric of lost causes in history. Fundamentally, the question which challenged those who had recourse to the social contract was, How make government responsible to man's social needs? When the question was interpreted as signifying, How can man be provided with a life of security and peace, or how can he maintain his property and foster his private business? it was merely a specification of what were taken to be the primary demands of social life at a given time. The clue to the significance of the social contract is revealed in those social structures which the political theorist believes are necessary for satisfying the urgent demands of social life. A government which is responsive to those demands must establish institutions in order to satisfy them and thus to secure the ends that effect a real community of interests. Accordingly the contract is achieved in those institutional forms which further the social life of a culture.

As a theory of liberal action, the contract stands in opposition to class distinctions and preferential treatment. Class distinctions set up social barriers which prevent large segments of society from actively participating in social life. Plato could find no higher virtue for the artisan than that of being temperate, or for the warrior than that of being brave. Social fulfillment remained the exclusive privilege of the guardians. Class distinctions involve invidious comparisons, and are the complement of preferential treatment. Yet, essentially, the contract is designed to obliterate artificial distinctions and to recognize the worth of men as social beings, that is, as beings who create values in the give and take of cultural life. Liberty, as contract theorists have seen, is a means by which this sort of life is established. Equality too, they have seen, is also an indispensable means to this end. And even if they do not always insist that men are equal in the civil state, yet one of their basic arguments for the contract is that they are equal in the state of nature. Liberty and equality are essential aspects of the liberal tradition. Few have realized, however, that their truly social character is to be found in neither of them alone, but rather in their interconnections as they develop into an organized form of communal life. This is none other than the ideal of fraternity.

Fraternity exists when all men share deeply in the values that are common to a culture. It is a harmonious organization of the powers of a society to promote the common interests of people. Fraternity loses its rich potentialities when it is converted into chauvinism or when it is equated with vague, sentimental feelings of the brotherhood of man. Chauvinism perverts the fraternal life by taking fraternity to the exclusion of liberty and equality, and making of it—as Napoleon did—an apology for nationalism. Sentimental, brotherly love, on the other hand, gives lip-service to the ideal, but has no institutional underpinning

117

which makes brotherhood a reality in cultural life. The Romans were able to convert fraternity from a merely moral ideal into a principle of political obligation by extending the *ius gentium* into the *ius naturale*. In practice, the social compact is engendered only as it respects the fundamental nature of *social* relationships among people, and it operates only as institutional life affords men and women the opportunity of social fulfillment. Institutions may—and in time do—become inert, frustrating, and a hindrance to social action. Yet a vigorous social life that penetrates beyond intimate, esoteric groups can be carried on only as institutions provide the structure by which the continuity of cooperative effort can be sustained and by which achievements that represent effective mass participation can be secured. When a working harmony between powerful institutions and widespread social fulfillment occurs, man succeeds in attaining that vitality of culture which at once challenges his energies and satisfies the requirements for a rewarding participation in a creative enterprise. When this occurs, fraternity is not just a vague mouthing, nor is it a tool in the hands of those who seek privileges. On the contrary, it is effective realization of social action.

The institutions which a culture can create depend, on the one hand, upon the material conditions available to a people for sustaining themselves and, on the other, upon their genius for envisaging the potentialities which by their industry they may realize. This they may do by leaving the vast majority economically depressed, politically disenfranchised, and socially ostracized. Or they may do it—although it has rarely been tried—by spreading as nearly as possible the available resources to all who need them, by encouraging widespread participation in political decisions, and by actively promoting the development of those talents which are consistent with the fullest sharing of communal values. Institutions, consequently, may be primarily for the benefit of the few, or they may be primarily for the benefit of the many. Only in the latter case do they measure up to what is required by the demands for a truly social existence.

For the present purposes I shall state dogmatically what seem to me to be the conditions that must be met if man is to build worthy social institutions. First, there must be the acceptance of common goals, for in the absence of these there can be only the submission of the weak to the powerful, whose special interests are promoted at the expense of those who are powerless. Secondly, there must be the recognition of the existence of other human beings as human. An individual can delight in things, but he cannot enter into social relationships unless he recognizes that others, too, can delight in things. If a man possesses no strong sense of social imagination, he cannot but run roughshod over others whose feelings he cannot understand. Finally, social life includes a willingness to resolve differences in ways which, as far as possible, are mutually satisfactory. In other words, there must be open to men avenues of communication in order that their claims can be assessed and that ways of adjudicating them can be satisfactorily arrived at. Violence is diametrically opposed to men's composing their differences peacefully, and the social relationship is annulled to the extent that violence is resorted to. If the substance of the social contract is to be justified, it will be then on the basis of these principles.

The principles above stated afford a point of departure for intelligent criticism of institutional life. Since they constitute what are considered to be the standards of the social relation, the degree to which actual institutions embody the ideals of social life may be assessed by means of them. Moreover, these principles underlie the liberal tradition, which is one that insists that these ideals be realized, not just for an elite, but for the large mass of people. Liberalism in the modern world comes to signify liberty, equality, and fraternity. Hence, by observing, on the one hand, the extent to which institutions embody these social ideals, and, on the other, the extent to which they are actually expressed through liberty, equality, and fraternity, it is possible to judge whether institutions further the ends of social life, and thus of the ideals of democracy. The upholders of the theory of the contract have explicitly observed its implications for liberty and equality, but they have only vaguely recognized its further implications for fraternity.

Liberty is power. It is the power of promoting organized interests, and thus of giving them institutional status. When a society sanctions, fosters, and gives expression to a set of interests, the liberty of these interests is established. They may then sensibly be said to constitute a liberty within that society. If a society really prizes freedom of speech, of the press, or of religion, that freedom will require auditoriums, facilities for gathering, publishing, and distributing news, or church assemblies in which people may actually worship. When anyone is prevented by economic status, by political creed, or by religious, ethnic, or racial discrimination from taking part in the activities that promote an interest, his freedom is abridged. In principle, the matter is as simple as that. A person who is unable to press the claims which he considers to be worthy of attention is excluded from the social processes by which liberty is established. When large numbers are thus excluded from entering into the social processes because there are no institutions to care for their claims, liberty is only pious vacuity.

"Liberty without equality is a name of noble sound and squalid result." Liberty represents power, and individuals or groups may, and do, possess power. The focal institutions which are typical of a culture provide the clue to the interpretation of the degree of liberty which that culture engenders. A society which is geared to the church, or to business enterprise, or to the development of a national state, expresses the liberties of those who find fulfillment in these organized activities. But those who serve without compensation adequate to their service do not, so far, enjoy the liberties of a society. The expression of a community of interests is that of a free society. In this kind of a society there must be *distribution* of power such that everyone is encouraged to develop both the capacities for the shaping of a culture, and the sensitivities for enjoying the rewards which it has to offer. He who serves a society without sharing in its benefits is a slave; whereas he who benefits without serving is a leech. Privilege, not liberty, results from the exercise of power in which there is no corresponding service. Equality is the condition of universal participation in a culture; it is that distribution of power which makes a community of interests possible. No society can arrive at basic agreements when its organized powers are so arranged that the many work for the advantage of the few.

Neither liberty nor equality are, however, sufficient conditions of community life. For it is not enough that liberties be distributed equally among men, since this may merely divide powers in a way that leaves a people prostrate and unable to get on with the business of its life. Unless there is a harmonization of powers to produce common ends acceptable to the whole population, there can be no virile community. Mere liberty promotes the interests of those who are already powerful; mere equality promotes the interests of those who are less powerful; but

120

fraternity promotes the interests of the community. The social contract can become a substantial justification of social action only as liberty and equality come to be realized in a fraternal society; otherwise, the contract can be nothing more than an inoperative form. The question, then, to which the contract must supply an answer is, How create those social structures to which people can consent, and which will provide a life of challenge and abundance?

The contract is not contained in some magical formula by which one says, "Yea," and thereby forms a community. Nor is it a technique by which a voter places his "X" on the ballot, and is thereby guaranteed that his interests will be cared for in the political structure. Hobbes used it to try to effect the security of the individual. Locke used it to try to regularize the institution of private property. The success of their undertakings depended not upon the myth of the contract, but upon the political genius of the time to establish successful institutions to carry out these ends. Rousseau came closer to establishing the principle of the contract, however much it became confused with a general will, together with curious mechanisms by which this will was supposed to be discoverable. But inasmuch as the nerve of the general will is merely the common good understood as the guide to political action, it can be trimmed of its romantic trappings and left standing as the social ideal which a culture needs to embody in ways pertinent to its own political problems.[5]

Both the meaning and the justification of the social contract are to be found in those fundamental agreements which are nothing other than community life. This life can be established only as people work together for common ends and share in the values that are implicated in the attainment of them. The common consent of a people must be continually established in the processes of mass communication by which people demonstrate *in their actions* whether or not they are in agreement with the prevailing directions of social organization. This fraternal life is expressed when people willingly co-operate in what

---

[5] Dewey attempts to cleanse the idea of the public from all contamination by the general will. Yet honesty forces him to observe: "Wants and impulses are . . . attached to common meanings. They are thereby transformed into desires and purposes, which, since they implicate a common or mutually understood meaning, present new ties, converting a conjoint activity into a community of interest and endeavor. Thus there is generated what, metaphorically, may be termed a general will . . ." (*The Public and Its Problems*, p. 153).

they take to be their common tasks. The contract is not an agreement between people and their government. It is agreement among themselves, which is administered by government. Or when governors are statesmen, they are leaders whose political insights are catalytic agents for permitting people to act together in ways which they find congenial to themselves. As Thucydides says in the funeral speech of Pericles, "And if few of us are originators, we are all sound judges of a policy." The statesman is the originator of public policy, but unless those policies can be put into practices that meet the needs of a people, it cannot agree to accept them. The test of the genius of the statesman is to be found in his ability to create institutions that facilitate social life, for here lies the evidence of whether agreement is actually reached. And here, consequently, is the empirical ground by which alone we can discover the degree to which the contract is in effect.

THE WORKING CONTRACT

The fatal shortcoming of the classical statements of the social contract are to be found in the absence of any connection between theory and practice. The fictional character of the contract as a historical event is symptomatic of a more basic difficulty—namely, how the contract is to be known. Hobbes provided the escape by man's right to return to a state of nature. Althusius and Locke had recourse to the principle of representative or majority rule. Finally, Rousseau's fanciful bit of procedure of canceling out particular wills in order to discover the general will is too preposterous to be given a second thought. He himself does not take seriously the suggestion that a direct voice vote is the way of determining fundamental agreements. Neither the direct, individual consent of all with all, nor a majority vote, provides a method of determining agreement. There is no way of providing a forum in the modern state by which all men can come together to decide upon whether they can agree to the setting up of a state. If, moreover, it is contended that the majority shall rule as if they constituted the body politic, this is in the final analysis no more than the fiction of *"as if."* The majority do not constitute the totality, and although they may act as if they did, they do so at the risk of potential rebellion. The possibility that the majority may become tyrannical suffices to dispose of this argument. If, again, it is argued that the majority may decide issues at stake because the minority always has the right to become a majority, the argument is again insufficient. It is insufficient because the agreement, if it be so, is only procedural; it is not substantival. A minority can always find grounds to refuse to accept the actions of the majority and to assert its own claims with violence, if necessary. By contrast to the vain rationalism of his predecessors, Hume's empirical analysis in tracing agreement to the emotional allegiance that individuals develop for the state seems vastly preferable. For no doubt without some such allegiance, political life would come to a standstill.

My alternative suggestion to both Hume and his rationalistic predecessors is that institutions are necessary to provide mass agreements which are pertinent to the conditions of modern life. When they are working arrangements that elicit men's respect, they constitute the only agreements that we can reasonably hope to find. In order to elicit this respect they must embody clarified purposes which serve the well-being and amenities of social life. Muddled ends and cross-purposes can lead only to conflict, inaction, and frustration, thus defeating the aims of a vigorous culture. Consent can be given only to those actions that further social relationships. It is manifested by the satisfactions that individuals take in their activities. When the vast majority take delight in their common tasks, when they participate in social affairs with a sense of mutual fulfillment, when they are gratified in the pursuit of their work, then they may be said to consent to the public institutions of which they are an intrinsic part. Institutions can thus provide both the limits within which the novelties that add richness to life can be ordered, and the routine which gives meaning to the daily affairs of human existence. This is to assert only in a more contemporary mode what Aristotle stated as the connection between habit and moral virtue. The test of moral virtue and of consent is one and the same—namely, taking satisfaction in social action. This being so, the degree to which a people consents to its institutions is a matter to be determined by the investigations of the social psychologist. It is strictly an empirical undertaking, but one which, of course, can be undertaken only by a psychologist with sufficient insight to recognize the importance and function of institutions. Consent, then, is not a solemn promise made at the ballot box or in a formal declaration of intent; it is the agreeable situation in which man may find himself and in which he may be able willingly and without compulsion to exert his energies to achieve richer harmonies which his fellow men may share in. That these harmonies in any large measure exist today only for the prosecution of war is a commentary upon our failure to come to agreements of a constructive nature, and consequently upon our failure to clarify our social purposes.

Consent cannot be compelled by law. However important a position the law may occupy in the process of adjudicating claims and composing differences, the law is itself only one institutional base which may or may not command respect. As Professors Sabine and Shepard have sensibly written:

A common law cannot flourish except where there exists a common mentality in which it can thrive, and it may be laid down as a general proposition that the thinner and weaker this common mentality is in a community, the narrower the range of interests that can reach an accepted valuation in that law. When the basis of common agreement is slight, the law must be more general; more must be left to local groups where a better basis exists.[6]

When there is general agreement on fundamentals, the law is easily adapted to its purposes; when these values are in dispute, it loses its effectiveness. Speaking from the English scene, one able student puts it in these words: "The power Parliament exerts is situate in it not by law, but by consent, and that consent is, as certain famous instances have shown, liable to suspension. . . . Where sovereignty prevails, where the State acts, it acts by the consent of men." [7] Consent cannot exist in the presence of basic conflicts in society. It disappears in the presence of revolution. But short of revolution, it ceases when there are large groups that do not share in the values that a society is capable of providing for its members. In truth, the law is but one institution for mass communication. It is a technique for providing for a stability of social action in order that men may reasonably count on how their projected actions will be received by the courts. When their projections fall outside the routine of accepted folkways, or outside the pronouncements of the courts, they must gamble on the outcome of their actions. After these actions have been initiated, the law can attempt to shape their novelty into a form that is socially acceptable. Where it fails, and where the

---

[6] Introduction to Krabbe, *The Modern Idea of the State*, p. lxxv.
[7] H. J. Laski, *Studies in the Problem of Sovereignty*, p. 13.

124

proponents of the novel are able to press their actions, the law is clearly seen to be not a means which can force consent.

In these troubled days, pressure groups are likely to be the originators of social action. The pertinent question is whether the existence of pressure groups is consistent with actions sanctioned by consent. The principles by which such actions are to be judged are clear. First, it is necessary to see whether what is proposed contains a worthy social purpose—that is, one which advances the interests of society without destroying other interests which are more valuable to it. Secondly, whether the purpose is thought out in terms of a program of action that is reasonably capable of being attained, and, thirdly, whether such a program of action, once instituted, receives acceptance from those affected by it. In the final analysis, consent must come from those whose lives are vitally affected by any program of action. All others may be expected to be indifferent to it, and consequently not competent to pass crucial judgment.

The meaning of consent is sometimes confused by making a spurious distinction between it and justice. There are those who say that the two constitute contradictory conceptions.

One is that the law is the will of the sovereign, and the other that law is eternal reason or immutable justice. . . . Now it is possible to construct a doctrine of restraints on the popular will in the interest of justice or reason; and it is also possible to construct a doctrine that what the people want, whether it be just or not, should prevail as law. But the combination of the two in the theory that law which judges make is both just and the will of the people, is a logically impossible feat.[8]

Granting that "courts must decide in the interests of justice, and not in accordance with the changing will of the majorities," [9] I fail to see how the interests of justice, when they are opposed to the basic interests of society, can for any length of time bind people whose needs are not being served. What can the distinction between justice and consent signify except that a people may be ignorant of the measures required to attain the ends which they intend, or that they may adopt means which are not adequate for attaining these ends? A society may wish to control inflation in the interests of a just economy, but the means it

---

[8] M. R. Cohen, *Law and the Social Order,* p. 137.
[9] *Ibid.,* p. 138.

adopts to control it may work grossly inequitable hardships on certain of its classes. Those who suffer from these hardships know that they suffer, and cannot consent, other than through sheer ignorance, to those measures. In truth, judgments arising through ignorance are no judgments at all; and *by their actions,* those who resent such measures are dissenting from them, whether they know it or not. Injustice always hurts someone. This alone is what makes injustice unjust, and this is what compels a portion of a society to withhold its consent in social action. When improvisations are substituted for social policies which can support rewarding activities, when in order to "solve unemployment" men are put to work which is neither productive for the ends of social life nor capable of challenging their capacities, these measures are (not to say stupid) both unjust and powerless to elicit general consent. A justice to which men cannot consent is one that pertains, not to the hard issues of the social scene (for which the courts are presumably the spokesmen), but to Utopia.

FROM CONTRACT TO STATUS

The truth of Maine's contention is a half truth. Men can live by contract only when it gives them status. They cannot contract obligations freely unless they can rely upon institutions which further and protect their mutual interests. Even man's most intimate relations, such as marriage and the family, may be furthered by institutional organization. In the less personal spheres of economic and political life, it is inconceivable that man should be able to accomplish much without the stability that institutions can provide. This is the reason for insisting that liberty is the organization of power, and that this organization makes possible extensive and effective action. The late Professor Morris R. Cohen's words on this subject are well worth quoting. He declares: "Real or positive freedom depends upon opportunities supplied by institutions that involve legal regulation. Our legislative forces may be narrowly partisan and the rules may be poor ones. But this can be remedied not by abrogation of all rules but by the institution of new ones." [10] Liberty must indeed be guided by rules, for since it is the organization of power, it can gain consent only as it is used for social

---

[10] *Ibid.,* p. 109.

ends. This is not liberty in a merely formal sense—that which gives one the right to submit to vicious forces in the social scene or else to accept even more vicious alternatives. It is liberty in the sense that man may maintain his dignity in a society which has a care for his social being. It is liberty which is consistent with equality, and ultimately with fraternity. It is a doctrine which prizes not individualism as an economic doctrine (which of course never could have developed extensively without an institutional base), but rather individuality as the dignity that man may develop by participating in a common life of values and reasonable hopes.

The nation-state is the obvious institution that provided for the development of economic individualism—that purely secular state, which of necessity broke its ties with the Church. Modern man found his basic orientation in the context of this secular state. Within it he developed his science, his industry, his high (as compared with the past) standard of material life, and those aesthetic and religious sentiments that were more or less in keeping with the structure of the nation-state. Although his economy was interrupted from time to time by sharp rises and subsequent falls, by and large it worked tolerably well. Moreover, he was able to fight nationalistic wars which catered to his vanity and sometimes even to his pocketbook. But modern man has come to find decreasing satisfaction in his economy, with its cycles of inflation and depression, harboring in their wake intensified miseries. Moreover, he has come to find warfare increasingly destructive of the values he cherishes. Thus, however much lip-service he may give to the state, actually he is becoming more reluctant to consent to its alleged authority. The solidarity of the nation is still a reality, but it is beginning to show a large number of fissures. The nation-state no longer provides that stability of life that modern man needs in order to invest it with wholehearted consent.

Major stirrings in contemporary life are suggestive of the kind of developments needed to regain men's consent to vigorous social action. On the other hand, new structures are needed to give the local community a feeling of solidarity and consummatory activity. The social scientists have documented the case for the disorganization of both urban and rural life. Megalopolis does not provide the cultural milieu for a life of integrity and social fulfillment. Nor does rural life provide

127

the farmer and his family with the opportunities of taking a part in those wider human affairs that would add to the significance of their position in the scheme of things. On the other hand, even if local communities were to achieve a cultural harmony within the region, their security would be threatened by our failure to resolve international differences. Peoples throughout the world are popularly demanding the elimination of war. They cannot consent to those agencies which are responsible for the disruption of their lives. Thus actual consent is increasingly being withheld from the alleged sovereignty of the nation-state, in part demanding decentralized authorities which can meet the requirements of regional communities, and in part demanding international controls for the prevention of war and for the promotion of peaceful trade among the nations of the world.

Until adequate institutions are established to make democracy work both in the community and in international affairs, modern man cannot consent to present political arrangements. The Tennessee Valley Authority has demonstrated how consent may be obtained for the promotion of a regional culture. The United Nations has yet to demonstrate how that consent may be obtained on the level of international relations. No pious resolutions concerning its high office will suffice; nor will an organization stifled by veto powers, dollar diplomacy, and inability to control fascist politics. The social contract is real only as people are able to get along with one another in achieving the positive goods that men can realize in participating in a common life. The social contract is the measure of a free society, composed of free men.

CONCLUSION

The social contract is a fiction when it is considered to be a historical event by which man once and for all set up a government which has binding authority over everyone. If the state of nature is identified with human interests that know no bounds other than those of their natural, inherent limitations, and if the civil state is identified with those interests that are controlled and furthered by the establishment of just institutions and measured by the degree of satisfaction that people take in participating in a common life, then the contract is both a historical reality and a principle of moral obligation. This contract is realized not in any formal promise, but in the actions of men who find that they can enhance their mutual relations through community life. The opening historical remarks of this essay have been directed to the proposition that the essence of the classical theories of the contract is the establishment of a community of interests. Hobbes so strait-jacketed the community as to make it inoperative; Locke gave it more latitude, even though he excluded the so-called natural rights of life, liberty, and property. Rousseau gave it complete latitude, but failed to devise the principle of institutional embodiment whereby man could give consent to political relations, not merely in theory, but also in fact. Because of this limitation, Rousseau needed no provision for the breaking of the contract. Yet the social contract is of necessity broken when large elements of a population are excluded from the values which a culture is capable of realizing. Participation is possible only as institutions provide for the harmonization of contract with status. Finally, it must be concluded that the conditions for status are absent in the contemporary world when local communities have no sense of real solidarity and when life is interrupted by international conflicts. The social contract is that moral prescription which demands that an intelligent and informed people manage to lead a rewarding life in ways that are mutually satisfactory. The ground of this obligation is nothing other than the establishment of social relations, which are, of course, their own reward.

Man and Citizen: Applications of Individualism in the French Revolution

R. R. PALMER

THAT INDIVIDUALISM has long been fundamental to Western civilization is widely agreed, at least among those who can agree on the terms used in discussing it. Individualism is found in the underlying rationalism of Greek philosophy and Roman law. It appears in the Christian insistence that every human being must be free to call his soul his own. Of the Renaissance it is often said that individualism was the very essence, and the same is said of the Reformation, in both cases with significant truth, and without denying that the Middle Ages were also in their own way individualistic, since the idea of individualism is sufficiently broad, or perhaps hazy, to include what in some lights seem to be opposites. In political theory the radical individualism of the seventeenth century is well known; Locke and Hobbes, disagreeing in much else, postulated a state of nature in which calculating individuals, fully formed without benefit of social institutions, decided, so to speak, to "join" society and "invent" government. The individualism of modern economic thought need only be mentioned. One may cite also, as bearing on both politics and economics, the Benthamite maxim that "each [person] should count as one and none for more than one." In other spheres the romantic movement brought a profound re-evaluation of individual feeling and creative powers. But at the same time romanticism may be said to have seriously modified the older forms of individualism, insofar as romantic philosophies dissolved the individual into the sources from which he might be presumed to derive

130

his moral being: his People, his Epoch, his State, his Class. Philosophies of this sort, often well removed from their romantic origins, but adhering to the principle of the "reality" of groups, may when carried to extremes become profoundly alien to the Western tradition. For they hold that groups, not persons, are the true individuals, the indissoluble entities, the protagonists of history, the bearers of value and right, the vehicles or even the determinants of reason and justice; and that persons are merely transitory reflections of such groups. ·

What is the place of the French Revolution in this long history of individualism? It is, perhaps, essentially this: that the French Revolution, coming at a climax in the history of individualist thought, was a supreme attempt to realize the principle of individualism in the domain of actual institutions. The present paper is offered as a study in applied ideas. It will contribute nothing to theory, or to the history of ideas in themselves, but the author hopes that it will show how one idea was applied in legislation in France between 1789 and 1794. No one to the author's knowledge has ever attempted a brief and convenient summary of such applications of the individualist principle. Nor is there any general conspectus even of large scope. One may read about the "atomization" of society produced by the French Revolution.[1] One may find an excellent study of the law of property and other civil law during the Revolution, in which the effects of individualism are abundantly clear.[2] And there are studies of the dissolution of gilds and other corporate bodies.[3] Nowhere are these materials brought together. To provide a simple and useful list of applications of individualism in the French Revolution is the aim of what follows.

[1] See, for example, some of the *dicta* in the works of Tocqueville or Taine on the Revolution, or the long introduction in H. Michel, *L'Idée de l'état: essai critique sur l'histoire des théories sociales et politiques en France depuis la Révolution* (3rd ed., Paris, 1898).

[2] P. Sagnac, *La Législation civile de la Révolution française* (Paris, 1898). See also G. Lefebvre, "Les recherches relatives à la repartition de la propriété et de l'exploitation foncières à la fin de l'ancien régime" in *Revue d'histoire moderne*, 1928, and "La place de la Révolution dans l'histoire agraire de la France," in *Annales d'histoire économique et sociale*, 1929.

[3] There is a large literature, within which may be noted P. Nourrisson, *Histoire de la liberté d'association en France depuis 1789* (2 vols., Paris, 1920); F. Olivier-Martin, *L'Organisation corporative de la France d'ancien régime* (Paris, 1938); a symposium entitled *L'Organisation corporative du moyen âge à la fin de l'ancien régime: études présentées à la Commission internationale pour l'histoire des assemblées d'états* (2 vols., Louvain, 1937); Martin Saint-Léon, *Le Compagnonnage*

131

What is meant by "individualism" hereinafter is chiefly a strong drive toward individual liberty. It is a philosophy which seeks to emancipate the individual from all involuntary dependency on collective groups. But the word is taken to mean also a way of looking at people, a habit of considering all human beings, not as primarily members of a particular people, church, class, or occupational body, but simply as specimens of the human race, or simply as "man." The individualist idea underlies all the better known conceptions of the French Revolution. Liberty is the liberty of the individual, equality the equality of individuals in the possession of legal rights, fraternity a free, voluntary, and enthusiastic coalescence of individuals into a body politic. The "nation" in Revolutionary parlance is the result of this free coalescence. It is not a *Volk* bound together by community of physical race or historic culture, into which persons are born by a destiny apart from their own will. It is a body made up of individuals in their capacity as citizens; it is presumed to exist by voluntary participation in a kind of contract; and what the members have in common is not race, language, or history but law and rights. The nation, thus defined, is sovereign, but the individual members are not subjects. They are "citizens," still in possession of their individual liberty; and the idea of citizenship, in which a new and stronger sovereignty and a new and wider liberty were asserted together, was probably the profoundest idea of the French Revolution, as it was the most immediately popular and most deeply felt—all persons, as we know, having called one another *citoyen* at the time.

The whole matter can be clarified by a little play upon words. The English "state" is a term of many meanings; still more so is the French *état*. By *état* may be understood either "state," "estate," "condition," "status," or "station in life," the last in the sense either of social status or of economic occupation, i.e., one's trade. The drive of the French Revolution was to disengage the individual from the *état* in every sense. It was to prevent every form of determination of individual life by any *état;* it abolished the "estates" of the realm, it repudiated the very notion of "status," it undertook to break up "stations in life" as lawfully

(Paris, 1901); Germain Martin, *Les Associations ouvrières au 18ᵉ siècle* (Paris, 1900); Grace M. Jaffe, *Le Mouvement ouvrier à Paris pendant la Révolution française* (Paris, 1924); J. M. J. Biaugeaud, *La Liberté du travail ouvrier dans l'Assemblée constituante (1789–91)* (Paris, 1939).

influential things. It held that all men were of the same *état* (in the sense of condition, status, or station), and that there was only one *état* to which men owed any loyalty or obedience, or from which they obtained any benefit—this *état* is what we call the state. Or again, the only *état* or status appropriate to a rational being, in Revolutionary doctrine, was the *état* of citizenship in a common *état* or state. The sovereign state grew in power not merely under external pressure but as an instrument of social reform. The state was used to destroy status. In the state all lesser collective interests were to be merged and lost. The Revolution thus exalted the individual and the state together, and with individualism went what has been recognized as the totalitarian tendency of the Revolution. But the Revolutionary doctrine of the state is not really totalitarian, for even from the sovereign state the individual is, so to speak, disengaged; he remains free, a voluntary, rational, and eagerly participating member, one who helps to make the state, not one to be made by it—in short, a citizen. We plumb here, of course, the Rousseauistic mysteries of the Social Contract and the General Will, which, however, like the mysteries of religion, contain depths in which the more we plumb the less we see but the more we feel.

If the French in 1789 were so set upon individualism, it was because, as Tocqueville observed long ago, they had up to then had so little of it in their social life. France before the Revolution (like most other countries of the Old Regime) was a kind of bundle of boxes, held together by the monarchy as by a kind of net. The boxes were the most solid part of the structure, and who a man was depended on which box he was in. Upon his box, *état*, classification, or group affiliation depended his legal rights, the kind or amount of taxes he paid, the function he performed in war, the place appropriate to him in the economy of peace, and the role he might play in public life, for example in those provinces where representative assemblies currently met. The most comprehensive of the boxes were the three "stations" or estates—clergy, nobility, and the "third" estate or *roture*—in one or another of which everyone had to fall. Other such boxes (if one can imagine a geometry in which boxes intersect) cut through the three estates, being geographical or territorial—provinces, *pays,* towns. Units of this kind, as corporate bodies, had arrangements with the royal government conferring specified laws, rights, or tax liabilities upon them, and hence collectively upon their members. Other boxes were vocational. The estates themselves were in a sense vocational categories; for the clergy was more a profession than a class, being recruited from all classes; and the nobility were debarred legally from most commercial pursuits, and favored in many governmental appointments.

The Third Estate was a world of boxes within boxes, of vocational bodies within town bodies, all in turn within the *état* of *roture* within provinces and within the country as a whole. Gilds of the several trades, and professional associations such as those of lawyers, had a strong corporate existence. Individuals usually might not practice an occupation unless they were members of the appropriate body, yet to become a member was difficult or expensive; it was as members of such bodies that they participated in municipal affairs, if at all; and through such bodies that their occupations were regulated by government. The farm population, too, lived in "boxes"; village communities possessed some common land, conferred rights and imposed obligations on their members, and sometimes were collectively responsible for taxes or road work, so that one individual might suffer from successful evasions by another.

As another kind of vocational bodies, not limited to the Third Estate, may be considered the organizations of certain government officials. Here corporate spirit was enhanced by the institution of property in office, and hence by inheritance of public position through the family. Best known of these are the thirteen *parlements* in existence in 1789; the members, noble in status, irremovable by the king, owners of their seats in their own right, had the exclusive collective privilege of dispensing royal justice at the highest level, and of remonstrating against legislation of which they disapproved.

All boxes, of every kind, endowed their members with distinctive rights or privileges which were literally "privy laws." In a sense every person, even the humblest, had his privilege. The poorest peasant by membership in a village community might have a right to gather firewood on the common lands, or by being a resident of Brittany have the right to buy salt without paying a tax. But some boxes, to be sure, were far roomier than others in the privileges they conferred.

The boxed-up, or corporate, character of French society at the beginning of 1789 made itself evident in the elections to the Estates-

General in February and March of that year, from which the Revolution was soon to follow. In the elections the nobleman, the cleric, and the *roturier,* though they might be neighbors on the same street, or even friends, proceeded each to a separate assembly to cast his vote. The theory was that each "station in life" should each send representatives of its own to take part in public deliberation; nor is it, in principle, an unreasonable theory, being in fact still in use, as at a conference on industrial matters where labor and management are equally represented, or labor, management, and the consumer, each being in effect counted as an estate, with no thought of representation of individuals by head. Nor was the theory as decayed in France in 1789 as is sometimes supposed, for although the three estates had not met for the country as a whole since 1614, they had continued to meet and to be active in certain important provinces.

In any case, in the elections of 1789, the nobleman, the cleric, and the commoner each went to an assembly of his own kind. The nobleman went directly, by personal right, to a district assembly called that of the *baillage,* where, with other nobles, he elected delegates to the Estates-General at Versailles. For the clergy the procedure was more complex: all active parish priests, and all bishops, went directly to the *baillage* assembly; but smaller corporate entities within the church, such as monastic houses and cathedral chapters, sent only delegates; the clerics assembled at the *baillage* chose delegates to go to Versailles. For the Third Estate the procedure was most complex of all, and representation by subgrouping the most apparent. In rural areas, the peasant proceeded to an assembly of his village or parish, which sent on delegates to the *baillage.* In the towns (except in Paris, where a more purely numerical or individualist system was used) the townsmen proceeded to an assembly of his gild or professional association; each of these chose delegates to a town assembly; this in turn chose delegates to represent the town collectively at the *baillage;* and at the *baillage* assembly the combined town and rural delegates, representing together the *tiers état* of the district, chose delegates to Versailles.

Hardly had the delegates thus elected convened at Versailles, each sitting in the house appropriate to his *état,* when the individualist principle made itself strongly felt. The three estates, as legally defined, did not in 1789 correspond to the actual divisions of influence or interest among the French people. In any case the house of the Third Estate refused to accept the legal classification. What they did was not to try to modernize the idea of organization by status (as some modern "corporatist" writers seem to wish they had done), but to repudiate the institution of legal status altogether. The Revolution, in a constitutional sense, is rightly dated from the Oath of the Tennis Court of June 20, 1789. At this time an unauthorized body of men stood by its claim to exercise the sovereignty of the nation, or supreme power of state; and the first use they made of this power was to "delegalize" status by asserting the equality of members of the three houses as individuals. It is to be noted also how the concept of the nation was used on this occasion to subordinate the claims of class, a use that became frequent in later times, often for purposes considered reactionary in the light of later philosophies emphasizing class. Concretely, shortly after June 20, 1789, the three houses of the Estates-General merged into one, the National Assembly, in which decisions were made by a majority of individuals present. This was enough to constitute a juridical revolution, although no new elections were held or even asked for; not until 1791 was there a general election in which, in the selection of national representatives, voters voted as individuals instead of as occupants of a station in life. Hence despite the emigration nobles and clergy remained proportionately more numerous in the National Assembly than in the country as a whole.

The next step, precipitated by popular violence and revolutionary *voies de fait*, was the equalization or individualization of legal rights. This is the significance of the Night of August 4 and the Declaration of the Rights of Man and Citizen of August 26. The events of June had transformed only the organization of the elected assembly. Now, in August, the new principles were applied to the country. In the famous night of August 4 privileges of all kinds were abandoned. Nobility and clergy, provinces and towns, surrendered their corporate rights; landed property was relieved of certain manorial encumbrances, and peasants of certain obligations arising from their status; "Feudalism" was declared "abolished." All the old boxes disappeared; Frenchmen were now all in one box, namely the Nation, and were all of one status, equally citizens of one state. And since all rights under the Old Regime had been in the nature of privileges, so that the repudiation of privilege left a kind of vacuum of rights, the Assembly proceeded to draft its historic Declaration. Here in seventeen articles was outlined the new "box" in which Frenchmen were to live. The Declaration asserted certain specific liberties of the individual, the legal equality of all individuals, and the sovereignty of the nation in the power to make and enforce law, which in turn it described as falling uniformly upon all individuals, and having individual welfare as its aim. The term "individual" was not employed, though then coming increasingly into use. The terms used in the Declaration were "all" and "every"—"man" and "citizen."

From then on the individualist principle was applied in many directions. It turned up in September when the Assembly, now drafting a new constitution, refused to provide for a bicameral legislature on the English model, fearing the reappearance of the nobility in politics as a collective interest. It destroyed the vested corporations of office owners, such as the *parlements,* compensating them as individuals for the loss of their property. It liquidated what was left of the old provincial estates and other provincial liberties and characteristics. France, first made legally uniform, was subdivided into administrative *départements,* each exactly like all the others, each being a territorial block of individual citizens. The old towns, with their several distinctive identities, were turned into the new *communes* organized under uniform national legislation, which recognized no difference between one town and another except in the number of its inhabitants.

Individualism showed itself plainly in the nationalization of the property of the church in November 1789. The immediate reason for this move was to find means to pay off the public debt. The individualist propensity is revealed in the arguments used, and in the subsequent disposition of the confiscated lands. It was argued that all ownership of property by corporate bodies was bad, since it kept masses of property out of circulation, immobilized in a mortmain. "Society," said one speaker,[4] "needs real proprietors," i.e., individuals. He argued likewise that only actual persons had rights by nature, corporate bodies having only rights created by law; that the state was not absolute over the individual, but that with respect to corporations it had "an absolute power not only over the conditions of their existence but over their existence itself." These arguments, plus the argument, often used in the

---

[4] *Moniteur, réimpression, II,* 84.

past by churchmen themselves, that church property belonged not to the clergy but to the laity as well, resulted in the placing of church lands and buildings "at the disposal of the Nation."

Thus was created the main bulk of the *biens nationaux,* or nationalized wealth. Church lands were supplemented from other sources in the following years. The royal domain was nationalized. Emigrés had their property confiscated, though no attempt was ever made to confiscate the wealth of former nobles as a class. When gilds and other similar corporate bodies were suppressed, their property was also thrown into the common pool. For a time the property of mere suspects was subject to confiscation. There was likewise a policy of breaking up the common lands of agricultural villages and putting them under individual ownership. The *biens nationaux,* drawn from so many sources, made up a significant fraction of the real estate of the country. No close estimate seems to be possible, but if church lands in 1789 constituted as much as a tenth of the area of France (the highest reliable figure), it may be loosely conjectured that the total of *biens nationaux* may have approached 20 per cent, some of it virtually wasteland. The *biens nationaux,* except for property confiscated from émigrés, represented wealth formerly under corporate ownership.

All this wealth, substantially speaking, was sold to individuals during the Revolution. Nationalization meant the opposite of what it means today. The policy through all phases of the Revolution was not to retain the nationalized property under public ownership, nor to let it out to concessionaires as was commonly done with crown domains in the monarchies of the time, but to raise cash by selling to private buyers. The Revolutionary authorities took pains to assure themselves that the buyers were really individual persons. Repeatedly the poorer peasants, unable to purchase under the conditions stipulated for sale, formed associations for the collective purchase of tracts of nationalized land. Such associations were repeatedly prohibited by the Revolutionary authorities, even by the democratic Convention in April 1793, and even when the stated purpose of such associations was to distribute land to individuals after collective purchase. Temporary associations of wealthier peasants and bourgeois for land purchase were in truth connived at; the principle of equality was thus somewhat roughly treated, but not the principle of private individual property. In general, the former corporate properties of the Old Regime wound up in the hands of individual owners.

The law of landed property itself was individualized, ownership becoming more absolute and more private. Formerly, under conditions popularly called "feudal," a given plot of physical ground had been subject to a plurality of rights that may be thought of as proprietary in character. What the "owner" had was a secure and hereditary tenure; he could inherit the land, bequeath it, rent it out, or sell it; he could live on it at will, cultivate it, and consume or sell the produce. But over the same piece of ground there was the right of eminent property, possessed by the owner of the manor or *seigneurie;* this meant that the ground in question yielded various forms of income, such as annual quitrents and mutation fees due in the event of inheritance or sale (the *lods et ventes*), payable by the "owner" to the manorial lord. In addition, the same ground yielded the tithes to the church, or to whoever it might be to whom the right of tithe had been conveyed. To the king it yielded, by a kind of historic right, the land tax called the *taille*. Furthermore, the same ground was subject to the collective rights of the local community; the owner was obliged to sow the crop required by the village system of rotation, or to admit to his own field, after the harvest was removed, livestock belonging to the other villagers or to the lord. All these rights, of owner, lord, king, church, and community were before 1789 equally valid, customary, and enforceable in the courts.

The Revolution swept all such rights away except those of the "owner," who thus emerged as an individual property owner in the modern sense, and except those of the king, which were transformed into those of the state. The tithe and the manorial fees were abolished in fact. Collective village rights resisted legal annihilation; many peasants sought to maintain them; compromises were made. But their scope and exercise were greatly reduced. The Revolutionary legislation concentrated control in the hands of the owner; it was argued that investment of capital would in this way be encouraged, and productivity of land and labor enhanced. To assist the landowner to raise capital the law of mortgages was clarified and interest was fixed at 5 per cent. To prevent a relapse into "feudal" confusion, i.e., to prevent doubt as to who the proprietor was, perpetual tenancies were forbidden and leases limited to ninety-nine years or three lifetimes. The principle of exclusive control by the owner was worked out in detail: if a fruit from a neighbor's tree fell on one's property the neighbor might not legally overstep the boundary to pick it up; or if a swarm of bees settled on one's land it became one's property as soon as the original owner ceased obviously to pursue it. Yet the new property right was not absolute. A landowner, for example, by Revolutionary legislation, could be required to clear and cultivate his property on pain of being bought out at a price fixed by the government. This enactment, justified at the time on grounds of agricultural production and public health, offers a curious precedent to policies in force in parts of Europe today, more or less under socialist auspices. In general, the Revolution left all final rights over land in the hands of only two parties, the proprietor and the state.

From property, in speaking of institutions in the eyes of the law, it is no great distance to the family. The Revolution undertook to liberate the individual from the family as from other group attachments. The family, especially in the aristocracy, was a kind of property-owning unit, almost a little "corporation" as the term was then understood. By laws of primogeniture and entail property remained concentrated in the same family generation after generation; individual members of the family had no freedom to dispose of it at will; family wealth was held in a kind of mortmain, perpetuating the economic foundation on which the family rested. The Revolutionary legislation put an end to primogeniture and entail. It required equal division of inheritances among all children. It allowed heirs to dispose of their inheritances as they chose. Individual freedom was thus favored at the expense of family solidarity. These measures were designed largely to undermine the aristocracy, for before 1789 primogeniture and the freedom to entail one's estate had been essentially privileges of the nobles; but in some parts of France somewhat the same situation could be found among commoners also. Whereas in northern France the law before 1789 required peasants and other *roturiers* to divide inheritances among children, in southern France, where Roman jurisprudence was influential, the law allowed great freedom in the making of wills, so that a father could leave the bulk of his property to a single child, and thus preserve family status. The Revolution abolished this *droit de tester*, requiring

140

in this case, as in the case of former nobles, equal division of inheritance among all children. The argument used was that, in southern France, some counterrevolutionary fathers were disinheriting patriot sons. In any case, whatever the motivation, whether to subvert the aristocracy or to foil reactionary fathers, the effect was to strengthen individuals at the expense of family power.

Other legislation cut into the family as a moral and disciplinary unit, always in the interest of more thoroughgoing individual freedom. Formerly, a family head could arrange with the authorities for the discreet confinement of a wayward child, even one fully grown, without legal formalities and without publicity. This had in fact been one of the commonest uses of the famous *lettres de cachet* in the last years before the Revolution. Nor was this convenience extended to the nobility only; Saint-Just was once locked up by his mother under a *lettre de cachet*, for purely private and family reasons. The Revolution, in abolishing the *lettre de cachet*, thus liberated the individual from another form of family control. Henceforth only the state, using legal process, had the right to place persons under confinement, and then only in the public interest. The Revolution also legalized divorce (having provided for civil marriage); it thus applied the principle that no individual could forego his freedom forever, and regarded marriage as a perpetually voluntary association of husband and wife. Toward children born outside the lawful family the Revolutionary legislation was generous. Taking the view that an illegitimate person was in a plight due in no way to himself, and that therefore his freedom and rights should not suffer, the law afforded legal procedure to such persons for the identification of their fathers, and prescribed that where paternity was established the illegitimate offspring should have an equal claim to the inheritance. This provision, it need not be said, proved short-lived; it was omitted in the Napoleonic codification, supposedly on Bonaparte's dictum that society has no interest in the propagation of bastards.

The individualism of the Revolution not only destroyed the theory of estates and hence transformed the constitutional structure of the country. It not only affected the distribution of property and even the nature of private property itself. It not only disassembled adult members of

141

the family into a group of individual persons. It destroyed all bodies known as "corporations" and "associations." It disapproved of all organized interests within the state.

The greatest of the corporate associations was the church. Deprived of its property, deprived of its income from tithes, deprived of its autonomous legal system, obliged (since shortly before the Revolution) to accept religious toleration, with its clergy no longer recognized as a distinctive estate and no longer dealing collectively with the government, with the very title of archbishop abolished and with bishops elected by the same persons, irrespective of religious affiliation, who elected corresponding civil officials, the church virtually ceased to be a distinct corporate organization, and became a kind of spiritual magistracy maintained and guided by the state. Such, at least, was the philosophy behind the Civil Constitutional of the Clergy. Smaller bodies within the church disappeared altogether, at least in law. Following the precedent of the Old Regime, which had broken up the Jesuits in France, the Revolution outlawed all regular clergy. It forbade the taking of monastic vows, and dispersed existing bodies of monks and nuns, offering them as individuals a small pension, but forbidding them to meet or take action together. The aim was in part to liberate individuals from an irrevocable commitment, but mainly to dissolve corporate bodies thought to represent an undesirable special interest.

A problem comparable to that of the church, if a microcosm may be compared to a macrocosm, was presented to the Revolutionaries by the Jews. Not very numerous in France, the Jews lived by their own law in an intense corporate life of their own, collectively detached from the rest of the population, partly by their own will and the needs of their religion, partly at the age-old insistence of the Christians. They were a privileged body in that they lived under the king's special protection, were subject to distinctive taxes, were exempt from certain obligations such as military service, and preserved their own socio-religious law together with their own means of its enforcement. The Revolution granted the Jews the same civic rights as everyone else, and imposed the same civic obligations. Its trend was to assimilation, to liberate the individual Jew not only from general social disabilities but also from the requirements of his own Jewish community. Jews, like Catholics, sometimes resisted such liberation from their own his-

toric mode of life. But the Revolutionaries, secular, rationalist, individualistic, thought of religion as a body of believed ideas, held pri-
vately within the mind of each individual person, and by freedom of
religion they meant freedom of the individual to accept or reject certain
religious doctrines. That a religion should be a community, great or
little, imposing its own special pattern of behavior or customs, or affecting individual life in any way other than by moral edification, was
foreign to the Revolutionary ideal. Religious freedom did not mean the
freedom of organized religious bodies.

On race the Revolutionary doctrine is clear. It was that race was at
most one of the many facts of life, of no legal or moral significance, and
without relevancy to the question of citizenship. It was to liberate the
individual from race as from other forms of *état,* or to disregard race as
it disregarded other collective patterns. The issue arose only with
respect to the Negroes of the French West Indies, and even there was
scarcely felt as a racial question. The practice of the Revolutionary
governments toward the Negroes was affected by various practical considerations, such as the need for a labor force in the colonies and the
degraded condition of most blacks in America at the time. But early in
the Revolution civic rights were given to mulattoes and free Negroes
in the colonies (as in France), and the Convention prohibited slavery
in all possessions of the Republic.

Judaism and the status of Negroes, though the policies adopted
toward them are highly illustrative of principle, were actually on the
periphery of life in France. To return to the main stream, and resume
the story of the Revolutionary attitude to corporate associations or collective groupings, one may note what happened to the schools, hospitals,
and charitable establishments of the Old Regime. To a large extent in
1789, though not exclusively, these institutions were church bodies,
staffed by regular clergy and financed from church property or from
tithes. They were therefore bound to disappear in consequence of
more general legislation. But all such establishments were in addition
abolished specifically. The universities were dissolved. In the preceding
century there had been a marked tendency for the government to
secularize and revivify the old universities of France. One would perhaps expect the Revolution to continue it, but from fear of the church
and from dislike of corporate and monopoly spirit, in education as else-

where, the Revolution simply put an end to the universities, nor were they reconstituted for over a century, despite the reputation of Napoleon on the subject.

In fact, while it is possible to argue that in content of education or theory of poor relief the Revolution marked an advance, if one is thinking of the number of persons actually educated or relieved, the Revolution was unquestionably a destructive movement. Individualism, arising in this case largely from fear of the church, dissolved the old institutions without successfully creating the new. The Revolutionary leaders disapproved of private foundations for education and charity; indeed they turned the wealth of such foundations into *biens nationaux*, to be sold off to private persons. They generously planned for the support of similar institutions at public expense. But in the financial stress of war and revolution their accomplishment fell far short of their aim.

The prevailing attitude was expressed, somewhat rhetorically, by the orator who, on December 24, 1792, laid a great program of public schooling before the Convention. Schools, he said, should be established uniformly throughout the country under government auspices. Then all else could be

left to nature and genius, which have no desire to be imprisoned by academic corporations, and which ask only for fraternity and help. All corporations tend to aristocracy. . . . Peoples who wish to be free, give encouragement to letters and the arts and sciences! But let liberty heap upon isolated individuals (*individus isolés*), who dare to speak the truth, the benefits which despotism heaped upon corporate bodies to provoke their adulation! [5]

Against the universities it was held, not merely that they were ecclesiastical bodies (a misfortune that could have been corrected by outright secularization), but that they were pernicious in any case, that they were gilds of the learned, inclined to monopolist attitudes, and that their practice of awarding degrees was medieval and invidious, creating a distinctive *état* in society. Somewhat the same arguments were turned against other corporate organizations in the arts and the world of learning. The French Academy was abolished. The Comédie Française virtually went out of existence. The Opera, or Academy of Music, lost its privileges, such as the right to receive a kind of royalty from any private person operating a theater in Paris. The Academy

---

[5] *Archives parlementaires*, LV, 394.

of Painting and Sculpture was suppressed, partly at the instigation of the painter David, himself a formidable Revolutionary. Painting became free; there were no more privileged painters; any painter could submit his work for exhibition in the biennial salons. The Academy of Science and the Academy of Inscriptions likewise went into the individualist chopper. The old academies were repugnant to the Revolutionaries as centers of professional privilege and special status; but, reorganized and transformed, they virtually reappeared as early as 1795, merged into the newly founded National Institute. As for the College de France, it passed through the Revolution undisturbed. From its origin it had been an institution of the kind the Revolutionaries favored: it was not a church body and hardly a corporate body, playing no collective role, awarding no degrees, and being mainly an aggrega- tion of individual professors paid by the government, whose salaries, indeed, the Convention substantially raised.

Nor did Revolutionary doctrine favor collective units in the economic mechanism of production and exchange. The bourgeois leaders of the Revolution, from beginning to end, from the Night of August 4, 1789, when the dissolution of gilds was resolved on, through the period of the Terror and beyond, were firm partisans of economic individualism and commercial freedom. During the Terror there was a good deal of regulation, but it was felt to be exceptional and temporary, and in any case was imposed directly by the state, with little recourse to interme- diate corporate bodies. The distaste of the leaders for all forms of collective economic action was not altogether shared by the rank and file, just as the program for individualizing landed property was not altogether shared by the mass of the peasantry. But the bulk of the population had no developed economic philosophy of its own, and in the end had to accept the decisions of the leaders.

The gilds, at the close of the Old Regime, were numerous and some- times influential. Only the masters for the most part had any power in them; journeymen were life-long wage earners, and apprenticeship was a blind alley. The masterships were closely held, and the new masters were typically the sons or sons-in-law of the old. There was thus a heredity of economic status. The masters generally enjoyed, within a given town, a monopoly of the right to open and operate a shop in their trade. There was no overwhelming popular complaint against the

145

gilds in 1789, only a general plea that they be reformed and opened up; some modern writers have wished that reform had been attempted, seeing in the gild a means by which employer and employee might be brought together and the class friction of modern industrialism mitigated at the start. Whether the gilds could have been readapted to the needs of modern society is open to question. They were town units, in a time of growing national and international markets; they were concerned with protecting their own work and methods, in a time of new inventions and machines; and the masters, though they stood above the wage-earning class, and were sometimes municipal notables, were in other cases already reduced to dependency on larger commercial interests, becoming skilled workmen like the journeymen whom they in turn hired.

In any case the Revolution abolished the gilds and confiscated their property. It proclaimed the "right to work," by which was meant the right of any individual to open a shop in any trade, or to seek employment in any shop, without having to belong to any organization or consult with any other person whatever. All association of persons in the same trade was regarded as bad. The Revolutionary leaders were of the opinion, like Adam Smith, that for whatever purpose men of the same trade might ostensibly foregather, they usually ended up by conspiring against the public, i.e., devising schemes to raise the price of the goods or services that they had to offer. Behind this view, in France, lay the whole Physiocratic movement.

As the gilds had become more exclusively organizations of masters or small employers, journeymen's associations had arisen beside them. These, composed of mere wage earners, were the real forerunners of the labor unions of later times. In France in the eighteenth century, where they were called *compagnonnages* (after *compagnon*, a journeyman), they were surprisingly strong. They were organized with dues and officials, and in a few trades extended throughout the country. They conducted strikes, imposed closed shops, and required payment by the masters of a stipulated wage. They were never legal under the Old Regime, but on the other hand the royal government had never actually suppressed them.

The Revolution brought with it a great deal of economic unrest, which expressed itself in waves of strikes and outbreaks of violence. Members of the National Assembly became alarmed. Having outlawed the gilds, and pronounced against all association of persons of the same trade, they now took action against the *compagnonnages* also. The legislation embodying this action is known as the Le Chapelier law of June 14, 1791; and since this is a matter of especial interest to the modern reader it seems well to quote from Le Chapelier's speech in support of his bill.

I appear to refer to you a violation of the constitutional principles which suppress corporations, a violation from which great dangers to public order may arise. Some persons have been trying to recreate the abolished corporations by forming assemblies by trade in which presidents, secretaries, syndics, and other officers have been elected. The aim of these assemblies, which are spreading through the kingdom, and have already entered into correspondence with one another, is to oblige those entering upon a productive enterprise, the former masters, to raise the price they pay for a day's labor. It is to prevent workmen and those who employ them in their shops from arriving at agreements between themselves at will, to require that registers be signed showing acceptance of a wage fixed by these assemblies, and of other regulations which they allow themselves to make. Even violence is being used to enforce these regulations; workmen are forced to leave their shops, though content with the wage they are receiving. Some establishments are deserted; in some there have been veritable revolts, and various disorders have been committed.[6]

He observed that the city of Paris had injudiciously authorized such a meeting of workmen. "All citizens," he said,

should doubtless be allowed to assemble, but citizens of a given profession should not be allowed to assemble for their alleged common interests. There are no longer any corporate bodies in the State. There is no interest except the general interest and the particular interest of each individual. It is not permissible for anyone to inspire any citizens with an intermediate interest, or to detach them from the common cause by arousing a spirit of corporate separatism.

Le Chapelier himself believed that wages ought to be higher; at least he said so repeatedly in the face of "murmurs" in the Assembly. But he did not want higher wages imposed by group pressure or agitation. "We must adhere to the principle," he insisted, "that free agreements between individual and individual are the proper means of determining the day's wage for each workman, and that it is then up to the workman to hold to the agreement he has made with the person who has employed him."

---

[6] *Moniteur, réimpression,* VIII, 661–662.

147

The bill was enacted, in a form generalized to apply to all vocational organizations, including those of employers. It affirmed that, "the destruction of every species of corporation of citizens of the same *état* and profession being one of the fundamental bases of the French constitution, it is prohibited to restore them in fact under any pretext or form whatsoever." Gatherings of persons of the same trade were forbidden to elect officers, keep records, pass resolutions, or petition the public authorities. If workers' coalitions were nevertheless formed, and "if the individual liberty of employers and workmen be attacked by threats or violence on the part of these coalitions, the authors of such violence will be prosecuted as disturbers of the public peace." Later in the same year, at harvest time, when rural landowners, farmers, and agricultural laborers came together to set wages for the season, the Assembly prohibited these associations also. The provisions of the Le Chapelier law remained in force in France for about three-quarters of a century.

That the individualist principle was aimed at employers as well as at workingmen is evident not only in the drafting of the Le Chapelier law, but in the preceding suppression of gilds, which were essentially associations of small employers. During the height of the Revolution, in 1793 and 1794, the association of owners of capital in stock companies was also prohibited. For a time the views of the small man prevailed; business was to be conducted by individuals or at most by partnerships. The fact that the great stock companies, such as the East India Company, were corporate institutions carried over from the Old Regime, each operating under the special law of its own charter, together with the practical fact that banking and financial interests had become generally counterrevolutionary by the summer of 1793, gave sufficient impetus for this legislation. But pure individualism did not long survive in this connection. One of the first acts of the Directory, in 1795, was to rescind the legislation against the formation of stock companies. The value of corporate association was now extolled. To revive French industry, said a speaker in the Council of Five Hundred, "citizens must have the opportunity to combine their efforts, personal and pecuniary"; or as it was put in the Council of Elders, "it is a matter of natural right, and allowed by the constitution, to engage in commerce either individually or in association with others, *ou seul ou en société*." [7] France entered the nineteenth century, as did less revolutionary countries, permitting investors of capital to combine for certain business purposes, while forbidding laboring men to combine for the collective purposes of labor. But it would be false to regard the prohibition of labor unions as a crude weapon of class struggle, for the provisions of the Le Chapelier law were only an aspect of the whole theory of society for which the Revolution stood.

This theory was stated concisely by a poet, André Chenier, also a Revolutionary:

Unwise and unhappy is the State where there exist various associations and collective bodies whose members, on entering them, acquire a different spirit and different interests from the general spirit and the general interest! Happy the land where there is no form of association but the State, no collective body but the country, no interest but the general good! [8]

It might almost be claimed, by one delighting in the appearance of cynicism, that Property and Sovereignty describe the program of the French Revolution about as well as Liberty and Equality. The Revolution, by blurring or blotting out all marks of status except property, left a glaring contrast between rich and poor. By destroying the intermediate bodies beloved by Montesquieu and Tocqueville, by trying to merge all other *états* into the state itself, it passed on to us the modern sovereign state as we have known it ever since.

Intentionally and deliberately, not merely as an unforeseen consequence, the Revolution declared the state supreme over all other forms of human association, and at the same time (except in the radical democratic period of 1793–1794) made the ownership of property the basis for full political rights in the state whose power it thus enlarged. By the constitution of 1789–1791, and again by the constitution of 1795, the vote was granted to a surprisingly larger portion of the male population, all things considered; but through systems of electoral colleges, property qualifications for office, or other sifting devices, the persons capable of occupying important positions in political life on the national level were reduced to a few tens of thousands. They were men of sub-

---

[7] *Ibid.*, XXVI, 509 and 512.
[8] Quoted by Nourrisson, *op. cit.*, p 86.

stantial means, "notables" of their communities, of either bourgeois or *ci-devant* noble background, and they remained the dominant influence in French society for a hundred years. They were almost a new "estate," distinguished mainly by wealth, in a country within which all estates were supposed to have vanished. But they were not a closed estate, not even an exclusive or invidious one; they welcomed new members; it was expected that any person might become a property owner, if sufficiently diligent and socially useful, a thought perhaps grotesquely expressed in Guizot's famous *enrichissez-vous!*

As for the Revolutionary leaders themselves, or at least the Jacobins, their ideal was what in this country is called Jeffersonian. They thought of property in terms of land, in a country still mainly agricultural; they wanted the largest possible number of individual owners, none too rich, and none too poor; they wanted each owner to be master of his own little domain; and they considered that such a society of independent landowners produced a reliable and responsible citizenry. And their ideal was that these citizen-proprietors should not have to belong to any special body—church, class, family, gild, or village—in order to do exactly as they pleased, within the law.

It was once observed by Coleridge that most men do not possess ideas so much as they are possessed by them. The French of the Revolution seem to have been literally possessed by an individualist mania; it was by insisting on individual liberty that they hacked down and disintegrated almost every organized institution that they had known. Yet it is impossible to say that they were merely doctrinaire, or that they were dizzy with ideas drawn from an excessive reading of Rousseau. The genius of Rousseau lay in fact in perceiving the fundamental practical issue. On the whole the French knew exactly what they were doing. It was because they had lived in a country where no one counted as an individual that they wished to create an order in which no one should count except as an individual. They seem to have reached, in 1789, a point of unbearable disgust with a world of hierarchy, privilege, favoritism, oligarchy, monopoly, special interest, legal differentiation, social categorizing, *état,* and status. They broke violently and even fanatically out of their boxes.

Their ideas had the defects of their qualities. The greatest and most constructive single idea of the French Revolution was the idea of citizenship—of citizenship running over a wide area, not confined as in ancient times to a city-state; and of true citizenship, that of free, rational, and responsible beings, not of mere "nationals" of a government. But the Revolutionaries idealized the conception of citizenship. They wished a society in which the public interest should transcend the petty bickerings of class or status. They held that the good citizen had no real interest except that of the common weal. They held, in effect, that no merely private interest is legitimate at all. They saw in politics, therefore, as Burke complained, not a perpetual effort to accommodate different interests all of which may be legitimate and honest, but a struggle between unselfish and selfish persons, between good citizens and bad.

This exaltation of civic spirit, this passion of *civisme*, this belief that no good citizen ever acts apart from the public, or associates with other citizens for purposes that not all citizens share alike, explains both the radical individualism and the glorification of the state and nation. It undercut all groupings except the political; it saw man, almost, as citizen only. It deprived all intermediate organizations, in which the interests of church, locality, or vocation might be represented, of moral character and of moral support. It gave irresistible momentum to the killing off of groupings for whose demise, in each case, other and more immediately practical reasons could also be adduced. For example, the University of Paris was killed off because of immediate fear of counter-revolutionary clergy; but in addition no need was seen for any such institution at all. Why should professors have interests different from other people?

The attitude toward class, as it embraces the individual, is what mainly distinguishes the older revolutionary movement, that of the French Revolution, from the revolutionary movement of more recent times, the one which has associated itself with the name of Marx, at least so long as this movement is in opposition. The seeing of man mainly as citizen, the denial of class or other special affiliation, the belief in a "people" whose members are supposed to fraternize rather than struggle, all of them ideas fundamental to the old revolution, are all of them heatedly rejected by the new. Nothing so irritated Marx, writing in 1849, as these notions of the "good old republicans" as he derisively called them. Nothing seemed to him so much of a dream as their particular dream of a classless society. This dream, he declared, was forever exploded by the class war which broke out in Paris in June 1848, a war which the traditional democrats, obsessed by their faith in a classless people, could not understand and by which they were horrified—"stupefied by the gunpowder smoke in which their fantastic republic had dissolved."[9]

And in truth the expectations of the French Revolutionaries, and of the older democrats of all countries, have not by any means come true. Since the industrial revolution a society of small, nearly equal, and stubbornly independent property owners is scarcely imaginable. Nor has the sovereign nation-state proved to be a purely beneficent institution. The older individualism is clearly of the past. We need bodies and associations of all kinds, both within states and among states, groupings that will take the sting out of solitary individualism and the edge off the exclusively sovereign state. What, then, remains of those principles of the French Revolution that have been traced here? What remains is the belief, let us hope indestructible, that it is after all only actual and individual human beings that are the bearers of ultimate rights, and only a totality of human beings that is the bearer of ultimate legal power; that this ultimate legal power, or sovereignty, is a just power only so far as it protects and advances the rights of identifiable persons; and that all other bodies, corporations, associations, class organizations, or parties are to be regarded, at least in political science, as subordinate or transitory, conveniences serving the interest of persons who have interests in common, but within a total community, and under law.

[9] *The Class Struggles in France* (New York: International Publishers, 1934), p. 56.

From Compact to National State

in American Political Thought

CHARLES M. WILTSE

WITH her long heritage from Magna Carta, her experience with administrative problems under colonial charters, and her relatively advanced economic development, the United States ran the full cycle from revolution to world power in a single century. This cycle included war of defense, war of aggression, and war to put down internal rebellion; it included the physical conquest and settlement of a continent; it included the successive dominance of a mercantile, an agrarian, and an industrial economy. In the same century, American political thought, paralleling the development of the society it described and criticized, turned from the social compact and the natural rights of man to a philosophy of power, realized in the sovereign national state.

I

The American Revolution was justified by those who participated in it in terms of two distinct lines of argument. One of these was purely legal: the acts of which the colonists complained were viewed as violations of the British Constitution, and resistance to them was therefore not rebellion.[1] The other followed the pattern of revolutionary theory that had been slowly building up since the sixteenth century. Government, so the argument ran, existed by agreement or contract, to which

---

[1] R. G. Adams, *Political Ideas of the American Revolution* (Durham, 1922); C. H. McIlwain, *The American Revolution* (New York, 1923).

the ruler was one party and the ruled the other. In the absence of any sovereign power to judge between the parties, each had necessarily to judge for itself if the instrument had been violated; and if it had, the compact stood dissolved. To establish their case, the Americans had only to show that the measures taken by Parliament and the Crown in the decade and a half before 1776 were violations of the agreement under which alone their allegiance was due. The terms of the agreement were vague, but by the eighteenth century they included the preservation of certain "unalienable rights," which appertained to man by gift of nature and whose very indefiniteness was their chief utility.

The constitutional argument was dominant until the outbreak of hostilities,[2] but to it was subjoined, before the end of 1774, a declaration of rights which might not be overstepped by any sovereign, be it prince or parliament.[3] Thereafter the rights of man and the violated compact became the primary arguments, and after the first shots were exchanged at Lexington no more was heard of the British Constitution. The Colonies were no longer protesting an unconstitutional exercise of power, but were resisting in arms the duly constituted authorities. The compact theory of the state was then their intellectual salvation, and it received its definitive expression in the Declaration of Independence.

Colonial charters, in themselves a form of contract between ruler and ruled, were replaced as rapidly as possible by state constitutions; but these too were contracts, drawn up by specially chosen representatives meeting in convention for that sole purpose, and ratified by popular vote. So also was the first political connection between the states a contract, styled "Articles of Confederation." Under it each state retained its "sovereignty, freedom and independence" but yielded the exercise of certain powers to a Congress representing them all. This time the contract was not between ruler and ruled, but was a joint agreement among sovereigns, establishing a common government with specifically delegated powers. The experiment survived the Revolution, but without conspicuous success. The league was too loosely knit. The

---

[2] See especially James Otis, *Rights of the British Colonies Asserted and Proved* (Boston, 1764); John Dickinson, *Letters from a Pennsylvania Farmer* (Boston, 1768); James Wilson, *Nature and Extent of the Legislative Authority of Parliament* (Philadelphia, 1774); Thomas Jefferson, *Summary View of the Rights of British America* (Philadelphia, 1774).

[3] "Declaration and Resolves," *Journals of the Continental Congress*, I, 63–73.

authority granted the Congress was not enough to permit good government. There were jealousies and squabbles, commercial rivalries and unstable currencies. The Confederation threatened to fall apart, and its members to become easy prey for reconquest from abroad. It was at this juncture that a general convention was called, and a new constitution drawn up.

The process of constitution making was the same as it had been for the individual states. It was not done by any existing body, but by a specially chosen group, to which each of the states was invited to send representatives. The delegates to the convention were instructed by their principals—the people of the states, acting through their "sovereign" legislative councils—to revise the contract under which the joint concerns were administered. They actually did a far more thorough job than had been contemplated, but the resulting document in the eyes of those who made and ratified it was still a compact even though its meaning was not so clear as to preclude debate.

The problem of the convention was the recurrent underlying problem of government itself: how to reconcile the liberty of the individual with a grant of powers sufficiently strong to preserve the state from external and internal attack. Among the framers there were some who feared most the tendency of a weak government to degenerate into anarchy, while others believed that the tendency of a strong government to absorb all power to itself and destroy liberty was the greatest danger. The federal structure that finally emerged was a compromise between these conflicting views. The Bill of Rights, added almost immediately by amendment, represented all that survived of the natural rights philosophy. The ratification by state conventions, however, was the logical outgrowth of the compact theory, and served to underline the role of the states as parties to the agreement.

The exigencies of practical politics and the problems of actual administration can never be fully anticipated, and it often happens that the very men who are most anxious to limit power in the abstract are the most ready to exercise it when it falls into their hands. The first decade of the new government was marked by international tension threatening war with England and with France, and by internal unrest following financial legislation that appeared to be in the interest of a class. The government was scarcely three years old before Congress

155

authorized the President to execute the law by military force if it could not be done through constituted channels,[4] and in 1794 an army was actually sent to western Pennsylvania to compel payment of a tax on whisky. Opposition to class legislation and to highhanded methods of enforcement presently became partisan opposition to those in power, and the election of 1796 saw the voters divided into Federalists and Republicans. The former, in defense of the course so far pursued, stressed the claims of the general government to power; the latter, in opposition, based their case on the liberties of the individual, for which the Revolution had been fought, and called upon the state governments to restrain the centralizing tendencies they detected in the national administration.

The Federalist victory that resulted in the election of John Adams over Thomas Jefferson only served to intensify the party cleavage, and to drive both sides to extremes. But the Federalists were in power, and in sheer panic they undertook to suppress the opposition. Resident foreigners and newly naturalized citizens were found taking sides with the Republicans; so the privileges of aliens were sharply curtailed, and naturalization was made much more difficult. The administration was criticized without restraint in the Jeffersonian press; so conspiracy to oppose the measures of the government, and publications tending to bring its officers into disrepute, were declared seditious. The Alien and Sedition Acts [5] represented precisely that type of arbitrary power that most of the founding fathers believed they were guarding against in framing the Constitution. If the general government could lawfully suppress even spoken and written opposition to its measures, it was in fact unlimited, and no better—perhaps worse—than the monarchy of George III.

It was the Alien and Sedition Acts that led to the first gloss upon the Constitution, made the states rather than the courts the defenders of individual liberty, and completed the transformation of the natural rights dogma into the far more powerful and effective doctrine of state rights. The basic issue was between a government of limited authority, restrained by some source of power other than itself, and a government

---

[4] 1 Stat. 264 (May 2, 1792).

[5] Four separate measures were so designated: the Naturalization Act of June 18, 1798, 1 Stat. 566; the Alien Act of June 25, 1798, 1 Stat. 570; the Alien Enemy Act of July 6, 1798, 1 Stat. 577; and the Sedition Act of July 14, 1798, 1 Stat. 596.

limited only by its own capacity—a state, sovereign in the nineteenth-century meaning of the term. Republican spokesmen did not deny that the limitation or exclusion of aliens and even the abridgement of freedom of the press were sovereign powers; Federalists did not deny the sovereignty of the states. The whole argument hinged on whether or not the powers in question had been delegated in the compact.[6] The disputed bills were passed by partisan majorities in both houses of Congress, and were signed by President John Adams, who had long been accused by his enemies of a preference for monarchy.

With partisan judges ready to apply the law to its utmost extent, the liberties of the individual seemed already lost; for those who protested could be held in violation of the very acts of which they complained. It was in this emergency that the opposition turned to the state governments to enforce what they conceived to be constitutional guarantees. A state legislature could not be considered an unlawful combination, and its criticisms, whatever their effect, could hardly be punished as the law prescribed. So Jefferson drafted a set of resolutions which were passed by the Kentucky Legislature in November 1798, and a similar set from Madison's pen passed the Legislature of Virginia some six weeks later.

The argument that emerged was simple, and in terms of the compact theory was logically sound. It is admirably summarized in the first of the Kentucky Resolutions:

Resolved, That the several states composing the United States of America are not united on the principle of unlimited submission to their general government; but that, by compact, under the style and title of a Constitution for the United States, and of amendments thereto, they constituted a general government for special purposes, delegated to that government certain definite powers, reserving, each state to itself, the residuary mass of right to their own self-government; and that whensoever the general government assumes undelegated powers, its acts are unauthoritative, void, and of no force; that to this compact each state acceded as a state, and is an integral party; that this government, created by this compact, was not made the exclusive or final judge of the extent of the powers delegated to itself, since that would have made its discretion, and not the Constitution, the measure of its powers; but that, as in all other cases of compact among parties having no common judge, *each party has an equal right to judge for itself, as well of infractions as of the mode and measure of redress.*

---

[6] *Annals of Congress,* 5th Cong., 2nd sess., *passim.*

The resolutions went on to show that the Alien and Sedition Acts represented an exercise of undelegated power, were unconstitutional, and therefore "altogether void and of no effect." [7]

The legislatures of other states took issue, with resolutions of their own.[8] The general tenor of those coming from Federalist strongholds was to the effect that the state legislatures were not the proper tribunals to pass upon the constitutionality of acts of Congress. In the opinion of the majority in Rhode Island, Massachusetts, and New York, only the Supreme Court was empowered to determine constitutional questions. Massachusetts went furthest of all, declaring the Constitution to be a "solemn Compact" to which the people rather than the states were party, but Madison explained away the distinction in his detailed *Report* of the following year. It was not as geographical entities that the states were to be regarded as parties to the constitutional compact, but as "the people composing those political societies, in their highest sovereign capacity." [9] Further refinements and emendations, including a second set of resolutions from the Kentucky Legislature embodying previously omitted portions of Jefferson's original draft, resulted in only one significant addition to the argument. This was the clause from Jefferson's pen which declared that "a nullification, by those sovereignties, of all unauthorized acts done under color of that instrument, is the rightful remedy." [10]

The doctrinal controversy thus set forth was still in full cry when Jefferson and the Republicans won the election of 1800. The victory gave a species of sanction to the tenets of the victors; and the doctrine of the Constitution as a compact, to which the people of the states in their corporate capacity were the parties, and of the infraction of which they were the legitimate judges, came in due course to be "the old Republican doctrine of '98," sanctified by time and hallowed by association with the great. The natural rights of man joined other forgotten doctrines that had served their turn; the abstraction of a social compact was all but forgotten. Both were forms of moral protest, useful when

---

[7] Jonathan Elliot, ed., *Debates . . . on the . . . Constitution* (2nd ed., Philadelphia, 1866), IV, 540–544.

[8] *Ibid.*, p. 547.

[9] *Ibid.*, p. 547.

[10] *Ibid.*, p. 545. Jefferson's authorship of this passage was not proved until the discovery of the original draft in his handwriting in 1832. See Richmond *Enquirer*, March 13, 1832.

no better bludgeon was at hand. The state rights formula after 1800 served the same purpose and served it better, because it combined the moral principle with a plausible and cogent legal case.

With the Republicans in power, it was the turn of the Federalists to protest, and they would have been less than human had they not used the theory their opponents had so carefully formulated. The state rights dogma had been developed as a defense of civil liberties against the exercise of arbitrary power by the general government, after the skillfully devised system of checks and balances had proved ineffective in the face of a partisan majority. The Federalists used it to defend a vested interest—to protect wealth against numbers. First it was the Louisiana Purchase, which Jefferson himself admitted was an act beyond the Constitution.[11] Then came the threat of war with Britain, and to forestall it, the Embargo—as clearly an act of class legislation as were the funding and banking laws of the Federalists. And finally, with James Madison, the very architect of the Constitution, in the presidency, came the war itself. It was a war reprobated by a third of the nation, including the commercial classes who controlled most of the national wealth. New England governors chose not to call their militia into the field, and when Congress threatened to draft an army regardless of local prejudices, the New England states added a new gloss to the Virginia doctrine.

The same New England Federalists who had denied through their legislatures in 1799 that the states had any right to judge infractions of the constitutional compact were now willing to declare the compact dissolved on the authority of the states. Those who had once indignantly rejected state interposition were now ready to pursue the Jeffersonian doctrine to its logical end. If the government existed only as the result of a compact between sovereign states, and each state was free to determine for itself whether or not the instrument was being properly carried out—if each state might refuse obedience to a law it held to be unconstitutional—then surely the Union was no more than a league held together by treaty, and each party to it might withdraw at will. The Essex Junto schemed for a Northern Confederacy in 1803–1804. New England statesmen talked darkly of secession when Louisiana was ad-

---

[11] Jefferson to John C. Breckenridge, August 12, 1803, *Writings* (Memorial edition, Washington, 1905), X, 411.

mitted to statehood in 1811; and by 1814 they were making overtures to the enemy for a separate peace. The state rights doctrine which had served for the expression of Republican protest in 1798 had been extended by the Federalists to justify the separation of the oppressed minority from the Union.[12] When the threatened conscription of 1814 brought sectional opposition to a head, yet another gloss was added. For though the Hartford Convention did no more than relieve the feelings of its members, it established the notion that a popular convention was the ultimate vehicle for the expression of original sovereignty.

II

The issue was still between liberty and authority, between individual freedom and collective power, but the terms of the defense against majority rule necessarily narrowed the contest to one between state and federal sovereignty. The nation was growing in wealth, population, and importance. Soil and climate, the conformation of the hills and the slope of the streams, the distribution of natural resources, the peculiar system of labor inherited by the South, all combined to give a sectional cast to economic interests. When those interests clashed, it was inevitable, under a system of majority rule, that the federal government would be on the side of the numerically stronger group, which would in time become by its own votes the economically stronger as well. It would then follow that the majority would adhere to a theory of government which conferred upon the national legislature the supreme power to make laws in the interest of the dominant group; and the minority would seek refuge in constitutional limitations, enforced by sectional power.

The question of state versus national supremacy was thus a legal problem of first importance, and the Constitution had been in operation scarcely a decade before commentaries and judicial interpretations began to accumulate. The state rights group, perhaps because their party was in power, was first in the field with an excellent edition of Black-

---

[12] Henry Adams, ed., *Documents Relating to New England Federalism* (Boston, 1877), pp. 338 ff.; F. M. Anderson, "A Forgotten Phase of the New England Opposition to the War of 1812," Mississippi Valley Historical Association, *Proceedings*, VI, 176–188.

stone, published in Philadelphia in 1803. The editor was St. George Tucker, Professor of Law at the College of William and Mary, and Judge of the Supreme Court of Appeals of the Commonwealth of Virginia, who added appendixes expounding in terse and unequivocal prose the legal version of the doctrine advanced in more popular form in the Kentucky and Virginia Resolutions. In Tucker's view any political connection that may have existed between the states when they were dependencies of the British Empire was dissolved by the Revolution. By that act they became separate, sovereign, and independent states. The Constitution was a compact between equals, each sovereign in its own right. By this compact a federal union was created, with specific powers granted by the contracting parties. The federal government was not a party to but a creature of the compact, and was answerable to the states severally, and to the people of the states, for the performance of its duties.[13]

For a generation Tucker's *Blackstone* was one of the most widely used law texts in America, and countless fledgling attorneys were brought up to accept the compact theory of the Constitution. In the very year that Tucker's work appeared, however, another Virginian, Chief Justice John Marshall of the Supreme Court of the United States, began laying down the precedents out of which was to be molded the legal theory of the national state. Though by birth he belonged with those who had formulated the doctrines of '98, and by party allegiance was affiliated with the Federalists who had conceived and carried through the Hartford Convention, Marshall set himself to destroy the doctrine that had served both groups as a vehicle of minority protest. The Chief Justice by 1819 was expounding a positive theory of national sovereignty: The general government is supreme, and within the limits of the Constitution its will is uncontrolled. It derives its powers from no compact between sovereign states, but "is emphatically and truly a government of the people. In form and in substance it emanates from them, its powers are granted by them, and are to be exercised directly on them and for their benefit." The powers of the government, to be sure, were limited by the specific delegations in the Constitution, but within its prescribed orbit, the "government of the United States . . .

---

[13] St. George Tucker, ed., *Blackstone's Commentaries with Notes . . . to the Constitution . . . of the United States* (Philadelphia, 1803), I, App. D.

is supreme; and its laws, when made in pursuance of the Constitution, form the supreme law of the land. . . ." [14] In 1803 Marshall had affirmed the power of the courts to set aside unconstitutional acts of Congress.[15] In 1810 and again in 1819 the inviolability of contracts was affirmed and the states were forbidden to interfere with any contractual obligations.[16] It was also in 1819 that the right of a state to tax an instrumentality of the federal government was denied; and five years later Marshall declared that only the general government could regulate commerce among the states.[17] In each of these cases, and in others of similar import, the Chief Justice expounded over and over again the principle of national supremacy within limits to be determined only by the Supreme Court. The federal government, in effect, was declared to be the sole judge of its own powers, and the doctrine of state sovereignty was denied.

The complete exposition of this theory coincided too closely with the Missouri Compromise to be overlooked by the leaders of the slave states. It coincided also with the shift of northern capital from commerce to manufacturing, and with the consequent rise of the protective tariff as a national policy. The sectional balance had swung from South to North and West, from the cotton to the industrial states, from slave to free soil, and the agrarian minority read its own economic ruin in a theory that made the will of the majority supreme.

Again it was the Virginians, led by the aged but still clear-headed Jefferson, who raised the cry of tyranny, and sought to overrule the Court. In pamphlets, speeches, and newspaper crusades, in the state courts and legislature, and on the floor of Congress a brilliant group fought a vigorous but losing battle. Ex-President Madison teamed with Jefferson. The erratic genius of John Randolph of Roanoke was a tower of strength, and younger men like Thomas Ritchie of the Richmond *Enquirer* and John Tyler won their spurs. But the major contribution was made by old John Taylor of Caroline, the man who as a member of

---

[14] McCulloch v. Maryland, 4 Wheaton 316 (1819).

[15] Marbury v. Madison, 1 Cranch 137 (1803).

[16] Fletcher v. Peck, 6 Cranch 87 (1810); Dartmouth College v. Woodward, 4 Wheaton 518 (1819).

[17] McCulloch v. Maryland, 4 Wheaton 316 (1819); Gibbons v. Ogden, 9 Wheaton 1 (1824).

the state Assembly had introduced the Virginia Resolutions in 1798.

For Taylor sovereignty was unlimited and indivisible. It could not, therefore, rest in the government of the United States, because even John Marshall admitted that the central power was limited. For the same reason it could not rest with the state governments. The only legitimate source of sovereignty in the American system was the people, for they alone could exercise unlimited power. The people of the United States as a whole, however, could not be sovereign because they had no original corporate existence. They became an entity only by agreement among the people of the several states, who were sovereign before there was any such compact. "The people of each state, or each state as constituted by a people, conveyed to a federal authority, organized by states, a portion of state sovereign powers, and retained another portion. . . . If each state, or the people of each state, did not possess a separate sovereignty, they had no right to convey or retain powers. If they had a right both to convey and to retain powers, it could only be in virtue of state sovereignty."[18]

Taylor went on to analyze the economic implications of what he regarded as a deliberate attempt to consolidate the government into one of supreme power. To his mind the rising clamor for a protective tariff of ever larger proportions followed logically upon the funding of the public debt in Alexander Hamilton's time, the creation of a national bank, and the denial to the state of any power to interfere, by taxation or restriction of contract. The end sought was clearly the creation of a national state with sovereign powers, which would be used to foster and further enrich a moneyed aristocracy at the expense of agriculture. The pure republicanism of the Revolution was being transformed into a class structure similar to that of England, and supported, like England's, by bribery and corruption in the form of legislation for the economic benefit of the ruling class.[19] So alarmed was he by what he saw that Taylor himself accepted a seat in the Senate, where he directed the losing fight against the tariff of 1824.[20]

---

[18] John Taylor, *New Views on the Constitution* (Washington, 1823), pp. 173–174. Cf. his *Construction Construed* (Richmond, 1820), p. 27.

[19] See especially *Tyranny Unmasked* (Washington, 1822).

[20] Henry H. Simms, *Life of John Taylor* (Richmond, 1932), pp. 201–202, 206–207; *Annals of Congress*, 18th Cong., 1st Sess., pp. 676–688.

Though he failed to arrest the consolidating tendencies he saw and feared, Taylor succeeded in two things: he showed that there was a consistent pattern behind economic legislation and Supreme Court decisions, which, consciously or not, rested upon a theory of government by and for the primary benefit of a capitalistic class; and he gave to the state rights doctrine a more profound philosophical content than it had previously possessed.

How deep an impression the state rights theorists and jurists had made was evident when William Rawle of the Philadelphia bar published his *View of the Constitution* in 1825. Rawle was a thoroughgoing conservative if any man was. A loyalist at the time of the Revolution, he had fled to England, where he studied law. Back in the United States he naturally drifted into the Federalist camp, and as United States Attorney for Pennsylvania had been responsible for the legal steps in putting down the Whisky Rebellion. Yet Rawle agreed with Taylor that the Constitution was "the act of the people of each state, not of the people at large." Each state, he declared, "must be viewed as entirely sovereign in all points not transferred by the people who compose it, to the government of the Union: and every exposition that may be given to the Constitution, inconsistent with this principle, must be unsound." [21] The states, moreover, had entered the Union voluntarily and might, in Rawle's opinion, withdraw from it at their own pleasure.[22]

Rawle's work was followed a year later by the first volume of James Kent's *Commentaries on American Law*. Consummate jurist that he was, Kent saw all too clearly where the historical weakness of the case for national sovereignty lay, and he set about to remedy it. Deliberately and consciously, he affirmed that the Union was not federal but consolidated; that the Constitution emanated not from the people of the several states, but from the people of the United States as a whole. He realized, however, the logical barrier presented by the original independence of the states; so he argued that the "association of the American people into one body politic took place while they were colonies of the British empire, and owed allegiance to the British crown." The case was thin, and he did not improve it by citing such

---

[21] William Rawle, *View of the Constitution* (2nd ed., Philadelphia, 1829), pp. 18, 31. The author states this edition to be unchanged in anything but arrangement of material.

[22] *Ibid.*, pp. 296–297.

transitory unions as the New England Confederation of 1643 and the Albany Congress of 1754. Somewhat better was the argument that the Continental Congress had preceded the Declaration of Independence; but to clothe the Continental Congress and the Congress of the Confederation with "the chief rights of political supremacy, the *jura summi imperii*," would have appealed to those who sat in either body as the final and most bitter irony.[23]

However unconvincing the historical evidence might be, Kent's work represented a distinct advance in the development of the theory of national sovereignty. He had asserted in terms more positive than even Marshall had used the supremacy of the general over the state governments; and he had offered as an affirmative substitute for the compact theory of the Constitution the doctrine of a united people creating for themselves a fundamental law. The Constitution expounded by Kent was a far cry from the document drafted a generation earlier by the founding fathers. As one of the ablest of Southern lawyers protested, the government through the process of judicial interpretation and legislative usurpation had ceased to be "one of enumerated powers and a circumscribed sphere." It was now bounded by the will of the congressional majority alone. Already the general government was "seeking out employment for itself by interfering in the domestic concerns of society," and threatened in time "to control in the most offensive and despotic manner, all the pursuits, the interests, the opinions and the conduct of men." [24]

III

The constitutional debate was given new impetus in 1828 by the passage of the "tariff of abominations," with the center of protest shifting from Virginia to South Carolina. It was South Carolina, with her disproportionately large slave population and her uneconomically high cost of cotton production, that was hardest hit by import duties averag-

---

[23] James Kent, *Commentaries on American Law* (New York, 1826–1830), I, 189–198.

[24] [Hugh Swinton Legaré], "Kent's *Commentaries*," *Southern Review*, II (August 1828), 94–95. For the authorship of the article see Linda Rhea, *Hugh Swinton Legaré* (Chapel Hill, 1934), pp. 95–96. A future Attorney General of the United States, Legaré was not at any time a follower of the extreme state rights school, and was an admirer of both Kent and Marshall.

ing more than 45 per cent on manufactured articles. Robert Y. Hayne in the Senate and George McDuffie and James Hamilton, Jr., in the House had aided materially in the fight against the tariff of 1824, appealing to state rights as well as to the standard free trade arguments. Since that time a steady agitation had been kept up in the state, with Dr. Thomas Cooper, president of South Carolina College, and Robert J. Turnbull, publicist and planter, furnishing the rationalizations.

Cooper had come a long way since he had been convicted under the Sedition Act in 1800. He had watched with academic detachment and sharply critical eye the gradual accretions of power to the general government, and he drew conclusions that Thomas Hobbes would have relished. "No man," wrote Cooper in 1829, "has any rights but such as depend on his relative force of body or force of mind. The universal law of nature is, the law of force." Societies were formed for mutual protection, upon agreed terms, which were enforced by the common power. Political rights "are what society acknowledges and sanctions, and they are nothing else." [25]

Inescapably it followed that without some adequate safeguard, backed by force, the majority would always oppress the minority. If, as Andrew Jackson was fond of proclaiming, the will of the majority was to govern, the minority would have neither rights nor privileges, neither property nor safety. The conclusion, after sundry biting references to legalized plunder in the form of tariffs, was obvious. "The only safeguard in our confederacy, is the absolute inviolability of state sovereignty," including "the expressed and declared right of withdrawing peaceably from the Union, whenever circumstances may render it expedient, or the persevering injustice of a majority, may render it necessary to do so." [26]

Though not published in the definitive form cited above until late 1829 or early 1830, Cooper's views had been widely broadcast by letter, newspaper paragraph, and lecture; and the substance of his creed, as expressed at an antitariff rally in the summer of 1827, had shocked the country. "Wealth will be transferred to the North, and wealth is

---

[25] Thomas Cooper, *Elements of Political Economy* (2nd ed., Columbia, 1829), pp. 360–361. The date is misleading. The book was not actually printed until March 1830, and was probably not publicly distributed until 1831. See *Southern Times*, March 15, 18, 1830.

[26] *Ibid.*, p. 365.

power. . . . It is in vain that the force of argument is with us; the hand of power is against us and upon us. . . . We shall, before long, be compelled to calculate the value of our union; and to inquire of what use to us is this most unequal alliance. . . ." [27]

Cries of "treason" were still gaining volume when Turnbull, over the pseudonym of "Brutus," began issuing a series of inflammatory newspaper articles, published in pamphlet form in October 1827 as *The Crisis*.[28] Turnbull went back to the Virginia and Kentucky Resolutions for the framework of his reasoning, but he went much further than the pacifistic Jefferson could ever have forced himself to go. To the familiar case for state sovereignty he added Cooper's analysis of power. If force is an attribute of sovereignty, and if the states are sovereign, it must follow that they may if need be defend in arms their integrity against the encroachments of the federal government. The states, declared Turnbull, may interpose forcibly to arrest a violation of the compact to which they are parties.

When the tariff of 1828 was passed over the united protest of the cotton states, unrest in South Carolina threatened to turn into revolutionary channels. It was at this point that John C. Calhoun, then Vice President of the United States, took over the leadership of the state rights movement. His aim and purpose was to establish the rights of the minority, by nonviolent means. His method was to transform the philosophy of protest from a negative to a positive doctrine, at the same time so grounding it in law and precedent as to give it clear moral sanction. If action should be required, it could then be taken under forms of law, and the burden of obloquy that would follow an illegal use of force would fall upon the general government rather than upon the state.[29]

With the whole voluminous literature of state rights to draw from, and the mature formulation of the case for consolidation as laid down by Kent and Marshall in his hands, Calhoun restated the theory in terms appropriate to the growing emergency. Thomas Jefferson had

---

[27] Dumas Malone, *Public Life of Thomas Cooper* (New Haven, 1926), pp. 308–309.

[28] Robert J. Turnbull ['Brutus,' pseud.], *The Crisis: or Essays on the Usurpations of the Federal Government* (Charleston, 1827).

[29] For background, see C. M. Wiltse, *John C. Calhoun, Nationalist, 1782–1828* (Indianapolis, 1944), pp. 375–386.

given to the doctrine popular appeal, but it had lacked in depth. John Taylor of Caroline had given it philosophical content but had buried it beneath an avalanche of words. Calhoun gave it breadth and background and literary form. He gave it place in the main stream of political and economic thought, yet took from it none of its cogency as a tract for the times.

In his first statement of the theory, in the *South Carolina Exposition and Protest* of December 1828,[30] Calhoun argued as Taylor had done, from the nineteenth-century concept of indivisible sovereignty, defined in Austinian terms as the power to make binding law. If the national legislature, through its majority, was indeed sovereign, then the tariff was legitimate, and could be opposed only by argument and, in the last resort, rebellion. But clearly the majority in Congress was not sovereign, for certain powers were forbidden to it in the Constitution, and the Constitution itself could be amended by the same power that created it—the states. Since sovereignty was indivisible, the states could not have surrendered it in part and retained it in part. They must, therefore, have retained it all, only delegating the exercise of it, in certain stated particulars, to the general government set up by agreement among them. The doctrine of the compact, drawn up and ratified by the people of the several states, was skillfully pointed to the end in view, and Turnbull's appeal to force was made to serve the purposes of peaceful protest. For the states were the original source of power. The general government was their creature only, and if it overstepped the limits assigned to it, there was no power but in the states themselves to compel obedience. A state, then, could refuse to obey an unconstitutional law—could "interpose her sovereignty"—and the general government could enforce its will only with the consent of the constitution-making power itself: the three-fourths of the states necessary to amend the instrument.[31]

The first Jackson Congress was to meet in December 1829, and the South believed it had been promised tariff reform. The question would undoubtedly be reopened at the first opportunity, and if it failed the

---

[30] R. K. Crallé, ed., *Works of John C. Calhoun* (New York, 1851–1856), VI, 1–59.

[31] For fuller analysis of the doctrine, see Wiltse, *op. cit.*, pp. 390–398; "Calhoun and the Modern State," *Virginia Quarterly Review*, XIII, 396–408; and "Calhoun's Democracy," *Journal of Politics*, III, 210–223.

way had been cleared to challenge the authority of Congress itself. It was Calhoun's *Exposition*, the authorship of which was not openly avowed but which was widely guessed, that must be answered by those who would justify national sovereignty, and it was precisely that task for which Daniel Webster prepared himself during the recess of Congress in 1829.

In common with other New England Federalists, Webster had made free use of the state rights argument, including the doctrine of the Constitution as a compact between the states, in opposing the Embargo and the War of 1812. When manufacturing replaced commerce as the dominant interest of his section, however, Webster had become the spokesman for industry, even as Calhoun had become the champion of the cotton planters of the South. The manufacturers owed their rise to the fostering hand of government, and their continued success, in their own view, required the continued exclusion of foreign competition. Only a strong central government, a national government sovereign in the full meaning of the term, could meet their demands, and so it was such a government that their lawyers set out to justify. Webster was already perhaps the foremost advocate of central power. In the *Dartmouth College* case and *McCulloch* v. *Maryland* in 1819, and in *Gibbons* v. *Ogden* in 1824—the three cases that, more than any others, had served Marshall as vehicles for the expression of his own political creed—Webster had been attorney for the winning side; and the language of the court had followed closely the arguments of counsel.[32]

Webster's second reply to Hayne, delivered in the Senate on January 26 and 27, 1830,[33] was in reality a reply to Calhoun's *South Carolina Exposition* of 1828, but it was couched in language designed to reach the common man. The thesis was a simplification in more popular form of that set forth by Chancellor Kent, whose friend and admirer Webster was. The whole case rested on a denial that the Constitution emanated from the people of the states, or that the states had by compact delegated certain powers to the general government.

It is . . . the people's Constitution, the people's government, made for the people, made by the people, and answerable to the people. . . . So far

---

[32] Claude M. Fuess, *Daniel Webster* (Boston, 1930), I, 252–253, 278.

[33] *Register of Debates*, 21st Cong., 1st sess., pp. 58–82; Webster, *Writings* (National edition, Boston, 1903), VI, 3–88.

as the people have given power to the general government, so far the grant is unquestionably good, and the government holds of the people, and not of the State governments. We are all agents of the same supreme power, the people. The general government and the State governments derive their authority from the same source. Neither can, in relation to the other, be called primary, though one is definite and restricted and the other general and residuary. . . .

It was easy, then, to buttress the case for federal supremacy by quoting the Constitution itself, and to establish the primacy of the Supreme Court as the final interpreter of the instrument.

Though Webster failed to convince a number of his fellow Senators, the evidence is strong that his frank appeal to the general public was more successful. His name became a byword, even in the South, and the words of his ringing peroration—"Liberty *and* Union, now and forever, one and inseparable"—soon appeared at the masthead of the widely circulated *National Intelligencer*.[34] The debate was, however, by no means over. With interruptions only for necessary business, it went on until well into May, with every shade of opinion being aired. Perhaps the most thoughtful and most realistic of all the speakers was Edward Livingston of Louisiana, who took the floor in mid-March. Belonging to the generation of the founding fathers, and himself a distinguished lawyer, Livingston agreed with Hayne that the Constitution was undeniably a compact between the states; but he followed Webster in denying that any state retained a veto over acts of Congress. He distinguished between "the ultimate sovereign power residing under all governments . . . in the people" and the more tangible "power to regulate the affairs of a nation, which resides in its government." This latter power had been in part retained and in part surrendered by the states, but that part which had been given up could not be reclaimed. The government was neither wholly federal nor wholly national, but it did possess the power to make and enforce law. Secession, though it might be justified on the ground that the compact had been violated,

---

[34] The circulation given to Webster's speech must have been enormous for that day. Gales and Seaton, publishers of the *Intelligencer*, had printed 40,000 pamphlet copies within four months, and at least 20 other editions were known to have been printed elsewhere in the same period. In addition, the speech was carried in full by many newspapers, including *Niles' Weekly Register*, which reached every corner of the land. See *National Intelligencer*, May 21, 1830; and *Niles' Weekly Register*, XXXVIII (March 6, 1830), 25–48. This is to be compared with a mere 5,000 copies of Calhoun's *Exposition* of 1828.

was nonetheless rebellion, and "must be at the risk of all the penalties attached to an unsuccessful resistance to established authority." [35]

Here, then, were three general views: (1) The Constitution was a compact between the states, which retained their sovereignty and might interpose to check the exercise of unconstitutional powers by the general government. (2) The Constitution was a fundamental law, drawn up and sanctioned by the people of the United States as a whole, the sovereignty being exercised by a majority of their duly elected representatives. (3) The Constitution was a compact between the states, which, however, retained their sovereignty only with respect to matters not specifically delegated to the general government, and had no control over that government other than through the ballot and the process of constitutional amendment. The second and third arguments did not differ in results. Under each a majority in Congress was for all practical purposes sovereign. It might if it chose vote the wealth of one class into the pockets of another, and make good its will by force.

Outside of Congress, too, the same debate was carried on, with skill and learning, and a dangerous tendency to mistake sectional interests for the results of intellection. For the issue reached down to the source of livelihood for planter and manufacturer alike. If the general government had no power to protect industry, then industry was doomed; but if the power were granted, then were the floodgates open and the will of the majority supreme—a majority already restive at the existence of slavery in the South. So the *Southern Review* examined the speeches of Hayne and Webster, and with convincing clarity showed that Webster was indubitably wrong.[36] With equal lucidity and skill and at even greater length the *North American Review* demonstrated the palpable misapprehensions of Hayne.[37]

The editor of the *North American*, however, had engineered a *coup d'état*. He produced a letter from the venerable James Madison, not only the principal draftsman of the Constitution and co-author of the *Federalist*, but also author of the Virginia Resolutions of 1798 and of the often quoted *Report* of the following year. As he grew older, Madison had grown more conservative—or perhaps his radicalism had never

---

[35] *Register of Debates*, 21st Cong., 1st sess., pp. 265–270.
[36] *Southern Review*, VI (August 1830), 140–198.
[37] *North American Review*, XXXI (October 1830), 469–546.

171

been more than the voice of Thomas Jefferson whispering in his ear. His mature position was hardly distinguishable from that of Livingston. The Constitution was "a compact among the States in their highest sovereign capacity"; it constituted the people of the several states "one people for certain purposes," and it could not therefore be "altered or annulled at the will of the States individually." The supreme power was divided between state and federal governments, and within their assigned spheres the acts of each were sovereign. As to the Virginia and Kentucky Resolutions and the debates and *Report* of that faraway time, they had simply been misunderstood. It was meant only that the states might act jointly to repudiate at the polls any Congress or President guilty of unconstitutional acts.[38]

The attempt to explain away the precedent of 1798–1799 was weak, but Madison's name carried great authority, and his own part in the proceedings made him almost invulnerable. The advocates of central power were jubilant, and the state rights leaders depressed—the more so as the House had voted down any revision of the tariff even as the Senate debated its own claims to sovereignty. Unrest in South Carolina again threatened to get out of hand, and young hotheads began to talk openly of rebellion. So in July 1831 Calhoun explained again that the doctrine of nullification—or state interposition as he preferred to call it—was lawful and constitutional, supported by precedent and by the authority of the founding fathers, Madison to the contrary notwithstanding. This time the document was signed, and gained much wider circulation than his earlier version of it. It was more popularly written, and was consciously pointed at the arguments advanced on the other side since 1828.[39] Still better was Calhoun's letter to Governor Hamilton of August 28, 1832,[40] which Webster called "by far the ablest and most plausible, and therefore the most dangerous" vindication of the state rights doctrine to appear.[41]

Before Webster could prepare an answer, the controversy was carried beyond the discussion stage by the re-election of Andrew Jackson. The tariff, which had been the occasion for reopening the debate on sovereignty in 1828, had long since been superseded in the eyes of the

[38] *Ibid.*, pp. 537–546. Also in Madison's *Writings* (Cong. edition), IV, 95–106.
[39] "Fort Hill Address," *Works*, VI, 59–123.
[40] *Ibid.*, pp. 144–193.
[41] Webster to Chancellor Kent, Oct. 29, 1832, *Writings*, XVIII, 526–527.

state rights theorists by the more basic question of a consolidated as against a limited or divided government. The Supreme Court, with no power to enforce its own decrees, offered no check to the executive will, and with the patronage at the disposal of the President a majority in Congress could always be bought. Yet if the executive were thus conceded the sole right of construing the Constitution, then there was no Constitution in fact, but a monistic state whose will was limited only by its power.[42] The debate in the Virginia Legislature in the winter of 1831–1832 on the question of slavery had underlined the isolation and the helplessness of the South in the face of a majority hostile in economic interest,[43] and her leaders saw their only possible safety in maintaining, even by force if need be, a constitutional theory that gave them power to protect their own. The election of 1832 meant to the state rights theorists that the doctrine of national sovereignty would be sustained. The result was filled with irony, for Andrew Jackson, who would exercise the powers that Marshall and Kent and Webster had so painstakingly justified, was anathema to all three; and the masses who approved the theory in approving Jackson were bitterly hostile to those very interests that would in the end be the chief beneficiaries of the national state.

The ballots were hardly counted before South Carolina, through a specially chosen convention of her people, declared the tariff unconstitutional and forbade the collection of duties within her limits. Machinery was carefully devised to throw the onus of using force, if force should be used, upon the general government. The whole procedure was given the cloak and form of law. An effective date was established far enough ahead to give Congress time to yield by modifying the tariff, and Calhoun was sent to the Senate to defend his state and her principles.

In its practical results the nullification episode was a stalemate, for the tariff was compromised and force was not used. In the realm of ideas, however, it marked the emergence of the national state in

[42] Calhoun to Virgil Maxcy, Sept. 11, Nov. 3, 1830, Maxcy Papers, Library of Congress. The impotence of the Supreme Court was demonstrated early in 1832 when state officials ignored the decision in Worcester v. Georgia, 6 Peters 515, and the President chose not to intervene. See A. C. McLaughlin, *Constitutional History of the United States* (New York, 1935), p. 429.

[43] See Thomas R. Dew, *Review of the Debate in the Virginia Legislature of 1831 and 1832* (Richmond, 1832).

America. Jackson's Proclamation of December 10, 1832, written by Edward Livingston, who was then Secretary of State, was a blunt denial of the whole theory on which the right of state interposition rested and an unqualified assertion of national sovereignty. The Constitution "forms a Government, not a league; and whether it be formed by compact between the States, or in any other manner, its character is the same. It is a Government in which all the people are represented, which operates directly on the people individually, not upon the States. . . ." It forms a nation, from which there is no right of withdrawal. "To say that any State may at pleasure secede from the Union, is to say that the United States are not a nation. . . ." The people of South Carolina were urged to recede from their untenable position, but the people of the nation were called upon to sustain the government should coercion be required.[44]

The reaction of the South was one of shocked surprise and of rebellious anger. There were numerous and able answers in the press and in the halls of state legislatures, but one is typical of them all. The Proclamation, so the answers ran, denied doctrines held to be fundamental in the South, and asserted others regarded as pernicious heresies. It confounded sovereignty with government, and implied that whoever controlled the latter might wield the former.[45] It was precisely there, however, that the critics erred; for sovereignty is neither more nor less than naked power, and the general government was sovereign to exactly the extent that it could enforce its will. Jackson made no further move until he got a public reaction, indicating how far his authority would be sustained. The reaction was satisfactory, and on January 16, 1833, he asked Congress to authorize military intervention in South Carolina at the discretion of the President.[46]

The request precipitated the clearest and most important of the debates on sovereignty, with Calhoun and Webster the protagonists. Both men realized that power, supreme and uncontrolled, was by

---

[44] The Proclamation and other documents in the controversy are in *Register of Debates*, 22nd Cong., 2nd sess., App., pp. 145–202.

[45] The particular reply followed here is one that appeared in December 1832 and January 1833 in several numbers of the Norfolk and Portsmouth *Herald*. Signed simply "A Virginian," the articles were written by Littleton Waller Tazewell, recently United States Senator from Virginia, and generally regarded as one of the foremost constitutional lawyers in the South.

[46] *Register of Debates*, 22nd Cong., 2nd sess., pp. 100–104, and App., pp. 145–154.

definition indivisible, and each avoided the pitfall of divided sovereignty. It must rest either with the states or with the national government. Calhoun's argument from history and precedent that it belonged to the states could not be broken down, as Webster well knew, and so he based his own contention, as he had in 1830, on a denial of the compact theory of the Constitution.[47] But aside from clarifying the issues and eliminating the middle ground, the debate was futile. It did, to be sure, serve the purpose of so dividing public sentiment as to make the actual use of force against the nullifiers hazardous, but it did not deter the Congressional majority from exercising sovereign power. The Force Bill was passed, authorizing the President to relocate custom houses, alter the procedure of the courts, and if need be employ an army to enforce the laws of the United States.[48]

The power was not used, because the tariff compromise and the discretion of South Carolina leaders secured rescission of the Ordinance of Nullification. The subsequent nullification of the Force Act by a state convention, however, was an empty gesture. It remained on the statute books until it expired by its own terms, a reminder to all who doubted that the national government was supreme.

IV

In the nullification episode thoughtful men on both sides glimpsed for a moment the abyss of civil war. Both sides drew back in patriotic horror, and for another generation the opposing forces were maintained in uneasy balance. It was, however, a generation of controversy on an issue already settled in fact. Tariffs, commercial restrictions, territorial rights, even slavery could be compromised, but sovereignty could not. So the state rights theorists kept their cause alive, lest silence be construed as surrender, while the majority took its sovereign power as proved, and exercised as much of it as seemed in the circumstances good.

It was perhaps fitting that the same year that saw the practical emergence of the national government as supreme saw also the definitive statement of the case for central power in Supreme Court Justice Joseph Story's *Commentaries on the Constitution*. With immense learn-

[47] *Ibid.*, pp. 519–587, 750–777.
[48] 4 Stat. 632 (March 2, 1833).

ing and consummate skill, Story demonstrated in sixty-five copiously footnoted pages that the Constitution of the United States was not a compact at all, but a "fundamental law," representing the will of the majority and creating a form of government under which the majority would rule. The whole literature of law and controversy from Coke and Blackstone to Webster and Calhoun was made to serve his purpose, and when he had finished, there was no more to be said.[49] Story, to be sure, was no more successful than Kent had been in his attempt to prove from history that the Constitution was the work of the whole people, acting through their majority.[50] But the point no longer mattered; for no argument on earth could change the fact that sovereignty was where the power lay.

The critics were as clear on this as were the defenders of majority rule, and they saw with at least equal clarity the ultimate result. "Whatever be the *theory* of our Constitution," wrote Abel P. Upshur in a review of Story's *Commentaries,*

its *practice,* of late years, has made it a consolidated government; the government of an irresponsible majority. If that majority can find, either in the pursuits of their own peculiar industry, or in the offices and emoluments which flow from the patronage of the government, an interest distinct from that of the minority, they will pursue that interest, and nothing will be left to the minority but the poor privilege of complaining. Thus the government becomes tyrannous and oppressive, precisely in proportion as its democratic principle is extended; and instead of the enlarged and general interest which should check and restrain it, a peculiar interest is enlisted, to extend its powers and sustain its abuses. . . .[51]

Only by the interposition of power could the abuse of power be restrained; in the states alone did the power to interpose exist.

Above all else the state rights theorists, like the natural rights philosophers of the eighteenth century, feared an absolute government; but they feared equally the excesses of democracy. They wanted a government strong enough to protect their property, but not strong enough to take it away. The "property" in their case was three million negro slaves.

It was Calhoun who gave the doctrine its definitive form, and made it, in his posthumous *Disquisition on Government,* a permanent part of the

---

[49] Joseph Story, *Commentaries on the Constitution of the United States* (Boston, 1833), I, 279–343.

[50] *Ibid.,* pp. 3–216.

[51] Abel P. Upshur, *Brief Enquiry into the True Nature and Character of Our Federal Government* (Petersburg, Va., 1840), p. 128.

176

stream of political thought.[52] Governments, he reasoned, are of two kinds only: absolute and limited or "constitutional." The absolute form knows no restraint but the will of the ruler, who might be a single individual, a group, or a majority. The limited government is a balance of interests which must proceed by compromise. The numerical majority alone is as absolute and as authoritarian as any monarch, and as inimical to liberty. The principle of constitutional government, as Calhoun unfolded it, came very close to functional representation, with the states or sections being conceived as economic interests. The welfare of the whole required the preservation of each of these interest groups, but government by a simple numerical majority would mean destruction of the weaker by the stronger. The solution was to require, in addition to the sanction of the majority, the concurrent sanction of a majority in each major interest group.

Calhoun's argument, in keeping with his mental powers, was abstract. Though a thorough economic realism pervaded his analysis, he was still concerned with government as it ought to be, whereas the problem of his section was how to preserve its interests under government as it was. Increasingly through the 1840's, with their successful venture into imperialistic war, power came to be centralized in the national administration. The theory of state sovereignty was simplified accordingly to achieve a more concentrated appeal. The doctrine of state interposition, or nullification, was tacitly dropped, and emphasis was placed on the terminable nature of the compact. When the Constitution was patently and willfully violated by a majority, and redress could not be obtained, any state injured by the violation might withdraw from the Union.

By 1850 the political and economic issues between North and South were approaching the final crisis, and the disruption of the Union was freely predicted in the halls of Congress. The state rights theorists had prepared the ground maintaining over a half-century of controversy their right to secede, but the sovereignty in fact rested with the majority and the majority would not have it so. Again it was Webster who announced the sovereign will, not argumentatively this time, nor as one stating a proposition to be proved, but in the blunt, unvarnished language of power. "There can be no such thing as peaceable secession.

---

[52] *Works*, I, 1–107. Though not published until after Calhoun's death in 1850, the *Disquisition* was written in 1845, and belongs to the era of the forties.

Peaceable secession is an utter impossibility." [53] A few days later William H. Seward, from the lofty pinnacle of the majority, condemned all legislative compromise as morally wrong, and appealed to a "higher law" than that of the Constitution to sanction what the majority intended to do.[54]

A compromise was reached in spite of Seward, but it did not last. For another decade the old contentions were dressed up again in new and appealing verbiage, but in the end the hostile parties faced each other in arms. President Buchanan, in his last annual message to Congress before yielding his office to Lincoln, referred once more to the state rights doctrine, which he pronounced "wholly inconsistent with the history as well as the character of the Federal Constitution"; but a convention had already been called in South Carolina to take that state out of the Union. Buchanan found a loophole for himself in his inability to discover in the Constitution any authority to coerce a state, but Lincoln did not search for authority. The sovereign power of the nation rested in his hands, and he exercised it. The rebellious South was beaten back into the Union, and the great debate was finally over.

What of the founding fathers, and their simple eighteenth-century philosophy? "What binds," wrote Orestes Brownson in 1865, "is the thing done, not the theory on which it was done, or on which the actors explained their work either to themselves or to others." [55] It was not the Constitution nor any gloss upon it but natural forces inherent in the world order that had wrought of such recalcitrant materials a united nation. It was not the labors of Madison and his colleagues but manifest destiny that had brought forth upon this continent a new world power. However men might explain or justify it, the fact remained. A century after the Stamp Act had been rejected by His Majesty's North American Colonies as arbitrary and unwarranted, the United States of America itself emerged as a true national state, whose sovereignty was undisputed and whose will was uncontrolled within the limits of its power.

---

[53] *Congressional Globe*, 31st Cong., 1st sess., App., p. 276. Also in Webster, *Writings*, X, 93. This was the famous Seventh of March speech, 1850.

[54] *Congressional Globe*, 31st Cong., 1st sess. (March 11, 1850), pp. 260–269.

[55] Orestes A. Brownson, *The American Republic: Its Constitution, Tendencies, and Destiny* (New York, 1865), p. 243. Cf. John W. Draper, *Thoughts on the Future Civil Policy of America* (New York, 1865), esp. ch. iv.

Marx and Weitling

CARL WITTKE

IN THE SUMMER of 1845 Karl Marx was living in Brussels, as a refugee. Urged on by Friedrich Engels, he had begun the research necessary for a two-volume *Critique of Politics and Political Economy,* which actually did not see the light of day until 1859. In the midst of his labors, Marx became convinced that it was of more immediate and vital importance for the future of "true" socialism to attack the existing systems of German post-Hegelian philosophy and the various brands of primitive communism which still blocked the way to a general acceptance of his own type of historical materialism and prevented the formation of a unified Communist League, which would spread the propaganda for his own more "scientific" scheme for the salvation of society.

The *German Ideology,* begun in 1845 as an exposition of Marx' views on historical materialism, was not published in complete form until 1932. His biographers have given ample space to an analysis of his theories.[1] Of equal interest and importance are the conflicts which Marx had with certain personalities whom he regarded as serious rivals and competitors in the formative period of the 1840's, when he was clarifying his own views on "true" socialism, and welding them into a closed "system."

Marx engaged in violent controversies with men like Karl Grün, a Westphalian who was an acquaintance of his student days; with Moses Hess, the "communist rabbi" who preached a simple, primitive Utopian

---

[1] See, e.g., Boris Nicolaievsky and Otto Maenchen-Helfen, *Karl Marx, Man and Fighter* (Philadelphia, 1936), chs. ix–xi; and Otto Rühle, *Karl Marx, His Life and Work,* tr. by Eden and Cedar Paul (New York, 1929), pp. 47–142.

formula for human happiness; [2] with Max Stirner, the theorist of individual anarchism; and with Wilhelm Weitling, the Utopian who, in contrast with the intellectuals, was the spokesman for a workers' "bread and butter communism."

Marx was determined to stamp out both the philosophical communism of a Hess or a Grün, and the handicraftsman's type of communism advocated by Weitling. The final clash between Marx and Weitling, which is the subject of this paper, not only illustrates the nature of the conflict between Utopian and "scientific" socialists, but also suggests the important consequences for the whole future of the communist movement that derive from the utter rout of Weitling's point of view.

Wilhelm Weitling, born in 1808, in Magdeburg, as the illegitimate son of a young soldier in Napoleon's army of occupation, was reared in extreme poverty, and never knew the protection and security which a home and family can give. His formal schooling ended with the elementary grades of the Magdeburg *Bürgerschule*. Apprenticed at an early age to a tailor, Weitling became equally proficient in ladies' and men's tailoring, a trade which he followed intermittently until his death in New York in 1871. As a young man, he traveled widely and worked as a journeyman in Leipzig, Dresden, Vienna, and other German cities. When his wanderings finally took him to Paris, he remained in the French capital from 1837 to 1841.

It was in this Parisian crucible of revolution that the young tailor became thoroughly aware of the problems and needs of the emerging proletariat and of the economic and social consequences inherent in the new factory system. It was here also that he absorbed the radical theories and "systems" of revolutionists like Babeuf and Buonarrotti, and of social philosophers like Cabet, Considérant, Fourier, Saint-Simon, Proudhon, and others, for Paris, at that time, was the intellectual center of the new radicalism.

The sources for Weitling's "system" are to be found in a mixture of rationalism, French utopianism, and religion. Lamennais' *Paroles d'un Croyant*, a little book in which a priest turned socialist put the red cap of liberty on top of the cross (in Heine's phrase), made an especially

---

[2] See Theodor Zlocisti, *Moses Hess, der Vorkämpfer des Sozialismus und Zionismus, 1812–1875* (Berlin, 1921).

deep impression on the embryo German communist during these Paris days, and the theories of these intellectuals slowly percolated down to the ranks of the workers, to which Weitling belonged. He entered upon the path of social revolution through the door of the workers' movement, and by way of the many secret societies which the radicals developed in France after the suppression of the workers' uprisings in Paris and Lyons in 1834 had driven the labor movement underground.

It was as a member of the Bund der Gerechten ("League of the Just") in Paris that Weitling achieved fame in the early history of communist activities in France, Germany, Switzerland, Austria, and England. He became one of the Bund's most influential leaders, and in 1838, he was officially commissioned by the Bund to prepare its first major publication, *Die Menschheit wie sie ist und wie sie sein sollte* ("Mankind as it is and as it should be"). This propaganda treatise was an attempt on the part of the author to integrate the rising labor movement with the new program of communism. It was written strictly in the Christian communist tradition, and with the fervor of a prophet, who had such faith in the potentialities of man that he believed that the human race was ready even then for social revolution.

After the suppression in the spring of 1839 of a revolutionary uprising in Paris, led by the disciples of Babeuf, the League of the Just was broken up, and Weitling moved on to plant the seeds of communism in the fertile soil of Switzerland. Here he labored with workers' organizations, promoted co-operative dining halls, founded secret communist societies, and published a radical journal. His magnum opus, *Garantieen der Harmonie und Freiheit* ("Guaranties of Harmony and Freedom"), the most complete exposition of his theories and principles, appeared in Switzerland late in 1842. It was written in language intended to reach the ordinary worker, and set forth the reasons why artisans and petite bourgeoisie were being depressed into the proletariat, as well as a plan for the thorough reorganization of society along communist lines.

A detailed analysis of the "system" which Weitling described in his major works is impossible here. His books must be read and analyzed in detail to feel the power of his eloquence in exposing the evils of the existing society, and to sense the religious fervor and assurance with

181

which, as a new Messiah, he unfolded his blueprint for a planned economy.

According to Weitling, the cancer gnawing at the heart of society was the unequal distribution and consumption of goods, the unequal apportionment of the labor necessary to produce them, and the vicious monetary system which sustained and perpetuated these inequalities. The kind of social organization which he advocated was expected to provide equal work, equal rewards, and equal educational opportunities for all. Private property and inheritance would be abolished and a social order brought into being in which that balance and harmony between man's desires and his capacity to produce and enjoy which existed in the "Golden Age" would be restored.

Weitling loved to write constitutions, and he wrote many during his lifetime. Nearly all of these "Constitutions of the Great Human Family" started with the assumption that society must be organized as a union of families (*Familienbund*). This large unit in turn was broken down into smaller administrative units, according to an intricate pattern for a hierarchy which had at its top a Senate, a Ministry, and a "Trio" who suggest Plato's philosopher kings. Parallel to the political structure, Weitling provided an occupational organization (*Geschäftsordnung*) to control and direct the economic life of the society, consisting of organizations of farmers and those engaged in industry. These administrative units again were arranged in a neatly ordered hierarchy whose members were elected by an extraordinarily complicated election procedure. Because of his great respect for education and science, and perhaps because of his own meager schooling, Weitling recommended an association of teachers and the learned (*Gelehrtenausschuss*) that would control all the appointments in agriculture and industry that required any appreciable amount of special training. An "Industrial Army," patterned on the military, was expected to furnish the training needed to carry on the ordinary activities of the people. The Senate and Ministry, at the apex of his highly complex triangle of administration, to be elected by a process which would sift the ablest in the community for positions of leadership, would establish general policies, apportion the tasks among the various crafts and services, and assume responsibility for such matters as health, food, housing, recreation, and the arts and sciences. In order to encourage invention and ensure progress, and to make sure that genius and talent were adequately recognized, Weitling outlined a plan for special *Meisterkompagnieen* ("master companies") of inventors, discoverers, and creative artists, who were to receive special privileges in his communist state because of the special contributions they could make to the advancement of the race. Space does not permit an analysis and description of the general regulations for the great communist society which would embrace the whole human family, nor of Weitling's educational and judicial reforms, though these matters are of greater importance than the mere structure of the new society.

Convinced that equality of labor and equality in the enjoyment of goods would not, of themselves, guarantee permanent happiness, and indeed might lead to intolerable monotony, Weitling unfolded a plan which he believed would avoid the blighting effects of the existing methods of exchange and at the same time give men an opportunity for self-expression and for the satisfaction of their legitimate individual desires. The solution proposed was a system of *Kommerzstunden* recorded in a *Kommerzbuch*. In essence this meant that members of the community might earn additional "labor credit" for work done voluntarily beyond regular hours and beyond their regular tasks, and could use this credit to pay for products which they especially desired and which were produced by others in the same manner. Thus, the individual could "satisfy his particular wants without destroying the harmony between the desires and capacities of all," and the products of workers and farmers, deposited in common storehouses, could be acquired in exchange for labor certificates. To hold such additional private production and exchange within proper bounds and in order to protect the needs of the community as a whole, Weitling provided an elaborate system of controls, which permitted the closing of certain occupations to such extra labor, raising the "hour cost" beyond the value of the actual work expended or placing temporary embargoes on the further production of surplus goods. In brief, this was a plan to exchange labor for labor and time for time; to eliminate the banker and the middleman; to base value solely on the amount of labor needed for production; to keep production and consumption in balance; to control prices and markets; and to avoid violent fluctuations in employment. Being a skilled craftsman himself, Weitling proposed to have the guilds of journeymen and masters decide what products were needed and guarantee their quality. His major emphasis was centered on the development of a co-operative handicraft system of production.

This brief and incomplete analysis of Weitling's brand of communism is sufficient to forecast the Marxian reaction. Yet its sponsor believed that his "system" would not only cure all the economic ills from which the race was suffering and become the "pivot" of an entirely new society, but also would be a long step forward toward "the realization of Christian principles" in a kingdom of heaven on earth. Weitling maintained that little preparation was necessary to bring the new order into being. "Humanity is of necessity always ripe for revolution," he wrote, "or it never will be."

In the spring of 1843 Weitling issued a prospectus for still another work, known as *Das Evangelium des armen Sünders* ("The Gospel of the Poor Sinner"). In it he undertook to prove that the religion of Jesus, far from being ignored or condemned by the social reformers, should be used to help emancipate mankind from existing injustices and economic and social maladjustment. It was the publication of this little book which led to his arrest; to his trial for blasphemy, because he had represented Jesus as the revolutionary hero of the underprivileged; and to a jail sentence of ten months in Zurich on the charge of being a public nuisance.[3]

Released at last after a period of confinement which had psychological effects from which he never fully recovered,[4] Weitling was pushed across the border into Germany, and finally made his way from Hamburg to London. Here his arrival was celebrated at a festival of workers, who welcomed him as a martyr of their sacred cause, but unfortunately, the English Socialists did little to help the refugee meet his ordinary living expenses. In due time, also, he found himself at odds with the leaders of the German communist club in London, whose theories, perhaps under the influence of English Chartism, were be-

---

[3] For brief, general accounts of Weitling's European career, see Emil Kaler, *Wilhelm Weitling, seine Agitation und Lehre im geschichtlichen Zusammenhange dargestellt* (Zurich, 1887); Wolfgang Joho, *Wilhelm Weitling: Der Ideengehalt seiner Schriften entwickelt aus den geschichtlichen Zusammenhängen* (Heidelberg, 1932); and F. Caille, *Wilhelm Weitling: Theoricien du communisme, 1808–1870* (Paris, 1905).

[4] See Ernst Barnikol, *Weitling der Gefangene und seine "Gerechtigkeit"* (Kiel, 1929).

coming less and less utopian, and more and more opportunistic and practical. Weitling, on the other hand, clung stubbornly to his role as a prophet of a sentimental, primitive Christian type of communism. "Revolutions," he insisted, "come like a thunder storm, no one can foretell their effects," and in them "reason will play a pitiful role; . . . the greatest deeds will result from the power of emotion. . . . It is nonsense to preach enlightenment to the hungry; . . . the eternal propaganda for peaceful evolution merely stultifies men's courage and zeal" for reform.

In 1846 Weitling moved on to Brussels. He had broken with the communists of London over questions involving the techniques of propaganda and the end results to be achieved by their movement. His distressing experience in England foreshadowed the coming break with Marx.[5]

In the middle 1840's Weitling was far better known in communist circles than the young man who was ten years his junior, and who was destined to become a world figure as the high priest of modern, scientific socialism. As yet, Marx had been relatively unproductive, whereas Weitling's three major works and his journal had made his name widely known in western Europe. Heinrich Heine called his *Die Menschheit* "the catechism of the German communists," and Marx, in 1844, referred to the *Garantieen* as the "brilliant, literary debut of the German working class" and rated it as superior in theory to the writings of Proudhon. When Engels read the magnum opus of the man whom he called the "social-democratic tailor," he thought it merited translation into English, and he gave due credit to its author's influence in initiating the workers of Germany in the tenets of radical reform. Weitling's books were in the library of the Communist Club of Berlin, and prior to 1846 Marx and Engels probably would have agreed with the verdict of several historians of the communist movement that this self-educated tailor was "the only really great communist of pre-Marxian times."[6]

---

[5] For the factional strife in London, see Max Nettlau, "Londoner deutsche kommunistische Diskussionen, 1845" in *Archiv für die Geschichte des Sozialismus und der Arbeiterbewegung* (Leipzig, 1922), X, 362–391.

[6] See Max Beer, *Karl Marx: Sein Leben und seine Lehre* (Berlin, 1919), pp. 435–439; Werner Sombart, *Der proletarische Sozialismus* (Jena, 1924), I, 25; Morris Hillquit, *History of Socialism in the United States* (New York, 1903), p. 161; and Charles Andler, *Le Manifeste communiste de Karl Marx et F. Engels* (Paris, n.d.), pp. 6, 162.

No proletarian author ever described the miseries of the poor more eloquently than Weitling, for he had experienced them personally, and the growing threat of industry reminded him of "an iron bodice crushing the tender forms of children."

The clash with the Marxists was inevitable. Slowly, but with increasing determination and conviction, Marx had evolved his materialist interpretation of history. He believed that not man's mind conditions his being, but his social being conditions his mind. He concluded that men were not free to choose the social form under which they lived, but that the pattern of production was the basic factor in determining the mode of life and even the morals of a particular age. In short, men's material relationships were fundamental for all their relationships. So he rejected the theories that dealt with the primitive but "golden" state of nature, or were related to primitive Christianity, or to a particular scheme of social ethics, for he could find in none of these a proper basis for communism. Moreover, Marx wished to divorce the labor movement altogether from the ritual and techniques of secret societies and direct it into channels of political action. He and Engels had discovered the "scientific" basis for their philosophy of economic determinism, materialism, the class struggle, and the inescapable proletarian revolution. Their brand of socialism was distilled from the French Revolution, large doses of Hegel and Feuerbach, French theorists like Fourier and Saint-Simon, and the impact of British industrialism. Marx explained all social institutions, whether political, legal, moral, or religious, by the economic structure of society, and maintained that even morality and religion were dependent on the processes of production and exchange of goods. Such a system left no place for sentimentalism, and the true Marxists would have no truck with what they regarded as idealistic rubbish.

Although several factors contributed to the break between Marx and Weitling, the religious aspects of the philosophical tailor's communism were the most important cause. Weitling was a simple son of the people. Though he had acquired an amazing amount of miscellaneous information, he lacked the formal training either to formulate or to comprehend an historic law of economic determinism. His own bitter experience taught him that man could not be free spiritually if he were held in economic bondage, but he flatly rejected a doctrine that made self-interest the sole motivation of life. He would not admit that man was

186

only a figurehead in the interplay of external, economic forces. For him, man was the actor and maker of history, and though he believed that progress was the law of nature, he insisted that man, by conscious effort and planning, must help make that law of progress function. Not unlike the Marxists and the Hegelians, he admitted that all things have within them the germ of change and revolution, but he emphasized man's obligation to direct this change in accordance with the principles of Christian self-sacrifice and brotherhood.

Thus, Weitling's appeal was to the emotions and the heart. He believed man had an inner desire to do good, and a capacity for unselfish conduct which could be nurtured by morality and religion, and he proposed to use the power of religious emotionalism to help establish a communist society which he regarded as practically synonymous with the good life of the practicing Christian. This faith sustained him, and he was confident that it would help others to penetrate the black night of their despair. Communism, according to Weitling, was not a mere matter of the stomach, but much more a matter of ethics.

Weitling was never an avowed atheist like Feuerbach, nor a materialist like Marx. He was an agnostic, and certainly not a churchman, but he was eager to use Christian faith and doctrine to stimulate and feed the emotions necessary for social revolution. Like most men, he had no solution for the riddle of the universe, and he could not explain the deep mystery of life. Yet he believed that "the mysterious emotions of love" frequently prove more powerful than reason, and he referred often to that "image of highest love," which men call God, as well as to an "eternal, omnipotent, unifying cause." His bruised spirit yearned for the balsam of religion, and his reason led him to agnosticism. Yet he was far from ready to dismiss the whole area of religious experience as a mere opiate for the people.

More and more, and especially after his shattering prison experiences in Switzerland, Weitling pictured himself in the role of a prophet, with a great mission to perform. As one of his contemporaries, Wilhelm Marr, pointed out, his type of communism was becoming a "social theology," "with its own sacred books, its prophets, its Messiahs and its heaven." Along that road lies the fanaticism of the martyr. Weitling's gospel, in Louis Blanc's phrase, was *"l'Evangile en action,"* a secular faith to be proclaimed by the prophet. He did not think that it needed

187

to be scientifically demonstrated. It was a faith comparable with the fervor of the Anabaptists, the Moravian Brethren, and the Levellers and Diggers of England, and Weitling, in many ways a more lovable character than Marx, constantly sought to dissolve his communism in Christian love, compassion, and the quest for justice.

It must be remembered that Weitling wrote before the days of Darwinian evolution and modern industrial capitalism. He knew nothing of large-scale industry. He was first and always a journeyman tailor, and he had little or no conception of the role modern capitalism, with all its faults, would play as an instrument of progress. He spoke for the guild craftsman whose status in the social order was being depressed by new forces which he did not fully understand, but which he felt would reduce his class to the level of a homeless, poverty-stricken proletariat. In Weitling were embodied some of the best qualities of his group—courage, industry, self-sacrifice, respect for honest work. He voiced the grievances of all the oppressed, but he planned especially for a state controlled by skilled artisans. He violently attacked the existing relationships between employer and employee, but he was not yet ready to preach the class struggle. He appealed to men of good will in all classes, and like Owen, Fourier, and Cabet, was as ready to propagandize the rich and powerful as the poor and impotent.

Another essential difference between Marx and Weitling must be emphasized. The former was a university man, with his doctor's degree from Jena, a neo-Hegelian, very much of a pedant, and capable, as Karl Heinzen once said, of mobilizing "the whole artillery of logic, dialectic, stylistic and learning." Weitling's study of Hegel, under Fröbel and Bakunin, ended almost before it began with the conclusion that all German philosophy was "the quintessence of German nonsense" and calculated to leave men in a "fog." He was not interested in abstractions; he was sure that experience was a better teacher than books; and he feared lest the "foxes and asses" among the German philosophers lay obscene hands on his communist movement to confuse the common people. In the spirit of the true craftsman, Weitling contended that "science and skill" are of equal importance. Engels was quite right when he accused him of having a strongly developed *Gelehrtenhass*.

Thus the conflict between Marx and Weitling represented the clash between a master of economics and Hegelian dialectics, who was an advocate of a class struggle preordained by scientifically discoverable economic laws, and a simple-minded prophet of the brotherhood of man, who regarded himself as the new Messiah capable of building a new kingdom in which science would be blended with Christian love. It is interesting to point out in passing that Marx always managed to keep away from direct contact with the proletariat about whom he wrote so vigorously. Weitling had no respect for what he called a "closet analysis."

When the two men met in Brussels, Weitling undoubtedly proved irascible and violent in argument. He was irritated and unhappy because of his experiences in London, which revealed that his influence was declining rapidly. His prison experiences in Zurich had made him unusually sensitive. He suspected treachery in the ranks, and he was constantly on the watch for secret enemies and plots. Marx, on the other hand, was noted for his intolerance; he would brook no opposition, and Carl Schurz was impressed by his "offensive, insufferable arrogance."

When Weitling arrived in Belgium, Marx was busy organizing the first communist party, and his efforts were making inroads in the ranks of Weitling's erstwhile followers. With the help of Gigot and Engels, he carried on a voluminous correspondence in three languages with communists in many places, in order to persuade them to accept his doctrine, and to purge the movement of all sentimentality. Unity was possible, he felt, only if the Marxists could crush both the philosophical communism of men like Hess and the artisan type of communism represented by Weitling.

Because of his reputation and his influence, the older leader could not be totally ignored, and so Weitling was invited to participate in the launching of the new party, which consisted, at the outset, of only seventeen of the faithful. A majority belonged to the bourgeoisie. These seventeen pioneers of modern socialism met twice a week under the guise of a workers' educational society to hammer out in long debates the communist gospel as presented by their leader. Weitling's early correspondence with Marx had been quite friendly, and was marked by the use of the familiar "*du*" form. Relations had become somewhat strained however when Weitling asked for financial help to publish the treatise on a universal language on which he had been working in

London, and had been brusquely refused, in the sharp, sarcastic language of which both Marx and Engels were masters.

The actual quarrel between the leaders of the old and the new communism broke out at a meeting in Brussels attended by Gigot, Weydemeyer, Seiler, Heilberg, and Marx' brother-in-law, Edgar von Westphalen. "Jupiter Marx," with pencil and paper in hand, seated himself at the head of the table to direct a discussion of the kind of propaganda best suited for Germany. According to the Russian, Annenkov, who also was present, he "spoke only in the imperative, brooking no contradiction." As Marx revealed his intention to rid the movement of all sentimental appeals to the emotions, the debate became heated and reached a climax when Marx turned sharply on Weitling to demand an outline of his program, and an explanation and defense of his methods of propaganda. Confused and embarrassed, and really without a specific program that could be compared with that of his young, aggressive adversary, the older man made repetitious statements, expressed complete satisfaction with his methods and his brand of communism, and indicated that apparently neither his influence nor his achievements were properly appreciated. At this point Marx angrily interrupted the speaker and denounced fantastic propaganda which would stir people to revolt without first providing them with a definite and complete program for social action. In the course of the tirade, delivered while the speaker stamped furiously up and down the room, Marx accused Weitling of plain ignorance, and sarcastically observed that the latter's confused system might be suitable for a benighted, backward country like Russia, but would not do at all for Germany. Both men lost their tempers, and Weitling in turn accused Marx of fawning upon people of means to get support for his movement. In spite of this altercation, it is interesting to note that some time after the quarrel Weitling sent Marx an article for publication, and the latter invited him to lunch.

The final, irreparable break, oddly enough, occurred because of the activities of young Hermann Kriege in far-off America. Kriege, an ardent disciple of Feuerbach and a friend of Robert Blum, who fell in the Revolution of 1848, had gone to the United States, after trouble with the Prussian police, to become the leader of a "Young America" group in New York, and to publish the *Volkstribun*. This little German radical sheet had some circulation in Europe, and its enthusiastic editor

190

corresponded regularly with some of the leading communists on the Continent. Always somewhat unstable, both politically and psychologically, Kriege had joined the land reform movement in his newly adopted fatherland, advocated free homesteads, accepted the support of Tammany Hall, and did not hesitate to appeal to men of means when he needed funds for his various undertakings.

The *Volkstribun* was anticlerical, anticapitalist, antirent, and against other things. Kriege followed a policy of opportunism and piecemeal reform, and defended his tactics on the ground that a democratic America presented a very different problem for the agitator than autocratic Europe. His paper, which was as short-lived as most of the radical press of the period, was written in the extravagant, rapturous style of a sentimentalist bubbling over with love for all humanity. To rigid doctrinaires, like Marx, the antics of the editor were those of a crackpot, and were making communism laughable.

The *New York Tribune* in an obituary notice of January 1, 1851, referred to Kriege, who died insane at the age of thirty-one and, as he had requested, was buried with an American flag draped across his breast, as "one of the most sincere, upright and generous men with whom it was ever our fortune to be acquainted"; but to orthodox Marxians he had never been more than a source of embarrassment, though Engels at one time considered him a "splendid agitator" and had sent him material for his paper. It was not long after, however, that Marx resolved to repudiate this eccentric coworker in the vineyard of proletarian revolution, and to call the renegade to account by bringing his case officially before the party council in Brussels.[7]

When Karl Marx attacked Kriege and charged that he had endorsed land reform, given away the *Volkstribun* instead of selling it, and accepted gifts from the bourgeoisie of New York, thus violating all orthodox communist principles, only Weitling refused to sign the circular letter drawn up to read Kriege out of the party. Copies of the letter of excommunication were sent to England, France, Germany, and the United States. The *Volkstribun* carried both the letter and an editorial reply. Weitling insisted that Kriege should be given reasonable

---

[7] Engels to Marx, Feb. 22, 1845, in *Briefwechsel zwischen Friedrich Engels und Karl Marx, 1844 bis 1883*, ed. by A. Bebel and Ed. Bernstein (Stuttgart, 1921), I, 15, 18; also 39, 43, 49.

191

latitude in adapting his techniques to American conditions. More important is the fact that Weitling believed the attack on the young New York German-American really was an attack on him, and was designed to rid the Brussels group of its last dangerous rival and competitor. He now proclaimed the *Volkstribun* a proper organ for the spread of communist doctrine, and dispatched a long letter to the editor, deploring a policy calculated to sow dissension between European and American communists, and reaffirming his belief in the power of love to deal effectively with social injustices. The letter was promptly published in New York. For a time Weitling seriously considered assuming the editorship of Kriege's paper, and he made his first trip across the Atlantic for that specific purpose, only to find that the *Volkstribun* had suspended publication just before his arrival.

The break between the Marxists and the older Weitling wing of the communist movement now was complete. Engels, in a fury "about the infamy of brother Weitling," renounced all connections with the "warm brotherliness," "gentleness," and "meekness" of such prophets of Utopia. Kriege, on the other hand, just before the suspension of his paper, had taken down the slogan "Up with the workers. Down with capital," which he had carried at the masthead of the *Volkstribun*, had apologized for ever having used the name "communist," and had joined the ranks of the Social Reformers who at the moment were operating with the support of Tammany Hall.

Marx and Engels followed their initial victory over the utopian dreamers with a purge of the communist movement intended to rid it of all who deviated in the slightest from the doctrine as proclaimed by the *pontifex maximus*. Engels made a trip to Paris to break whatever little influence Weitling still exercised among the German workers there, and especially among "the little tailor clique." He not only painted the former leader of the League of the Just as a reactionary, but did not hesitate to spread the false charge that Weitling was not the author of the books which carried his name.[8] In a letter to Marx, Engels referred to the small following which their rival still had among the journeymen in London as "asses." Similar attacks were made on August Willich and Fritz Anneke, other prominent radical German Forty-eighters who later published German papers in the United

---

[8] See *Briefwechsel, Engels und Marx*, I, 23–29, 40, 49–50, 88.

States, and they too were accused of "trying to sow dissension in our ranks."

Weitling came to America to stay, after having played an insignificant role in the German Revolution of 1848 and 1849. In the United States he published a radical paper known as *Die Republik der Arbeiter* and managed to keep it alive through five difficult years; organized a Workingmen's League which had featured, among other objectives, a program of social insurance and old age pensions; sponsored the first German labor congress ever held in the United States; and finally saw his whole movement collapse largely because of his foolhardy efforts to establish a communist colony in Iowa. Marx and Engels continued to keep a sharp eye on "the poison of this king of the tailors," [9] and threw their support to men like Joseph Weydemeyer when the latter established a rival organization among the workers in New York along more orthodox Marxian lines.[10]

The events in Weitling's career between the years which marked his break with Marx in Brussels and his death in New York, in 1871, lie beyond the scope of this paper, and will be fully described in a projected full-length biography of the forgotten "social-tailor." It is interesting to speculate however on what might have happened in the history of communism and in the history of modern Europe if the efforts of men like Weitling to bridge the gap between materialism and humanitarianism had been more hospitably considered at the Brussels conference, and subsequently. Marx and Engels had the education and the scientific training to enable them to forge their theories into the system which became one of the most powerful forces in the modern world. Weitling was not equipped for such a task, for his head was not equal to his heart. Nevertheless, in spite of his extravagant language and nebulous references to a new Messiah who would lead the children of God into a new Canaan, he had a conviction that a system utterly divorced from concepts of morality, social ethics, and the motivation derived from religious emotions, and frankly espousing the amoral principle that the end justifies the means, would turn into the devil's own philosophy and result in a new kind of tyranny.

---

[9] *Ibid.*, pp. 145, 171, 384, 398, 422.
[10] See Karl Obermann, *Joseph Weydemeyer, Pioneer of American Socialism* (New York, 1947), especially ch. ii.

John Morley on Liberty and Compromise

MILTON R. KONVITZ

N O DISCIPLE of John Stuart Mill was more loyal to the root thoughts of the master than was John Morley. When Mill died in 1873, Morley spoke of him as his intellectual father [1] and said that he bore to the memory of Mill the affectionate veneration of a son.[2] Of all the writings of Mill which Morley absorbed,[3] none were rated by him higher than *The Subjection of Women* and *On Liberty*, which he considered the notable fruits of the ripest and loftiest part of the author's life,[4] books written after Mill's "grand moral climacteric." [5] Although Morley considered *The Subjection of Women* more important than *On Liberty*, because in the former Mill attempted to apply to a difficult subject the abstractions he had formulated in the latter,[6] he described *On Liberty* as a work belonging to those rare books that, after hostile criticism has done its best, are still found to have somehow added a cubit to a man's stature.[7] One is aware of the impact of Mill at almost every stage in the development of the mind of Morley, and especially in his Liberalism, which he defined in terms typical of Mill: "Respect for the dignity and worth of the individual is its root. It stands for the pursuit of social good against class interest or dynastic interest. It stands for the subjection to human judgment of all claims of external

---

[1] Morley, *Critical Miscellanies* (1886) (London: Macmillan), I, 37.

[2] *Ibid.*, p. 38.

[3] Morley never adopted the mild theism found in Mill's *Three Essays on Religion* (1874); never gave up his agnosticism.

[4] Morley, *Crit. Misc.*, I, 81.

[5] *Ibid.*, p. 78.

[6] *Ibid.*, p. 75.

[7] Morley, *Recollections*, I, 61.

194

authority." [8] Here in three short sentences one finds the amalgam of thoughts and aspirations characteristic of both Mill and Morley: belief in the liberty of the individual, joined, on the one hand, to utilitarianism, and, on the other hand, to empiricism. They belonged to the school of Locke, Hume, Adam Smith, Bentham, and James Mill, "whose method subordinates imagination to observation, and whose doctrine lays the foundations of knowledge in experience, and the tests of conduct in utility"; [9] they added, however, to the teachings of the school a belief in "unchecked liberty of thought, unbounded freedom of individual action in all modes not hurtful to others." [10]

Mill had been dead only a year when Morley wrote *On Compromise,*[11] in which the conclusions of *On Liberty* serve as postulates.[12] The problem Morley posed for himself was this: Granted the formulations and conclusions of *On Liberty,* how far should one permit himself to go in his self-assertions, in his tenacious hold on principles, in the earnestness of his convictions? [13] Mill had taught that one should distrust his own bias and his own supposed knowledge—this distrust is an essential quality of tolerance and is one of the foundations of the doctrine of liberty. One must be fair towards the opinions from which one differs; for no one has a monopoly on knowledge or wisdom: we live under a dome of many-colored glass. But a person sees more truth in one doctrine than in another. How far should one go in loyalty to the opinions which he accepts? Can one combine earnestness in his own opinions with tolerance for the opinions which one rejects? [14]

Morley was aware [15] of the fact that Mill himself had anticipated that his doctrine of liberty might be construed as checking the free expression of disapproval. Mill met the problem by saying that we have a right to act upon our unfavorable opinions of another, not for the purpose of oppressing his individuality, but rather to express our own individuality. Among the permissible ways in which one may express

---

[8] *Ibid.,* p. 56.
[9] Morley, *Crit. Misc.,* I, 40.
[10] *Ibid.,* p. 62.
[11] First ed. published 1874; new ed. 1877. References are to the 1891 reprint of the latter ed., published by Macmillan, London. The book is out of print.
[12] *On Compromise,* pp. 241–242.
[13] *Ibid.,* p. 242.
[14] Morley, *Crit. Misc.,* I, 62.
[15] *On Compromise,* pp. 273–275.

his disapproval, Mill enumerated the following: (1) to avoid the company of the person whose opinions we disapprove ("though not to parade the avoidance"); (2) to caution others against him; (3) to give others a preference over him in the distribution of offices ("except those which tend to his improvement").[16] Except for the parenthetical limitations, what difference is there between the response of one imbued with the principles of Mill and the response of one who is a stranger to these principles, in the face of a person of whose opinions or conduct they disapprove? Morley, in commenting on this matter, stated that the differences are notable; for the person not imbued with Mill's principles would be sure that he is right and the other person wrong, and he would proceed to make the other person smart for his error—he would act from "the officious principle"; while the follower of Mill, not ever being sure that he is absolutely right and the other person altogether wrong, would feel the responsibility of censorship much more seriously; he would reflect carefully about the conduct or opinion of which he disapproved; his disapproval would have "an austere colour, a gravity, a self-respecting reserve."[17]

Admitting, then, as Mill did, that there are limits on tolerance, and that there are permissible ways in which one may show his disapproval of another's conduct or opinion, how is one to know when the limits have been reached—when the occasion has been presented for the earnest demonstration of one's own opinions and the austere disapproval of the opinions one has rejected? An answer to this question is sought by Morley in *On Compromise*.

It should be noted that this question is not on all fours with the question of limits on the province of government. Mill limited the province of government to the repression of acts that directly and immediately injure others than the doer of them. So long as conduct is self-regarding, it may not be interfered with. He formulated his principle thus:

that the sole end for which mankind are warranted, individually or collectively, in interfering with the liberty of action of any of their number is self-protection; the only purpose for which power can be rightfully exercised over any member of a civilised community, is to prevent harm to others. His own good, either physical or moral, is not a sufficient warrant. He cannot be right-

---

[16] Mill, *On Liberty* (1859), Everyman's edition, p. 134.
[17] *On Compromise*, p. 275.

fully compelled to do or forbear because it will make him happier, because in the opinion of others to do so would be wise or even right. These are good reasons for remonstrating with him, or reasoning with him, or persuading him, or entreating him, but not for compelling him, or visiting him with any evil in case he do otherwise. To justify that, the conduct from which it is desired to deter him must be calculated to produce evil to others.[18]

Assuming, then, that there are actions whose consequences do not go beyond the doer of them—self-regarding conduct, with which government or unorganized public opinion may not interfere—how far may a person go in showing his disapproval of another's opinions or conduct, or in pressing the rightness of his own opinions, or in attempting to actualize them in conduct?

Mill, it has been correctly said, "had one of the attributes of the sceptic, a sense of the incompleteness of any formulated truth, of the possibility that the opposite of what he was affirming was true also." [19] This may be said also of Morley. Skepticism of this breed may be rooted in empiricism and the principle of utility, and its fruit may be intellectual and moral nihilism. Mill and Morley both avoided eating of this fruit. They, however, saw the danger—Morley even more than Mill. *On Compromise* shows how at least one of them combined skepticism and earnestness, empiricism and militancy; how love of liberty and respect for individuality combined with a spirit of combat and a zeal for causes; how belief that my neighbor's asserted principles are always only "one set of partialities, passions, and prejudices" [20] led to the belief that I must correct or counterbalance them by the assertion of my own partialities, passions, and prejudices—for, from the standpoint of individual liberty, my neighbor has no greater right to assert his opinions than I have to assert mine, to perpetuate his notions than I have to innovate mine.

II

All schools of thought, said Morley, agree that there are occasions when it is necessary to compromise—necessary in the interests of truth itself. Thus there are times when one needs to stay the formation of

[18] *On Liberty*, Everyman's edition, pp. 72–73.

[19] Crane Brinton, *English Political Thought in the Nineteenth Century* (1933), p. 90.

[20] Mill, *Dissertations and Discussions* (1859–1875), I, 404.

opinions, or exercise reserve in expressing them, or delay an attempt to realize them. The wise exercise of self-restraint in these three provinces of compromise needs to be differentiated from cowardice, hypocrisy, self-illusion, and indolence.[21]

There is the difference, in a word, between expedience and principle. But let it be noted at once that principle

is only another name for a proposition stating the terms of one of these larger expediencies. When principle is held in contempt, or banished to the far dreamland of the philosopher and the student . . . this only means that men are thinking much of the interests of today, and little of the more ample interests of the many days to come.[22]

A moral proposition may be a "supreme and indefeasible" expediency, as contrasted with a narrow expediency of ordinary politics; [23] it may be a statement of the order of facts of the future, as contrasted with the assumed need of the existing order of facts.[24]

There is, however, a proper dread of broad principles—a dread which springs from attachment to a high standard of evidence, or from a deep sense of the relative and provisional quality of truth, or from distrust of the rational judgment in comparison with the emotional or mystical forces in man.[25] Generally, however, the dread of principle is caused by deference for the *status quo* as the last word and final test of truth and justice. While in physical science accurate reasoning is demanded,

in morals and politics, instead of admitting that these subjects have equally a logic of their own, we silently suspect all first principles, and practically deny the strict inferences from demonstrated premises. Faith in the soundness of given general theories of right and wrong melts away before the first momentary triumph of wrong, or the first passing discouragement in enforcing right.[26]

True moral principles are at bottom only noted generalizations from experience, recording certain uniformities of antecedence and consequence in the region of conduct.[27] But Morley noted that in his own day, when old hopes had grown pale, when strong sanctions had become weak, and when vivid faiths had become very numb, there was a decisive reluctance to commit one's self; the sense of personal responsibility had lost sharpness of edge; [28] it was a day of small calcula-

---

[21] *On Compromise*, p. 4. [23] Page 16. [25] Page 18. [27] Page 26.
[22] *Ibid.*, p. 6. [24] Page 14. [26] Page 19. [28] Pages 36–37.

tions and petty utilities, without vision of the true expediencies.[29]

Where ideas are subordinated to the *status quo*,[30] a situation is found where one may think one doctrine true and the contrary doctrine morally beneficial.[31]

In other words, they think error useful, and that it may be the best thing for society that masses of men should cheat and deceive themselves in their most fervent aspirations and their deepest assurances. This is the furthest extreme to which the empire of existing facts over principles can well be imagined to go. It lies at the root of every discussion upon the limits which separate lawful compromise or accommodation from palpable hypocrisy.[32]

Erroneous opinion or belief, in itself and as such, can never, said Morley, be useful.[33] It may, however, be expedient to let errors alone at a given time, for, Morley quoted Condorcet, "the passage from error to truth may be accompanied by certain evils."

No doubt we should destroy all errors, but as it is impossible to destroy them all in an instant, we should imitate a prudent architect who, when obliged to destroy a building, and knowing how its parts are united together, sets about its demolition in such a way as to prevent its fall from being dangerous.[34]

But error as such has no provisional utility;[35] "for all good habits in thought or conduct there are good and real reasons in the nature of things."[36] Once we have satisfied ourselves that a doctrine is false, the only question should be the selection of means to displace it; and we should not for a moment feel embarrassment in dealing with it because of the notion that the doctrine may be useful to someone else.[37]

Suppose a subject is not ripe for practical treatment. Does it follow that we are in the meantime entirely relieved from the duty of having clear ideas about it? Not at all, said Morley. "It is precisely because we believe that opinion, and nothing but opinion, can effect great permanent changes, that we ought to be careful to keep this most potent force honest, wholesome, fearless, and independent."[38] We must make every effort to achieve clear ideas even if the time for their effectuation may seem remote; otherwise, because of some unforeseen development or in the natural course of things, we may find ourselves called upon to propose a solution, though the question has not been adequately discussed; then the question is settled in a slovenly, imperfect, "and

---

[29] Page 43. [32] Page 48. [35] Page 73. [38] Pages 96–97.
[30] Page 40. [33] Page 56. [36] Page 63.
[31] Page 45. [34] Quoted at pp. 57–58. [37] Page 84.

often downright vicious manner." [39] *There should never be compromise in the formation of opinions.* In our own minds we should never acquiesce in second-best opinions. We should be guided, in the formation of our opinions, by "the great truth, that it is worth while to take pains to find out the best way of doing a given task, even if you have strong grounds for suspecting that it will ultimately be done in a worse way." [40] *In the formation of opinions the minority owes no respect to the majority:* "a man is answerable at his own peril for having found or lost the truth." [41] There must always be the free and vigorous use of the intelligence.[42]

The conditions which make against frank declaration of our convictions are of rare occurrence; [43] the duty to express the truth as one sees it gives way only when such expression will inflict keen distress on those to whom a person is bound "by the tenderest and most consecrated ties." [44] Only one relationship in life justifies us in being silent where otherwise it would be right to speak; namely, the relationship between child and parents.[45] In all relationships, however, there is the "tact of seasonableness." [46] But this tact, which puts a reserve on speech, must itself be subject to rigorous limitations; for only rarely should one feel himself bound by tact not to speak the truth. "Consider," said Morley, in a passage that deserves to be widely known,

the triviality of life and conversation and purpose, in the bulk of those whose approval is held out for our prize and the mark of our high calling. Measure, if you can, the empire over them of prejudice unadulterated by a single element of rationality, and weigh, if you can, the huge burden of custom, unrelieved by a single leavening particle of fresh thought. Ponder the share which selfishness and love of ease have in the vitality and the maintenance of the opinions that we are forbidden to dispute. Then how pitiful a thing seems the approval or disapproval of these creatures of the conventions of the hour, as one figures the merciless vastness of the universe of matter sweeping us headlong through viewless space; as one hears the wail of misery that is for ever ascending to the deaf gods; as one counts the little tale of the years that separate us from eternal silence. In the light of these things, a man should surely dare to live his small span of life with little heed of the common speech upon him or his life, only caring that his days may be full of reality, and his conversation of truth-speaking and wholeness.[47]

---

[39] Page 99.   [41] Page 117.   [43] Page 119.   [45] Page 165.
[40] Page 100.   [42] Pages 140–141. [44] Page 149.   [46] Page 182.
[47] Page 198. Cf. Bertrand Russell's "A Free Man's Worship," first published in 1903; reprinted in *Mysticism and Logic* (1929), ch. iii.

The season is never—or almost never—unripe for the announcement of the fruitful idea.[48] Is there a limitation on the duty to push the idea to active conquest? "In so far as it can be done by one man without harming his neighbors," said Morley,

the time has always come for the realisation of the idea. When the change in way of living or in institution is one which requires the assent and coopera- tion of numbers of people, it may clearly be a matter for question whether men enough are ready to yield assent and cooperation.[49]

In the endeavor to convert a theory into practice, it often is expedient to defer to the views of the majority, to move slowly, to bow to the conditions of the *status quo*, to practice "the very utmost sobriety, self- restraint, and conciliatoriness." [50]

This reserve in any attempt to actualize one's views does not, how- ever, mean that we are to accept the *status quo* as a despotic authority of a heavenly dispensation, that we are to accept "the plenary inspira- tion of Majorities." [51] It would merely be the worst of political blunders "to insist on carrying an ideal set of principles into execution, where others have rights of dissent, and those other persons whose assent is indispensable to success, as it is impossible to attain." [52]

The counsel to bide one's time in the attempt to put theory into practice does not carry over, however, to the free expression of the theory. The question whether we can get a majority to agree with us is relevant only when we are eager for instant change; but there are many preliminaries before change is effected.[53] In the meantime one must speak as a minority, aware of the fact that in a world where progress is made only slowly and gradually,[54] the "history of success, as we can never too often repeat to ourselves, is the history of minorities." [55] Force should not be substituted for persuasion; otherwise the conscience of society will be weakened and hypocrisy will be bred.[56] The absence of coercion, "or the leaving people to think, speak, and act as they please, is in itself a good thing. It is the object of a favourable presumption. The burden of proving it inexpedient always lies, and wholly lies, on those who wish to abridge it by coercion, whether direct or indirect." [57]

---

[48] Page 216.
[49] Pages 216–217.
[50] Page 103.

[51] Page 118.
[52] Page 122.
[53] Page 225.

[54] Page 233.
[55] Page 226.
[56] Page 246.

[57] Page 254.

The presumption against coercion becomes, as the lawmen would say, an irrebuttable one when the force is directed against ideas or against conduct in the self-regarding sphere.[58]

Outside the self-regarding sphere, conduct may be regulated by the majority; but the minority have the right and the duty to express their dissent; there is always the duty not to tamper with veracity as one sees it, from whatever motive; for to tamper with veracity is to tamper with the vital force of human progress.[59] For the new order of things, when it comes, will be of little worth unless it will have been shaped by generations of honest and fearless men.[60] The man who hides his candle under a bushel out of fear, timidity, tenderness, or whatever motive, does for ideas with which he agrees "the very thing which the acute persecutor does for ideas which he dislikes—he extinguishes beginnings and kills the germs." [61]

In action, then, outside the self-regarding sphere, there is need of compromise. But compromise, to be legitimate, must not mean the suppression or mutilation of ideas, in order to make them consistent with current prejudices.

It is legitimate compromise to say:—"I do not expect you to execute this improvement, or to surrender that prejudice, in my time. But at any rate it shall not be my fault if the improvement remains unknown or rejected. There shall be one man at least who has surrendered the prejudice, and who does not hide that fact." It is illegitimate compromise to say:—"I cannot persuade you to accept my truth; therefore I will pretend to accept your falsehood." [62]

Since a sound principle is a larger expediency, one should not abandon it for the sake of a seeming expediency of the hour; one should not sacrifice the greater good for the less, defraud the future by truncating our ideas. "It is better to bear the burden of impracticableness, than to stifle conviction and to pare away principle until it becomes mere hollowness and triviality." [63] Although in the endeavor to convert theory into practice, it may be necessary to defer to the views of the majority, to move slowly, to bow to the conditions of the *status quo*, to practice conciliation, one should not refrain from expressing his dissent, one

---

[58] Page 251.
[59] Pages 141–142.
[60] Page 200; cf. 215.

[61] Page 218.
[62] Page 209.
[63] Page 265.

should not conform to language implying the acceptance of notions one really rejects.[64]

III

In brief, it appears that: (1) There should never be compromise in the formation of opinion, in the sphere of thought. There is the duty ever to search for true principles, regardless of the question whether or not one will ever have an opportunity to apply them. (2) Only rarely should one exercise reserve in expressing his settled views. The season is almost always ripe for the announcement of the fruitful idea. (3) The formation and expression of opinions are like self-regarding acts: they are outside the legitimate sphere of restraint by government or public opinion. (4) Insofar as the conversion of theory into practice is not a self-regarding act, one must yield to the will of the majority, and one may accept compromises, provided always that one does not hide his candle under a bushel, or pretend to accept views which in his heart he rejects. (5) The search for and expression of truth are the vital forces of human progress; the wheels of history are moved forward by the energies of honest and fearless men, who keep awake the conscience of society. (6) The majority members of a community should not insist on imposing their will upon any other portion, "except in matters which are vitally connected with the maintenance of the social union." [65] The root of Liberalism, it should be remembered, is respect for the dignity and worth of the individual.[66]

On Compromise does not answer all relevant questions,[67] but it does

---

[64] Page 103.   [65] Page 102.   [66] *Recollections*, I, 56.

[67] Would Morley accept the "clear and present danger" doctrine as a limit on freedom of expression? He probably would accept it, if joined with the rule that there is strong presumption against the application of the doctrine to any given set of facts, and that the burden to rebut the presumption rests with the government. Morley's statements are not altogether free from ambiguities and contradictions. He wrote with a verve and force that gave color to his books but detract from straight, logical analysis and demonstration. But the fundamental principles and direction of his thought stand out clearly enough when he is read with sympathy. The judgment, however, that Morley was a *philosophe* rather than a philosopher, and that he was "better when dealing with broad principles than in detailed analysis or constructive suggestion," is quite correct. See Kingsley Martin, *Encycl. of the Soc. Sciences*, XI, 13, 14.

explicate some fundamental principles of *On Liberty*, consistently with the three cornerstone ideas of Mill and Morley: individualism, utility, and empiricism. Read together (as they should be) [68] they represent the most cogent statement of Victorian Liberalism.

It may be of interest to observe that Morley's position comes close to that of Jefferson.[69] In the realm of action, where acts are not self-regarding, progress can be made only by compromise. "I am sensible," wrote Jefferson,

how far I . . . fall short of effecting all the reformation which reason would suggest, and experience approve, were I free to do whatever I thought best; but when we reflect how difficult it is to move or to inflect the great machine of society, how impossible to advance the notions of a whole people suddenly to ideal right, we see the wisdom of Solon's remark that no more good must be attempted than the nation can bear.[70]

Compromise is the price to be paid for majority rule, if one is to live in a community in which changes are effected by persuasion rather than by force. In the realm of practice there must be "gradualism by majority rule through the strategy of compromise." [71] Compromise is necessary in all things joint, all things public—all acts that are not self-regarding. But in all things individual—the formation and expression of opinion, the doing of acts essentially self-regarding—there must be no compromise. The Bill of Rights marks the line between the two realms—the line between the private and the public, between theory and practice, between ideals and actions, between ends and means. "Democracy is not a goal, it is a going. Democracy is whatever can be arrived at democratically." [72] Men, says Professor Smith,

who find the justification of compromise in furthering the process of compromise and who find the justification of ideals in what ideality is surplus to action, rather than in what is realized through action, such citizens are our safest custodians of the civilization already achieved and are the harbingers of what further perfectibility may be in store for mankind. They are the truest children of Jefferson, for such citizens, and apparently they alone, can

---

[68] While *On Liberty* has been widely reprinted, *On Compromise* has been printed in several editions only and is not as readily available. See note 11, *supra*.

[69] T. V. Smith, "Thomas Jefferson and the Perfectibility of Mankind," *Ethics*, LIII (1943), 293.

[70] Quoted by Smith, *ibid.*, p. 298.   [71] *Ibid.*, p 302.   [72] *Ibid.*, p. 309.

face full-bodied ideality without fanaticism and can survive the mediocrity of practice without cynicism.[73]

Certainly Morley was such a citizen, and one of "the truest children of Jefferson." [74]

---

[73] *Ibid.*, p. 310.

[74] For an interesting comparison between Jefferson and Danton, see Morley's essay on Robespierre, *Critical Misc.*, I (1886), 71.

The Vital Disequilibrium in
Croce's Historicism *

KATHARINE GILBERT

I N HIS RECENT VOLUME *Il ritorno alla ragione* [1] Guido de Ruggiero appraises the "Crocean phase" of philosophy interpreted as history. The judgments expressed in the book are partly a development and critical re-examination of those in the earlier *Storia del liberalismo europeo* and partly the outgrowth of the author's active participation in the political crises in Italy in the last few years. To the double derivation of the book corresponds a twofold judgment on Croce. De Ruggiero gives Croce first place among the scholar-liberals who remained true to the principle of freedom during the Fascist regime. "If among us Italians," he says,

only a fraction of the cultured capitulated to the enemy, while the majority kept intact the values of the Western tradition (in contrast to what happened in Germany) the largest share of the credit goes to Croce. He knew how to keep alive the flame of that tradition with his unremitting philosophical, literary, and historical labors and by a keen watch on the enemy's distortions and misrepresentations damaging to that culture. [2]

De Ruggiero goes on to praise Croce's severe repudiation of his former friend, Gentile. Croce saw focused in that one man, he says, the danger threatening a whole generation of lovers of learning. [3] Then after touch-

---

* During the writing of this paper I have had the privilege of consulting Professor Napoleone Orsini, friend and editor of Croce.

[1] Laterza, 1946.

[2] *Op. cit.*, p. 12.

[3] *La critica*, November 1947, prints Croce's diary written on the day that Gentile was murdered. It records the deep grief of a friend as well as a political estrangement.

ing on Croce's championship of good taste in the midst of rhetoric, sophistry, and occultism, and his infusion of life into moral discussion, the author concludes by saying summarily that the valor of Croce's example and his fortifying of faith in the gray days of servitude are too recent and well known to need recounting.[4]

But the other part of De Ruggiero's judgment on Croce moves in the opposite direction. The participant in Italy's crises praises Croce's personal attitude and perseverance as giving courage and hope to members of the Underground and Action Party. But the reflective writer deplores the trend of Croce's theory, calculated, he feels, rather to breed pessimism and nostalgia than to sustain the hope and courage his example furnished. The particular point of the objection is that Croce's historicism leaves no room for the justification of a genuine moral act. It is too retrospective. Its content is precedents and probabilities, whereas a moral agent must be able to reject what has been and what is likely to be, in order to affirm and invent a better future. Historicism is like the settled and static bed of a river, container of diverse currents, but unable to favor or further any one of them. As historicism furnishes no spring for a better future, so it fails to establish ideals and norms. The lack of transcendent values in Croce's philosophy, we are told, means the absence of the vital disequilibrium between experience lived through and the will to good. "Croce's historicism lacks the notion of a distinction between spiritual planes, the real and the ideal, which alone can give life to a fertile dialectic and create a passage from history accomplished to history yet to be." [5]

To the charge that his historicism drives out morals, Croce has made a variety of replies. Far from preventing moral action, he rejoins, historical reflection gives the moral agent wisdom. It frees his mind from the confusions of passion and thus enables him to aim straight at the mark. As the rational order of a well-designed tragedy subjects the easily disturbed soul of the spectator to a beneficial catharsis, so following the solution of the problems of men of former times clears out the obstructions of doubt and perplexity in one required to act in the present.[6] Any philosophy must allow that the moral agent, set for

---

[4] *Il ritorno alla ragione*, pp. 12, 13.
[5] *Ibid.*, p. 14.
[6] *La storia come pensiero e come azione* (1943), p. 31.

choice, is rooted in the past and much bound by the surrounding culture. For Croce's philosophy, the facing of that conditioning past and present with will and power to understand frees a man from them. Record becomes converted into counsel. When the collection of historical material has been domesticated and judged, the import of the facts in relation to human welfare shines out; chronology has become history; history, philosophical wisdom. Its role as ideal premise for a new life appears.

This rejoinder does not seem to De Ruggiero to meet the objection. No explanation of the creative act with moral intent is given in it. All that Croce has done is show how, granted the moral act, study of the past may make it more intelligent. His historiography paralyzes history, says De Ruggiero,[7] meaning by the first the intellectual reworking of the records, and by the second the succession of events due to emerge after the labor. Only the personal attitude of Croce, fusing with his theory, saves the Crocean philosophical product from sterility. For Crocean historicism, even when tied with action as its ideal premise, merely brings thought up to the point before decision, and then stops. No provision is made for free will. De Ruggiero, for his part, believes that moral action issues from an order of reality distinct from history. Continuity such as Croce teaches, making the new blossom out of the old through the virtue of critical thought, seems to him an academic formula incapable of illuminating human behavior.

Because the new process is grafted on to the preceding one, there has to be a cut between the one and the other as in all grafting. The concrete man, set in the middle to mediate that passage [from the one to the other], must occupy a post above history, on that ideal summit of which Nietzsche used to speak where humanity's supreme values are concentrated, and whence man judges the past and the inadequacy of what is before him to what ought to be, and draws from the vital disequilibrium between the real and the ideal the impulse to set himself new tasks and to get ready a new action. Continuity between what has been done and is to be done only reëstablishes itself, or better, is conquered, at the price of this fracture by means of which the dialectic of the spiritual life is stirred to life. Croce has wished to ignore this fact. He has wished to deny that meta-historical summit on which perennial philosophy has concentrated its gaze. By so doing he has demonstrated that he prefers to a beacon which from its lofty position illuminates all life, a portable lantern which lights up the road of historical research.[8]

---

[7] *Op. cit.*, p. 19.
[8] *Ibid.*

The sharp divergence between these two philosophers is the more instructive in that they share the idealistic bent and professional concern with the history of the growth of liberalism in modern Europe while differing on the necessary presuppositions of the moral life. De Ruggiero insists that without an element of philosophical transcendence the moral act can never occur. Man must inject into history "the leaven of those values that surpass history." Croce, on the other hand, claims that transcendence makes talk of human good and evil proceed in a vacuum. In a spirited final appendix to his autobiography (May 1945) addressed *"Agli amici che cercano il 'trascendente'"* Croce asks how he can return to or possibly encourage a return to the deluding dreams of a realm outside time. He has not only made the trial of belief in two transcendents, a supernatural Heaven and a Communistic State, but has thought through by a strenuous effort of reflection all their "recesses and meanderings," and has finally dismissed as empty them and their kind.[9] The terms descriptive of moral life require the contrast of evil and good and the notion of struggle, and these in their turn require the historical process. Those who rest their hope for morality in a "transcendent" Croce compares to the Jesuit poet Hopkins when he wrote:

> . . . I have asked to be
> Where no storms come,
> Where the green swell is in the havens dumb,
> And out of the swing of the sea.

The true Utopia, the true place of soul's desiring, Plato's Ideal Republic, says Croce quoting Vico, is history.

But Croce attributes to his critics another invalid standard of moral judgment. Remembering Ruskin, one might call this other false criterion the anachronistic pathetic fallacy. Persons and actions of past centuries are turned into symbols of what someone loves or hates today. Thus for historical judgments are substituted mere affective expressions.[10] These affective expressions are outside history, like transcendent ideals. But in this case the evaluation rests on nothing more substantial than the speaker's feeling, reflecting passively the currents of emotion and prejudice around him. Persons unfamiliar with the actual occur-

---

[9] *Contributo alla critica di me stesso* (Laterza, 1945), pp. 83, 84.
[10] *La storia come pensiero e come azione,* p. 35.

rences and cultural postulates of the time of Caesar or Napoleon denounce them as tyrants, fusing those names with the figures of living hated men of action. These natural emotional attitudes, using the common material of ancient story and current conflict, however much they reflect credit on men's good hearts, are not valid judgments. Valid judgments must always be purified by the discipline of reflective study of history.

If, then, Croce rejects a morality based either on the mythology of religion or of rationalism, or again on sentiment lacking the catharsis of historical perspective, he is bound to demonstrate the possibility of a "vital disequilibrium" between the moral and the nonmoral within the historical process as he understands it. How men like ourselves, wholly contained within moving history, can decide present moral issues has to be clarified. Only so can his philosophy do justice to the main facts of human experience.

Now Croce unquestionably distinguishes spiritual planes and assigns to moral action a specific character. The difference between the economic or vital level of action and the moral is labored from his early *Philosophy of Practice* to his postwar essays. Certain descriptive terms are favored in the earlier works; others later; the marks overlap; but on the whole they converge toward a single general sense. De Ruggiero may be objecting, then, to ambiguity or inconsistency in Croce's use of terms, or in his nullification of a categorial distinction in its historical application. It is important, however, before examining further De Ruggiero's charge to know what Croce claims the moral to be. The characters of the moral for Croce may be listed as follows: (1) in the moral act, the agent wills the universal; (2) promotes liberty; (3) creates life; (4) and exercises a unique vocation; (5) the good is always relative, and opposed to an evil, historically determinate.

The moral function, as universal, stands in immediate relation to the economic, which for Croce is always aimed at the particular good of a particular person. Man must first live before he can live well, Croce says, repeating Aristotle. Pressed by the want of food, shelter, and mate, the individual acts in the interest of survival and comfort. When he transcends this immediate and concrete orientation, guiding now his action and reorganizing his personal desires in the light of the happiness of all, he enters the moral sphere. The *entrepreneur* becomes

210

a philanthropist; the laborer, a champion of the universal rights of man and of the general dignity of work.

But the elementary logical distinction between the particular and the general does not at all cover the full import of the term "universal" as applied to moral action by Croce. This is not saying that Croce's deeper import is easy to come by. The commentaries on and amplifications of such broad assertions as: "The ethical form is . . . volition of the *universal*" [11] and "This faith, this impulse, this enthusiasm, that characterizes those epochs that are highly historical, what is it if not a working faith in the ethical universal . . . ?" [12] are often bafflingly vague. For example:

What is the universal? Why it is the Mind. It is Reality insofar as this is truly real as unity of thought and will. It is Life understood in its depth as that unity itself. It is Liberty, if a reality so conceived is perpetual development, creation, progress. Apart from the Mind, nothing is thinkable under a truly universal form. . . . And the moral man, in willing the universal, or that which transcends him insofar as he is individual, turns himself toward Mind, the real Reality, true Life, Liberty. [13]

But if such ranging phrases as "real Reality" and "Life in its depth" seem to obscure rather than clarify the meaning of morality as universal, Croce makes it plain that the sweep of his terms he deems required for the precise rendering of his intention. Moreover he notes that a reader who cannot infuse abundance of meaning into the wide terms from previous study cannot hope to find them meaningful, when thus held aloft in abstraction. Because what makes a volition moral is never a particular motive or achievement, the nature of the moral universal can only finally be grasped by reliving in thought its slow working in philosophy and history. Croce says virtually this: To the question, What is the universal? the answer must be that it has been our constant theme throughout the philosophy of Mind. It operates not only in the practical world but in everything the mind does. One who has not understood its meaning yet will never understand it. We must not expect to understand the branch of a tree without understanding the central position and use of the trunk. The universal, says Croce, is no *deus ex machina* to be hastily introduced as a solution at a final move-

---

[11] *Filosofia della pratica* (5th ed., 1945), p. 291.
[12] *Etica e politica* (1945), p. 282.
[13] *Filosofia della pratica*, p. 292.

211

ment of philosophy but "the force that has animated it from the first to the last scene." [14]

Here, in spite of further vagueness and a proud refusal to stop for detailed elucidation, is a clue to the meaning of moral universality in Croce. It is the methodological principle of his philosophy, i.e., dialectical history. Now since philosophy is for him history made intelligible by reflection, it follows that one may search in Croce's rendering of historical characters and events for the explicit operation of the method. Though universality is not confined to any one place or time, being the way of the whole, certain men, acts, and times do, in fact, illustrate the method of the whole more vividly than others. Two examples will help: Mazzini and Galeazzo Caracciolo: "whole men," peculiarly representing the spirit of "universality" in moral history.

In conformity with his professional thoroughness as a historian, Croce pictures Mazzini within the frame of the events in Europe between 1830 and 1847: Belgium's liberation from Holland, English electoral reforms, progress toward more liberal constitutions in Portugal and Switzerland; on the other hand, Austria's suppression of attempts at freedom in Italian cities, Russia's dismemberment of Poland, and in general the moves and countermoves of kings and insurgents in the web of the liberal movement in Europe at that period. Croce sees most of the events and men as possessing limited relevance, i.e., as bound to a faction or interest and as standing for a code, measure, or side. Mazzini, on the other hand, he sees otherwise. Croce sets him in relief against the particular conflicts and attachments, as the meeting point of all the patriots in Europe, as one perceiving what is possible to a "will that really wills," rising above factions, strokes of fortune, and calculations, and becoming a creative force. Croce says of Mazzini, using the word that shows its relevance here, that he saw the need of awakening in man "the sentiment of the universal." The context is:

Mazzini saw that there is something more fundamental than the politics manipulated by statesmen, something that must be done when the other cannot be done, and before the other is done; that is, to awaken in man the sentiment of that universal, the ideal, and with it the consciousness of the mission that is assigned to each one, and of the duty that is derived from it, and of the dedication of one's entire self to this duty which potentiates forces and renders possible what to men of little faith seems impossible. [15]

---

[14] *Ibid.*

[15] *History of Europe in the Nineteenth Century,* tr. by Furst (1933), p. 116.

This greatness of Mazzini, Croce goes on to say, is moral greatness, not acute reading of events nor intellectual ability. But why call this dominant trait of Mazzini's temperament, "universality"? That it contained the moral virtues of faith, courage, unselfishness, and persistence is obvious. But the reasons for using the term "universal" are less clear. Two may be found: (1) Though as a strong and independent person Mazzini leaped out of and ahead of the common level of political behavior, he was even so united to, and a spear-head of, a historical continuum, a "universal" line of connection, viz., the gathering human momentum for freedom in Europe at that date, what Croce calls in a striking phrase "the new conscience of the peoples." [16] The empirical conflicts of kings and popular groups, of nation against nation, could be read as interplay on the surface of events; the new element of will to freedom has to be underread or overread. But it is there and at work, a persisting force. (2) Mazzini's personal resolution. His exemplification of the will to freedom had a steadiness not explicable in terms of outer happenings or calculable probabilities. A ground bass in Mazzini's character, holding his acts and words to one end, a source of behavior lying deeper than biological adaptation or rational computation, in fact, his peculiar vocation, fused with a superindividual power in the history of mankind that makes for freedom. In the uninterpreted political context Mazzini's ways look highly individualistic. They seem the result of personal bravery flouting dominions and powers and the counsels of prudence. But actually he was more integrated with the forces that control events than the majority of the realistic participants in the conflicts of the day, e.g., Metternich or Louis Napoleon. In Croce's language, he joined the "Reality" that is "Creative Mind." Because he did this with "inflexible resoluteness," "trying and retrying and never giving up, rebelling, accepting eventual or even certain defeat and rebelling once more, with the generosity of sacrifice in the certain consciousness of final victory," [17] he not only joined the universality of Mind but became a determinate member of it.

Through this reference to Mazzini we have been trying to elucidate Croce's conception of the moral plane as volition of the universal. Our interpretation may be summarized thus: Universality as a mark of "the moral" means complete commitment and peculiar contribution to the

[16] *Ibid.*, p. 110.
[17] *Ibid.*, p. 115.

ideal of liberty, which is the major force at work in the history of peoples. Croce's treatment of the Neapolitan Calvinist, Galeazzo Caracciolo,[18] is concerned with another period and other conflicts. But it may serve to supplement and at the same time confirm the inferences drawn from the account of Mazzini. Of Caracciolo, Croce says, not that he was fitted to awaken "the sentiment of the universal," but that he was "what is called a whole man." In the concrete, Caracciolo's moral universality appears as the constancy of a rich and powerful young man of the world to an austere religious ideal. The strong social forces pushing Caracciolo's moral decisions and habit away from the ideal were the Catholic and Imperial sympathies of an affectionate father and wife, their repeated solicitations to remain in the prosperous and pious tradition of the family and kingdom, the rising threats of persecution from the Jesuits and the ever more diligent Popes, and the loss of money, position, family, friends, and country entailed by the new allegiance to Calvinism. Caracciolo's constancy or wholeness, his moral universality, is likened by Croce to a soldier's loyalty.

He bore himself toward the faith with the same loyalty, directness, and intrepid courage as a cavalier and a soldier toward his true military duty. This moral character of his, rather than doctrine or reasoning, made it evident to him that the principle accepted in the teaching of the Waldenses, i.e., justification by faith, permitted no compromise with the Church of Rome, and that it was not a question merely of abolishing abuses and reforming customs, but of denying and repudiating the Church in its very essence. What does justification by faith mean in substance, translated into modern philosophical terms, and freed from its mythological wrappings? No more nor less than the exclusive authority of the moral conscience, this interior voice that has absolute value, commands, does not stoop to bargaining, and itself alone approves and disapproves, alone redeems, alone makes strong.[19]

Caracciolo's religious constancy in the face of temptation, suffering, and persecution immediately strikes the attuned reader as parallel to Mazzini's inflexible resoluteness, his "trying and retrying and never giving up," his disposition of will drawing its power from profound levels of consciousness. But the parallel to the second element in moral universality is less evident. Is the ideal of liberty that called Mazzini the same as the ideal of Calvinism? For the reader who has not undergone the catharsis of historical discipline, the two ideals would seem dissimilar.

---

[18] *Vite di avventure di fede e di passione* (1936), pp. 181–281.
[19] *Ibid.*, pp. 195–196.

But Croce, precisely because he has immersed himself in the thoughts of the men of both times and knows the rational language of both epochs, sees a single moral universal operating amid the diverse conditions. He admits the harsh censorship and severe penalties inflicted by Calvin, a harshness and heaviness perhaps even worse than that of Rome because more fanatical and more modeled on the dark-hued enthusiasm of the Old Testament prophets. But Croce goes on to claim a difference between Romanism and Calvinism lying deeper than the analogous spirit of persecution and intolerance. Rome looked backward. It opposed change and progress, prevented free thought, and made a favorable soil for compromise and servility. Calvinism nourished a new moral attitude. Its rigors steeled men's tempers and made them resourceful and industrious. One's work was interpreted as one's divine vocation; success in it, a sign of grace. Calvinism's encouragement of initiative and hard work, Croce claims, even had something to do with the spread of new thought and independence in the modern world—Holland's and England's fight for freedom, the colonization of America and the later history of the United States—and it "finally lent a hand to the modern ethics of Kant." [20] Thus does the molding hand of Croce bring together the religious ideal of Calvin and the general ideal of liberty, which is the major force in the history of peoples.

There should have been coming to light in the tracing of these two cases what some of Croce's vague attributes for the moral plane mean. First one perceives Mazzini as a genuine historical figure embracing without reservation the desperate cause of liberty in Italy in 1830. Then Mazzini's acts and words melt into a larger landscape, philosophical and perennial in nature, where Italy's freedom becomes continuous with Europe's, with humanity's, and with the Life and Spirit that works through men for men's elevation and enlargement. Caracciolo starts out as a rich man's favorite son in the stirring Neapolitan kingdom of 1550; becomes the devoted adherent of a new religious faith; the faith becomes the free conscience, then the free thought, of modern Europe, then widens into the source of energy for the increase in the liberty of institutions and peoples in the new world, and finally identifies itself with the affirmation of the infinite value of human spirit. All this expansion followed our effort to demonstrate moral "universality." But

---

[20] *Ibid.*, pp. 210–211.

more has resulted. The explanation of the meaning of "universality" has involved in its course the explanation of other terms and phrases listed at the beginning of our analysis of Croce's conception of the moral challenge by De Ruggiero, viz., promotion of liberty, of life, and exercising a vocation. And this is as it should be; because for Croce moral ideas interpenetrate. A just exposition of any of the major ethical notions should carry one into an understanding of the whole moral world, its universal nature. The word "liberty" for him is the prerogative name for the good. But attention to his explanations of the meaning of "creation of life" will bring us out at approximately the same place.

Insofar as the idea of creation of life is not left deliberately vague by Croce to cover all that one could wish to mean by that expression, it means making conditions favorable for doing one's special work,[21] that is, helping on the fulfillment of a life-long call of conscience, putting into practice one's vocation. You create life when you give a plant root room, air, and sun and pull out the encroaching weeds. The moral obligation to create life is met among human beings when a boy with an aptitude for handicraft is supplied with tools and training and freed from interfering hardships or inappropriate dictation. One may use this moral criterion in respect to one's own task and aptitude. In this case conditions favorable to life are created when one limits oneself to the requirements of one's special capacity and avoids forcing it into alien channels. For example, the poet must not preach, the farmer must not muddy the waters of politics. To know one's function and its duties—that is the moral law in respect to creation of life. Immediately it becomes clear that the notion of the creation of life interacts with that of exercising a vocation and with that of opposing evil, two other marks of the moral for Croce. Evil is the injury to special activity through unclear conception or rampant enthusiasm. One gives both oneself and others living and working conditions by remaining in bounds.

As the idea of moral "universality" only took on the special color intended by Croce when the moral agent's volition was seen to spring from a deep and steady sense of vocation and when such resolute work contributed to human liberty and spiritual enrichment, so the idea of the creation of life can only shed its biological connotation and belong

---

[21] *La storia*, pp. 42–46.

to ethics when a similar deepening and widening takes place. This can be seen by reference to our two illustrations. Mazzini belongs to the class of the morally great, according to Croce, when and insofar as he acted as an apostle of liberty, stirring up men's love of country and of independence, setting an example of devotion, and founding "Young Italy," an organization which nursed "the religious sources of virile and combative character." [22] But Mazzini killed life, i.e., operated against his moral vocation when he added to his work as practical leader that of a doctrinaire committed to Saint-Simonism. He could not think well, Croce says, and he compromised his contribution to human liberty by espousing and propagating an ideology. He functioned pathologically and compromised the ideal of life and liberty when he set his program in the inept frame of a democratic Utopian theory.[23]

The case of Caracciolo conforms more exactly to the moral ideal of the promotion of life. Caracciolo's native endowment was not intellectual and he did not try to be a philosopher. His bent was practical, and in elevating and consecrating the particular good of his endeavor in Geneva to the moral and religious level of universality, he did not blur the limits of his place and powers. He promoted the life of free conscience by standing rocklike in his faith, by assiduous devotion to works of mercy, and by helping converts arriving from foreign countries to adjust themselves to the new community.

So far in this study we have been preparing to test the validity of De Ruggiero's charge that Croce fails to make the moral plane of experience distinct by examining the various marks Croce assigns to the moral and by watching these function in his historical judgments. Are we now prepared to say that De Ruggiero is wrong? Have we been able to show Croce providing a theoretical basis for the required "vital disequilibrium" between the real and the ideal?

We must repeat, with new right and emphasis, the assertion and surmise we stated at the beginning of the analysis. Croce unquestionably distinguishes spiritual planes and assigns to moral action a specific character both in his doctrine of categories and in his historical judgments. But, even so, De Ruggiero may have reason in his dissatisfaction.

[22] *History of Europe,* p. 116.
[23] *Ibid.,* pp. 117–118.

If Croce defines and applies an ethic such as we have outlined, what does De Ruggiero require that he does not receive at Croce's hands? He requires a theoretical basis for the function of moral decision in action. He demands a philosophical demonstration, which is different from historical accounts and definitions, of the operating moral crisis. Coming closer to Croce's terminology, we may say that the critic doubts the ability of history past to bring into being, i.e., to deliver, a new history, in the strictly moral sense. De Ruggiero diagnoses Croce's deficiency as caused by the lack of a transcendent element. The moral will not only moves toward human betterment, for De Ruggiero, when activated by power in disequilibrium with normal mentality; there must be space between the mover and the moved. We have tried to show that this cannot be the correct diagnosis of the alleged deficiency. For in an intelligible sense Croce's system contains a transcendent. He provides an operative ideal, and a commitment to it, that issues in persistent modes of action. Croce's ideal of moral universality is, indeed, sometimes almost unmanageably sublime. Although in theory Croce insists on the immanence of all values, in practice he gives their pure essence religious finality. The religion of liberty, he says, sums up and goes beyond all the institutionalized and dogmatic religions that man has known. Beyond these, it gives purity, depth, and power to the best that these postulate.[24] We have noted that when Croce has defined the moral plane in general terms, he tends to invoke in the discussion Mind, Reality, Life, terms which thus written with capital letters proclaim their Heavenly Habitation. We turn then to the alternative suggestion made at the beginning of the paper concerning the possible justice of De Ruggiero's objections. Is the alleged failure of Croce due to "ambiguity or inconsistency in Croce's use of terms or in his nullification of a categorial distinction in its historical application"? [25] In this flickering of points of view and application of terms, this wavering of method and failure to think with vigorous consistency when passing from theory to practice, a doubleness reflected even in a literary style that sometimes brings opposites disconcertingly together, we may find the source of the difficulty.

There is indeed at first reading a confusing fluidity of movement from

---

[24] *History of Europe*, p. 19.
[25] Page 210.

218

historical description to judgment on history, from history to logical category and back again, from linear order, by virtue of which the categories are resolved from individual to universal and from the theoretical to the practical, to the circular or cyclical order by means of which all the categories recur at different levels and operate as complements only. If De Ruggiero could accept a formula from a dubious but apt source, he might repeat Callicles' impatient complaint to Socrates in the *Gorgias*: "O Socrates, you are . . . running riot in the argument. . . . You, in your ingenuity perceiving the advantage to be thereby gained, slyly ask of him who is arguing conventionally a question which is to be determined by the rule of nature; and if he is talking of the rule of nature, you slip away to custom." Croce is an agile and fertile writer and before one knows it, he has apparently passed from the intrinsic morality of category to the quite different *mores* of a historical period; and from the call of conscience absolute to the call of opportunity and possibility temporal. Conscience in certain contexts compromises with Time's forelock. He treats voluntary action both as product of fate and maker of fate; both as historical configuration and shaper of a time. Moral obligation becomes in his quick hands now accommodation to the factual situation for the sake of realization of a good end; now defiance of the trend of the times to the point of martyrdom. Dialectic, the law of historical movement, seems now to be propelled by the faith of good men, ensuring moral progress; now to be the swinging pendulum of events with values lost.

We turn to illustration. Our hypothesis will be that basically and increasingly Croce means by history (the core of his theory, and the crux of the problem) the process of the creative activity of minds as grasped in their attendant circumstances; and further that the important moments of history are human energies in action, determined by the utter commitment of able men to the cause of freedom. The constancy of Caracciolo to Calvinistic Protestantism in Geneva in the sixteenth century, already reviewed, would be part of such an important moment. But in the context of his story there is a significant defense of the Calvinistic doctrine of predestination, which seems at once to assert and deny free individual moral action. Croce says:

Here exists in germ a great thought, which is neither more nor less than the concept of history as such which in its course condemns and destroys indi-

219

viduals and generations and peoples, and from the hecatombs makes rise—thanks to great men or the elect—the ideal values of thought, beauty and moral dignity which live eternal. [History] therefore does not unfold for the salvation or happiness of individuals, but precisely as Calvin meant, for the greater glory of God.[26]

Croce notes the "fierce archaism" of this Calvinistic doctrine and its unsympathetic direction for the modern mind. The mythology of election through the arbitrary will of a transcendent God has to be stripped off. But its austere truth remains a part of modern philosophy, Croce insists; i.e., the principle of free competition or enterprise and the victory of the better by a superindividual law. Liberalism, which is the true political philosophy, is aristocratic. Like Calvinistic predestination it is hostile to the leveling egalitarianism brought in by the Enlightenment.

There is a tendency here for the meaning of history, as given in the hypothesis, to fly off from its peculiar moral intention. The virtue furnishing the key of such history was freedom. Of course liberty is notoriously difficult to define. But there is a distinction between moral liberty, and indeed all the freedoms which it is a moral obligation to promote, and, on the other hand, free competition in general—a distinction which Croce himself at times emphasizes. This difference it is possible to assert, however hard it may be to draw a precise line in the concrete case. Croce wrestles with the wide scope of the term in the beginning of his *History of Europe in the Nineteenth Century.* He runs through a dozen or more specifications: opposition to foreign rule, feudal privilege, ecclesiastical oppression. It may refer to juridical guarantees, the right of free association or speech or press, the reform of the franchise, economic or political equality, or the concept of strong personality and self-realization brought in by the Renaissance. After his comprehensive enumeration, Croce concludes thus:

Any qualification [of the word liberty] would cloud the concept. And those cold and superficial observers were wrong who wondered at it or made it a jest and, accusing the concept of empty formalism, asked in irony or sarcasm: What is liberty anyway? Liberty of whom or of what? Liberty to do what? Liberty could not accept adjectives or empiric delimitations because of its intrinsic infinity.[27]

---

[26] *Vite di avventure,* p. 212.
[27] *History of Europe,* p. 12.

In watching closely the Crocean argument concerning the nature of liberty, that liberty which gives sense to history and specific quality to the good, and which delivers the moral act, the reader's mind is divided. Certainly most of the definite content laid into the frame of the concept of liberty by Croce has to do with the enabling of man in his unremitting pursuit of the higher values. But the nonacceptance of adjectives or empiric delimitations because of intrinsic infinity opens the door to dangerous company. Croce makes the Renaissance add to the concept of liberty not only a new sense of the individual in respect to his political and religious rights but, for example, the philosophy of technical discoveries and the formation of the modern idea of industry. This leads us directly to a dyad, or possibly a triad, difficult to resolve.

Croce teaches the doctrine of two histories: economic and ethico-political, autonomous with respect to each other and yet synthesized by "dialectic." The idea central in economic history is technical competence within a limited context. The executive force of the prince in peace and war, the production of food in agriculture, the financial prosperity of a business, the skill of medicine in healing, of architecture in building, and of all types of engineering in furnishing material utilities at a minimum of expenditure of energy, are the typical values and standards.

This "order of facts," this relatively autonomous economic history, exalts the neutral fact of achievement. A surgical operation requiring to be performed, nothing is relevant but a surgeon's skill. His honesty belongs to another "order of facts" which—everybody knows—we must not introduce at the door of the operating room. Again, "business is business." Croce says that a businessman who mingles justice with his industrial enterprise will not only ruin his enterprise but injure society.[28] The crucial instance for Croce's separate order of economic-political history is that of the ruler. Praising Machiavelli for the important intellectual discovery of the independence of state-good from moral-good, Croce sets out its implications. "Political honesty is nothing but political capacity."[29] States are, so to speak, natural forces, necessary for the ongoing of history. They have no honor to be saved or to

---

[28] *The Conduct of Life,* tr. by Livingston, p. 259.
[29] *Ibid.,* p. 251.

be lost. They have only vital interests to be preserved in the best way possible. Well-meaning but foggy-minded persons criticize statesmen for devoting all their energies to the maintenance and strengthening of their countries. The "bald truth" is, Croce says again, that states are huge and magnificent animals, whose "chief desire is to endure" and whose virtue is to save their skins and develop their force.[30] Croce, writing about 1920, applies the Machiavellian principle to World War I. He describes the changing attitudes of the belligerents: cringing, flattering, bullying, boasting, decoying, according to their changing fortunes in the struggle. And then he says: "The Germans made a great mistake, but it was a mistake of political method not of political theory." They thought straighter than others and tied their action to their theory more courageously. But they failed in the instinct of secrecy which is necessary for political success.[31]

But having grasped history in this economic and realistic sense, we are immediately asked to reconcile with it a second order of facts constituting moral or ethicopolitical history. Applied to the state, this new way of viewing history makes the State the true Church, with men's souls as well as bodies in its keeping. This autonomous moral State must deny any political rights to separate ecclesiastical organizations. The education of the citizens, in the arts and philosophy as well as in sports and technics, is an essential part of its function. All the moral well-being of the members of the body politic can be delegated to no one or nothing isolated from federal authority, this also being the business of "the state."

Croce himself is aware that the two definitions of the state—a politician's speciality with the state a force, and a philosopher-king's duty with the state a nursery of humane life—are not easily reconciled. The key to the difficulty is historical dialectic, he says. But this key, also, is hard to use.

To be sure, the principle of dialectic which keeps the world in motion through the clash of opposite tendencies seems made to reconcile such uncongenial orders of facts. The dialectic of practice is the war of good with evil, the conquest of the exclusively economic demand by the high moral will. But on Croce's own showing, the dialectical warfare

---

[30] *Ibid.*, pp. 266–267.
[31] *Ibid.*, p. 260.

does not so much resolve the conflict, as intensify the distinction of kinds of function. When Croce actually brings the moral dialectic, the war of good against evil, on the stage, one sees not two champions, but a general principle of order, operating at all points in history and life, doing precisely one thing: keeping every cobbler at his own last! There is no moral intention, he says, that can be added as a distinct kind to others; its "kind" is to underline distinctions. For every particular pursuit carries its point by a single-minded drive. The thing to be done presents itself as all that has value, as the beloved becomes the whole world to the lover. It follows that in the impulse toward the accomplishment of a legitimate and proper end, there is often an overshooting of the mark; the individual effort spreads exuberantly toward an interest that excludes all others and fills the whole field. Then arises the need for moral action, i.e., the ordering and restraining of particular activities to their proper place and limits. Moral activity prevents encroachment. Croce remarks that by a profound human instinct every individual sees the violation of his special obligation not only—if he is an artist—as the ugly or—if he is a scientist—as falsehood; but also as moral violation, as his particular kind of evil-doing.[32] Goodness becomes the decorum of the *métier*. The upshot is that the synthesizing dialectic actually precipitates us down again from the moral plane to the economic plane, but with the addition of feeling the special work to be done as a holy vocation. The poet is to write poetry, and not oratory; but he is to do it with the earnestness of a priest.

The same ambiguity obstructs a clear comprehension of the operation of the dialectic in the movement of history, as in the reconciliation of planes. The dialectic prescribes progress through conquest of old barbarisms and insensitiveness by new humanity and insight. But it equally prescribes the distinctness of historical periods: "Let every age keep to its own moral last!" One wonders whether the great dialectic really does confer any supervening moral power on the philosophical historicist after all. We have already noted how Croce defends the persecutions and obscurantism of Calvin as right in his period—the religious decorum of 1550. Another illustration may be given. Reviewing *La libertà di coscienza e di scienza* by Luzzatti in 1909, Croce charges the author with historical irrelevance and the anachronistic pathetic

---

[32] *La storia*, pp. 44–45.

fallacy for cutting across the peculiar temper of times, places, and conditions to lift for absolute praise instances of conspicuous religious toleration, such as that of Roger Williams in Rhode Island or Spinoza in the seventeenth century, and for absolute blame the procedures of the Holy Office in the Inquisition. In this way, he says, poetry and not history, is made. He continues:

Which was right: Diocletian or the Christians? Innocent III or the Albigensians? Gustavus Adolphus or Wallenstein? the Catholics or the Protestants? Bruno or his executioners? Neither the one nor the other; and both the one and the other, if it is true that later historical reflection both denies and includes them all. And each strove as it was able to and was under obligation to.[33]

If history condones all by the very principle of its historicity, then a morally colorless historical continuum covers with gray the succession of constellations of events. And, even though it is contrary to Croce's best thought, the notion of a fate ruling all suggests itself. Indeed, from time to time Croce, taken with this phase of his thinking, does write as if the course of events were determined by a Logic of Events, Necessity, or unconcerned Deity that carries men blindly along, unaffected by their hopes and aspirations. "Fate drew them on with its super-individual force," he says of those thoughtful men before 1914 who ineffectually raised their voices against swollen rhetoric and imperialistic programs. "Fate drew them on. . . . The wind was blowing in that direction." [34] It adds to the confusion, rather than rectifies the amoral naturalism, when Croce occasionally makes this blind Fate God. Who caused World War I? he asks. All the nations constructed syllogisms to prove that the responsibility lay on other nations; individuals did the same. But the author of the world was really responsible, Croce says, "because he and no one else arranged that European life, after passing through so many trials and experiences, should still pass through this." [35] Croce asks again: Who carries out social programs? And his answer is the same, God. We are attracted by the good-will in schemes for increasing or reducing the population, for free trade or protection, unionism, communism. But these things are not for us. "It is His task and not

[33] *Cultura e vita morale* (1926), pp. 95–99.
[34] *History of Europe*, p. 346.
[35] *Ibid.*, pp. 345–346.

ours: that is to say, it is the task of History which brings things to pass, as it has always brought things to pass. . . ." [36]

We have said that De Ruggiero has reason in his dissatisfaction, not because Croce does not believe in a distinct moral plane, but because he is ambiguous and sometimes nullifies distinctions in the application. The use of the idea of liberty "without adjectives or empiric delimitations" as functionally identical with Fate or a Deity careless of human life seems an apt illustration. However, among the various conflicting and wavering views that Croce in his multifarious writing, and rich and growing thought, furnishes us, there always stands out the view of the concrete historical person, morally constrained, and in vital disequilibrium with states of affairs that are valueless or evil. Moreover, when thinking in this vein, Croce does not have to secure his vital disequilibrium by passing like his friendly critic De Ruggiero "al di là dello storicismo" to a meta-historical vertex.[37] Rather he presses deeper into history itself and the relations of its determinative categories.

We shall end then with an example that shows Croce pondering again the attitudes and fates of nations in the two World Wars. He stresses now a moral principle that overcomes the principle of order which keeps every person and period in its proper sphere. It is precisely the principle which requires a man to subordinate his peculiar trade or vocation to the demands of threatened liberty. Why did Germany fail? and, Why was Germany wrong? he asks in the light of this other principle. Because Luther first, and Bismarck later separated the kingdoms of thought and action. Croce shows how deceitful in its potentialities for Germany was the encouragement given to German professors and scientists in the nineteenth century to live lives wholly devoted to the laboratory or study. Its falseness was its apparent promotion of liberty. Because by an implied contract, the princes left the scholars to their scholarship, on condition that men of ideas should not apply their ideas to what princes might be doing, each class developed in a kind of enfeebling purity. The scholars became pedants, impotent to do or know anything in the surrounding political world. And the politicians became masters of their craft, set to gain political force and that alone, narrow, menacing, and menaced by what was to come. The

---

[36] *Conduct of Life,* tr. by Livingston (1924), p. 287.
[37] *Il ritorno alla ragione,* p. 30.

lack of lively interchange was in truth the death of both forms of activity.

What became the German habit of mind, economic and realistic, was embodied and promoted by Bismarck, man of utility and power. Over against it Croce places the spirit of the epoch in the country of Cavour. Cavour, he says, furnished Piedmont "the independent, uninterrupted, tenacious, and guiding activity of a moral conscience." He assumed command "active and gay" like one who knows what he has to do and is able to do it, ready for the fight, lover of liberty, hater of despots, and scorner of cabals.[38] Croce is fond of saying that history moves from above down,[39] and Cavour and Mazzini and Garibaldi were, he claims, the particular formative influences operating from "above" in their social area, which made the Italian *Risorgimento* a model for emulation by liberals everywhere. The location of their moral freedom was "immanent," i.e., in the mind of living persons; its quality was "transcendent," i.e., complete—passing beyond common expectation. The completeness of this spirit was embodied in Italian thinkers as well as in men of action. "German philosophy had no martyrs, as . . . had the Italian which derives from this its quarterings of nobility." [40]

In the last number of *La critica* (November, 1947) Croce refers once again to the gravity of German renunciation of interest in political liberty, that separation of compartments of duty promoted by Luther by virtue of which individuals restrict themselves to their individual vocations.[41] Freedom possesses an importance which tops all and constrains all. This seems to be Croce's last word, in spite of other directions of his thinking in various passages of his writing. And Croce's historicism is not inconsistent with that last word. History is not research into the past for the past's sake, but equally a vivification of the present and a moving force to intelligent action. Two statements of his about history, the first also from the last number of *La critica*, and the other earlier, but in harmony with his present statements, support our conclusion: "The one and only history—as all intelligent Italians know—is the clarification of present problems, thanks to inquiry into

---

[38] *History of Europe*, pp. 211, 216.

[39] "Considerazioni sul problema morale del tempo nostro," *Quaderni della 'Critica,'* I (1945), 1.

[40] *History of Europe*, p. 77.

[41] Page 75.

and comprehension of the correlative facts of the past"; [42] and: "The moral flame . . . gives [the historian] the light by which to understand events." [43]

---

[42] Page 76.
[43] *Etica e politica* (1945), p. 342.

The Political Typology of
Moeller van den Bruck

ALBERT R. CHANDLER

T HIS STUDY is limited to the political typology of Arthur Moeller
van den Bruck as found in his major work, *Das dritte Reich* ("The
Third Reich").[1]

Political typology is as old as political theory. Plato often speaks of
"the one and the many." His "one" is a generic "Idea" or type; his
"many" is the multiplicity of concrete individuals that imperfectly embody the Idea. In *Philebus* 16 and 18 he refines upon this conception
in two ways. First he speaks of the many individuals as "infinite," not
in the sense of the modern mathematical infinite, but in the sense that
thought can set no limit to their number. Second, he demands that a
definite number of subtypes be interposed between the single generic
type and the infinity of individuals.

Applied to political thought this means: (a) We cannot get anywhere by trying to think of individuals one by one. These are unlimited
in number and therefore not intellectually manageable. (b) We cannot
get far by thinking only of the essence of humanity—which is one of
the "ones" of which he speaks. (c) To get somewhere in our political
thinking we must think of *kinds* of men, that is, we must form and use
a political typology.

I say "typology" rather than "classification" because the former term

---

[1] Dritte Auflage bearbeitet von Hans Schwarz, 26. bis 30. Tausend (Hamburg:
Hanseatische Verlagsanstalt, c1931). Moeller's preface is dated "Berlin, in December, 1922." Schwarz's "Preface to the Third Edition" is dated "Berlin, in November,
1930." Dr. Goebbels' endorsement is on the jacket.

better expresses the mode of thinking of both Plato and Moeller van den Bruck. In classification we think of a multitude of individuals and devise ways of dividing them into classes. For administrative purposes college students are divided into freshmen, sophomores, and other classes. Precise criteria are set up to determine whether any particular student belongs in one pigeonhole or another—so many credit hours, such and such grades, such and such required courses passed. These criteria may be marginal distinctions of slight importance in themselves. The traditional *types* of freshman and sophomore are quite another thing—the inexperienced and gullible but eager freshman, the lordly sophomore, the "wise fool," exaggerating and exploiting the superiority gained by a year's experience. These traits are not marginal but central and socially significant. The types with which Plato and Moeller van den Bruck deal are central and socially significant characters.

Plato, with his usual flexibility, uses different typologies in different dialogues. His most complete and systematic political typology is the one he presents in Books VIII and IX of the *Republic*. The types are (1) the philosopher-king, fit to rule the ideal state; (2) the timocratic man, dominating a militaristic state; (3) the oligarchic man, the man of wealth, dominating a commercial state; (4) the democratic man, full of unbridled impulses, rejoicing in the unbridled liberties of the democratic state; (5) the tyrannical man, the slave of his own worst impulse, enslaving the whole population of the state, He gives a psychology of each type, the pattern in which the personality is organized or disorganized. He gives a sociology of each type, deriving it from its predecessor through the influences of biological variation, education, and experience with the social environment. Each psychological type implies and is implied by the type of state which it tends to produce and in which it flourishes.

Moeller's political typology is more complex and less neatly organized than Plato's. Like Plato's it is correlated with actual or hypothetical forms of the state. Like Plato's it has psychological and sociological aspects. Unlike Plato he includes much historical material in his discussion and focuses his interest upon the problems of a particular country at a particular time—namely Germany in the period following World War I.

The chapter headings of *Das dritte Reich* are as follows: "Revolutionary," "Socialistic," "Liberal," "Democratic," "Proletarian," "Reactionary," "Conservative," "The Third Reich." These headings might lead us to expect that the first seven chapters would define seven political types and that the eighth would define their relation to the Third Reich. In fact, we shall find the situation more complex because of the presence of subtypes and mixed types. For instance, he distinguishes three types of Socialist, and he considers that most of the types he mentions have become tinged with Liberalism.

Like Plato, Moeller deals with the interrelation and interplay of his types. Writing as a German in 1922, he was concerned with the ways in which conflicts among these types had brought Germany into a desperate condition. Even more he was concerned with ways in which some of these types could be modified and blended to secure for Germany a better future.

I shall expound Moeller's typology, adding very few critical remarks. Undoubtedly my readers will be willing and able to provide their own criticisms.

REVOLUTIONARY

Moeller distinguishes three kinds of revolution and therefore three types of Revolutionist. He is of course especially interested in the German overturn of 1918, but he insists this was not a real revolution. He merely calls it a revolution because there is no other convenient term for it. In this broader sense any violent change of government by forces within the nation is a revolution, and those who bring it about are Revolutionists. The overturn of 1918 was not sufficiently German nor sufficiently constructive in its results to be classed as a real revolution. Those who made it did not represent a definite psychological type of Revolutionist. They were half-hearted Socialists, joined by moderates of other parties. They were not temperamentally Revolutionists but ordinary men who happened to have to make a pseudo revolution under pressure from the victors of World War I.

The second type of revolution, a *real* revolution, is one which brings political maturity to a *Volk* ("people"). It gives a people a national organization, a national spirit, the capacity to form and execute national policies. Such a revolution is achieved by a people only once. England

230

and France had their respective revolutions in the seventeenth and eighteenth centuries. Their firm national policies brought them victory in World War I. Germany remained politically immature. Neither the empire of Wilhelm II nor the Weimar Republic was sufficiently nationalistic to preserve the people from the influences of Marxism and "Liberalism" (to be defined later).

To achieve this *real* revolution, which will bring political maturity to the German people, a new generation must arise that will be devoted to the eternal German ideals abandoned by the preceding generation. This new generation must revive the energies of the German people and find the political form in which the German spirit can be adequately embodied. The man of this type is not a Revolutionist by temperament, but a *Conservative* (to be defined later) who may have to make a revolution because conservatism has been abandoned.

A third type of revolution is that desired by extreme radicals. These men are temperamentally Revolutionists—men for whom the past has no value, who wish to wipe it out with sudden violence. They have no idea how to *build* a future, but expect the millennium to arrive automatically when the remnants of the old order are destroyed. Moeller gives little consideration to this type because he thinks the main struggle will be between Conservatism and Liberalism.

SOCIALISTIC

Moeller distinguishes three main types of socialism, with national subdivisions under the second type.

The first type is the Socialism of Marx and pure Marxists. Marx was a materialist. He saw that men had never been persuaded to conform to ideals of social justice—their egoistic desires for material satisfaction had always held them back. He decided to appeal to men at the material level, to interpret all social phenomena in terms of the production of material goods. Although he attacked Utopias in general, he offered a materialistic Utopia, in which men would have their material needs satisfied and would have no more problems except to regulate their digestion. He developed the well-known doctrines of the proletariat, surplus value, internationalism, the class struggle, and the dictatorship of the proletariat as the predictable outcome of the class struggle. The pure Marxist, then, would be the type of man who can be satisfied with such an outlook on life.

The various Socialist parties have modified Marxism in various ways, in practice if not always in words. "Each people has its own Socialism." In Germany the Social Democratic Party has been perverted by Liberalism. It has talked of liberty, equality, fraternity, and also of evolution and adaptation. It has been satisfied to play the parliamentary game and accept small favors in behalf of the working class. It has taken the internationalist doctrine with sufficient seriousness to be victimized by foreign propaganda. It has lacked consistency, intellectual power, and boldness. In England and France the Socialist parties have made similar concessions, but their underlying nationalism has been stronger. In Russia the Bolshevist party in its triumph has been more Russian than Marxian. It has abandoned internationalism and pacifism to build up Russian military power. It has had to compromise with foreign capitalism to obtain needed goods, and to compromise with domestic capitalism in its "New Economic Policy." The dictatorship in the Kremlin is more tsarist than Proletarian. Thus the Socialist party members in various countries are persons of the sort who can be content with Marxian theory, but yield to the pressure of circumstances and of other types of thought in practice.

Moeller's criticisms of these Socialistic types are important because they are made from the point of view which he later defines as "Conservative" and holds up as his ideal.

Marx, being Jewish, could not share the *national* feelings of Europeans nor understand European problems. His intervention in European affairs was therefore doomed to failure. Lacking access to the higher values, which are distinctively national, he concentrated on the material values sought by the Proletariat, which seemed to him an international class.

The Marxian predictions of increasing productivity, increasing concentration of capital, intensified class struggle, and final transfer of power to the Proletariat were refuted by the World War and the economic enslavement of Germany by her foes. The predictions were based on rationalistic calculation, but such calculation is always limited by incalculable factors in human affairs. The state is no mere device of one class to exploit another; there have always been states; history

232

begins with hostility between groups that have banded themselves together to assert themselves (*sich zu behaupten*). Still less is it possible that with all the complexities of modern life men should ever in the future live in a stateless condition. Economic conditions do not produce states, but vice versa. Man is not controlled by circumstance, which control would make the future calculable. Man *makes* circumstances, and the future is incalculable—though a prophet deeply at one with the inner life of a people may make valid prophecies. Man sets up a scale of values, in which material values are the lowest. Marxists err in subordinating the higher values. They err in ignoring races. They err in ignoring the problems of overpopulation that lead to disequilibrium between states. It never occurred to the German Social Democrats *dass es auch einen Kampf der Nationen geben könnte, aus dem das deutsche Volk als das besiegte hervorgehen würde, obwohl es als das Volk eines übervölkernden und besonders arbeitsamen Landes das Recht auf den Sieg besass* ("that there might be a World War from which the German people might emerge the losers, although, *as the people of an overpopulated and especially industrious land, it had the right to victory*"; p. 62). (The italics are mine.)

Moeller considers that these defects and failures discredit pure Marxism and the extant Socialist parties. But he sees the need for a new type of Socialism that shall be national in spirit and solve national problems by national means. In the depressed economic conditions in Germany, the educated classes share the insecurity of the Proletariat and see the need for social solutions. Particularly the problems of overpopulation must be attacked. He speaks of "corporative" organization—not in the sense of American corporations, but as organizations including employers and employees in the same industry, such as Mussolini later set up. He speaks of the growing preference among youth for the *Führergedanke*, the "idea of a Leader." Moeller does not speak specifically of the Nazi party, which was still in its infancy when he was writing in 1922, but the common elements are evident.

The third, and ideal, type of Socialist is then a nationalistic socialist—a man who shares in the aspiration toward a close-knit and powerful national life. The meaning of this ideal will become clearer in the ensuing discussion of "Proletarian" problems and the menace of "Liberalism."

LIBERAL

Moeller found good types of Revolutionists and Socialists as well as bad ones; but for him all Liberalism is bad. What he defines as Liberalism is really the perversion and misuse of Liberal ideas for private gain. Such men as Jefferson, Franklin, Lincoln, Holmes, and Brandeis are beyond his horizon. Liberalism is his great bogey, his chief scapegoat. The motto of his section on it is, *An Liberalismus gehen die Völker zu Grunde* ("Through Liberalism Peoples Perish").

Historically he traces Liberalism back to the Greek Sophists, the skepticism of Rabelais and Montaigne, the rationalism of the seventeenth century, the "Enlightenment" of the eighteenth century, and the Freemasonry of the eighteenth and nineteenth centuries.

Liberalism speaks of liberty, equality, and fraternity, of utility, humanity, and progress. It promotes parliamentary government, the contests and compromises of political parties. But these lofty phrases and impressive institutions are a false front behind which selfish men seek wealth and power. These men are not bound by ideals or principles in their own conduct; they use them as propaganda to control the masses and manipulate national policies. They have national and international affiliations. They use nationalism, internationalism, pacifism, and militarism from time to time as suits their momentary interests. They have no principles, no loyalties that are not subject to compromise, if compromise will gain them financial profit or political influence. The moral unity, the communal loyalty, of each nation is disintegrated by these false slogans and secret intrigues. Political parties and churches are corrupted by them.

The "Liberal" whom Moeller thus indicts has much in common with the "Bourgeois" of Marxian propaganda and the "Jew" of Hitler's and Rosenberg's propaganda. But he does not coincide with them, for economics and race play only minor roles in Moeller's thought; his interpretation is mainly cultural and "metaphysical."

Many Liberals are incapable of religious experience, and develop a prejudice against all revelation, a childish hatred of all tradition, which, they think, is a hindrance to "progress."

Liberals are little men, no one of whom would dare seek power by himself. But by forming cliques and political parties each can achieve a sense of sharing in power. Ambition to belong, to participate, arising from a sense of inferiority, is a basic motive in Liberalism. This arouses an envy of power, a hatred for the genius, the great man, who can do and dares to do what the many cannot and dare not do. Envy of power explains the hatred for dynasties, in which, if personal distinction is not always inherited, at least the prerequisites for its formation as well as its privileges are transmitted. Envy of power explains the hatred for the Papacy and for the claims to infallibility set forth by Louis XIV and Pius IX.

Liberalism rises to power when Conservatism decays, as in the times of the later Louis's in France and the later Georges in England. Napoleon and Bismarck drove the Liberals to cover. But the romanticism and dilettantism of Wilhelm II were Liberal, not Conservative traits, and Liberals profited by his favor.

Moeller considers the ending of World War I a masterpiece of Liberal deception and destruction. Wilson's talk of "peace without victory" and the promise of a just peace in his Fourteen Points were thrust aside after Germany's surrender, and the 440 articles of the Treaty of Versailles impose slavery, not justice, and do not bring peace. He declares that the youth of Germany have learned to see the fraudulent character of the whole Liberal movement, and to recognize in it their real enemy. The coming battle is between Liberalism and Conservatism.

DEMOCRATIC

The motto of Moeller's chapter on Democracy is, *Demokratie ist Anteilnahme eines Volkes an seinem Schicksal* ("Democracy Is Participation of a People in Its Destiny"). But what kind of "participation"? The German term is just as ambiguous as my translation of it.

Moeller distinguishes three types of Democracy—three ways in which the people participate or seem to participate in the formation of policy.

The first form he discusses is the Democratic form of government introduced into Germany by the "revolution" of 1918. It is an instance of *Liberal* Democracy since it includes parliamentary government, popular election of representatives, political parties, free press, and other "Liberal" features. But it is a pseudo Democracy for various reasons. It does not express the will of the German people but of their enemies, since it is carrying out the Treaty of Versailles. The German people have never respected the Reichstag; they have not felt that they really influenced policy by voting for representatives every few years. A representative may think otherwise than his constituents, and he may vote otherwise than he thinks. Therefore the system is a fraud.

The people of Germany know that improvement in their political situation can come only through the guidance of *individuals* capable of *leadership*—but the people see no such individuals. (Evidently Moeller did not "see" Hitler as a "leader" in 1922.) German youth, loving the extraordinary, despise the mediocrity of the Republic even more than its corrupt practices.

Moeller's first type of "Democrat" encompasses those who approve a *Liberal* Democracy, either because they profit by it or because they are deceived by its claims.

His second type of Democracy is found in the early history of the Germans. *Die Demokratie war das Volk selbst* ("Democracy Was the People Itself"; p. 138). It rested on a common blood and a tribal organization. It functioned through popular assemblies and the election of dukes and kings as military leaders. These leaders were part of the people and naturally expressed their will. His second type of Democrat is therefore the primitive German.

As political conditions became more complex, the nobility lost touch with the people, and the widening gap led to the Peasants' War in the sixteenth century. This breach was gradually and partially healed. After the Thirty Years' War, the people were helpless, and absolute monarchs preserved them by acting *for* them. Prussia was more Democratic than it is reputed to have been. The nobility was loyal to the king and the king was loyal to the *Volk*—his motto was *Ich dien* ("I serve"). The inclusion of parliamentarism in the Empire of 1870 was a mistake; it did not promote real participation by the people—for the reasons given above. Thus the primitive German Democracy was lost and never fully recovered.

A third type of Democracy is an aspect of the rejuvenated Germany, which is the object of Moeller's aspiration. It would rest on the unified national sentiment of the people and on the guidance of great leaders who would express the people's real will. It must be nationalistic Democracy and *geführte Demokratie* ("led democracy"). A true Democrat would be the kind of person who aspires to bring about such a condition.

The question of monarchy, republic, or dictatorship is secondary. Not the form of the state but the *Geist* ("spirit") of the people constitutes Democracy; its basis is *Volklichkeit. Volklichkeit* is one of those cryptic terms in which Germans delight. "Folkishness" would mean nothing in English. I suppose the German term means that each individual deeply feels the experience and sentiments and aspirations of the whole people. A *Liberal* Democracy would ruin Germany; an *ideal* Democracy would be one aspect of its salvation. What is needed is that all sixty million Germans should share a single will—but it must be "a nationalized will, the will of a nation that knows what it wills, and does what it must to recover its freedom" (p. 153).

PROLETARIAN

Marx took the Proletariat as he found it—a mass of workers exploited by capitalists. He found a Proletariat in all nations and conceived it as an international class. He conceived "surplus value" as the device by which the capitalist exploits the worker. On these bases he developed his doctrines of class struggle and the inevitable triumph of the Proletariat.

Moeller accuses Marx of ignoring the sociological origins and the psychological traits of the Proletariat. Surplus value would not enable the capitalist to exploit anyone if there had not been surplus men for him to exploit. In every form of society there are men who cannot fit into its pattern—apprentices who are incompetent to become masters, and the like. These men remain at the bottom of society, unable to participate in its higher activities and values. "Proletarians are what remains at the bottom. There are always proletarians" (p. 190).

Finding themselves in this position, men think and feel in certain ways. They feel excluded from society. They tend to think in materialistic terms—of more wages, more goods. They think in momentary terms—of some immediate betterment, not of a long past and a long future. To think and feel thus is to have "the Proletarian consciousness." Having

237

this consciousness, Proletarians were easily converted to Marxian doctrines. These doctrines were economic and materialistic; they showed no respect for the past, and promised the inevitable triumph of the international Proletariat.

Thus we arrive at the first Proletarian type—the Marxian Proletarian. Moeller does not consider him a bad fellow—but misled. He does not hate and scorn him as he does the Liberal.

The World War and the Treaty of Versailles have tended to change this type. They showed the Proletarian that he cannot rely on the aid of the Proletariat of other nations. He sees that the Treaty of Versailles forces him to work as a slave of other nations to which Germany as a whole is enslaved. It convinces him "that in this world one people is the natural enemy of another people, that every people thinks only of its own ego . . ." (p. 200). Thus he feels himself to be primarily German rather than Proletarian, and begins to think nationalistically. In so doing he begins to think in higher terms than materialistic and momentary ones. In short, he ceases to have the Proletarian consciousness, and thus ceases to be Proletarian in the political sense. That seems to be what Moeller means by his chapter motto, "He Is Proletarian Who Wishes to Be So," that is, one may choose to rise to the level of nationalistic thinking, or to linger on the level of Proletarian consciousness.

The second Proletarian type is the Proletarian in the process of turning toward nationalism. This type is met halfway by the man from a higher social level who finds himself deprived of the specialized work for which he is qualified, deprived of economic security, and thus in danger of being pushed down to the Proletarian economic level. This man recognizes the Liberal as the source of his woes, and so turns toward Conservatism. Thus the rightist and the Proletarian share a common misery and learn to respect each other. Both see in Liberalism their common foe.

The Proletariat knows it cannot produce leaders; it rejects Liberal Democracy; it might accept Conservative leadership. To command the confidence of the masses a leader must know their innermost wishes and feelings. He must have a kind of mental superiority that enables him to act in line with the will of the masses, as if his will and theirs were identical; yet in fact he must guide them. Moeller thinks that all divisions among Germans, such as those between Revolutionaries and

Reactionaries, must be overcome, for all Germans face the same fate. One uprising ruined Germany; perhaps another will be needed to bring nationalistic values to the top.

The Proletarian cannot be saved by a world-wide dictatorship of the Proletariat; that is an idle dream. He can be saved by nationalism. He deserves a place in an integrated society that depends on industrial enterprise and proletarian labor. This will be a more modest place than Revolutionary Socialism offers him, but more genuine, more justified, more permanent, and therefore more valuable (p. 194). Only Conservative nationalism can give him this place. The Proletarian in process of becoming nationalistic is a welcome and indispensable ally of the Conservative.

REACTIONARY AND CONSERVATIVE

Throughout the earlier sections of the book the noble figure of the Conservative has repeatedly appeared on the horizon. This is especially true in the section on the Reactionary, which consists mainly of comparisons with the Conservative. For this reason I shall combine the sections on Reactionary and Conservative in my discussion.

The Reactionary is the kind of man who wishes to restore things just as they were at some previous period—usually the period of his own youth. In 1922 German Reactionaries thought they could restore things by restoring the old *forms* of political and economic life. They thought the revolution could be erased from history. The Conservative saw that the people had had an experience in the revolution that was needed for their knowledge of themselves and the world. The Conservative sees eternal laws of politics that apply in spite of changing conditions; he is not concerned with restoring old forms.

The Reactionary remembers the world superficially as it *was;* the Conservative sees it profoundly as it will always be. "Anyone is Reactionary who still thinks the life we led before 1914 was fine and great, even magnificent. Anyone will be Conservative who yields to no flattering self-deception and honestly confesses that it was horrible" (p. 219). The reign of Wilhelm II was a mixture of remnants of the past and features supposed to be "progressive." Its policies were vacillating and ineffective. The Reactionary would meet the present crisis by reviving the policies that failed to prevent it. (So American Reactionaries today would revive the policies of 1921–1929.) The Conservative sees that the changes that have occurred cannot be reversed.

Revolutions are interludes in history. They expose the defects of previous policy but they do not in themselves establish a new order. Revolutionists inevitably relinquish their power to men who have the experience and insight in political matters to get things going again. Such men are Conservative; they make *connections* with the past but do not try to restore it as a whole.

Reactionary regimes like those of nineteenth-century Austria and Russia, and France under the Bourbon restoration, use force to supply their deficiency in ideals. The Conservative seeks *power* that will come from his own nature—power over men, peoples, events, customs, and institutions that comes to him through his possession of a comprehensive ideal that is not merely personal or temporary (p. 233).

The Reactionary is a decadent form of Conservative. He is merely rationalistic and never had a vital and penetrating understanding of Conservative ideals. The negligence of Reactionaries helped to produce events that provoked the revolution. In the resulting crisis the Reactionary is a dangerous man because he hinders the union of rightist and leftist forces that is needed to destroy Liberalism.

Conservatism is complex and does not lend itself to any short definition. The Conservative has a characteristic relation to *time*. He is vitally related to past, present, and future—and to eternity. He is conscious of a precious heritage from the past, to be transmitted to future generations. He is conscious of a present situation with which he must deal skillfully so that in these novel circumstances this heritage may be preserved or enhanced, not corrupted or destroyed. He is conscious of eternity, for the ideals which command his allegiance are eternal, though they must be embodied in different forms in different times.

The Conservative rejects the bondage of the Reactionary to the external forms of the past. He rejects the Liberal's concentration on present gratification, his lack of respect for the past, and his naïve or hypocritical promise of inevitable progress in the future. He rejects the Revolutionist's delusion that the destruction of past forms will automatically usher in a utopian future.

The Conservative is endowed with insight—insight into ideals, insight into realities. His insight into ideals gives him criteria for choosing policies. It preserves him from the greed, self-indulgence, and pettiness of the Liberal, and from the materialism of the Marxist. His insight into realities preserves him from the delusions of equality and human brotherhood, from the delusions of progress and Utopias, and from the Reactionary delusion that a past situation can be reinstated. The Conservative has insight into such realities as the perennial impulses and passions of men, the superiority yet also the deficiencies of the Individual, the inferiority yet also the violent demands of the masses; he has insight into the natural relations of strong and weak, and into the results of courage, circumspection, decisiveness, and their opposites. He knows there are unchanging factors in life—such as love, hate, adventure, enterprise, trade, competition, conflicts between individuals and between peoples, and the will to power.

Conservative political thought seeks to make secure the conditions for the growth of values (*Wachstumsbedingungen für Werte*). It seeks stability. It binds men together. It needs inviolable persons, symbols, and traditions that sanction its power. It requires the acceptance of a whole series of generations. The Holy Roman Empire and the Catholic Church are achievements of this Conservative sort.

The insight of the Conservative is intuitive, not rationalistic. By reason you can prove anything. Richelieu used it to support absolute monarchy; the Revolutionists of 1789 used it to support absolute Democracy. When every man does what is rational (from his egoistic point of view), the results are most irrational. "Values cannot be verified or calculated. They are due to grace (*Gnade*). They burst into being spontaneously and daemonically" (*dämonisch*, implying uncanny and imperative motivation—not malice; p. 246). The Conservative has the natural gift of judging and inferring, and of recognizing what is real. He has the manliness to forego self-deception. By devoted service to his people and his state he acquires a sound knowledge of human nature. He is guided by insight rooted in character, which leads to the preservation of life—not by abstract reasoning, which leads through Liberalism to disintegration. The Conservative's knowledge of human nature gives him both a high and a low opinion of men. Glorious things can be achieved *with* men banded together to defend their

241

existence and fight for their future and their freedom. But if they are turned loose to follow their egoistic desires, they soon turn life into filth.

The Conservative avoids the rigidity of the Reactionary, who loses touch with present reality. He avoids the unlimited relativism of the Liberal, who has no principle that he will not abandon for profit. Conservatism is the art of national self-assertion according to the current condition of the world (*die politische Kunst, das Volk als Nation zu behaupten—je nach der Weltlage, in der es sich befand;* p. 231). The Conservatives of Rome in the first century B.C. were Republicans. The Republic fell, but Conservatism reasserted itself under the form of the Empire.

The Conservative is a nationalist because he is realistic. He sees that to think in terms of individual men, as Liberalism does, brings disintegration. He sees that there is no validity in the ideas of an international class, or of humanity as a whole. He sees that "the life of men is preserved in nations. Therefore he seeks to preserve the nation to which he belongs" (p. 275). (Note, however, that the Holy Roman Empire and the Catholic Church, which he cites as great Conservative achievements, are *international* in their ideology.)

To sum up, we may say that the Conservative is a man who grasps the continuity of life in past, present, and future; who is endowed with insight into eternal ideals and persistent facts of human nature; whose insight is rooted in character and experience, not in abstract reason; who seeks to create stable conditions in which values may flourish; who is faithful to eternal ideals but flexible in applying them to changing situations; and who subordinates all other ends to the preservation of his nation.

Perhaps a third type should be added to the Reactionary and the true Conservative, namely the Liberalized Conservative. This type would be illustrated by post-Bismarckian Conservatives, who did not stiffen into Reaction but softened into some degree of Liberalism. Moeller considers that Wilhelm II himself was essentially more Liberal than Conservative. But this is only one of many possible hybridizations that need not be separately labeled.[2]

---

[2] Moeller's political types may be tabulated as follows: (1) Revolutionary types— (a) any persons who overturn a government, (b) persons who bring about the

THE THIRD REICH

Moeller's section on the Third Reich adds little to our knowledge of his typology.

The Third Reich is to be the product of the Conservative spirit. It will embody the eternal German values in a political form appropriate to the situation in which it will arise. This Conservative spirit will not operate through extant Conservative parties alone. Passages scattered through the book indicate the following alignment of types: The Conservatives will welcome to their ranks Socialists of the third type, Democrats of the third type, and Proletarians of the second type, who have all become nationalistic. This combination of groups will function as Revolutionaries of the second type, who know how to achieve the political maturity of the nation. Reactionaries and Liberals will have to be converted or overridden.

This program largely foreshadows the actual development and success of the Nazi movement.

We are told that the Conservative does not wish to preserve Germany merely because it is German—that might too easily fall into the Reactionary error of preserving something that is outworn. He wishes to preserve Germany *weil es Mitte ist, weil nur von ihr aus Europa sich in Gleichgewicht halten lässt* ("because it is the midpoint from which alone Europe can be kept in equilibrium"; p. 302). (This seems to contradict the bald national egoism of an earlier statement that the German wishes to preserve Germany because it is the nation he belongs to.)

A nation is a community that shares the same values. Conservatism preserves traditional values insofar as they preserve the nation's power of growth, and incorporates new values insofar as they enhance the nation's power to live (p. 303). Moeller never tells us *what* the German values are. He asserts in an untranslatable sentence of cryptic verbiage

---

political maturity of a nation, and (c) persons who expect to produce the millennium by overturning a government; (2) Socialistic types—(a) pure Marxists, (b) members of Socialist political parties, and (c) National Socialists; (3) Liberal types; (4) Democratic types—(a) Liberal Democrats, (b) Primitive Germans, and (c) nationalistic Democrats; (5) Proletarian types—(a) Marxist Proletarians, and (b) Proletarians turning toward nationalism; (6) Reactionary type; and (7) Conservative type.

that they are mysterious, fragmentary, inconsistent, yet tending toward unity, etc., etc. (p. 308):

> In keinem Lande sind die Werte so rätselhaft, so unbegriffen und unge-grieflich, so unausgetragen und bruchstückhaft abgebrochen und wiederum in sich vollendet, bald innige Geständnisse, bald wilde Weltstürmereien, zart oder gewaltig, erdhaft oder entschwebend, ganz wirklichkeitsnahe oder ganz raumweit und dem Anscheine nach Ausdruck von lauter Unvereinbarkeiten —wie in Deutschland. . . . Und in keinem Lande drängen diese Werte so zu einer Einheit hin, zu der wir seit unserem ersten Reiche nicht mehr gelang-ten und die wir in unserem zweiten Reiche verfehlten—und die uns nun für ein drittes Reich aufegegeben ist. . . .

Rationalism having been condemned throughout his book, it is fitting that he should end on a note of fervent irrationalism: "The beast in man creeps forward. Africa begins to spread its darkness over Europe. We must stand guard at the threshold of values" (p. 322).

MOELLER'S BOOK AS PROPAGANDA

The importance of *Das dritte Reich* as a forerunner of Nazi ideology has been widely recognized. The jacket of the third edition (1931) displays an endorsement by Dr. Goebbels: *Ich begrüsse die Verbrei-tung des für die politische Ideengeschichte der NSDAP bedeutungsvol-len politischen Werkes "Das dritte Reich."* ("I welcome the circulation of the political work *The Third Reich,* which is significant for the de-velopment of the political ideas of the National Socialist Party.")

Gerhard Krebs has discussed Moeller's relation to the Nazi move-ment in his article, "Moeller van den Bruck: Inventor of the 'Third Reich.'"[3] It would be superfluous for me to repeat his analysis. But it may be of interest to compare Moeller's book with Hitler's *Mein Kampf* and Rosenberg's *Myth of the Twentieth Century* with reference to its effectiveness as propaganda.

Moeller's scapegoat is the Liberal; he blames Liberalism for most of the woes of Germany and the world. His "Liberal" has much in common with the "Jew" of Hitler and Rosenberg. But Moeller rarely mentions the Jews and does not go in for anti-Semitism, except to re-

---

[3] *American Political Science Review,* XXXV, 6, December, 1941, pages 1085–1105. See also Aurel Kolnai, *The War Against the West* (New York: Viking Press, Inc., 1938). Kolnai discusses or mentions Moeller in passages beginning on pages 112, 138, 142, 326, 329, 333, 348, 397, 525, 531, 549, 571, 580, 647, 650.

mark that Marx, being a Jew, could not appreciate European problems. His "Liberal" is an abstract and shadowy figure compared to the vivid depiction of the Jew in the writings of Hitler and Rosenberg; it is therefore less effective as propaganda.

Moeller's ideal is the "Conservative"; since his Conservative is *nationalist* he has much in common with the "Nordic" of Rosenberg and Hitler. Here again Moeller's figure is far less vivid, picturesque, and emotionally exciting than the other.

Russia in all its aspects, and Communism wherever found, are targets of Hitler's and Rosenberg's attacks. Moeller, by proposing a rapprochement with German communism and hinting at a rapprochement with Russia, fails to gain the psychological advantage of these two bogeys.

Rosenberg was relentless in his hostility to Catholicism and scolded the Protestants for retaining the Jewish Old Testament and too many features of Catholicism, and for maintaining international ties. Moeller has nothing to say on these topics. His attitude is more like the tactical silence of *Mein Kampf* in this respect. Which policy was better propaganda I would not venture to say.

Moeller contents himself with vague demands that space be secured for Germany's "surplus" population. Hitler and Rosenberg are more definite in their proposals that territory be seized in Russia and her border states; they therefore make a stronger appeal to hate and greed.

On the whole Moeller's volume is too moderate on some points and too vague on others to be as effective propaganda as the masterpieces of Hitler and Rosenberg.

On Sabine's Philosophy of Value

JULIUS R. WEINBERG

IN HIS JUSTLY FAMOUS *History of Political Theory*, his Presidential address, and his Howison Lecture, Professor Sabine has defended a view of moral evaluation similar in essential respects to that of Hume. Like Hume he holds that no fact implies any other fact and no fact implies any value. But, although he agrees with these negative views of Hume's, it would not be correct to say that he would subscribe to Hume's positive theory of moral judgment. That moral evaluations are the expression of individual or collective human preferences or sentiments is too simple.[1] We can say only that "sentences about intrinsic value are linguistically primitive."[2] Hence "what ethical realism actually proves . . . is that the values in an ethical system must be postulated as values. There is in them an element of choice, limited in use, of course, by the requirements of logical consistency."[3]

There is only one way I find myself able to render these two statements consistent, and that is to suppose that when one judges that some state of affairs "ought to be" or that some act "ought to be" performed, the statement is *linguistically primitive* for him, but that his statement can be characterized as the expression of a choice that he has made. It is not, of course, necessary that the choice be the result of conscious deliberation (although it might have been), nor, on the other hand, is it necessary to suppose that the choice results from conscious or unconscious motivations such as the desire for pleasure,

---

[1] *History of Political Theory*, Preface.
[2] Howison Lecture, "Social Studies and Objectivity," *University of California Publications in Philosophy*, XVI [6] (1941), 137.
[3] *Ibid.*

prestige, or the like (though these are plain possibilities to be considered). What is necessary is only that the significance of an evaluative judgment is to be found in human choices, however these choices have been caused. I say that I can only render the two statements consistent in this way, because it is necessary to provide some account of the meaning of evaluative judgments and the alternative to supposing that a linguistically primitive judgment has a substantive referent is to suppose that it has subjective or social causes which can be analyzed, even though this fact be concealed from the person who is engaged in evaluation. The supposition that there is a substantive referent for linguistically primitive moral judgments is inconsistent with the notion that they express choices that may be laid down as postulates merely.

Now as these views derive largely from Hume, it will be well to review the arguments which led Hume to his own conclusions in the matter. If this is undertaken, it will become clear, I think, that we can accept most of Hume's negative arguments without being forced to his conclusion that, since moral judgments cannot be excogitated from facts, they must rest on sentiment alone.

Hume urges that "a reason should be given, for what seems altogether inconceivable, how this new relation [sc. ought, ought not] can be a deduction from others, which are entirely different from it." [4] That the answer can only be that reason, in the sense in which Hume takes it, can discover no relation between fact and value is a foregone conclusion. But that *reason* must be so understood has nowhere been actually shown by Hume or by his followers in these matters.

That reason cannot discover an agreement or disagreement of relations of ideas or matters of fact where moral judgment is concerned depends, for Hume, on the passionate or volitional character of those judgments. Reason is inert while moral evaluations, being based on the passions, have a potential or actual effect on our behavior. Again, the passions are original facts and, implying nothing beyond themselves, cannot be said to be "true or false, and [to] be either contrary or conformable to reason." [5] This argument proves not that reason alone cannot make moral distinctions but only that moral distinctions alone

---

[4] *Treatise,* Bk. III, pt. I, 1 *ad finem.*
[5] *Ibid.*

cannot rouse us to act or to refrain from acting on a distinction discovered by reason. This, however, is not the main issue.

Taking the question more generally we may argue as follows: (a) That x has the characteristic ϕ will, admittedly, never imply that x ought to have such a characteristic. But it is certainly possible that if x is ϕ, it is what it ought to be. Hence, while we may not suppose that any characteristic or combination of characteristics of a possible act or state of affairs will ever *imply* a value which this character does not possess as fact, it may yet be that some factual characteristics of acts or states have value. So if such characteristics do in fact characterize an actual action or state of affairs, such a state of affairs will be what it ought to be. Hence, while we may not discover by way of deduction or any problematic inference what ought to be from what merely is the case, we might yet discern in an act or state (actual or merely imagined) the presence of moral value.

(b) It is also possible that characteristics, when mutually isolated, may lack any moral quality but, when existing in combination, may possess moral quality. In this case, although we could not discover any moral quality in these characteristics, taken distributively, they may reveal such a quality when they are combined in certain special ways.[6]

Some people are inclined to deny this. But such a denial requires, for its proof, a metaphysical proposition which, I think, has often been *tacitly* assumed, but for which there is not the slightest evidence. This tacit assumption is, of course, that no characteristic can belong to a complex, or to the relation (or relations) which constitutes the component (or components) of the complex, which is specifically different from the qualities and relations which are the constituents of the complex. Consider, for example, malice defined as pleasure in the contemplation of another's misfortune. The bare cognition of another's misfortune is quite neutral, ethically speaking. And again, pleasure, if it could exist quite alone, might be ethically neutral. But it is commonly thought that the combination of pleasure and contemplation of misfortune is not ethically neutral but definitely *wrong*.[7] Now it is plain that, whatever the relation of such a pleasure to such a contemplation may be, it is not a bare conjunction but something which more inti-

---

[6] Cf. G. E. Moore, *Principia Ethica*, ch. i.

[7] I owe this example to C. D. Broad's *Five Types of Ethical Theory*.

mately binds that emotion with that particular cognition. And so it is quite plausible to suppose that such a complex is a case of the ethically wrong or *ipso facto* possesses a quality (in addition to its factuality as such) which is the quality of being ethically wrong.

Now as far as I know, this supposition would be impossible only if the metaphysical proposition I enunciated above were intuitively or demonstratively certain. And I am sure that it is not.

(c) That a state of affairs ought to be has, in the history of thought, been taken to be connected causally in some way with what is the case in this world. But this unfortunate association of two distinct categories constitutes no reason for rejecting the substantive character of moral distinctions.

The fact is, as Broad has pointed out,[8] that Hume took *reason* in a very narrow sense and only thus was enabled to achieve such an easy triumph. Just as he urged that a conception of body that could be reduced neither to an intellectual intuition nor to a relation of particular sense-given qualities must be accounted for in terms of imagination, and just as he held that a relation of causal connection that could not be excogitated by way of a philosophical relation of ideas or discerned in sense-given relations of qualities must be accounted for in terms of an impression of reflection, so here he seems to pass too easily from the absence of a deductive or empirically discernible moral quality in acts or states to the view that the passionate side of human nature must be the basis of moral judgment. Hume may have been right, but his failure to allow to reason any function other than logical intuition and demonstration and his unwarranted limitation of perception to imagination and sensation ought to make us hesitate to accept his positive views about moral judgments, however convinced we may be about the definitiveness of his negative arguments.

II

I should like now to indicate another possible interpretation of the meaning of judgments involving ethical predicates. But before I embark on this task I shall find it necessary to make some preliminary remarks on the methods of analysis which are characteristic of some

---

[8] *Ibid.*

leading views in this field. Accordingly, I shall begin by some criticism of the methods of Moore and writers who are in general sympathy with his approach to the problem.

The method of Moore seems to be this: many propositions are plainly significant and true, but we do not yet know precisely what such propositions mean. An analysis, similar in certain respects to Plato's dialectical method, considers a number of possibilities, and after rejecting all but one, concludes that probably this is the right analysis. In ethics, specifically, there are significant and true judgments made by ordinary people whose significance and truth can best be defended by an analysis of their meaning. Now when a number of people make judgments of the form "This state is good" or "That action is right," Moore assumes that such people are not wholly mistaken about the admittedly undetermined meaning which they wish to express. That is, he assumes it to be very improbable that they are really expressing merely that they feel in a certain way about such an act but imagine that they are expressing something quite different from a feeling. And he has an argument about reducing ethical attribution to mere belief which, so far as it goes, seems to me quite conclusive in showing that one meaning of such a doctrine is utterly incoherent.

Now naturalistic views in ethics have been very badly stated and defended even more ineptly, so that it is difficult to understand what such views amount to. The simplest, and in many ways the most plausible, form of naturalism maintains, at any rate, that people *can* be utterly mistaken about the character of value judgments. I think their argument to this conclusion ought to run somewhat as follows:

It is possible that a feeling becomes so fused with action of a certain kind that it is taken, by the percipient, as a characteristic of the action by a kind of projection. Just as we say that *red* is a *warm color,* so we may say that the sight of someone inflicting pain on another is a wrong action. While the two cases are far from parallel in all respects, they yet may be sufficiently similar to show how fused association of a feeling with the perception of a given action may take place. And the difference between the two cases brings out an important point. In the case of the *warm color,* careful introspection might permit a distinction of two confused sensations because warmth is a localized sensation and felt as such, whereas the sentiment of disapprobation is not localized, so that its confusion with the associated action may be infinitely more difficult to dissolve and, indeed, it may be impossible. Now if such were the case, it would be possible not only for a man to be completely mistaken about the meaning of his own moral judgments, but also impossible for him ever to see *in his own moral judgments when he was making them* the confusion of a nonlocalized sensation with a perception of some human action. It would, on such a theory, nevertheless be possible for a man to understand that moral judgments might very well have such a character, and perhaps *indirect* empirical evidence might very well support such a hypothesis.

Such being the case, Moore's type of argument is not convincing. We cannot therefore argue from the two propositions, (1) that *x is right* does not explicitly signify, and is not consciously intended as meaning, the *judger has a certain feeling about x* and (2) men are not commonly so completely mistaken about the content of their own thoughts as to misapprehend a subjective feeling as the objective quality of an actual or contemplated state of affairs, to the conclusion that values are objective. Indeed (1) is quite consistent with the negation of (2) in theory and in fact.

How, then, can Moore's general conclusion be saved from the bad arguments he used to support it? It seems to me that two lines of argument are possible: (1) to admit that there is the greatest possible danger in misapprehending subjective feelings as qualities of objective states of affairs, and yet to maintain that the occurrence of such a misapprehension must be shown for each particular type of case; (2) to show that, in the type of case under discussion, the arguments for subjectivity are based on some groundless assumption to which alone the alleged facts urged in support of the position owe their plausibility. It is, then, possible to appeal to the reflective experience of adult educated men in order to bring to each man's consciousness the significance of the moral judgments which he makes.

Now the feeling theory, as I have restated it, is, in many respects, quite analogous to the arguments about the selfish motivation of all human action. And it is analogous also to some arguments of popular psychoanalysis to the effect that apparently nonsexual thoughts are, covertly, sexual in character. These theories are, prima facie, so implausible (unless we accept some very doubtful and extravagant pieces

251

of metaphysics) that the *onus probandi* lies on the proponents of such theories rather than on their critics. And the point is not, of course, that we are incapable of any self-deception in all these matters, but rather that, if such theories were true, we would be incapable of anything else.

The fact is, as far as my own experience goes (and I suspect it is true for others), that I commonly am able to discriminate between pseudo-moral attitudes and "genuinely" moral attitudes I have taken from time to time. That is to say, I can apply a series of tests to my attitudes. These tests are attempts to discover in these attitudes indications that they have been caused by personal or social psychological disturbances of which the attitudes are rationalizations. Some attitudes survive these tests; others are annihilated by them. Such experiences would be quite inconsistent with the doctrine that all ostensibly moral attitudes and judgments are cases of self-deception.

I suspect that some who hold the view that all facts must be ethically neutral are thinking in a somewhat different way. They are supposing that, since man is, *in all probability,* the descendant of a form of animal life with which few persons (if any) would associate ethical qualities, therefore man individually or in groups possesses no ethical qualities. Now this view can be refuted if it can be shown that, as a matter of fact, men have distinctive qualities which brutes do not possess. It can also be challenged if it can be shown that the brutes possess ethically significant characteristics. But it might be open to serious question if it could be shown that an ethical characteristic could emerge when certain severally distinct nonethical characteristics of animals in process of evolution would be such as to constitute (in combination) an ethical characteristic when their evolution proceeded to just the right degree.

Hence, there is little reason to accept the negative arguments of the ethical subjectivists. And this is just about as far as argument and analysis can go in these matters. But the proponent of the reality of ethical characteristics should carefully guard against certain misunderstandings. Chief among these is the following: To say that there are ethically significant facts is sometimes interpreted to mean, e.g., that the universe is, or is created and conserved by, a being possessing ethical characteristics. Now this is certainly not necessarily involved in such a view. Historically it is true that the doctrine that there is an objective content of ethical judgment has usually been associated with a doctrine about the moral economy of the universe. Yet even this must be qualified, for from Plato to G. E. Moore, many philosophers holding such views have insisted that good and right do not depend on the mere being or mere volition of a deity (although, of course, some writers have held this).

Now that some of the difficulties have been removed, the outline of a positive approach to the problem may be indicated. And it is best to discuss the problem in this order: the logical and epistemological problems, and the ontological problems.

The arguments of Hume establish this much about moral cognition (cf. Hume's results concerning causation and substance). If intuition be limited (as it ought to be for the sake of precision if nothing else) to the discernment of ostensible identities and resemblances of ideas and/or impressions, a moral quality of goodness, or rightness, or praiseworthiness (or their opposites) is not intuited. If necessary inference be limited to explicative reasoning, it is equally impotent to provide cognition of moral values. A fortiori, the various forms of problematic inference of the factual sciences are incapable in the matter in question. It remains then that moral judgments are quite unverifiable in their ostensible form or that they are like perceptual judgments. For perceptual judgments are, it has been made pretty plain, neither intuitive nor inferential in character. We seem to have a conception (not a *definition*) of a physical object, and in certain perceptual situations we appear to have prima facie exemplification of such a concept. The perceptual situation constitutes evidence for an existence for which we have, at best, an implicit definition. No amount of additional evidence would transform the conviction that there is such an existence into an apodeictic inference. Now ethical judgments are like perceptual judgments in a number of ways. We have no definition of the right, the good, the worthy. Yet we can easily put upon any state of affairs or act a set of conditions which distinguish it from facts to which moral judgments could not apply. We cannot ever be sure that moral judgments are true, i.e., we cannot ever be certain that the statement "x is good" conforms to the known conditions of goodness. But we can, in advance, specify the kind of evidence which would be favorably or unfavorably relevant to this statement, just as we can do the same things about perceptual judgments.

The analogy between moral and perceptual judgments goes even further than I have suggested. We have criteria which confirm the existence of perceptual objects and we have criteria which would disconfirm such existence. Analogously, we have criteria which confirm the objectively valuable character of states of affairs and of actions and we have criteria which would reject the ostensible objectivity of moral judgments. Such criteria of confirmation and disconfirmation are rarely (perhaps never) definitive. Yet the very fact that they continue to be employed by persons who are adequately informed suggests very strongly that we have some conception of the objectively valuable, just as the use of criteria of perceptual assurance strongly suggests that we have a conception of an objectively physical object.

Now it is true that ethical judgments will initially possess distinctive features which cannot be reduced to the factual or logical features of our conceptual thesaurus. In this sense they may be called intuitive. But they are not intuitive in the sense that they refer to a simple quality or to a definable complex of qualities and relations.

Turning to the ontological side of the question, we must consider that moral values are not first-order predicates or relations. Now this should not disturb us in the least. For no simple predicates or relations could possibly constitute the quality or relation to which value judgments are addressed. Such judgments are applied only to things or aggregates of things which already have many determining qualities and which stand in many determining relations. Hence value predicates have to be second-order predicates, at least, in order to involve objects whose complexity is sufficient to constitute objects of evaluation. Value predicates are like the so-called dispositional predicates of things in this respect. But they are like dispositional predicates in another respect as well. A dispositional predicate always involves, I think, a hypothesis which cannot be explicitly elucidated in terms of other predicates. And value predicates are hypothetical in just this sense.

The fact that we cannot explicitly define the quality of good or of right does not seem to me to be a conclusive argument for anything. We cannot explicitly define chairs, fields of force, or electrons, or genes, but very few philosophers would, for this reason, reject these concepts.[9]

Since such a view as I have been suggesting is obviously open to the

---

[9] I owe some of these reflections to my friend William Henry Hay.

objection that it is quite valueless unless it, at least, states some characteristics which are morally valuable, it is necessary to suggest a tentative list of conditions which are severally necessary for an ultimately valuable state of affairs or for a valuable action. The problem of right action is very complex and I do not have the skill to resolve it. It will suffice to indicate the general outline of the former.

Some of the conditions which a completely good state of affairs for men would possess are, I feel sure, these:

1. Satisfaction of animal needs.
2. Opportunity for satisfaction of distinctly human needs.
3. Attitudes of equal right to these opportunities as widely distributed as the opportunities themselves.

I believe that men have come, in the course of development of civilized society, to discern these conditions as requirements of the objectively good life in and of society. Sometimes prophetic insight has brought moral perception to a sudden and sharp focus. Sometimes such conditions have emerged from the protracted reflections of philosophers and statesmen. Until the Enlightenment, there was considerable confusion of these conditions with special religious or political concerns. But, in general, their persistence, their adoption by singularly able minds throughout West European History, and their resistance to criticism profoundly supports the assent which given individuals give to them.

This list of conditions does not pretend to be exhaustive or even relatively complete. Furthermore, it is highly abstract. What distinctively human needs there are is, to a great extent, a function of the degree to which a civilization has progressed in respect to the arts, political organizations, and the economic situations which these developments necessarily involve. But anyone with a reasonable knowledge of the culture in which he lives will be able to discern existing needs and to anticipate needs in a foreseeable future. Ethical theory as such, in contradistinction to its application, cannot go much further than the indication of the final form of the conditions of ultimately valuable states of society and acts of men. Knowledge of matters of fact must supply the specific content of these conditions when they are applied to existing societies and individuals. But the conditions which I have set forth do contain a feature to which I should like to call attention. In addition to the satisfaction or enjoyment of needs, it is necessary, in order to be a complete realization of value, that these satisfactions be fairly distributed and that there be a general approval of fair distribution. A society in which all existing needs were satisfied and in which all goods were equally distributed would not be as valuable as one in which there was, in addition, a general consensus of the justness of such a state of affairs.

We can agree with Professor Sabine's view that facts do not imply values and that we do not have unerring moral intuitions of moral qualities. We can also afford to concede that basic value judgments are linguistically primitive. Moreover it does not destroy the case for a substantive solution of the analysis of value judgments to admit that choice and preference are accompaniments or even ingredients of moral judgment. Our position is, however, that basic moral judgment is not exhaustively reducible to preferences, choices, or volitions, or feelings of other kinds. The arguments that such a reduction is possible appear to us to be based on an incomplete survey of kinds of cognition of which human beings are capable or on too severe conditions of validity to which all judgments are expected to conform.

Values, Objectivity, and Democracy

FREDERICK L. WILL

IN HIS LECTURE "Democracy and Preconceived Ideas"[1] Professor Sabine has discussed with his customary clarity and understanding the historical background of one of the questions in the philosophy of democracy which in recent years has been of the greatest theoretical and practical importance. This is the question of the philosophical grounds of democratic ideals and institutions, of the basis or warrant upon which the values of democracy can be affirmed to be good, worthy of our allegiance, and preferable to the values of alternative forms of political and social organization. In its formative period in the seventeenth and eighteenth centuries, he observes, democratic social philosophy was grounded in a whole set of preconceived ideas, a whole metaphysical view encompassing the nature of man and his place or status in the world. One of the most important points in this view, in fact the central point of all, was its conception of man as possessing, in his "reason," a unique faculty capable, if cultivated properly, of grasping and establishing certain fundamental principles "of necessary truth and of necessary good." Such a metaphysical view lay behind, and to its devotees seemed to guarantee, that central tenet of early democratic philosophy, "the belief in the essential reasonableness of human nature and of human action." From it grew, as the democratic philosophy developed, faith in education as a means of reform and progress, belief in political and economic individualism, proposals for the extension of the suffrage, and so on. And now, in the middle of the twentieth century, when the goodness of democracy and the com-

---

[1] The Walter J. Shepard Foundation, Ohio State University, 1945.

placency and safety of democrats have been challenged by vigorous antidemocratic movements on both the right and the left, it must be admitted that the metaphysical grounds upon which democratic ideals and proposals one time rested will no longer support them. The development of science and philosophy in the past hundred and fifty years has rendered those preconceived ideas of an earlier age inacceptable. In place of the older idea of reason as "a transcendent endowment, serene above the physical and social forces of life, providing a frame of reference within which human purpose finds a fixed value as right or wrong, true or false," it has put a radically different idea of intelligence as "an organic process, a factor in human behavior, arising from the commerce of the body with its surroundings, involved from first to last with purpose, will, and passion." On what grounds, now that the older metaphysical ones are no longer safe for human habitation, can the edifice of democratic ideals be built?

The warrant or authority of democratic ideals, Professor Sabine goes on to say, is not to be found in various of the places where some philosophers have been most busily searching. It will not be found in some alternative metaphysics devised as a substitute for the older exploded one, for metaphysics, in his positivistic view, is apparently a kind of systematic intellectual deception, "after all a manner of speaking, a system of words in which men have already enshrined the hopes and aspirations they pretend to prove." Nor will it be found in the established or establishable propositions of science, since "hopes and ideals are not facts to be seen or theorems to be proved." No, moral values "in the last resort are matters of choice"; and the warrant, therefore, if warrant it is, of moral values generally and democratic values specifically lies in the hearts, the wills, the desires of men. "At some point," he believes, "a nation confronts its final conviction about what it is possible for human life to be and what they desire that it should become, and upon that choice they build their civilization and so they make their place in history. On that conviction it has to stake its life and fortune." [2]

It is to the positive philosophy implicit here, to the philosophical preconceptions implicit in Professor Sabine's description of the quarter in which the grounds of democracy are to be found, that I wish to ad-

[2] *Ibid.*, p. 19.

258

dress myself in this essay. First I wish to consider the main features of the view as it has been expressed in this and other writings, next to call attention to some of the philosophical and practical difficulties which it involves, and, finally, to show how these difficulties can be avoided by a correction of those features of the view upon which the difficulties depend. In doing so I hope that I shall seem to the readers of this festival volume to be honoring Professor Sabine in a way in which this distinguished scholar and philosopher, and my former teacher, may very appropriately be honored. That is, by dealing seriously with his philosophical views and evaluating them, so far as I can, with the same kind of careful critical analysis and the same deep concern for fundamental intellectual and moral values which have characterized his career as a teacher, philosopher, and educational leader.

II

In the beginning several things had best be made clear. First, no dissent will be made here from Professor Sabine's judgment concerning the inutility of metaphysics, as that subject is ordinarily conceived and cultivated, as a foundation for the moral ideals of democracy. Ideals and aspirations, it will be agreed without argument, have their grounds and derive their force from sources other than the study of the generic principles of reality, the essence of being *qua* being, or the nature of Transcendent Reality, if such transcendence there be, beyond the more homely world of objects and events with which we are, whatever our speculative metaphysics may be, in undeniable and intimate commerce.

And secondly, in these days, when the word "democracy" issues feelingly from the mouths and appears on the banners of various groups whose allegiance to what would ordinarily be regarded as indispensable features of democratic practice is not visible to the naked eye, it seems desirable to indicate briefly what kind of democracy and democratic ideals are considered here as worthy of inquiry into their philosophical grounds. It is not the kind of democracy which reaches its full flowering in the alleged benevolent dictatorship of any minority clique or party, either with or without an attendant chorus of *Ja's* from the regimented beneficiaries. Rather it is the kind which has been celebrated in the liberal tradition in the past century and a half, and which was fought for sincerely by many in the English, the French, and the American revolutions. What it is cannot be distilled into a concentrated essence and conveyed tightly bottled in a few words. It means, in politics, government which, as Jefferson put it in the Declaration of Independence, derives its just powers from the consent of the governed, and not, as we may add in our own day, in a fake or rigged election in which the voters must give their consent to keep their jobs, their ration cards, or their freedom from the processes of re-education practiced in government work or concentration camps. It means, then, government by consent when that consent is freely given; and that implies a multitude of things, such as the right to be informed, the rights of minorities to discuss and criticize, and freedom of speech and of religion.

It implies also, in the broader social field, if consent is to be freely given, the right of the governed to that education which is necessary for them to understand and make up their minds about the fundamental issues which come before them, and, if the government is to be genuinely responsible to the will of the governed, that they have the means to make the economic and other social arrangements which seem to be necessary or desirable to their good and to be not incompatible with those other democratic conditions already laid down. Each one of these conditions involves in its realization multitudes of other conditions, some of which change with time and circumstance and all of which are the subject of investigation by the legislatures, courts, and other instruments of government, as well as other social institutions and groups, including the university seminar, the labor union, the platform committee of the political party, and the local Parent-Teacher Association. Were this a disquisition on the nature and conditions of democracy, such a characterization of the conditions of a democratic society would obviously be as inadequate as it is admittedly incomplete. Here it may suffice to indicate that the kind of democratic society whose philosophical basis is being considered is that in which the governed are citizens and not subjects, where they have the right and the responsibility, the privilege and the joy, of arranging their own lives and affairs, public and private, as they see fit, and where, in the words of Professor Sabine, independence of judgment and action are taken to be both normal and right.

If one leaves off searching for metaphysical grounds of judgments of the worth of democracy, and agrees further with Professor Sabine that "hopes and ideals are not facts to be seen or theorems to be proved," what kind of philosophy of democracy may he have? What does this latter agreement commit him to concerning the grounds of ethical ideals? It means, as Professor Sabine made clear in his *History of Political Theory*, that he recognizes with Hume a radical distinction between the kind of evidence or basis which is available for and employed by these three types of expression or affirmation: (1) truths of reason, or of logic, such as are exemplified in pure mathematics; (2) truths of fact, such as are exemplified in the assertions about the world made in the natural sciences as well as in other areas of experience; and (3) judgments of value or worth.[3] In the systems of natural law, and in many other segments of early modern rationalism, the terms "reason" and "reasonable" had been employed in connection with all these three types of affirmation without the realization, which was clearly expressed in Hume's philosophy, that the grounds of these three things were fundamentally different. When "reason" is employed to mean the process of establishing necessary and demonstrative truths in the manner of logic and pure mathematics, then no affirmations of matters of fact or existence are decidable by reason alone, one way or other, since the denial of none is self-contradictory; and the same must be admitted of all judgments of value. "For in these cases," as Professor Sabine writes in his exposition of Hume's philosophy,

where a way of acting is said to be right or good, the reference is not to reason but to some human inclination, or desire, or "propensity." Reason in itself dictates no way of acting. It may show, by adducing knowledge of causes and effects, that the result of acting in a certain way will be so and so; the question will still remain whether, when the reasoning is finished, the result is acceptable to human inclination or not. Reason is the guide of conduct only in the sense that it shows what means will reach a desired end or how a disagreeable result can be avoided; the pleasantness of the result is in itself neither reasonable nor unreasonable. As Hume put it, "reason is and ought only to be the slave of the passions and can never pretend to any other office than to serve and obey them." [4]

And so, writing two hundred years after Hume had set forth these things, Professor Sabine indicated his general agreement with this portion of Hume's philosophy in the pithy pronouncement that so far as

---

[3] Pp. viii, 597–606.
[4] *Ibid.*, p. 600.

he could see "it is impossible by any logical operation to excogitate the truth of any allegation of fact, and neither logic nor fact implies a value." And further, that, "As for values, they appear . . . to be always the reaction of human preference to some state of social or physical fact. . . ." [5]

It is in the light or context of the philosophy just outlined that one must understand the above-cited pronouncements about the difference between hopes and ideals and facts and theorems, and the conclusion with respect to democratic ideals that at some point a nation confronts its final conviction about what it desires that human life should become. The main outlines of this general philosophical position have now become familiar through the development of empiricism or positivism during the past two centuries and have been emphasized in the renascent positivistic movements of the past twenty-five years, first in Europe and then in America. And much that is contended for concerning knowledge and values in this position remains, in spite of the Kantian and Hegelian counterrevolution, well considered and sound. Indeed the question which now appears is not so much whether what Hume explicitly said in the above main points is true, as whether it is the whole truth, and whether the partial truth by itself is not as misleading in some respects as it is illuminating in others. It is a question, here, of whether what has been said about the bearing of the "passions" and "inclination" upon valuation, though in many ways correct, is not put in such a way as to obscure the way in which human intelligence or reason can be and is employed in discriminating the better from the worse in human life and in choosing the better.

The answering of these queries requires that one first see, a bit more clearly and in detail, what is involved in this view of the basis of value judgments, and for this purpose I now turn to two public addresses delivered by Professor Sabine on kindred subjects previously to the Shepard Lecture on democracy. The general topic of both these lectures was that of method in the social studies. In his Howison Lecture of 1941, bearing the title "Social Studies and Objectivity," he confronted the problem of method raised by the intimate and apparently indissoluble connection between inquiry into social matters and judgments concerning values. "In all branches of social study," he said,

---

[5] *Ibid.*, p. viii.

there is actively present a suspicion that detachment [from questions of value] . . . is not really possible—perhaps is not even desirable—and that valuations, sometimes of individual scholars but more especially those widely accepted valuations that characterize an age, a nation, or a party, must have a share in shaping the patterns into which facts seem significantly to fall.[6]

Assuming that the suspicion just referred to is correct, and that hence "social studies must include an element of valuation, an attitude of preference and conviction toward the human interests at stake," he proceeds to ask a question of the very first importance, that is, whether this admitted fact is compatible with the objectivity of such studies. If the idea of a completely neutral history, economics, sociology, or politics must be given up as unrealistic, and these studies must inevitably concern themselves with values and valuation, must they for that reason cease to be objective as the natural sciences are? Or may they succeed in being objective in their own way, by dealing scientifically or objectively with values themselves?

The negative answer to the above rhetorical questions is foreshadowed in the treatment of Hume's philosophy in the *History of Political Theory* and the criticisms of the Hegelian dialectic made there, and also in Professor Sabine's presidential address to the Eastern Division of the American Philosophical Association in 1938.[7] The argument of this address combines neatly with that of the Howison Lecture on social studies and objectivity. The central positive thesis of the former address is the proposition, contrary to much of the philosophy of the nineteenth century, that the sciences, natural, social, humanistic, and historical, are, on the side of method, essentially one; and that, particularly, the difference in subject matter between the natural sciences and the social studies does not require or justify the employment in the latter of fundamentally different methods or principles of evidence and proof than those which are legitimate in the former. The general logical principles, he affirmed in the summation and conclusion of this address, are "the same in every subject." These principles, which can be no more circumvented or flouted in history than in mechanics, involve among other things veridical observation to discriminate fact from artifact, deduction either by implication or probability of the consequences of proposed explanatory hypotheses, and

[6] *University of California Publications in Philosophy,* XVI [6] (1941), 128–129.
[7] "Logic and Social Studies," *Philosophical Review,* XLVIII (1939), 155–176.

263

the detection of bias in the development and employment of hypotheses. "When the limits of these operations are reached—" he said,

and obviously in particular cases they may be reached in any subject—the limits of knowledge are reached too. There the historian, the economist, the anthropologist, and the student of government, like the natural scientist, has no word but *non possumus;* no conclusion is forthcoming. The vain hope that there is some epistemological trickery to circumvent this conclusion is in reality an invitation to sentimentality, to intellectual darkness, and in the end to barbarism.[8]

When this conclusion, and the general view which it represents, is applied to the question of the objectivity of the social studies, it eliminates one of the alternatives mentioned in the preceding rhetorical questions. Although the argument is not put exactly in this fashion, the essence of the reasoning seems to be that since the social studies do involve value judgments, and since such judgments are based solely neither on logical reasoning, nor on factual evidence, nor on a combination of these, as scientific statements always are, it is not possible for these studies to become objective in the way the sciences are, by dealing scientifically with values. There are those who have tried to provide such a "substantive" solution to the general question of objectivity and value judgments, to show that one may "have evidence for his valuations as compelling as for his facts"; in American philosophy this alternative has been tried both by the pragmatists and by the ethical realists.[9]

But just as the above argument gives general methodological grounds why this alternative is unworkable, so a specific examination of the views of each shows it to contain fatal errors and weakness. Pragmatism, for example, succeeds in making the substantive solution look plausible by using words like "unified," "resolved," and "ordered" to describe the results of inquiry. These words are sufficiently vague so that they can be used, in contexts of factual inquiry, to refer to the relation between factual evidence and the hypotheses confirmed by them, and, in contexts of value judgment, to the relation between states of affairs valued as ends and also as means to valued ends. In this way the essential difference between factual evidence and valuation is obscured, and in the obscuration a mistaken case can be made out for the view that

---

[8] *Ibid.,* p. 176.
[9] "Social Studies and Objectivity," *loc. cit.,* p. 134.

value judgments are made on the same rationale as scientific.[10] The ethical realists are guilty of errors of a different sort, one which is specifiable most briefly being its dependence upon an outworn and inacceptable view that objective knowledge is procurable through rational intuition or the intellectual perception of essences. At the time of Descartes, with the understanding of mathematics which was possible in his day, this was a very plausible view. But experience in both science and philosophy since that time shows that intuitive self-evidence is not a usable guide to what is objective in the way that objectivity is pursued in the sciences. "Apparent self-evidence and necessary truth are so different that one is not an index of the other, and in practice self-evidence proved itself a snare and a delusion." [11]

But the alternative, granting the impossibility of resolving issues about values with the same methods which suffice to deal with issues about logical implication and about facts, is not general skepticism about the use of such methods in the study of social matters, but rather a wise circumspection in the use of the methods with matters to which they are appropriate and a recognition of where they cease to suffice. The position of the scholar in these fields should be that of one who recognizes the *non possumus* mentioned above, and it is illustrated by two very eminent American historians, the late Carl Becker and Professor Charles A. Beard. Professor Beard put the matter strikingly when he wrote that all written history must include " 'an act of faith,' a selection and arrangement of historical fact in the light of some belief about the pattern of meaning . . . [which] is in the nature of the case beyond the scope of positive verification by the facts." [12] This alternative, this way of looking at the matter, involves at the outset the recognition that in the form of "valuation or moral preference" the social studies contain inescapable elements which it is quite appropriate to speak of collectively as an act of faith, since evidence cannot be expected for it.[13] Interest and aspiration, upon which valuation and moral preference rest, are not objective in the way that the occurrence of a fact is objective; and because of this some values must simply be postulated as intrinsic. "Such postulates," Professor Sabine said in words

---

[10] *Ibid.*, pp. 137–141.
[11] *Ibid.*, pp. 134–135.
[12] *Ibid.*, p. 127.
[13] *Ibid.*, p. 134.

which bring the discussion around in a full circle to the concluding passages of the Shepard Lecture, "are the result of choice, which is extralogical. . . . Logically a judgment of value is *sui generis;* and if the value is intrinsic the judgment has simply to be taken or rejected as any other postulate is taken or rejected." [14]

What the social scientist can do, and the same would presumably apply to any other person, scholar or otherwise, who must deal with issues involving questions of values, in being objective, is to recognize himself and make clear to his audience the limits of his objectivity. Since he can neither cultivate complete objectivity and neutrality with respect to values in the way the natural scientist can, nor deal with values scientifically, the next best thing is to recognize clearly when he is being scientific and objective and when he is not, so that he may not pass off upon himself or upon others valuations or preferences disguised as objective, scientifically verified facts. In this matter, as in other forms of salvation, it appears, the beginning of wisdom is the recognition of sin, and the cultivation of the capacity, since the sinless life is impossible, to recognize a transgression for what it is and to refuse to deceive oneself or others into believing it to be an act of righteousness. This, Professor Sabine concluded, is what logic has to offer which bears upon the objectivity of the social studies; and it is the same thing which it has to offer in all other cases, namely, clarity. But in this case it is clarity concerning that feature of the difference between the neutral sciences and the social studies which has been under scrutiny here, that is, clarity about the ultimate postulates of value upon the basis of which the social investigator is operating. On this alternative, from this point of view, he said,

the essence of objectivity in social studies, or anywhere else, is simply clarity: the clearest possible distinction between what evidence warrants and what goes beyond evidence, and the frankest possible avowal of what is assumed for which evidence is lacking. This might be called an analytic, as distinguished from a substantive, solution. In my judgment it is the only one which the case admits of.[15]

---

[14] *Ibid.,* p. 142.
[15] *Ibid.,* p. 134.

III

But is this so? Is it true that clarity about one's fundamental postulates of value is all that objective method can provide in these cases, and that in general in moral judgments, and in particular in choosing between democracy and alternative types of social organization, this is all that a sound method which restricts itself to that for which there is adequate evidence has to offer? And if this is not so, what is wrong with the analysis of these matters which leads to such a conclusion? This conclusion, as the preceding exposition was intended to make clear, rests upon a comprehensive theory of knowledge and value which at many points is well considered and illuminating and is therefore a redoubtable object for critical attack. Obviously it is impossible, within the limits of this essay, for me to criticize the above conclusion by exposing at their origins what appear to be the basic misconceptions in the comprehensive theory from which it derives. What I wish to do instead, in the remaining portion of this essay, is to call attention to certain difficulties, practical as well as theoretical, in the conclusion and to suggest how these difficulties are in fact genuine inadequacies in the theory which render it unsatisfactory as the ground for a sound philosophy of democracy. The general burden of the criticism to be made is, first, that this view does not provide the kind of grounding or basis for which one is looking in the philosophical inquiry into moral preferences and judgments. And second, that if one feels dissatisfied with the sufficiency of the basis which it does provide, he is justified in so doing. For it does appear that there is more to be had.

Where this view fails signally to furnish the kind of basis one wants for holding that democratic ideals, say, are better than totalitarian ones is in its incapacity to provide a proof, evidence, or an objective reason—because it holds that such things cannot in principle be provided—that in holding these things to be better he is right. What it offers instead, itself a thing of value but a very different piece of goods, is the possibility that one may be clear, by means of the accepted canons of logic, about what, in such a judgment of value or goodness, one is accepting without evidence or proof. There does not seem to be any need here for a further analysis of what Professor Sabine means by the word "clarity" in his pronouncements about the limits of objective method, for what he is referring to by that term seems already fairly definitely determined. What he is saying by means of this term is that objectivity about matters involving values consists in being able to discriminate between what one can demonstrate by logic or establish by empirical methods, on the one hand, and what one prizes or values on the other, since these latter processes always involve somewhere postulates about intrinsic values which are, and must be by their very nature, taken without evidence. Valuation depends ultimately upon the wants, desires, or inclinations of human beings, and these things are matters, in Hume's terms, not of reason or understanding, but of the passions.

The tricky, or at least key word here seems rather to be "objective." Valuations, it is claimed, are not objective. But why, and in what way, are they not? Basically because they are not susceptible of proof in the way theorems are demonstrated or matters of fact empirically confirmed or established. But why, and in what way, again, are such things only to be regarded as objective? The complete answers to these questions lie, of course, in the comprehensive theory of knowledge and value to which reference was made above, and can hardly be treated definitively without reference to the foundations of that theory. Every theory of knowledge is in a way an elaborate definition of the term "objective," an attempt to specify the kind of grounds upon which some things can be determined to be genuinely objective and others not. But without examining the detailed grounds for the above theory, or elaborating another to be installed in its place, one can properly and usefully ask how the conclusions to which it leads correspond to some readily available, pertinent evidence.

Now what does a man mean who says that only theorems which can be proved and facts which are scientifically testable are objective? The first thing to notice is that such a person is not giving a nominal definition of this term. He is not saying just, "Let us agree to use the word 'objective' to refer to things establishable in the above ways. From now on, when we use this term, we shall mean only that the things to which it is applied belong to one of these large classes." If this were all he is saying, if all he is doing were making a stipulation about linguistic usage, there would be no argument. And when, on the basis of such a stipulation, he went on to say that judgments of value or worth are not objective, but hence presumably are in the class of the subjective, there would be little to contest, for this would be merely to express in this language the apparently sound discrimination that such judgments are not a priori truths of the kind demonstrated in logic and mathematics, nor the kind of factual truth pursued in the natural sciences by their various and sometimes intricate methods. But there would be little point in any such person then arguing that value judgments are not objective *because* they are not determinable in the above scientific ways, for such an argument would, in this language, be an obvious and fruitless tautology.

The "because" here is indeed just one indication among others that the person who speaks in this way means to convey more than is contained in the above analysis, means to say something further about the character of value judgments, and something positive, about what they are as well as what they are not. And what is it? People use the terms "objective," "nonobjective," and "subjective" to speak about an enormous variety of things, ranging from a species of nonrepresentational painting, through examinations invented by educational psychologists, to dreams, illusions, and hallucinations. It does not seem that the speaker in question means to say that value judgments are not objective in exactly the way that dreams, illusions, and hallucinations are not. For it is characteristic of a dream or illusion, for example, that though it is nonobjective in the sense that it leads one to make judgments that are false, the judgments in question are genuinely objective in intent; they affirm something which can be checked and decided upon in some way which is generally valid. The deluded dreamer may judge that he is conversing with Socrates or Chiang Kai-shek, but it is possible by further experience to establish that this judgment is false, that, for example, neither was available for consultation at the time and, besides, neither speaks English. The drunk man, who in a normal sober condition never would dance well, now capers awkwardly about the floor in the confidence that the wine has brought him a miraculous ease and grace of movement. To others now, and to himself tomorrow, it can be established by obvious means that this judgment was unfortunately and embarrassingly false.

No. The man who is speaking about the nonobjectivity of value judgments does not mean that they are nonobjective in this sense of being mistaken but subject to revision and correction which will substitute objective judgments in their place. He means that they are nonobjective because they are in principle not objective; by their very nature it is impossible for them to be objective, and impossible therefore for them to be made more objective by revisions, or for more objective ones to be substituted for them. It seems, without traversing the analytic road through the many various usages of "objective" and cognate terms, that what he intends to convey is more like that which is conveyed when the psychologist says that his way of examining students is more objective than, say, an essay-type examination, or when a person speaks of varying moods, whims, or appetites as being not objective. He does not mean to convey that we will all wake up some morning and find that all value judgments are dreams, drunken delusions, or illusions of perspective. He means that valuations are, like moods, whims, and passing appetites, the kind of thing about which it is not sensible to argue whether they are correct or incorrect; they are what they are, they are matters of our inclinations and tastes, and about such things, as the woman remarked when she kissed the cow, *non est disputandum*.

Professor Marker read the examination in a temporary slump, after a bad night, and gave it an "F." If he had read it on another day when he was his normal, optimistic self, it might have got a "C." No wonder that even the students realize that such evaluations are subjective, and not to be compared with the scientific objectivity of calculating the ratio between the true and false choices, or better yet, having a machine "process" the examination, untouched by human hands or minds. Professor Pangloss greets each morning with a cheer. "Oh! what a beautiful morning!" he feels with the natives of the operatic Oklahoma, and has, with them, a "beautiful feeling" that everything is going his way and is for the best. But Professor Weltschmerz sees things differently. The mornings look bad to him each day, the skies baleful. He does not deny that the sun does shine, glaringly, on occasion, when it is not obscured by gray clouds, nor that flowering plants do continue to reproduce, nor that birds do chirp and chatter. But what is beautiful about it, what is going his way, or is for the best in the best of all possible worlds, he cannot see.

About such matters who is to say? Clearly it is not sensible to try to argue which of these men is right: whether it is true, as Professor Pangloss says, that the morning is promising and beautiful, or whether

270

Professor Weltschmerz is right in holding the contrary. For what these men are saying are not arguable, objectively decidable affirmations, but rather expressions of mood, feeling, or inclination. How the morning looks to you depends upon how you feel. Whether the sun is shining or not is an objective matter. But whether it is shining beneficently or hurtfully, or whether there is an over-all harmony in the whole concert of nature, depends upon who you are, how you feel, or what is your point of view. The same things affect different people differently. Some like them one way, some another, just as some men like Scotch whisky and others prefer rye. What is of utmost importance in dealing with such matters is not to confuse the objective with the nonobjective, but to be clear when one is making statements for which evidence can be given and when expressing valuations which in the end must depend upon one's tastes and preferences as a human being.

To be sure, not all tastes and preferences are trivial. For this reason it is not quite fair to discuss all value judgments with the gravity which is proper to the moods of professors or to varying human tastes for potable distilled spirits. Nevertheless, when one considers these judgments with all the gravity appropriate to the grandest of them, he must admit that one's judgments about the relative values of democracy and monarchy, like one's preferences for classical music or monogamy, are at bottom matters of taste or inclination. At bottom, in the case of a far-reaching choice like that of democracy, it is a matter of what, in the light of the known relevant facts, one desires that life shall become, of what path of life and personal development he prefers to others. And if one finds that people do differ about these fundamental matters, if on the basis of the relevant scientific information the basic preferences for the democratic or authoritarian ways of life still diverge, then upon a clear recognition of these divergences objective method, in its dealing with such issues of moral value, must rest. It cannot legislate ultimate moral postulates.

IV

In the history of philosophy there are many cases of philosophers who, on the basis of a theory which was in many ways a great and illuminating advance in the understanding of knowledge and things,

271

were nevertheless led by the theory into most peculiar perplexities. For the theory, sound as it was in many ways, involved misconceptions which at the time of its conceiving were difficult to detect and which somehow led its advocates, by a process which seemed to them to be valid reasoning from true premises, to question some of the more obvious facts of life which, without the prodding of the theory, they would hardly have dreamed of doubting. Such, I take it, was the experience of Descartes, who was early led by his reasoning about knowledge and what can be believed with confidence into the peculiar predicament in which only the assurance of the existence of a good God could render indubitable the belief that there was any world besides himself and that perceived physical objects were not just a part of an illusory dream. And such seems to be the case of the man who on the basis of the kind of reasoning depicted above despairingly concludes that values are at bottom a matter of feeling and inclination and hence that value judgments cannot be established by any objective method.

Now in a sense all value judgments are indeed all like moods, whims, and passing appetites: like them in the sense that they are not certifiable by the techniques of demonstration and verification cultivated in the mathematical and empirical sciences respectively; and like them also in that they do seem to depend upon the capacity of things to satisfy human desire or appetite, to make life and experience more satisfying, more pleasant, or more deeply and enduringly happy. But in another way value judgments are not all like moods, whims, and passing appetites; for there is no necessity in the recognition of the above facts for holding that all desires and all things which satisfy human desires, tastes, or appetites are on the same level and cannot be discriminated between. On the contrary, it is one of the stubborn facts of human life, sometimes obscured by complicated philosophical theories, that though a taste for Scotch or rye may be one of those things which depend upon differences between tasters and are not objective, some things have demonstrated well their general capacity to bring satisfaction or happiness into human life in such a way that we know that they are a general and enduring human good. For this reason we can recommend them to others who may not have heard about them, or for some other reason have failed to recognize their value. To them we can say, honestly and objectively, if we choose to speak in this manner, "These

272

things are good. Not because you want them, for you may not want them; you may indeed have a positive distaste for them. Furthermore you may be very clear about not wanting them. We know you; you know what you like and you know what you don't like; and perhaps you don't want and don't like these things. Nevertheless, they are good."

What we mean, further, is that though the person addressed has at present no appetite or appreciation for the things whose value is extolled, we have evidence from experience, from our knowledge of human nature and the conditions of human life, that these things, if given an opportunity, will prove themselves in his own experience. This evidence may be the well-established proposition that these things generally have, under these circumstances, so proved themselves, or it may rest on different, though still experiential, grounds. And if one objects that, as some present philosophers now insist, the broad rationale of the procedures by which such knowledge is derived is the same as that generally in the empirical sciences, there is perhaps no issue to be argued, at least until one knows with some definiteness what the rationale of general scientific method is conceived to be. At present it does seem that any scheme of describing a general way of knowing which is followed in all inquiries in which genuine knowledge is won from experience must result in a description so very broad and indefinite that it obscures at least as many important distinctions as it clarifies important similarities. And one of these distinctions is that between the kind of testing which one does in testing the merit of a piece of music, a way of behaving, or a bowl of soup, and the kind which he does in testing an allegation of scientific fact, such as, for example, that lead is soluble in sulphuric acid.

One cannot deny the obvious fact that human beings do differ in appetite, taste, and capacity to appreciate many things. But it is necessary here to insist upon another aspect of human nature, namely, that human beings differ in their appetites and tastes for some things much less than for others and, further, that in their capacity to appreciate many things they differ even less than in their *de facto* appetites, and about some things little if at all. This is an empirically establishable fact about human nature, and upon this, or something like this, the objectivity of value judgments, and hence the objective ground of moral imperatives, seems to depend. Because of it one can say about specific values, sometimes with great assurance, sometimes with only a small degree of probability, that even though a man has no appreciation of or interest in a thing now, if that thing is given a fair opportunity it will prove itself in his experience in such a way that, once he has developed an appreciation for it, he will recognize its value as others have, and will see that it would have been a matter of genuine loss in his life had he missed it. Nor does there appear to be any room for cavil in the fact that, since some capacities for appreciation differ among men, values in some cases at least can be guaranteed to prove their worth only with some degree of probability. This does not make valuations subjective in the sense that they are not susceptible of direction and guidance by objective method. The man who concludes that, because probability judgments are involved in ethics, that subject is beyond objective method in its fundamental valuations seems to be reasoning like the man who would say that the danger of death from lightning in the United States is not objective since in one year only one out of an approximate three hundred thousand is killed by being struck.

With what justification, after all, do we guide the morals, appetites, tastes, and appreciations of our children as we bring them up? With what justification, indeed, if objectivity in dealing with values is in principle impossible, and if our basis in doing this is merely that we have certain desires about what they should be and become which, in our position of superior power over their plastic, pliant natures, we are able to satisfy in a greater or less degree? There can be and surely often is more justification than this. For we are altruistic with children, as we are not with the wood we are forming into a cabinet, and are concerned therefore with guiding and disciplining the child's desires, in cultivating his tastes, so that he will more successfully find the goods of life and avoid the evils, and that in his own interests as well as those of the community he will pursue not simply what he wants, but what it is wise for him to want.

This applies to a great and wide variety of aspects of the cultivation of human life, from the guidance of culinary tastes, through the appreciation of literature, music, and other arts, to the development of habits of personal and social morality. We do not rest content with the child who wants nothing in the way of food except sandwiches and milk, even though we are assured that nothing further is necessary for his health; nor are we content later, if his literary taste is solely for comic books, or when, bursting from adolescence, his general physical appetites are more noteworthy for their strength and insistence than for their nicety and discrimination. In each of these things we have evidence, genuine and objective evidence, that a life in which the appetites remained unguided, uncultivated, or unrestrained would be, in these respects, in comparison with that which education of desire and taste makes possible, a poorer and less satisfactory one, and that hence, when confronting values of the above sort, we can judge objectively between better or worse even though all claimants to the decision are clearly the object of inclination and desire.

We know that goodness for a man, in morals as in aesthetic experience, is not always just a matter of what he wants, and that there often is some point in disputing about tastes. We know that it is the case that a life in which the literary tastes are nurtured solely on the cartooned adventures of mounted cattle herders or moving picture actresses is vastly inferior, in this respect, to the life which is possible when one has learned to enjoy the richer emotions, the brighter joys, the deft artistry, and the broader insights of the finer literature of the present and the past. We are little tempted to grant, as we should not grant, that with such values objective method is not competent to deal, and can contribute, when issues of valuation arise, only a clear understanding of what are the clearly neutral matters of fact involved and what are the fundamental aesthetic or moral postulates which are and must be taken without evidence.

In these and many other obvious ways we do illustrate in our daily lives the fundamental truth, which has been insisted upon by a variety of philosophers since Plato, that goodness is not solely a matter of inclination and desire, and that it is possible to employ objective methods in the determination of the fundamental decisions about values which the pursuit of the good life entails. Reason does indeed sometimes function as a servant of the passions. No one can deny it. But if one is to describe these things metaphorically it is not correct to say, as Hume was led to, that in its relations with the passions reason is only the slave, and the passions the master. For in its service to the passions, to inclination, appetite, and desire, reason often resembles more the Prime Minister than the slave, directing, guiding, shaping, and cultivating them to the end that the decisions of state which the passions must make will be enlightened and not blind, and that the ends pursued will be not only good because they are desired but desired because they are good. Such would seem to be a more apt metaphorical analogue of the fact that value judgments need not be, and are not all, in some incurable way subjective. For in some cases when a man affirms that a thing is good, or that one thing is better than another, there are ways of finding out objectively whether what he is saying is true. He is not merely sighing or groaning, or uttering ecstatic cries, or issuing disguised imperatives. He is saying something which is capable of being true or false; and there is in some cases evidence sufficient to determine that the assertions he has made are as a matter of fact justified and what he has said can be believed to be true.

V

Upon a basis of this kind, finally, democratic ideals and practices can be philosophically justified. They can be justified on the ground not merely that they are what we want, if we do want them, but also that they are good, and that when one affirms that they are good he is saying something that is the case and can be determined to be so by a fair and honest method. These ideals and practices are good, and preferable to the various authoritarian and totalitarian alternatives which at present likewise invite the allegiance of men, because in their working they do display, for those who honestly wish to find out, that they have capacities superior to their rivals for making life more deeply and broadly satisfying. And it is not just in our own lives, we who happen to have a taste for democracy and who thus differ from others whose tastes and inclinations turn in contrary ways, that they have these capacities. For though men do disagree profoundly concerning the values of democratic ideals and practices, it is happily the case that value judgments are not all basically incorrigible; there is a bar before which tastes and appetites can be argued fruitfully to some decision. And so one may maintain to those who are doubtful of the values of the democratic life, that if they will try them they too will find that our allegations of its superiority are not mistaken. Once they have tasted the flavor which life possesses when men have the rights of free men to direct their own

276

affairs, to deliberate openly upon fundamental social matters, to criticize, correct, and depose lawfully those in power, and to diverge from
the beliefs of the majority, they will discover that in the judgment
against democracy they have indeed been choosing the worse because
they did not know the better, and they will not, if the opportunity is
open, choose it further.

If the democratic ideals and practices to which we proclaimed our
allegiance in the recent war, and which we now champion in an uneasy
peace, are good, not only for us but for mankind generally, they can
have this kind of justification. And to the extent that it is wanting for
any part of them, we must be prepared to consider afresh whether
they deserve the advocacy and support which we have been giving
them, and also indeed whether they are what we really want for ourselves. The practical consequences of these conclusions for the conduct
of both the domestic and foreign affairs of a contemporary democracy
are many and important, but they cannot be traced out here. It is an
old story in democratic as well as nondemocratic societies that the "old
order changeth" and "new occasions teach new duties," but it is not an
easy lesson to keep learned and to apply. Moral ideals and practices
must continually demonstrate in a changing world their capacity to
make their contribution to the goodness of life. Unless our advocacy
of democracy is either dishonest or misled, unless it is but another form
of that stubborn ideological imperialism to which individuals and nations so easily incline, it must persistently and openly submit its program to this test of performance.

In following this practice we in America shall surely find that various
elements of the methods, traditions, and ideals which we have prized
highly must now have their value reassessed. We must be prepared for
the discovery that some things which we have thought to be necessary
features of the good society are not so, that if they once were, they are
no longer, and may now be a serious obstacle thereto, or, less seriously,
may be incidental features which recommend themselves to us because
of our peculiar geographical, economic, or sociological conditions but
which cannot be recommended on objective grounds to others. Some
of our values, on the other hand, will surely be revealed, despite time
and change and assaults from the right and the left, to be worthy of
the judgments which we and our democratic forebears have made of

them. And still other things which at one time seemed either unrelated to the realization of democratic ideals, or positively opposed to them, will turn out to be now important ingredients of democratic practice, to be so important, perhaps, that a recognition of their value is one of the primary conditions on which the survival of modern democratic society depends.

Realizing and remembering these things, we should be less apt than we now are in our advocacy and defense of democracy to behave as if political, economic, and social arrangements which have the sanction of custom, habit, or entrenched practice in our own society are thereby certified to have their archetypes in Utopia and to be indispensable features of any good society. In our allegiance to our own ideals we should be less liable either to spiritual pride, to a finicky insistence upon social incidentals, or to a dead conservatism which vainly hugs the cold remains of social institutions after their moral life has fled. On the other hand, if the democratic ideals and practices we endorse and advocate have been tested in the manner described above and their merits therewith sustained and approved, we have the enheartening assurance that they have the support, not only of our desires, or our fortunes or military power, but also of honest moral judgment. These things, we can be confident, when they are given the opportunity to display their value, and men are taught to know and appreciate them, do not fail, in a fair, objective way, to prove that they are good.

Reason, Morality, and Democracy

G. WATTS CUNNINGHAM

O NE of the subtlest among current irrationalisms is grounded in the assertion that the meaning of words is by convention. If this assertion be strictly true, any use of a word is as satisfactory as another if it is as clearly formulated and as consistently maintained; the only question then at issue in linguistic usage is that raised by Humpty Dumpty and the only plausible answer is that given by him, namely, that the function of words is to serve the will of the user. Thus, to ask what democracy is or who is a democrat is to ask a question which is meaningless unless it be construed with reference to some occasional use of the words "democracy" and "democrat."

It is indeed true that all symbols, verbal or other, are by convention; they are instruments created, consciously or otherwise, for a purpose. But the meaning of symbols is not thus by convention, since it includes what is meant and this is quite independent of the fact that it is meant; the symbols employed to symbolize it are determinate in respect to it, and do not determine it. There is no proper language, to be sure, but there is a proper use of language, namely, to refer to what is meant; otherwise, language could not perform any function outside of Bedlam. Humpty Dumpty was absolute master of his words only because he was absolute master of his universe of discourse; and this, it should be remembered, was Alice's looking-glass room. Symbols which are useful for purposes of communication, even for purposes of significant soliloquy, must symbolize something which is not brought into being by the circumstance that it is symbolized.

The word "democracy" is no exception to this rule. The word itself

279

is a product of Greek invention, but not what it means. That is the state of affairs, whatever it is, to which it refers and which lends to the word a significance not delimited by any biographical or cultural contexts. It remains in reference in the midst of divergent views about it and renders the historical controversy about democracy something more intelligent than an incoherent series of unrelated soliloquies. And the "proper" use of the word is in principle determinable through its exploration.

I

Those who regard themselves as democrats (and they are the ones who should be privileged to say what democracy *prima facie* is) think of democracy as at once a way of life and a form of government. The form of government is the institutional implementation of the way of life, which is said to be that which generates and maintains the welfare of the people. Thus, what is meant by the word "democracy" as used by the professed democrat may be shortly described as the way of life within which the "welfare of the people" is the objective of both individual and group behavior.

Having said this, however, one has said nothing precise or final about democracy. One has only thereby raised the question, What is this welfare and by what individual behavior and institutional machinery is it nurtured and sustained? But this is the crucial question in the debate, and in its answer lies the final answer to the question what democracy is.

In the present discussion, attention will be centered primarily on the first part of this question. What, we are to inquire, is to be understood by the phrase, "welfare of the people," as desiderated by the democrat? That such an inquiry is concerned with only one aspect of the general problem is obvious, of course, but that it is also concerned with what is logically fundamental is clear on little reflection. Any given view of the end necessarily entails some specification of the means, and some view of the end is presupposed in any specification of the means. If the welfare in question be identified with economic goods without remainder, for instance, and if the people whose welfare is in question be taken collectively rather than distributively, the details of its implementation must be construed in very different terms from those demanded if the people be taken distributively rather than collectively and their welfare be understood to include also what Aristotle calls "goods of the soul." On the other side, radically different views of the welfare of the people are entertained by those who regard the exercise of civil liberties as relatively unimportant and subsidiary to legislative enactment or dictatorial fiat in its implementation and by those for whom the exercise of such liberties is foundational to good government. Thus, the present discussion is concerned with the fundamental issue, and in conclusion reference will be made to implications of the analysis in respect to means.

There is at least initial agreement among professed democrats that the welfare of the people must be measured in terms of both economic and moral goods. If people are to live well they must first of all live, it is agreed all around, and from this tautology it follows that they must in any case be guaranteed the necessities of life. To these the democrat would add at least some of the luxuries, agreeing in principle with Aristotle that "it is impossible, or at least difficult for a person to do what is noble unless he is furnished with external means." But, agreeing once more with Aristotle, the democrat insists that the desiderated welfare cannot be adequately evaluated in terms of economic goods, however rich, but includes moral goods as well. And these moral goods he regards as indispensable; for him, as for the Christian, a man ultimately profits nothing if he gain the whole world at the price of his soul.

The democrat, then, prizes the welfare of the people in the sense in which such welfare is both economically and ethically estimable and regards moral values as logically prior. Consequently, when one asks what democracy is and who is a democrat, one is asking a question which is basically ethical in its connotation. One is asking, ultimately, what is the nature of moral values and by what means they are generated and maintained among men. For, as viewed by the professed democrat, discussions concerning the best form of government or proper social and economic legislation touch the fundamental matter only when they are extended, beyond economics, to include those values indicated by the words "good" and "evil" and their congeners— "right" and "wrong," "just" and "unjust." Thus, for example, the ques-

281

tion whether that form of government which governs least is the best form ultimately runs to ground in moral considerations.

It is precisely because of different views about this subject matter that professed democrats are currently divided into two hostile camps engaged in the unrewarding exercise of casting verbal stones at each other in the name to which all alike have sworn allegiance. What one camp disapproves in the name of democracy is approved by the other in the same name because, in last analysis, of two radically different conceptions of that aspect of the meaning of the word "democracy" which lies in the realm of moral values. Underlying the differences in economic theory, which are in the forefront of the controversy, are differences in ethical theory; on one side the welfare of the people is not also by the people, while on the other it is both of and by the people. And the only way out of the semantic confusion is through clarification of the end in whose name the loyalties of all have professedly been baptized. What is at issue is the nature of the morally good life and how it may be implemented in human society.

II

In the long history of the debate about morality in Western ethics, two questions have been mainly to the fore. These are: What is the status of moral good and evil? and, What is the matrix of moral good and evil? To these questions sundry answers have been proposed but, despite important differences in detail, they may with tolerable accuracy be classified as either absolutistic or relativistic with reference to the first question and as either rationalistic or irrationalistic with reference to the second. According to the absolutist, moral values are universal, the same for all under all circumstances and in all cultures, and even in an important sense eternal and immutable; according to the relativist, on the other side, they develop in the evolution of mankind and are, consequently, the creatures of circumstances and cultures. The matrix of good and evil is for the rationalist functionally linked with reasoning, whereas for the irrationalist it lies beyond the reach of reason in some nonrational realm of sentiment or fiat or faith.

Clearly, these two questions are logically linked. And, what is of primary concern here, the question at issue between rationalists and irrationalists is logically fundamental; an answer to it entails and is presupposed by an answer to the other question. It has figured prominently in the historical debate because of its importance, and disagreement on the proper answer underlies divergent theories of good and evil. It is therefore of special relevance to the present inquiry.

In the historical debate it has been considered under various formulations. The elderly Protagoras and the young Socrates discussed it in Plato's dialogue as the problem of the teachability of virtue; Aristotle considers it as the problem of practical wisdom; the Christian thinkers debated it as the problem of the reasonableness of faith; for Spinoza it is the problem of "affects" and ideas; for Hume it becomes the problem of the relation between sentiment and reasoning; and for Kant that of the relation between pure and practical reason; ideas and ideals are the alternatives for the Hegelians, and they remain so for the pragmatists though within a universe of discourse with radically different epistemological assumptions; the will to truth *versus* the will to power is the Nietzschean formulation of it, which is but an adaptation of Schopenhauer's distinction between the will in choice and the will to live; and for the contemporary semanticist it is the question whether declarative sentences in which the word "good" and its congeners appear as grammatical predicates are or are not merely emotive collocations of words indicative, if of anything, of the relatively unimportant biographical fact that something is liked or disliked by some person or some group of persons. But however formulated, the question has remained in principle the same throughout. It is whether reasoning is or is not competent in the business of living as distinguished from the business of making a living—is or is not functional, that is, in the determination of moral good and evil. This is the question in respect to which no significant social philosophy has succeeded in remaining neutral.

For the sake of clarity, it is important to note what precisely is here asked. It is not whether every individual exercises his reason in the determination of what on each occasion he accepts as good or rejects as evil; it is, rather, whether any individual can make a reasoned judgment about the moral value of what on occasion is accepted as good or rejected as evil. That all of us most of the time and most of us all of the time accept as good or reject as evil what is so designated by our catechisms and mores is, of course, a patent fact; but it is also a patent fact that, not infrequently, serious questions are raised whether what is called good or evil by our catechisms or mores is properly so called. What is here being asked is whether or not reason can, in principle at least, be of assistance when we become thus querulous about the proper application of our moral terms.

The answer to this question must be sought in an analysis of our linguistic procedures when we apply such terms. What is it that we actually call good or evil, and why? How do we actually go about resolving our doubts about the proper application of the words? Complete answers to such questions cannot be attempted here, but the following observations are relevant to the present purpose.

Apparently at least, the situations to which we apply the words "good" and "evil" in their broadest scope are desiderative situations—situations, that is, in which desires and aversions actually function. Anything which can be said to be good or evil is so only in relation to some desiderative agent, earthworm or man; if a thing is desired or averted it is so far forth good or evil, and vice versa. Apart from a desiderative situation, there is neither good nor evil. At least, this seems to hold in the empirical application of the words; and it must hold from the standpoint of the angels, or good and evil as we empirically understand them are not there envisaged. If it be significant to say with Browning that "all's well with the world," then we must suppose that "God is in His heaven"; or if, as Russell would have it, "omnipotent matter rolls on its relentless way . . . the trampling march of unconscious power," it has no relevance to what we call good and evil nor they to it. As we human beings ordinarily use the words, at any rate, "good" and "evil" find application only within desiderative situations or what are assumed to be such.

It may be and has frequently been denied, however, that the words in their moral connotation are applicable to every desiderative situation. Those who take this position would distinguish good and evil from moral good and evil, limiting the latter to desiderative situations of a certain sort. And it is evident that much can be said in support of this position on the basis of such considerations as, for example, that when we speak of what is good or evil for an earthworm and what is good or evil for a normal human being we are speaking of significantly different subject matters.

284

Whatever may be the proper answer to the question thus raised, it is clear that some desiderative situations involve a technique of behavior not characteristic of others. This is the technique of means and ends. The distinction between means and ends depends on choice, but in many desiderative situations choice is apparently not operative. Hence the technique is not characteristic of all desiderative agents, but only of some; we do not hesitate to say that normal human beings employ it, but only poetic license will permit us to say the same of an earthworm. It is also clear that this type of desiderative situation is the one in which good and evil in the moral sense come to fruition in human affairs. It is therefore of exclusive concern here, and for convenience it will henceforth be referred to as the moral situation, but without prejudice to the further question whether or not it may alone be properly so called.

In the light of these remarks the main question before us may be shortly stated thus: Is reasoning competent within the moral situation? And this is equivalent to asking whether or not it can aid in the determination of means and ends in respect to their moral value.

The crux of this question lies, of course, in the problem of ends. It is generally admitted that means are relative to ends and that, consequently, the determination of means is with reference to ends; it is also generally admitted that genuine as distinguished from spurious ends must be determined with reference to means; and it is generally admitted, further, that reasoning is competent here. Everyone knows that men do not gather grapes of thorns or figs of thistles and that, if they are ever to gather grapes or figs, they must learn that grapes come only from grapes and figs from figs. But what about the moral value of means and ends? Can reasoning help us here? If so, it must be able to determine the moral value of ends since that of means is dependent on them.

III

Those who deny the competency of reasoning within the moral situation attack it mainly at this point. They maintain that there must be some ultimate end by reference to which means and ends are evaluated morally, or a moral standard is lacking, and that reasoning is powerless either to determine or to evaluate such an end. Agreeing thus, however, they differ on the important question concerning the source and warrant of this end. The answers proffered are mainly three, which, taken together, probably exhaust the possibilities. These are the answers given by hedonists and fideists and voluntarists—the three main historical types of irrationalism in ethical theory.

The details of this controversy are here irrelevant and may be left on one side. But the fundamental inconsistency which besets irrationalists, of whatever persuasion, is important for the present purpose and calls for comment. What, then, is the inconsistency, and what is its significance?

The inconsistency is exhibited in the double-talk among the irrationalists about their supposedly nonrational ultimate ends. Not only do they insist on reasoning about such ends, but they tend to assume that the moral value and the warrant of the postulated ends are somehow grounded in their reasonableness.

Thus Hume, for example, having asserted that pleasures and pains are ultimate ends for which no reasons should be asked or can be given, immediately admits that not every pleasure is morally good and not every pain is morally evil. The morally important task of distinguishing between pleasures and good pleasures, pains and evil pains, he attributes to "a pleasing sentiment of approbation" with which we are supposedly endowed and which warrants "a preference to useful above pernicious tendencies" of qualities and actions. But it turns out that a good deal of reasoning is employed by this "sentiment" in performing its task, enough at least to determine which tendencies are useful and which are pernicious in the business of living and are therefore worthy of being preferred or rejected; and this seems to be the morally important matter. Nor is Hume's inconsistency here exceptional among hedonists; on the contrary, it is typical. No hedonist, so far at least as my knowledge extends, has ever stood squarely on the dictum that pleasure alone is morally good and pain alone is morally evil; even by the Cyrenaics, who among the hedonists perhaps most nearly approached consistency, it is at least tacitly assumed that pleasures and pains must be put to trial in the court of reasoning before any verdict can be rendered concerning their moral value. And the verdict is everywhere rendered, not in favor of pleasures and pains per se, but in

286

favor of reasonably warrantable pleasures and pains. It is not pleasure and pain as ultimate ends in terms of which moral value is defined by the hedonists, but pleasure and pain functioning as means and ends in the technology of human behavior.

According to St. Augustine, turning now to the most articulate tradition of fideism, "we could not say that one thing was better than another, if we are to judge truly, unless a conception of the good itself had been impressed upon us, by reference to which we might approve something as good, and prefer one good to another." And to see this good, we must "see God, not good by a good other than Himself, but the good of all good"—a vision which is ultimately derived only from revelation properly understood. Thus, by hypothesis, reasoning can have nothing of importance to say about moral value; the "conception of the good itself" is not a rational conception but a postulate of faith. Nevertheless, we find St. Augustine arguing at great length about good and evil and even assuming that what reason has to say here is the primary warrant for preferring his "conception of the good itself" to others. And this is beyond doubt characteristic of the Augustinian tradition in its orthodox formulation; nor is there any doubt that amazement would be expressed by representatives of that tradition that they should be numbered among the irrationalists. The fact remains, however, that in the tradition two incompatible things are being said: that the good which is God is ultimately derived from revelation, and that the reasonableness of the good which is God is its only guarantee. The conception of reason in this context as *fides quaerens intellectum* is but a verbalization of the fundamental inconsistency.

Irrationalists of the voluntarist ilk are of many sects, theological and secular. But the pure form of the doctrine, unmixed with theological assumptions or halfhearted compromises, is expressed in a blustering passage supposedly from the pen of the late Joseph Goebbels: "Intellectual activity is a danger in the building of character. . . . I put on my helmet, I draw my dagger and declaim heroic verse." Here is the art of posturing exhibited in its naked essentials: reasoning about good and evil is not only futile and decadent, it is positively dangerous. But is this art of posturing also the art of living? To make it so reasoning must be invoked, and it is invoked. When one asks the inevitable question, Why these particular trappings—a helmet rather than a laurel wreath, say, or a dagger rather than a pen, or heroic rather than pastoral verse—in the business of living and building character? it soon appears that mere posturing will not serve for an answer but is only the outward show of hidden assumptions. These, we learn from the major prophet of the art, have to do with a superior race and a new nobility—ultimately, the Will to Power. Sometimes, indeed, this is demoted from the exalted status appropriate to capital letters and made subservient to him whose will is strong; thereupon, "Plato blushes for shame and all free-spirits kick up a shindy," and the supposed halo about the countenance of Zarathustra takes on the form of a cheap adornment donned to impress the willful. In the full light of the "great Noontide," however, such antics on the part of "free-spirits" seem somehow quite unbecoming and Plato's blushes are without cause. For it is written that the creator of moral values, even though beyond good and evil, must be intelligent about his loyalties, that the new nobility must "learn to become procreators and cultivators and sowers of the future" and so to redeem the past by making amends to their children for being the children of their fathers. On the occasion of such preachments, Zarathustra emerges from his cave of meditation, glowing like the morning sun through gloomy mountains and with a new table under his arm, a prophet of calculated foresight rather than of blind willfulness; and, despite the helmet-and-dagger heroics of some of the neophytes, this seems to be an important part of the prophet's message. Other voluntarists speak in various languages, to be sure, but *mutatis mutandis* they exhibit essentially the same inconsistency.

Thus in fact do irrationalists in ethical theory indulge in talking at cross-purposes with themselves. What is the theoretical significance of the fact? That lies in the consideration that the double-talk is inescapable. If, as is by hypothesis agreed, there is some ultimate end (pleasure, or the good itself, or the will to power, or whatever) in reference to which alone human conduct is morally valuable and for which reasons can neither be given nor asked, it follows as a corollary that moral evaluation of conduct is not amenable to reasoned considerations except in the form of apologetics; all that can consistently be said in the premises is to the effect, "This is what I like or believe to be good or will to be good, and I hope [with whatever exhortation or propaganda, of course] others will like it or believe it or will it too."

But, if one is to say anything that is morally important and compelling, one must say much more than this; one must say, "This is what I like or believe to be good or will to be good, and others are reasonably obliged to like it or believe it or will it too." Hence, the double-talk.

IV

But one cannot have it both ways. Either there is an ultimate end which is beyond the powers of reason to determine and evaluate, or there is no such end. If there is and if moral values are determinable in reference to it alone, then it is futile to reason about moral matters so far as moral obligation is in question; by hypothesis it is the end which ultimately justifies all means and ends, and also by hypothesis this end is beyond reasoning's competency. On the other hand, if there is no such end then it is without warrant to say there is and irrationalism in ethical theory must be disavowed.

An irrationalist who would seek a way out of this dilemma by remaining consistently by his fundamental thesis could achieve only an esoteric doctrine bought at a great price. Since by hypothesis no reason could be advanced why the end postulated is preferable to another, the moral values defended would be of concern only to himself and to any others who happened to be similarly predisposed; in respect to the end itself there would be no obligation whatever save by proposal or, *in extremis,* force. Thus his moral discourse would be either a soliloquy or a hortatory or edifying conversation with a few congenial spirits or, perchance, a threat to the peace; it could have nothing to do with the sort of obligation which is commonly supposed to be fundamental in the moral experience of mankind, since the notions of duty and right are foreign to its underlying premises. And this is a very high price to pay for mere consistency—too high, indeed, to be paid by anyone who is not willing to do violence to experience in behalf of theory. So far as I know, no irrationalist has been quite willing to pay the price; but the sole alternative seems to be rejection of the basic assumption upon which ethical irrationalism rests.

That assumption lies in the main thesis that there is an ultimate end of conduct which is intrinsically valuable and with reference to which alone all other values are determinable. This is but another way of

saying that in last analysis the end justifies the means and is itself justified without reference to means. But this presupposes that ends and
means are in principle separable, and here is the basic assumption.
Should it be rejected?

Fundamental in every desiderative situation is the desiderative agent.
In the moral situation as above delimited, the agent is a person with
the capacity to choose among alternatives. By virtue of this capacity,
the desires and aversions of the agent are translated into means and
ends. Thus arises a double relativity of means and ends: they are
relative to the agent who wills them, and so are factitious, and they are
interchangeable, an end on one occasion becoming a means on another
and vice versa. On the fatal night at Inverness, for example, the death
of Duncan was an end; but it was a means in the context of "the imperial
theme," apart from which it would have been neither. This relativity
of means and ends underlies the theory, sometimes asserted as the fact,
of the relativity of morals; and because of it we can, as we frequently
do, act as if means and ends were separable not only from each other
but from fact as well.

But equally fundamental in every desiderative situation, and therefore in every moral situation, is the causal order of objects and events.
Human beings cannot act as disembodied spirits; if there is a desire
there also is something desired, if there is an aversion there also is
something averted, and what is desired or averted is not thereby created
or destroyed. Thus desires and aversions, and *ipso facto* means and ends,
are inseparably linked with factuality; whether as end or means, the
death of Duncan is to be the death of a man who is a king bound by
ties of fealty to other equally substantial men with swords of steel.
Because of this linkage with fact, means and ends are linked with each
other; they are as inseparable as are causes and effects, which in fact
they are.

Thus means and ends are factitious but inseparable—factitious as
designed to serve the purposes of conduct, inseparable as bound by the
chain of causes and effects. Their factitiousness is the source of irresponsible behavior, as their inseparability is the ground of responsible
behavior. If we tilt with windmills, it is because our ends are such that
we can entertain them in abstraction from means; if we are ever to learn
better, it will be by recognition of the fact that such unrewarding

exercise springs from loyalty to abstractions. In the business of living, if the business is to be either practically efficient or morally valuable, the technique must be that of ends-means rather than that of ends and means; not only must means be justified by reference to ends but ends must also be justified by reference to means, and this is but another way of saying that in the evaluation of human behavior the final appeal must be to the consequences entailed by the ends-means commitment. If forgetfulness of this leads in practice to futility, it leads to double-talk in ethical theory. And the fact must enter, openly or surreptitiously, into the construction of any theory which can claim for itself compulsion stronger than unreasoned emotive appeal or less brutish than arbitrary force.

V

Of the several species of rationalism in ethical theory, the one which alone seems to me finally defensible and which I should wish to advocate builds openly on the inseparability of means and ends in human conduct and seeks in the fact justification of the assertion of reason's moral competency. According to this type of rationalism, moral good and evil arise in empirical situations where the technique of behavior is that of ends-means; and reasoning is held to be competent here, because such behavior is necessarily committed to consequences with reference to which alone it can be morally evaluated and which reasoning alone is competent to determine. Whether the desired is also the desirable or the averted is also the detestable is the moral question at issue in the moral situation; and this question must be answered, so far as it can be answered, by reasoned consideration of the causal nexus in which what is desired or averted is embedded. In this sense and, as I think, only in this sense the rationalist can say that reasoning determines moral good and evil.

But this type of rationalism is not without its difficulty. In respect to moral values, certainly, there is warrant for Hume's assertion, "It is impossible there can be a progress *in infinitum;* and that one thing can always be a reason why another is desired." It is this consideration that led Hume, as it has led irrationalists generally, to postulate a nonrational end as the basis of moral reasoning; and it underlies Aristotle's conception of a "chief good," though he would not place it ultimately beyond reasoning's reach. The type of rationalism here defended, however, is committed from the beginning to the exclusion of ultimate ends from ethical construction: in the technique of ends-means there are no ultimate ends. Nevertheless, there must be something other than practical efficiency by reference to which moral values are determinable; otherwise, for example, the ends of the intelligent bandit would be even better than those of a blundering philanthropist. If this something is not an ultimate end, what can it be?

The only alternative is an ultimate fact—ultimate, that is, for moral evaluation. And such a fact is ready to hand within the moral situation, namely, the moral agent himself. Through the purposes of the moral agent desires and aversions become means and ends, and it is of the ends-means conduct that moral good and evil are predicable. Thus the moral agent may be said to be the creator of moral values, and therefore the basic moral fact; whatsoever is of good or evil report is so in respect to him about whom the report is proclaimed. It is to this fact that the rationalist may, and in last analysis does, appeal in his moral judgments. Nor is it easy to see how the appeal can be escaped; since every good or evil is somebody's good or evil, appraisal of it cannot finally be made without reference to the person whose good or evil it is. The theologically minded verbally escape it, but only by identifying the moral agent with God; while Kant, who more than most berated the moral value of consequences of behavior, was driven to it in the most significant formulation of his Categorical Imperative where the moral end becomes the moral agent. And such appraisal is embedded in our maxims and incorporated in our laws: if giving pauperizes the giver, it is not philanthropy we commonly agree, and if homicide is in self-defense, it is not murder in the opinion of our courts.

Thus the rationalist agrees with Nietzsche that "men have given unto themselves all their good and bad" and he would agree, further, that the "creating ones were first of all peoples" and "the individual himself is still the latest creation." But he would understand all of this in a sense radically different from that intended by the irrationalist.

According to Nietzsche, the creating ones are the elite and their creation is in "the aristocratic mode of valuation." The double-talk above noted becomes particularly troublesome in the details here, but what can consistently be intended is tolerably clear: the creating ones are only those in whom the will to power is especially strong, strong enough at least to make Plato blush for shame, and their creative technique is that of fiat—they say, simply, Thus shall it be! and thereupon see that it is good. As the rationalist views the matter, however, the creating ones are all moral agents, those in whom intelligence is sufficiently strong to convert desires and aversions into means and ends, and their technique is that of ends-means—they say, Thus so far forth should it be! and thereupon hope that it is good. Though central for both, the moral agent is conceived by the Nietzschean as self-centered and irresponsible in his creative activity and by the rationalist as self-centered but responsible both to himself and to all other moral agents.

It is not difficult to discern the divergent directions in which these alternatives lead. On the one side, moral values are made completely relative to the arbitrary will of their creators and consequently in principle incorrigible; on the other side, moral values are made relative to the reasoned perspectives of their creators and consequently in principle corrigible. Both accept the integrity and defend the freedom of the moral agent, but the freedom defended is of the irresponsible few on the one side and of the responsible many on the other. And these differences are of far-reaching importance for social theory: the one view entails an aristocracy of power, the other a democracy of intelligence.

If it is false that there are ultimate ends of human conduct, the Nietzschean alternative falls with the abstraction on which it is based; and with this remark it may be left on one side. But something remains to be said, in conclusion, concerning the democracy entailed by the other alternative. And what can here be said will turn around the two questions: What are the marks of a democratic individual? and, What is the test of a democratic society?

VI

In his opposition to democracy John Adams, the second President of the United States, stressed the obvious "physical, intellectual and moral inequalities" among men and urged that, since these "are founded in the constitution of nature," there is a "natural aristocracy among mankind." And from all of this he concluded that, since a democracy is a society in which sovereignty resides in "the whole body, assemblage, congregation . . . of the whole people" and must be exerted "by the whole people assembled together" presumably as in a New England town meeting, a genuinely democratic form of government "has seldom, if ever, existed but in theory." But his conception of democracy is very different from that entailed by the view before us and overlooks the main subject matter.

On this view the dictum of Fichte, if for the purpose it may be taken without commitment to the metaphysical context in which it was finally construed by the author, states the fundamental matter: "Not merely *to know,* but according to thy knowledge *to do,* is thy vocation . . . thine action, and thine action alone, determines thy worth." The moral values, as the moral value, of each moral agent are his own creation; his desires and aversions are synthesized and purified in the crucible of action and thereby his goods, as his good, are determined.

Since this holds of all persons and not of a select few only, it follows that there is a moral equality among men. But it is important to note in what sense this may be concluded from the premises. The conclusion is not warranted if it is understood to say that all are equally worthy regardless of what they do, that the behavior of one is on a par with that of any other; here is where reasoning and evaluation of consequences enter into the reckoning. Nor must the conclusion be understood to exclude the individual differences which loom so large in the mind of John Adams or to deny that the fruitage of the conduct of one is more or less socially significant than that of another. What must be understood is, rather, that all are equally creators of moral values and that the worth of each lies in this creative activity; as a point of reference for moral appraisal, each is an ultimate fact. The equality in question, in short, belongs to each by virtue of his centrality in the moral situation.

It follows also that each moral agent is free, but responsibly so. As the creator of moral values, he is free; as bound by the technique of ends-means in his creative activity, he is responsible. He is free to seek the satisfaction of his desires and to escape the dissatisfaction of his aversions, but only within the limits set by the structure of his action; he is free to make behavioral commitments, but responsible to and for the consequences entailed by his commitments. He is, in short, a responsibly free agent.

And his responsibility runs in two directions. On one side, he is under obligation to himself as a purposive agent, to his "ideals" through which his passing desires and aversions are transformed into means and ends; and not the least important part of this obligation is to fashion his ideals in the strong light of factual considerations and thus avoid the fallacy of the reification of his desires and aversions. On the other side, he is under obligation to all desiderative agents and, especially, to all moral agents who are on an equality with him in respect to their creative function. And both obligations obtain, whether he recognizes them or not.

Whoever recognizes them and strives to bend his attitudes and behavior to them deserves and, as I think, alone deserves to be called a democratic person. And his marks are mainly two: he strives to be objective in his appraisal of himself, and he strives to be tolerant in his appraisal of others. He honors his own individual worth, but he measures it in terms of his deeds and not of his good intentions; he respects the integrity of others, but he holds them responsible for what they do and estimates their worth in terms of consequences instead of professions. He claims for himself the right to exercise his intelligence, and he defends the right of others to do likewise; with Whitman, he will "accept nothing which all cannot have their counterpart of on the same terms. . . ." To expect him to love his neighbor is doubtless expecting too much, but to say that he should love his neighbor as himself is only to express the fundamental commandment; if he be a snob, at least his snobbishness cannot be such as to place in jeopardy his own moral integrity or warp his judgment of the moral integrity of his peers.

And his tolerance, it may be noted in passing, is far-reaching. In the realm of conduct, its limits are fixed by the moral integrity of himself and his peers; only conduct which transgresses these limits is intolerably wrong. In the realm of opinion and beliefs, its limits are fixed by truth and principles; only opinions and beliefs which transgress these limits are intolerably erroneous. But this, being interpreted, is to say that its limits here are not firm, since our ignorance outruns our knowledge and our knowledge consequently is subject to amendment; opinions and beliefs concerning which there is not a reasonable doubt are in principle included, but it is difficult to say in detail what these are. Certainly, opinions and beliefs about the "truth" and "principles" concerning which F. J. Sheen, for instance, insists we must be intolerant or threaten "the foundation of all stability" are not among them. The assertion that "about these things we must be intolerant" makes sense only on the assurance that as opined or believed they are absolute and are infallibly known to be so, but there is no such infallible knowledge about these things. On the premises before us, such "truth" and "principles" are progressively specified in the empirical processes of research and intelligent behavior and are consequently subject to revised formulation from time to time in the course of experience at the behest of reasoning. Intolerance about them is, therefore, itself intolerable; indeed, one intolerance which can consistently and with assurance be entertained in these premises is intolerance of intolerance of precisely these things, since the latter intolerance is inextricably linked with the abstraction of ultimate ends. And it is not irrelevant to remark that the "hounds of the Lord" during the bloody days of the Inquisition were thus intolerant in their zeal to save the heretics from error and wickedness, since this historical fact is but a tragic example of the harm that "good" men do because of the theoretical abstraction. The same criticism, *mutatis mutandis,* applies to the Nietzschean or the Marxian or any other who seeks the ground of his "truth" or "principles" beyond the reach of "unenlightened" and uncensored intelligence and predicates his practice on the assumption that the end justifies the means.

Any society which is so organized as to respect and foster the democratic way of life thus briefly indicated deserves to be called a democratic society, whatever its form of government. And if the word "democracy" in its social application is still to be used in reference to the organization of society for which the "welfare of the people" is the objective, a society thus organized alone deserves to be called democratic.

This is not the sort of society in which "sovereignty" resides, for whatever reason, in a select few who, for whatever reason, take it upon themselves to govern for the welfare of the people. It is, rather, the sort of society in which "sovereignty" resides in the people taken distributively and as moral equals, that is, as moral agents; for the welfare in question is a product of social behavior, the creation of moral agents interacting with respect each for the other's integrity and all for the integrity of intelligence, and is consequently the welfare by the people as well as of them. It cannot be handed down from above, it must be achieved from below; it is not made by edicts and executive orders, it

296

is grown through behavior at the grass roots intelligently oriented toward distant horizons. In such a society the function of government is that described by Walt Whitman: "to train communities through all their grades, beginning with individuals and ending there again, to rule themselves. . . ." And of such a society the guardian genius remains an educated mind, but only provided such a mind is multiplied as far as may be and education is concerned with fundamental issues in theory and practice and not merely with the production of gadgets— with the business of living and not merely with the business of making a living.

This sort of democracy is not a gift of nature, unfortunately, but it is not beyond nature. The "realities" to which scheming politicians every- where appeal to buttress their schemes, Adams's "physical, intellectual and moral inequalities" and Whitman's "pervading flippancy and vul- garity, low cunning, infidelity," stand in the way; and they are formi- dable obstacles. But reason, too, is a reality; and, if adequately nurtured, its power is strong. Though it is true, as Aristotle observed, that most men "are moved by necessity rather than by reason, and by fear of punishment rather than by love of nobleness," it is also fortunately true that necessity and punishment may be made to serve rational ends and men may thereby be moved by reason and a love of nobleness. Though responsible freedom is not a natural right, it may be and on occasion has been a social achievement; it must be bought with a price, but the price is neither prohibitive nor contrary to nature. That price is not only eternal but also intelligent vigilance.

Such a society meets the acid test which must be met by any society which can claim to be democratic. It not only tolerates dissenters within its borders, including the minority of one celebrated by John Stuart Mill, it even looks hopefully to them for further insight into truth and principles. Only when the implementation of their opinions and beliefs resorts to force rather than to argument does it regard the dissenters as intolerable; otherwise, they constitute an indispensable part of the body politic. And any society which cannot meet this test, which is so organized that dissension is alien to its genius and must be removed by "liquidating" the dissenters, can be said to be democratic only in a sense which differs radically from the meaning of the word entailed by the preceding analysis and renders the distinction between a democratic society and a totalitarian one quite indiscernible.

Heroes and the Way of Compromise

HENRY ALONZO MYERS

IN A BRIEF and pointed imaginary conversation between Frederick the Great and the utopian pacifists of his own time, William James once epitomized the almost comic clash between the attitude of the hero and that of the extreme advocates of moderation. " 'Dogs, would you live forever?' shouted Frederick the Great. 'Yes,' say our utopians, 'let us live forever, and raise our level gradually.' "

History in the making today offers to the student of human affairs another chapter, already half-written, in the ancient conflict between extremism and moderation. We are perhaps too close to our world to determine the prime cause, if indeed there be one only, of its division into warring camps. One clue, however, is to be found in the events leading up to World War II: the worship of half-truths which made some peoples seek the heroic life as a national ideal while others sought to live by compromise alone.

Frederick, in spite of his fierce scorn, must have been clever enough to see how much he owed to the moderate men of his own time, who served him as foils. Looking back on the events of the past thirty years, we can see that our own Fredericks owed much of their success in enthralling the spirit of great nations to the fortune which made them loom large against a pale background of peoples who seemed to have lost the courage to face the fact that a willingness to die is sometimes the price of a life worth the living. The hero is always dramatic; the moderate, colorless by contrast, and especially so when he loudly proclaims his revulsion from every form of the heroic spirit.

What happens to a world in which the lines are sharply drawn between extremists and moderate men? Part of the answer is already

298

written. First, the extremist forces his way of life upon his fellows. In the pursuit of his goal, whatever it may be, life is a bright coin which he is willing, at any moment, to exchange for glorious death; he scorns those who believe that a long and peaceful life is the only reasonable goal. In dealing with him, moderate men discover that compromise is not true compromise, but appeasement. Those who make this discovery have a choice between two equally extreme courses of action. Either they may themselves take heroic measures against the fanatic who will not compromise or they may persist in the error of appeasement until it becomes nihilism, the denial of the heroic in life which men sometimes pay for by losing their freedom and even their lives.

Living witnesses to this process, all the great nations were committed during World War II to the heroic way of life. Each was determined to fight on to victory or to death. Some sincerely believed that the moderate way of compromise is the only true way for men and for nations; but first, before they could think of ideal procedures, there was a job to be done, someone to be blotted out, someone with whom compromise was impossible.

After World War II, what? Freed from the menace of some of the new Fredericks, the moderates will presumably go back to the business of raising their level gradually. For some time they will have a new respect for *some* heroes, for those who successfully led them against the would-be world conquerors; but this new respect may easily vanish in the inevitable reaction against "blood, sweat, and tears." Will our utopians increase the power and menace of the remaining Caesars by again insisting that the way of compromise is always the best way of life?

We cannot correct the past mistakes which brought Caesarism into our world. The generation which turned moderation itself into a new form of extremism by refusing to find a place in their scheme of things for the heroic human spirit has done its work. But it is never too late to bring the lessons of experience to bear upon the future. A better understanding of human nature may yet save us from repeating old mistakes.

299

II

Dramatic poetry is a wonderful storehouse of the lessons of experience and possibly the best source of information concerning heroes and the heroic spirit. By an apparent paradox of intellectual history, the doctrine of the Superman, which exalts intensity of experience, and the philosophy of moderation, which aims chiefly at a long and complete life, were both derived from a study of the tragic hero. In the *Poetics* Aristotle describes the extremism of the tragic hero as an error, a failure to find the moderate way, which causes his downfall. In *The Birth of Tragedy* Nietzsche concluded that only as an aesthetic phenomenon is life eternally justified, a conclusion which he expanded in his later writings into the view that life is worth the living only for the Superman, only for the tragic hero who lives dangerously, who risks all to gain all, who touches the heights and depths of experience.

The Birth of Tragedy was Nietzsche's first book. In tragedy he discovered the apparent explanation of his youthful admiration for Richard Wagner's heroic music; from a study of tragedy he derived the conclusions that have strongly influenced so many movements in modern society, movements ranging in intensity from the violence and brutality of the Nazi party to the relatively mild "strenuous life" advocated by Theodore Roosevelt.

According to his own account, Nietzsche at first undertook his study of tragedy to answer a question which seemed more likely to interest the scholars and philologists among whom he moved than to unsettle the world of affairs. Did their interest in tragedy indicate that the Greeks were a pessimistic or decadent people? Nietzsche decided, on the contrary, that tragedy represents the highest degree of affirmation and acceptance of life. In the years which saw the production of the great Attic tragedies the Greeks were a strong people, capable of facing reality at its worst without flinching.

In seeking the answer to his question Nietzsche contracted a raging fever of hero worship. The question of Greek pessimism widened out in his mind into the more important question of whether life is worth living. Most spectators of a great tragedy leave with a sense of reconciliation, with the feeling that life, though terrible, is just. On this

300

point Nietzsche made an important reservation. Life is worth living, he decided, only for the extremist, only for the hero who reaches the heights and depths of feelings. Upon completing his study of tragedy, the future prophet of the Superman was prepared with the outlines of his message. Do you wish to make life worth living? Then love your fate; live dangerously and on the heights; be an extremist, a hero, a superman.

Nietzsche was fascinated by the intensity of the hero's experience, but Aristotle was more deeply impressed by its brevity. The simple fact revealed by tragedy is that heroes always live dangerously and usually do not live long. A comparison of Aristotle's remarks on the tragic hero in the *Poetics* with his theory of the golden mean in the *Nichomachean Ethics* shows the important influence of his study of dramatic poetry on his doctrine of moderation. Since heroes usually do not live long, the extremism which brings about their end is an error of judgment, a tragic failure in conduct. It is an error and a failure because happiness is not to be found in intensity of feeling but only in full self-realization, which requires a long and complete life. "For one swallow does not make a summer, nor does one day; and so too one day, or a short time, does not make a man blessed and happy." Virtue is the very opposite of the error of the tragic hero; it lies in the habit of choosing a mean between extremes, in the moderation which usually secures length of life.

Individual temperament is probably the only explanation for the paradoxical manner in which Aristotle and Nietzsche drew opposite conclusions from the same evidence. Quite clearly, one placed the highest value on the duration and completeness of experience, and the other placed it on intensity. The tragic hero, whose experience is intense, narrow, and brief, is a failure in the eyes of Aristotle and the ideal man in the eyes of Nietzsche.

The opposition between the cult of hero worship, which leads to Caesarism, and the philosophy of moderation, when it is carried to the extreme of nihilism,[1] turns on the question of which quality of experi-

---

[1] Aristotle himself never carried his doctrine of moderation to the extreme of nihilism. At the risk of inconsistency, he admitted that the virtuous man will sometimes prefer a swallow to a summer: "It is true of the good man too that he does many acts for the sake of his friends and his country, and if necessary dies for them . . . since he would prefer a short period of intense pleasure to a long one of mild

ence—intensity or duration—is more desirable. The whole truth about
human nature, as an answer to this question, can be derived from the
same evidence from which the contradictory half-truths of hero worship
and nihilism have been derived.

III

The tragic hero has enough in common with other men to make his
fate significant to them, and at the same time is unusual enough to
excite and hold their interest. His difference, which is the secret of his
dramatic interest, is his intensity, which is first manifest in his unyielding purpose. The first quality which distinguishes the hero is the will
to do or die, the uncompromising spirit which makes him pay any
price, even life itself, for his object. It is this quality which Wolfe at
Quebec has in common with Marlowe's Tamburlaine, which Stonewall
Jackson shares with Melville's Captain Ahab. In itself it is without moral
significance, for the unyielding hero may be either a saint or a sinner in
the eyes of the spectator. But unyielding character is the spring from
which heroic and dramatic actions flow.

The hero's attitude toward life is that of Ahab toward the whale; not
even the gods can swerve him from his purpose. "Swerve me? Ye cannot swerve me, else ye swerve yourselves! Man has ye there. Swerve
me? The path to my fixed purpose is laid with iron rails, whereon my
soul is grooved to run. Over unsounded gorges, through the rifled
hearts of mountains, under torrents' beds, unerringly I rush! Naught's
an obstacle, naught's an angle to the iron way!" Such intensity demands
concentration, and Ahab's purpose is centered on a single object, Moby
Dick. "Ay, ay!" he cries, "and I'll chase him round Good Hope, and
round the Horn, and round the Norway Maelstrom, and round per-
dition's flames before I give him up." And so it always is with heroes:
each has his favorite phantom, always something specific, never an
abstraction. The hero does not die for love, or for power, or for success,
or for revenge: he dies for Juliet, or for Abbie, or for Rautendelein,
or for Desdemona; he dies to be Duncan's successor or for "infinite
riches in a little room"; he dies to climb the tower that he has built. The

enjoyment, a twelve-month of noble life to many years of humdrum existence, and
one great and noble action to many trivial ones."

302

hero is indeed always a monomaniac to some extent, but he is different from his fellow men only in degree, not in kind, only in the intensity with which he pursues his object.

In life and in drama the heroic is marked by an uncompromising will; in both, moreover, the difference between the simplest and the greatest is that the greatest brings the widest range of feeling and the highest intellectual power to bear upon his inflexible purpose. Such is the difference between Grant in the Wilderness and Lincoln in the White House, between Tamburlaine and Hamlet. Grant's determination to fight it out on one line is as firm as Lincoln's will to carry through the war, but Lincoln adds to fundamental determination an intellectual power made manifest in his brooding on the meaning of events, as in the Gettysburg and Second Inaugural addresses, and a wide range of feeling which carries him into the hearts of all the actors in the national tragedy. His acts of kindness to delinquent soldiers, his concern for the point of view of his opponents, his letter to Mrs. Bixby—make more pointed, more heroic, more valuable his determination to save the Union. We rightly value the heroic according to its cost to the hero; and a Hamlet, to whom the cost is so great as to make him seem at times weak in will, displays a richer heroism in one moment of tortured struggle than can be found in all the thoughtless, insensate fury of a Tamburlaine.

IV

Such is the nature of the hero; what are its inevitable consequences? If we may trust the testimony of all serious drama, the outstanding consequence is that the hero lives intensely but not long. Life is the price we must all pay for experience; most of us dole it out in little sums over a long period of time; the hero gladly pays in a lump sum.

A more profoundly significant consequence is that the hero always gets what he wants—and always pays the full price. Oedipus finds the unknown murderer, at a cost; Wolfe takes Quebec, but falls in the moment of victory; Ahab throws the harpoon, and dies; Romeo comes back to Juliet, in death. The hero can have anything he wants, for a price; but not even a hero can get something for nothing.

Drama reveals these consequences in many ways—by showing that the hero falls as far as he rises or that he is brought down by the very forces which bring him to the top. The great turn of the wheel of fortune which carries the hero to the extremes of joy and grief, often in one moment of dazzling intensity, is the dramatic symbol of the endless little ups and downs, the little sorrows and joys, of ordinary men. The hero's great moment contains within itself rise and fall, fortune and misfortune, triumph and disaster. As Ahab at last faces the white whale alone, he cries: "Oh, now I see that my topmost greatness lies in my topmost grief." Othello's fate is wonderfully balanced in the moment of his discovery of Desdemona's innocence. For him this discovery means sheer exaltation; and yet this exaltation must come to him balanced by the horror of his own crime. Joy and sorrow are balanced with a terrible nicety, that wonderful balance which Edgar in *King Lear* notes in speaking of the death of his father:

> his flaw'd heart,—
> Alack, too weak the conflict to support!—
> 'Twixt two extremes of passion, joy and grief,
> Burst smilingly.

All these qualities suit the hero to the purposes and necessities of dramatic poetry. Some attempts have been made to dispense with the hero in serious drama. Maeterlinck says in a famous essay on tragedy:

I have grown to believe that an old man, seated in his armchair, waiting patiently, with his lamp beside him . . . I have grown to believe that he, motionless as he is, does yet live in reality a deeper, more human, and more universal life than the lover who strangles his mistress, the captain who conquers in battle, or "the husband who avenges his honor."

That the old man is as tragic as the hero, no one should question: he too has his moments; he too pays for what he gets. If it were not so, if he were not tragic in this sense, then the hero of tragic drama could have no universal significance. The trouble with the old man in the armchair is that he is tragic but not dramatic. His life has meaning but lacks every other dramatic quality; intensity, suspense, surprise, reversal, heightened diction, power to excite basic feelings—all are missing. When we think of the tragic in terms of the two-sided nature of feeling which is the basis of the common destiny of men, one man is as good an illustration as another, but only the intense hero makes drama possible, and makes it possible for it to end within two hours.

After we have looked at enough heroes, we can readily understand Aristotle's reaction to their way of life. He sees the hero for what he is, if the ultimate standard of conduct is length and completeness of life: a man not "eminently good and just, yet whose misfortune is brought about not by vice or depravity, but by some error or frailty." No doubt this tragic flaw is simply the essential nature of the hero—his extremism. No hero ever chose the golden mean in a critical moment; no hero would ever sacrifice his purpose, or any part of the "iron way" to the dictates of the kind of reason and virtue which bring length of life.

V

Great drama itself is not an adverse criticism of the way of heroes. Only confirmed Aristotelians believe that it is. Through his hero the dramatist is enabled to present the essence of life; and from the character of the hero and his fate we may draw our own conclusions. One famous exception is Ibsen's *Brand,* which was deliberately intended to be an attack on the heroic way of life. Brand, the fanatic priest, demands of all those about him, of his family and of his parishioners, the same heroic devotion to God and negation of the world which he himself seeks to practice. These demands result ultimately in the ruin of his family, the revolt of his flock, and his own death. But Ibsen is able to make the case neither better nor worse for the hero than have all great tragedies. Particularly interesting about the play, however, is what Ibsen, as a great dramatist, thought about the nature of the hero. This is revealed in two phrases, one positive, the other negative. "All or nothing," says Brand again and again to his followers in demanding their devotion. And warning them ever and again of evil, he repeats: "The devil is compromise."

From *Brand* we might conclude that Ibsen ascribed the woes of mankind to the iron way of heroes. But in *Peer Gynt,* his poetic satire on the Norwegian character, he wrote an even more impressive criticism of the way of compromise. The play was written out of the depths of Ibsen's indignation with Norway for her failure to ally herself with Denmark in the Danish-Prussian war. Peer Gynt is the opposite of Brand. "Enough," is his motto, not "all or nothing." His method is to go around obstacles and to abandon projects, ideals, and objectives

305

when they seem to demand the ultimate risk. Since, in following this method, he wanders over the face of the earth, he seems to have led a richer life than Brand, who fights it out with the devil of compromise within the narrow confines of his parish. In the end, however, Peer is revealed as one who stands for nothing, a man without principles or character, a nonentity. Like the objects of Thoreau's pity, he has frittered away his life in detail. One could say to him, as to the little mouse who was granted his wish to have wings: "You're nothing but a nothing; you're not a thing at all."

All drama reminds us that it is a serious mistake to underestimate the power of the heroic or to assume that people see only the unpleasant consequences of the way of heroes and none of its compensations. The reverse is more often true. "Hero worship" is a familiar term, but there is no similar familiar term to denote reverence for the moderate man. Great drama excites not only pity and terror, but also awe and admiration, and other feelings that lie so deep that we cannot easily name them. Most of the power of the dramatic to excite deep feeling rests in the hero. In him we see ourselves on a larger scale, often ourselves as we should like to be, for who would not like to be firmer of purpose, more intent intellectually, capable of deeper feeling? While we hunger for more of life, we cannot resist the appeal of the hero's intensity. We necessarily have our moments when Aristotle's golden mean seems to be indeed a kind of "golden meanness," a doctrine for the half-hearted who shrink from the farther reaches of experience, a prescription for a long life and a dull one, a guiding principle for a world of old men dozing in armchairs.

VI

Powerful indeed is hero worship. If drama were possible only in the form of tragic poetry, one might agree with Plato in ruling poets out of the ideal state. Tragedy by itself is an incomplete picture of life; since it presents only heroes to us, it needs comedy as an antidote to the unbridled hero worship which at times it might otherwise cause. Comedy, which teaches us to know a fool when we see one, teaches us also that not any fool can be a hero. The ordinary man, taking his stand on a trivial issue in his efforts to ape the hero, succeeds in being merely sullen. Or if he is, like Nietzsche, a gentle and serious young scholar, an intuitive but humorless philologist, too long fed on a diet of tragic poetry and Wagnerian music, he goes forth as a prophet to trouble the world with dreams of life aesthetically justified by a race of tragic heroes and to bring himself to madness.

To go with Oedipus, we need the Dionysos of *The Frogs;* to go with Hamlet, we need Falstaff; to go with the Cid, we need Orgon. A main effect of *The Frogs* is to show what happens to Dionysos, a sturdy but moderate middle-class soul who sets out to play the part of Hercules, a hero. If the point sinks in, we think twice before aping the way of heroes. As for Falstaff—he is neither a hero nor a fool: he knows how his kind of person should behave on a battlefield; and so, without shame, he lies down to play dead until the heroes have done their work. Orgon *is* a fool, who would never escape the machinations of Tartuffe were it not for the intervention of the King's officer. His folly, which takes the form of worship of the extreme forms of piety, makes him an ideal dupe for a hypocrite.

We may thank the comic spirit for deflating the pseudoheroic in life, and enlist it always in our service against the triumph of the simplest kind of hero, who has intensity of purpose without a correspondingly great capacity for thought and feeling. Such heroes, who are always without humor themselves, flourish in the absence of laughter. Meredith long ago pointed out that the comic spirit is an enemy of the sentimental, of the puritanical, and of the bacchanalian: it is even more strongly the sworn foe of the pseudoheroic and of the kind of hero whose brutality is the result of a will unguided by thought and feeling.

VII

Between great science, which seeks to show us *nature as it is,* caring nothing for what *it should be,* and great poetry, which has always shown us *human nature as it is,* caring nothing for what the reader thinks *it should be,* there can be no quarrel. But science in its beginnings had to contend with the pretensions of poets in the realm of nature; and today men neglect the solid realities of poetry for the vaporings of rhapsodists, who rest their dreams of progress toward Utopia upon their faith in the ability of science to do the impossible. It pleases us to smile at the pretensions of the philosopher-poet, Heraclitus, who thought that a new sun is born each day in the heavens. We see the folly of trying to make poetry do the work of mathematics. But the rhapsodists of our world are not poets who seek to take over the province of science; rather they are the pseudo scientists who, either in ignorance of or in defiance of the storehouse of wisdom to be found in poetry, would persuade us that the changes which man has been able to effect in his environment foreshadow even more wonderful changes in human nature itself. We have much to learn from both science and poetry. Science has taught us that the same old sun rises daily; the ancient wisdom of poetry is that it shines, and will always shine, upon the same old race of men—upon moderate men, heroes, and fools alike.

On one point Nietzsche was truly inspired: he saw that there is no place in a culture for tragic poetry once men have convinced themselves that they can change the basic conditions of their lives. For tragic poetry steels us to face evil as an inevitable aspect of experience; and it has no place in our culture if we believe that science and technology can free us from evil. Tragic poetry teaches us that each man pursues his own specific good, and that all too often the desire of two or more men for the same object makes conflict a brute fact in human affairs. Of what use is tragic poetry if we are bemused by the Socratic dream of a universal good acceptable to all and sharable by all? Tragic poetry teaches us that fanatics who seek an absolute good for mankind bring down upon men, by an inevitable recoil, their deepest sufferings. Of what use is tragic poetry, if mad men, lusting for personal power, convince us that paradise on earth will be possible once we have submitted ourselves to their wills?

This is the ancient wisdom of poetry which history today confirms: human nature is unchanging, and heroes, fools, and moderate men are always with us. Each of us, indeed, may be fated to play all of these roles in turn, and sometimes more than one role at once. There is often a comic view of even the admirable hero: the Socrates of *The Clouds,* snub-nosed, bald, homely as a gargoyle, absent-minded and absurd in his reasoning, is based upon life, as is the Socrates of the *Dialogues.* The world has decided that Plato has given us the truer measure of the man, but we should not forget the other portrait. Such twin-portraits are often possible. When Rostand sought to follow Hugo's injunction to create heroes who would exhibit the contrast of the sublime and grotesque to be found in life itself, he wrote *Cyrano de Bergerac,* calling it an "heroic comedy" in order to point out that the heroic and the comic can in unusual instances go hand in hand. Cyrano, who says that he seeks "to be always admirable in all things," is a hero to outdo the ordinary hero, who is extreme in one thing only. "Everything to excess," a principle that is fantastic, yet heroic, guides Cyrano's every act. When he fights, he fights a hundred men; when he is generous, he gives away all his money; when he is witty, he composes a ballade while fighting a duel. Spectators are so carried away by a blend of laughter and admiration that at the end no one can say which symbol is truer to the man, the grotesque, huge nose which makes him comic in appearance or the heroic plume which he wears in his hat, carrying it in death still unsmirched.

VIII

Are all men likely ever to agree that either intensity or duration is the higher value in experience? Not until the past is a completely false guide to the future; not until tragic poetry is completely out of touch with human nature. Since we have no grounds on which to predict the coming of a new kind of man, except the say-so of those romantic utopians who mistake science for magic, we must continue to think in terms of men as they are. In a world in which the fanatical extremist is a hardy perennial, always to be reckoned with, we must fortify ourselves with wisdom for the moment when our turn may come to play, as best we can, the part of heroes.

Since most men prefer a long life even at the expense of stretches of dullness, the Aristotelian golden mean points to the sensible course for men and nations most of the time. But if only one issue in a lifetime compels the moderate man to take an heroic stand, that is the one moment that fixes his place in history as either a man or a nonentity.

The trick is to know the right time and the right issue. No rule is possible. The simple hero is driven on by inflexible character. The fool mistakes the time and is merely sullen over trifles.

The moment when moderate men take a stand is always grave, but

309

it is not a time for despair. All is not lost. What is lost is the delusion that men can live by compromise alone. This delusion is an empty and negative form of extremism. It is nihilism—the heroic negation of the heroic in life. If we were to follow it consistently, we should become zeroes and tempt others to take our places. The world of human nature abhors a vacuum. When some men shrink altogether from the heroic, others are tempted to use it in its worst form.

Finally, in order to act wisely we must free ourselves from the half-truths designed to prove that the justice of our individual fate depends upon our choice between moderation and heroic action. All universal meaning in tragic poetry depends upon our recognition that in respect to justice the fate of the tragic hero is the same as that of the moderate man. Nietzsche was wrong in assuming that life can be justified only by living intensely. On the other hand, it is the tender sentimentalist, never the hero himself, who shrinks from the grand reversals which turn life into drama and history; and Aristotle was right in recognizing the compensations of heroic deeds, even if that recognition does invalidate his general criticism of the tragic hero. The Ahabs and Lincolns, the Cordelias and Antigones, accept their fate because they know its inner reality, the exaltation which accompanies suffering or dying for principles. The death of the hero is an affirmation of the unalterable conditions of life, a memorable symbol for multitudes who show their own acceptance by living.

There is justice in life for both the hero and the moderate man. The very surface of events points to it. What the hero gains in intensity, he usually loses in duration. What the moderate man gains in duration, he usually loses in intensity. But there is a deeper reality which unites heroes and moderate men in a common destiny. Both are subject to the fixed conditions whereby sorrow is the price of joy. Through the two-sided nature of human feeling, with its poles of good and evil, each pays for what he gets. The hero takes all, gives all, in one grand moment. The moderate man pays a little, lives to doze in his chair, and pays a little more. The choice between intensity and duration cannot upset the just equation whereby men pay with their lives for experience.

"Clear and Present Danger" in Free Speech Cases: A Study in Judicial Semantics

ROBERT E. CUSHMAN

IN 1919 Mr. Justice Holmes wrote the opinion of the Supreme Court in a case in which one Schenck was held properly convicted of violating the Espionage Act of 1917 by distributing pamphlets urging people to resist the draft.[1] Schenck claimed that he had merely exercised his constitutional right of free speech and free press. In rejecting this contention Mr. Justice Holmes observed: "The question in every case is whether the words used are used in such circumstances and are of such a nature as to create a clear and present danger that they will bring about the substantive evils that Congress has a right to prevent. It is a question of proximity and degree."

This was the origin of the famous *clear and present danger* test which has been either applied or discussed in some twenty-five Supreme Court cases in which issues of freedom of speech, press, or religion were involved. Two of these cases were decided in the 1946 term of the Court.

In three cases in which the Court applied the test of clear and present danger Mr. Justice Frankfurter has dissented on the ground that the test was either improperly applied or was irrelevant to the issue on which the case turned. In *Bridges* v. *California*,[2] in 1941, the Court set aside the conviction of Harry Bridges on a charge of contempt of court. Bridges had published a threat of a west-coast shipping strike unless a

---

[1] Schenck v. United States, 249 U.S. 47, 1919.
[2] 314 U.S. 252.

California appellate court in a case then pending reversed a lower court decision unfavorable to Bridges' union. Mr. Justice Frankfurter agreed that the test was applicable but felt that clear and present danger to the administration of justice, sensibly interpreted, had been shown. In *West Virginia State Board of Education* v. *Barnette*,[3] in 1943, which overruled the well-known Gobitis case,[4] and held a compulsory school flag-salute law unconstitutional, Mr. Justice Frankfurter, who had written the Court's opinion in the Gobitis case, insisted that the clear and present danger test could not properly be used to determine the validity of a legislative enactment. In substance he accused the Court of what argumentative theologians used to call "grasshopper exigesis."

But to measure the state's power to make such regulations as are here resisted by the imminence of national danger is wholly to misconceive the origin and purpose of the concept of "clear and present danger." To apply such a test is for the Court to assume, however unwittingly, a legislative responsibility that does not belong to it. To talk about "clear and present danger" as the touchstone of allowable educational policy by the states whenever school curricula may impinge upon the boundaries of individual conscience, is to take a felicitous phrase out of the context of the particular situation where it arose and for which it was adapted. Mr. Justice Holmes used the phrase "clear and present danger" in a case involving mere speech as a means by which alone to accomplish sedition in time of war. By that phrase he meant merely to indicate that, in view of the protection given to utterance by the First Amendment, in order that mere utterance may not be proscribed, "the words used are used in such circumstances and are of such a nature as to create a clear and present danger that they will bring about the substantive evils that Congress has a right to prevent." . . . The "substantive evils" about which he was speaking were inducement of insubordination in the military and naval forces of the United States and obstruction of enlistment while the country was at war. He was not enunciating a formal rule that there can be no restriction upon speech and, still less, no compulsion where conscience balks, unless imminent danger would thereby be wrought "to our institutions or our government."

In 1946 Mr. Justice Frankfurter scolded the Court more vigorously and at greater length for applying the clear and present danger test in the case of *Pennekamp* v. *Florida*.[5] This was another contempt of court case similar in its central issue to the Bridges case. Newspaper editorials had impugned the integrity of judges currently sitting. He declared:

[3] 319 U.S. 624.
[4] Minersville School District v. Gobitis, 310 U.S. 586, 1938.
[5] 328 U.S. 331.

312

It does an ill-service to the author of the most quoted judicial phrases regarding freedom of speech, to make him the victim of a tendency which he fought all his life, whereby phrases are made to do service for critical analysis by being turned into dogma. "It is one of the misfortunes of the law that ideas become encysted in phrases and thereafter for a long time cease to provoke further analysis." Holmes, J., dissenting, in Hyde v. United States, 225 U.S. 347, at 391. . . . Words which "are used in such circumstances and are of such a nature as to create a clear and present danger that they will bring about the substantive evils that Congress has a right to prevent," . . . speak their own condemnation. But it does violence to the juristic philosophy and the judicial practice of Mr. Justice Holmes to assume that in using the phrase "a clear and present danger" he was expressing even remotely an absolutist test or had in mind a danger in the abstract. He followed the observation just quoted by the emphatic statement that the question is one "of proximity and degree," as he conceived to be most questions in connection with the large, undefined rights guaranteed by the Constitution. . . .

"Clear and present danger" was never used by Mr. Justice Holmes to express a technical legal doctrine or to convey a formula for adjudicating cases. It was a literary phrase not to be distorted by being taken from its context. In its setting it served to indicate the importance of freedom of speech to a free society but also to emphasize that its exercise must be compatible with the preservation of other freedoms essential to a democracy and guaranteed by our Constitution. When those other attributes of a democracy are threatened by speech the Constitution does not deny power to the States to curb it. "The clear and present danger" to be arrested may be danger short of a threat as comprehensive and vague as a threat to the safety of the Republic or "the American way of life." Neither Mr. Justice Holmes nor Mr. Justice Brandeis nor this Court ever suggested in all the cases that arose in connection with the First World War, that only imminent threats to the immediate security of the country would authorize courts to sustain legislation curtailing utterance. Such forces of destruction are of an order of magnitude which courts are hardly designed to counter. "The clear and present danger" with which its two great judicial exponents were concerned, was a clear and present danger that utterance "would bring about the evil which Congress sought and had a right to prevent." . . . Among "the substantive evils" with which legislation may deal is the hampering of a court in a pending controversy, because the fair administration of justice is one of the chief tests of a true democracy. And since men equally devoted to the vital importance of freedom of speech may fairly differ in an estimate of this danger in a particular case, the field in which a State "may exercise its judgment is, necessarily, a wide one." Therefore, every time a situation like the present one comes here the precise problem before us is to determine whether the State court went beyond the allowable limits of judgment in holding that conduct which has been punished as a contempt was reasonably calculated to endanger a State's duty to administer impartial justice in a pending controversy.

Mr. Justice Frankfurter has thus challenged a re-examination of the clear and present danger test in cases involving freedom of thought and expression. He may be correct in his charge that the Supreme Court has been reading its own meaning into Mr. Justice Holmes' famous phrase, and has applied the test of clear and present danger in cases to which Mr. Justice Holmes would not have applied it. One need not, however, accept Mr. Justice Frankfurter's assumption that the Supreme Court is irrevocably bound to the Holmes interpretation of the clear and present danger test, and is *ipso facto* announcing unsound doctrine by deviating from it or applying it to new situations.

An analysis of the expansion of the clear and present danger concept as a judicial standard by which to measure the validity of restrictions which may be placed on freedom of speech, press, and religion may usefully turn around three main questions. First, what did Mr. Justice Holmes, with whom we must associate Mr. Justice Brandeis, mean by his test of clear and present danger? Second, what did the rest of the Court on which Holmes and Brandeis sat think of the clear and present danger test? For quite obviously they did not accept Holmes' view of it, and yet they did not entirely discard it. Third, what is the present Court's interpretation and use of clear and present danger?

Let us examine first the Holmes concept of clear and present danger. It may well be that Mr. Justice Frankfurter, who was closely associated with Holmes for many years, may know more about Holmes' own view of the clear and present danger test than the rest of us are able to glean from his few laconic comments in his opinions. However, Holmes' official connection with clear and present danger may be summarized as follows: In three wartime free speech cases (all arising under the Espionage Act) Holmes spoke for the Court. These were the cases of Schenck,[6] Frohwerk,[7] and Debs.[8] Holmes, as we have seen, announced the clear and present danger test in Schenck's case. He applied the test in the other two cases without calling it by name. In all three cases the test of clear and present danger was held to be met, and the convictions of the defendants were sustained. In two cases, those of Abrams [9] in 1919 and Gitlow [10] in 1925, Holmes wrote dissenting opinions urging that the publications of Abrams and Gitlow created no clear and present

[6] *Supra,* note 1.
[7] Frohwerk v. United States, 249 U.S. 204, 1919.
[8] Debs v. United States, 249 U.S. 211, 1919.
[9] Abrams v. United States, 250 U.S. 616, 1919.
[10] Gitlow v. New York, 268 U.S. 652, 1925.

314

danger and that their convictions should have been set aside. Holmes concurred with Brandeis in dissenting on the same ground (clear and present danger) in three cases (Schaefer [11] and Pierce,[12] which were wartime Espionage Act cases, and the Anita Whitney case [13] in 1927). Brandeis wrote no opinion for the court in which the clear and present danger test was applied. He concurred with Holmes in the five cases in which Holmes either used or commented upon the test. In *Gilbert* v. *Minnesota* [14] in 1920, involving a conviction under state law for discouraging enlistment in the armed forces, Brandeis dissented on the ground, among others, that the clear and present danger test had not been met, but Holmes went along with the majority.

While there is not as much to go on here as one might wish, two points stand out fairly sharply from the combined utterances of Holmes and Brandeis in these cases. It is clear, in the first place, that Holmes and Brandeis did not regard or use the test of clear and present danger as a guide or standard by which to measure the validity of statutes per se. In every case in which they applied the test or objected because it was not applied, they regarded the statute under which the defendants had been convicted as a valid exercise of legislative power. No one questioned, nor did the Court even discuss, the constitutionality of the Espionage Act of 1917 in the enforcement of which the six wartime free speech cases already mentioned arose. Holmes and Brandeis did not contend that the New York Criminal Anarchy Act under which Benjamin Gitlow was convicted was not a valid exercise of the states' police power, or the California Anti-Syndicalism Act under which Anita Whitney was convicted. This does not mean that the two justices would not have held void a statute which arbitrarily abridged freedom of speech and press. It merely means that in doing so they would not, so far as we can discover, have applied the test of clear and present danger.

In the second place, the test of clear and present danger emerges in the thinking of Holmes and Brandeis as an *administrative standard* to guide law enforcement officers and judges in applying laws to concrete cases. To repeat Holmes' original statement in the Schenck case, "The question in every case is whether the words used are used in such cir-

[11] Schaefer v. United States, 251 U.S. 466, 1920.
[12] Pierce v. United States, 252 U.S. 239, 1920.
[13] Whitney v. California, 274 U.S. 357, 1927.
[14] 254 U.S. 325.

cumstances and are of such a nature as to create a clear and present danger." In every instance their attention was riveted, not so much upon the words of the statute being enforced, but upon the concrete nature and consequences of the speech or publication which was alleged to violate the statute. What the two justices did was to announce a *rule of reason* to govern the enforcement and interpretation of laws under which issues of free speech and press might arise. While analogies are always suspect, it may be recalled that in the Standard Oil Company case [15] in 1911, the Supreme Court had read the "rule of reason" into the judicial interpretation of the Sherman Act. The Court there held that the words of the Sherman Act, "Every contract in restraint of trade is hereby declared illegal," were, in their actual enforcement, to be applied only to such contracts in restraint of trade as were in fact "unreasonable." Holmes joined in that decision. Very similar was the doctrine announced by Holmes and Brandeis in their dissent in the Gitlow case. Their position was that the broad language of the New York Criminal Anarchy Act forbidding all speeches and publications advocating the overthrow of government by force and violence could be validly applied only to those speeches and publications which in fact created a clear and present danger to the security of the state. And this was also the position taken in the Whitney case.

To sum up: Holmes and Brandeis regarded the clear and present danger test not as a measure of the validity of statutes affecting speech and press, but as a guide to keep prosecutors and judges from applying these statutes to cases in which no clear and present danger to the state could be shown.

The rest of the Supreme Court did not accept the Holmes-Brandeis theory of clear and present danger. We may turn then to the question, What was the "official" Supreme Court view of this matter during the period in which Holmes and Brandeis were on the Bench? The question may be answered by a series of statements.

1. The Court went along with Holmes in the three wartime free speech cases in which he wrote the opinions (Schenck, Frohwerk, and Debs). This is not significant. The three defendants were all held to be validly convicted, and the rest of the Court, agreeing with this result, were content to let Holmes' remarks about clear and present danger

---

[15] Standard Oil Co. v. United States, 221 U.S. 1, 1911.

316

stand as a bit of rationalization. It is unlikely that in these first cases they fully grasped the significance of Holmes' doctrine.

2. The rest of the Court, however, was not willing to use the test of clear and present danger as Holmes had stated it and would have applied it. In the other three wartime free speech cases (Abrams, Pierce, and Schaefer) the convictions were sustained, over the protest of Holmes and Brandeis that the test of clear and present danger had not been met. The majority said nothing whatever about clear and present danger. They did not repudiate the test; they simply ignored it.

3. By the time *Gitlow* v. *New York* reached the Court in 1925, the clear and present danger test could no longer be ignored. It had captured the imagination of lawyers and laymen alike, and furthermore we were then embarked upon a wave of witch hunting which was bringing to the Court issues of free speech and press far more difficult and complicated than those which stemmed from the war. Would the Court adopt the clear and present danger doctrine, or would it reject it? The Court did neither. It resorted to the familiar judicial device of "distinguishing" the rule practically out of existence. Without overruling or even criticizing Holmes' statement of the doctrine in the Schenck case, the Court hit upon a device by which the clear and present danger test was relegated to so narrow an area that it fell far short of serving as the Holmes-Brandeis "rule of reason" for free speech cases.

What the Court did was this. It declared that where a criminal statute forbids acts or conduct, and a person is prosecuted on the theory that his speeches or publications amount to such criminal acts, then the government must show that what he said or printed constituted a clear and present danger of bringing about the forbidden consequences. Words are punished in these cases because they amount to deeds, which are forbidden. Schenck was not indicted for publishing a forbidden pamphlet, because no statute forbade the publication of a pamphlet. He was indicted for obstructing the draft, and his conviction was sustained because the pamphlet which he published created a clear and present danger that the draft would be obstructed. His words were not forbidden words, but forbidden incipient acts. They were act words. This, said the Court, is all that the clear and present danger test means or ever meant.

Having thus pushed Schenck, Mr. Justice Holmes, and the clear and

317

present danger test into this narrow corner, the Court in the Gitlow case went on to say that a wholly different situation was presented by a statute which by its terms forbade language believed by the legislature to be dangerous either presently or by reason of its general tendency to bring about conditions which the state might properly forbid. Such a statute was the New York Criminal Anarchy Act. It explicitly forbade speeches or publications which advocated the overthrow of government by force and violence. This was a proper exercise of the states' police power and every presumption of constitutionality attached to it. The crime created was not the crime of overthrowing government by force and violence, but the crime of using words, spoken or printed, which advocate such overthrowing of government. In enforcing this act, said the Court, it was not necessary to show that Gitlow's flamboyant pamphlet created a clear and present danger of the overthrow of government —nobody claimed that it did—it was merely necessary to show that Gitlow's pamphlet advocated such overthrow. In short, Gitlow was convicted because he published, not dangerous words, but forbidden words.

Thus the Court emerged, as it has so frequently done, not with one rule or standard, but with two. It preserved a badly mutilated clear and present danger test applicable to a very limited category of free speech cases. It placed beside it a doctrine which upheld broad restrictions on speeches and publications the general tendency of which seemed to the legislature objectionable, and further upheld the enforcement of these prohibitions against any and all technical violations of the law regardless of clear and present danger. Speeches and publications which were clearly not dangerous could be punished if they fell in a group banned by the legislature because of its general "bad tendency."

Without commenting on each case which has recently come before the Court, let us review the present status of the clear and present danger doctrine. The present Court is using the clear and present danger test in three clearly distinguishable types of cases involving freedom of speech, press, and religion.

First, in five important cases decided since 1940, the Court has applied the clear and present danger test, as it did in the Schenck case, to determine whether particular speeches or publications actually constituted forbidden acts or conduct. In *Contwell* v. *Connecticut*,[16] one of the early Jehovah's Witnesses cases, a part of the charge against Cantwell was that, by accosting people and persuading them to listen to his phonograph records attacking organized religion, Cantwell was inciting breaches of the peace. Mr. Justice Roberts held that Cantwell's religious activities created no clear and present danger of such breaches of the peace. Other and broader points were also dealt with in the Cantwell case. The Bridges,[17] Pennekamp,[18] and Craig cases,[19] in 1941, 1946, and 1947, respectively, all dealt with alleged contempts of court arising from publications attacking or threatening judges or courts. Here, again, the Court found the crucial issues to be whether the publications of Bridges, Pennekamp, and Craig were of such a nature as to create such a clear and present danger of obstruction or perversion of the administration of justice as to spell out contempt of court. In all three cases the Court found that clear and present danger had not been shown, and the convictions were reversed. The case of *Hartzel* v. *United States* [20] in 1944 was practically identical with the Schenck case, except that Hartzel's conviction was set aside. Mr. Justice Murphy addressed himself to the question whether Hartzel's pamphlet created any clear and present danger of insubordination, disloyalty, or mutiny in the armed forces, or obstruction of recruiting. In each of these five cases an effort had been made to punish what I earlier labeled "act words," and in each case the Court found a lack of clear and present danger that the words would develop into or produce the forbidden acts.

Second, in *Taylor* v. *Mississippi* [21] in 1943, the Court applied the clear and present danger test as a "rule of reason," applicable to the enforcement against Taylor of a broadly drawn state sedition act. The act forbade the oral or printed advocacy of doctrines calculated to encourage disloyalty to the state and national governments. Taylor, a Jehovah's Witness, publicly urged people to refuse to salute the flag. Mr. Justice Roberts, speaking for the Court, did not hold the Mississippi

---

[16] 310 U.S. 296, 1940.
[17] Bridges v. California, 314 U.S. 252.
[18] Pennekamp v. Florida, 328 U.S. 331.
[19] Craig v. Harney, decided May 19, 1947.
[20] 322 U.S. 680.
[21] 319 U.S. 583

statute void, but did hold that Taylor's speeches created no clear and present danger to our institutions or our government, and Taylor's conviction was set aside. A similar use of the test appears in *Thomas* v. *Collins* [22] in 1944, in which the conviction of Thomas, the President of the United Automobile Workers, was set aside on the ground that the charge against him of violating a Texas statute requiring the registration of labor union organizers was not, in the circumstances of the case, justified by clear and present danger. Again the Court did not hold the act itself invalid.

One is tempted to include in this group the case of *De Jong* v. *Oregon*,[23] decided in 1937. De Jong, a Communist, helped organize and then addressed a meeting of Communists, but no unlawful conduct or speeches occurred at the meeting. He was nevertheless convicted under the Oregon Criminal Syndicalism Act. In an opinion by Chief Justice Hughes the Supreme Court set aside the conviction, but did not invalidate the statute. The test of clear and present danger, however, was not mentioned in the opinion, which was grounded rather on a straight due process point. In fact, it is interesting to note that neither Chief Justice Hughes nor Chief Justice Stone, both of them stalwart defenders of freedom of speech and press, ever made use of the clear and present danger test. They did not reject or criticize it, they simply seemed to prefer the more general test of due process of law.

Third, beginning in 1940, the Court in several cases has used clear and present danger as a test of the validity of statutes themselves, rather than a test of the validity of their application to concrete situations. In each of these cases the Court held the questioned statute bad. The Thornhill [24] and Carlson [25] cases in 1940 held unconstitutional an Alabama statute and a California county ordinance which in broad terms forbade all picketing. In the Thornhill case the Court said that the statute was "invalid on its face." Mr. Justice Murphy said:

Abridgment of the liberty of such discussion [of the nature and causes of a labor dispute] can be justified only where the clear danger of substantive evils arises under circumstances affording no opportunity to test the merits of ideas by competition for acceptance in the market of public opinion. We

[22] 323 U.S. 516.
[23] 299 U.S. 353.
[24] Thornhill v. Alabama, 310 U.S. 88.
[25] Carlson v. California, 310 U.S. 106.

hold that the danger of injury to an industrial concern is neither so serious nor so imminent as to justify the sweeping proscription of freedom of discussion embodied in section 3448.

In the Barnette case,[26] in 1943, the Court overruled its earlier decision in the Gobitis case, and held invalid an order of the West Virginia State Board of Education compelling school children to salute the flag under penalty of expulsion. In the majority opinion, Mr. Justice Jackson stated:

> It is now a commonplace that censorship or suppression of expression of opinion is tolerated by our Constitution only when the expression presents a clear and present danger of action of a kind the state is empowered to prevent and punish. It would seem that involuntary affirmation could be commanded only on even more immediate and urgent grounds than silence. But here the power of compulsion is invoked without any allegation that remaining passive during a flag salute ritual creates a clear and present danger that would justify an effort even to muffle expression.[27]

How has the Court rationalized this new use of the clear and present danger test as a limitation on *lawmaking* rather than on law *enforcement* or *application?* The answer is to be found in the recent emergence of a new and vitally important judicial doctrine in the constitutional law of civil liberty. The steps by which this has come about may be traced as follows: First, by the nineteen-twenties the American judicial mind, and especially that of the Supreme Court, had been fully won over to the doctrine that legislative exercises of the police power must be presumed by the courts to be valid, and should be upheld as long as the question of their validity is reasonably debatable. Mr. Justice Holmes had devoted a lifetime of effort to the accomplishment of this bit of judicial education, and it was no small achievement. In the numerous cases in which the police power had been used to promote social and economic progress the doctrine had the wholesome effect of restraining judges from substituting their own social and economic opinions for those of the legislature. The doctrine came to be associated with Holmes' name, and was widely heralded as an important asset of liberalism.

---

[26] *Supra,* note 3.

[27] See also the dissenting opinions of Justices Black and Douglas in *United Public Workers* v. *Mitchell,* decided February 10, 1947. The Court here held valid the provisions of the Hatch Act restricting political activity upon the part of federal employees against the charge that it violated their rights under the First Amendment. The dissenting justices declared there was no clear and present danger to justify the restrictions.

Second, the mounting volume of legislation aimed at the suppression of various kinds of minority opinion and its expression soon placed the liberal-minded judge in a most uncomfortable dilemma. These repressive measures were clearly exercises of the states' police power and were designed to protect the public security against some real or fancied danger. The disciple of Holmes' broad judicial tolerance found himself in the unhappy position of muttering pious incantations about the presumed validity of any exercise of the police power which could be thought fairly debatable, when in fact the statutes involved placed pretty severe restrictions on freedom of speech, press, or religion. I cannot believe that this is not the explanation of Mr. Justice Frankfurter's widely criticized stand in the flag-salute cases. A life-long admirer of Mr. Justice Holmes, what Frankfurter says in substance is that if the school authorities in Pennsylvania or West Virginia decided in their legislative wisdom that school children should be expelled from school if they refuse to salute the flag, the Supreme Court of the United States must presume that they knew what they were about and should defer to their judgment.

Third, the Supreme Court has recently extricated itself from this dilemma by a bold stroke. It has announced that the four great guarantees of civil liberty in the First Amendment, freedom of speech, press, religion, and assembly, are more important to our democracy than are other parts of the Constitution. They occupy a *preferred* place in our scheme of constitutional values. Therefore, a statute passed in the exercise of the police power, or any other power, which *on its face* appears to restrict any one of these four great civil liberties will *not* be presumed to be constitutional. On the contrary, it will be presumed to be *unconstitutional,* and the burden of proof will rest squarely upon the shoulders of those who defend it. Constitutional lawyers will readily realize that our present Court did not originate the idea that some provisions of the Constitution of the United States are more important and fundamental than others, not only intrinsically but legally. Nearly fifty years ago in the Insular Cases [28] the Court faced the difficult question whether our Bill of Rights in its entirety "follows the flag" into the island possessions we had just acquired. The Court found a practical solution of

---

[28] Hawaii v. Mankichi, 190 U.S. 197, 1903; Dorr v. United States, 195 U.S. 138, 1904.

the problem by holding that some of the rights protected by the federal Bill of Rights were "fundamental" in nature and must be respected by Congress wherever federal power is exercised; certain other rights, however, such as the right to jury trial are "formal" or "procedural" and apply of their own force only in territories of the United States which the Court classified as "incorporated." Later in the revolutionary line of decisions beginning with *Gitlow* v. *New York* [29] in 1925, the Court again held that certain provisions of the Bill of Rights are "of the very essence of a scheme of ordered liberty" and must therefore be regarded as a part of the "liberty" protected against state abridgment by the due process clause of the Fourteenth Amendment. Other provisions, however, such as those guaranteeing jury trial, grand jury indictment, etc., are not of this vital and fundamental nature and are, therefore not binding upon the states through assimilation into the broad guarantee of due process.[30] Thus the present Court has ample precedent for singling out the civil liberties protected by the First Amendment and giving them a preferred status, from which arises a presumption of unconstitutionality against any legislative restriction of them.

Fourth, in order to assume successfully the burden of proof imposed by this presumption of invalidity the Court insists that it must be clearly shown that some clear and present danger to the security or welfare of the state or nation demands the restrictions which the legislature has placed upon any of the four freedoms protected by the First Amendment. This new use of the clear and present danger test is stated by Mr. Justice Rutledge in his opinion for the Court in *Thomas* v. *Collins* [31] in 1944. He said:

The case confronts us again with the duty our system places on this Court to say where the individual's freedom ends and the State's power begins. Choice on that border, now as always delicate, is perhaps more so where the usual presumption supporting legislation is balanced by the preferred place given in our scheme to the great, the indispensable democratic freedoms secured by the First Amendment. That priority gives these liberties a sanctity

---

[29] *Supra*, note 10.

[30] See the careful classification of the provisions of the Bill of Rights into these two categories in the opinion of Mr. Justice Cardozo in Palko v. Connecticut, 302 U.S. 319, 1937.

[31] *Supra*, note 21. While the Court, as above noted, did not hold the Texas statute void per se, the doctrine under discussion is clearly stated in the majority opinion.

and a sanction not permitting dubious intrusions. And it is the character of the right, not of the limitation, which determines what standard governs the choice.

For these reasons any attempt to restrict those liberties must be justified by clear public interest, threatened not doubtfully or remotely, but by clear and present danger. The rational connection between the remedy provided and the evil to be curbed, which in other contexts might support legislation against attack on due process grounds, will not suffice. These rights rest on a firmer foundation. Accordingly, whatever occasion would restrain orderly discussion and persuasion, at appropriate time and place, must have clear support in public danger, actual or impending. Only the gravest abuses, endangering paramount interests, give occasion for permissible limitation.

This, then, is the Court's new interpretation and use of the test of clear and present danger. It does not replace or in any way restrict the earlier uses to which the test had been put; it adds to them. In doing so it uses the test for a new purpose and in a new context. It makes clear and present danger, or the absence of it, the acid test of the validity of legislation restricting the four guarantees of the First Amendment. Whether Holmes and Brandeis would have gone along with the new doctrine or not we have no sure evidence. Mr. Justice Frankfurter thinks they would not have done so. It is hard to believe, however, that these two justices, who placed so high a value on our civil liberty and who took so seriously the judicial task of protecting it, could have brought themselves to object to a doctrine, no matter how it is labeled, which insists that the liberties most vital to our democracy shall be abridged by legislative action only under the pressure of the most compelling necessity.

George Holland Sabine: A Bibliography

(1904–1947)

COMPILED BY JOHN MANSLEY ROBINSON *

BOOKS

1906

The Beginnings of English Associationism. Doctoral dissertation, Cornell University, 1906. Typewritten, 172 pp.

1917

Philosophical Essays in Honor of James Edwin Creighton. Edited. New York: The Macmillan Company, 1917. xii, 356 pp.

1922

The Modern Idea of the State. Authorized translation of H. Krabbe, *Die moderne Staats-idee;* with an introduction. With Walter J. Shepard. New York and London: D. Appleton and Company, 1922. lxxxi, 281 pp.

1929

On the Commonwealth. Translation of Marcus Tullius Cicero, *De re publica;* with an introduction and notes. With Stanley Barney Smith. Columbus, Ohio: The Ohio State University Press, 1929. ix, 276 pp.

1937

A History of Political Theory. New York: Henry Holt and Company [c1937]. xvi, 797 pp.

1941

The Works of Gerrard Winstanley. With an appendix of documents relating to the Digger Movement. Edited, with an introduction. Ithaca, New York: Cornell University Press, 1941. 686 pp.

---

* We are grateful to Mr. Robinson, a graduate student in philosophy at Cornell, for compiling the Sabine bibliography.—EDITORS

ESSAYS AND ARTICLES

1904

"The Oxford Movement." Guilford Prize Essay, Cornell University. With the pseudonym E. J. Tucker. Typewritten, 22 pp.

1905

"A Study in Tonal Analysis. I." With I. Madison Bentley. *American Journal of Psychology*, October 1905, XVI, 484–498.

"Radical Empiricism as a Logical Method." Discussion. *Philosophical Review*, November 1905, XIV, 696–705.

1906

"Hume's Contribution to the Historical Method." *Philosophical Review*, January 1906, XV, 17–38.

1907

"The Concreteness of Thought." *Philosophical Review*, March 1907, XVI, 154–169.

"The Material of Thought." *Philosophical Review*, May 1907, XVI, 285–297.

1912

"Descriptive and Normative Sciences." *Philosophical Review*, July 1912, XXI, 433–450.

"Professor Bosanquet's *Logic* and the Concrete Universal." *Philosophical Review*, September 1912, XXI, 546–565.

1915

"The Social Origin of Absolute Idealism." *Journal of Philosophy*, April 1, 1915, XII, 169–177.

"A New Monadology." Discussion. *Journal of Philosophy*, November 25, 1915, XII, 650–657.

1916

"Liberty and the Social System." *Philosophical Review*, September 1916, XXV, 662–675.

1917

"Rationalism in Hume's Philosophy." In George Holland Sabine (ed.), *Philosophical Essays in Honor of James Edwin Creighton*. New York: The Macmillan Company, 1917. Pp. 42–60.

"Philosophical and Scientific Specialization." *Philosophical Review*, January 1917, XXVI, 16–27.

1920

"The Concept of the State as Power." *Philosophical Review*, July 1920, XXIX, 301–318.

1921

"What Is the Matter with Representative Government?" *North American Review*, May 1921, CCXIII, 587–597.

1923

"Pluralism: A Point of View." *American Political Science Review*, February 1923, XVII, 34–50.

"Bosanquet's Theory of the Real Will." *Philosophical Review*, November 1923, XXXII, 633–651.

1924

"Henry Adams and the Writing of History." *University of California Chronicle*, January 1924, XXVI, 31–46.

1925

"The Philosophy of James Edwin Creighton." *Philosophical Review*, May 1925, XXXIV, 230–261.

1927

"The Sixth International Congress of Philosophy." *Philosophical Review*, January 1927, XXXVI, 10–21.

1928

"Political Science and the Juristic Point of View." *American Political Science Review*, August 1928, XXII, 553–575.

"The Significance of the Brookings Graduate School." *Journal of the American Association of University Women*, October 1928, XXII, 9–13.

1930

"Academic Freedom at the University of Pittsburgh." With Carl Wittke. *School and Society*, January 11, 1930, XXXI, 65–66.

"The Pragmatic Approach to Politics." *American Political Science Review*, November 1930, XXIV, 865–885.

1931

"The Colloquium Heptaplomeres of Jean Bodin." In *Persecution and Liberty; Essays in Honor of George Lincoln Burr*. New York: The Century Company [c1931]. Pp. 271–309.

"Are State Universities Different?" *School and Society*, September 12, 1931, XXXIV, 349–357.

1932

"Hegel's Political Philosophy." *Philosophical Review*, May 1932, XLI, 261–282.

1933

"Rudolph Stammler's Critical Philosophy of Law." *Cornell Law Quarterly*, April 1933, XVIII, 321–350.

1939

"What Is a Political Theory?" *Journal of Politics*, February 1939, I, 1–16.
"Logic and Social Studies." *Philosophical Review*, March 1939, XLVIII, 155–176.

1940

"The Historical Position of Liberalism." *American Scholar* [December], 1940, X, 1, 49–58. Reprinted in Caroline F. Ware (ed.), *The Cultural Approach to History*. New York: Columbia University Press, 1940. Pp. 212–222.

1941

"Social Studies and Objectivity." Howison Lecture, 1941. *University of California Publications in Philosophy*, XVI, 6, 125–142. Berkeley and Los Angeles: University of California Press, 1941.

1945

"Carl Lotus Becker." Introduction to Carl L. Becker, *Freedom and Responsibility in the American Way of Life*. New York: A. A. Knopf, 1945. Pp. vii–xlii.
"Democracy and Preconceived Ideas." Shepard Lecture, 1945. Columbus, Ohio: The Walter J. Shepard Foundation, Ohio State University. 21 pp.

1947

"Freedom and Reform." Discussion. *Philosophical Review*, September 1947, LVI, 569–581.

BOOK REVIEWS

1910

Cassirer, Ernst. *Das Erkenntnisproblem in der Philosophie und Wissenschaft neueren Zeit*. *Philosophical Review*, November 1910, XIX, 647–664.

1912

James, William. *Some Problems of Philosophy*. *International Journal of Ethics*, January 1912, XXII, 217–221.

Seth, James. *English Philosophers and Schools of Philosophy.* *Philosophical Review*, November 1912, XXI, 687–692.

1913

Stewart, Herbert Leslie. *Questions of the Day in Philosophy and Psychology.* *Philosophical Review*, July 1913, XXII, 434–437.

Perry, Ralph Barton. *Present Philosophical Tendencies.* *International Journal of Ethics*, October 1913, XXIV, 89–94.

1914

Rickert, Heinrich. *Die Grenzen der naturwissenschaftlichen Begriffsbildung: Eine logische Einleitung in die historischen Wissenschaften.* *Philosophical Review*, January 1914, XXIII, 65–70.

Bradley, F. H. *Essays on Truth and Reality.* *Philosophical Review*, September 1914, XXIII, 550–557.

1915

Strich, Walter. *Prinzipien der psychologischen Erkenntnis: Prolegomena zu einer Kritik der historischen Vernunft.* *Philosophical Review*, May 1915, XXIV, 325–329.

1917

Sellars, Roy Wood. *Critical Realism: A Study of the Nature and Conditions of Knowledge.* *Philosophical Review*, January 1917, XXVI, 87–91.

Teggart, Frederick J. *Prolegomena to History: The Relation of History to Literature, Philosophy and Science.* A notice. *Philosophical Review*, March 1917, XXVI, 228–230.

1918

Laski, Harold J. *Studies in the Problem of Sovereignty.* *Philosophical Review*, January 1918, XXVII, 82–87.

1919

Teggart, Frederick J. *The Processes of History.* *Philosophical Review*, March 1919, XXVIII, 208–211.

1920

Laski, Harold J. *Authority in the Modern State.* *Philosophical Review*, May 1920, XXIX, 276–282.

Krabbe, H. *Die moderne Staats-idee.* *Philosophical Review*, July 1920, XXIX, 379–383.

1923

Sellars, Roy Wood. *Evolutionary Naturalism.* *Philosophical Review*, January 1923, XXXII, 93–95.

McDougall, William. *The Group Mind*. *Philosophical Review*, May 1923, XXXII, 317–322.

1925

Babbitt, Irving. *Democracy and Leadership*. *University of California Chronicle*, April 1925, XXVII, 219–224.

1926

Kropotkin, Prince. *Ethics: Origin and Development*. *International Journal of Ethics*, January 1926, XXXVI, 205–207.

Vogel, Paul. *Hegels Gesellschaftsbegriff und seine geschichtliche Fortbildung durch Lorenz Stein, Marx, Engels und Lassalle*. *Philosophical Review*, November 1926, XXXV, 582–583.

1927

Hocking, William Ernest. *The Present Status of the Philosophy of Law and of Rights* and *Man and the State*. *International Journal of Ethics*, April 1927, XXXVII, 307–311.

MacIver, R. M. *The Modern State*. *Philosophical Review*, May 1927, XXXVI, 258–262.

1928

Catlin, G. E. G. *The Science and Method of Politics*. *Philosophical Review*, May 1928, XXXVII, 266–269.

1931

Lief, Alfred (ed.). *The Social and Economic Views of Mr. Justice Brandeis*. *International Journal of Ethics*, April 1931, XLI, 377–380.

Martin, Everett Dean. *Liberty*. *Journal of Philosophy*, June 4, 1931, XXVIII, 329–331.

1932

Jordan, E. *Theory of Legislation; An Essay on the Dynamics of Public Mind*. *Philosophical Review*, September 1932, XLI, 537–539.

Friedrich, Carl Joachim (ed.). *Politica Methodice Digesta of Johannes Althusius* (*Althaus*). *American Political Science Review*, October 1932, XXVI, 940–942.

1933

Grieg, J. Y. T. *The Letters of David Hume*. *American Historical Review*, January 1933, XXXVIII, 323–325.

Hocking, William Ernest. *The Spirit of World Politics*. *International Journal of Ethics*, October 1933, XLIV, 140–141.

Hook, Sidney. *Towards the Understanding of Karl Marx*. *Journal of Philosophy*, November 9, 1933, XXX, 634–637.

Cohen, Felix S. *Ethical Systems and Legal Ideals*. *Cornell Law Quarterly*, December 1933, XIX, 164–165.

1934

Gibson, A. Boyce. *The Philosophy of Descartes.* *Philosophical Review,* May 1934, XLIII, 312–314.

Bonner, Robert J. *Aspects of Athenian Democracy.* *American Political Science Review,* October 1934, XXVIII, 931–932.

1935

Haller, William (ed.). *Tracts on Liberty in the Puritan Revolution, 1638–1647.* *Philosophical Review,* July 1935, XLIV, 391–392.

1937

Swabey, Marie Collins. *Theory of the Democratic State.* *American Political Science Review,* December 1937, XXXI, 1143–1144.

1938

Strauss, Leo. *The Political Philosophy of Hobbes, Its Basis and Genesis.* *Philosophical Review,* January 1938, XLVII, 91–92.

Hook, Sidney. *From Hegel to Marx.* *Philosophical Review,* March 1938, XLVII, 218–221.

Baur, Ludovicus (ed.). *Nicolai de Cusa: Opera omnia. V. Idiota.de sapientia, de mente, de staticis experimentis.* *Philosophical Review,* July 1938, XLVII, 441–442.

Klibansky, R., and Paton, H. J. (eds.). *Philosophy and History. Essays Presented to Ernst Cassirer.* *Philosophical Review,* November 1938, XLVII, 644–647.

1939

Bridgman, P. W. *The Intelligent Individual and Society.* *Philosophical Review,* March 1939, XLVIII, 221–223.

Plamenatz, J. P. *Consent, Freedom, and Political Obligation.* *Philosophical Review,* September 1939, XLVIII, 538–540.

1940

McIlwain, Charles Howard. *Constitutionalism and the Changing World.* *Yale Law Journal,* December 1940, L, 354–357.

Fraenkel, Ernst. *The Dual State: A Contribution to the Theory of Dictatorship.* *American Political Science Review,* June 1941, XXXV, 547–548.

1941

Osborn, Annie Marion. *Rousseau and Burke. A Study of the Idea of Liberty in Eighteenth-Century Political Thought.* *Philosophical Review,* September 1941, L, 538–540.

1942

Gilmore, Myron Piper. *Argument from Roman Law in Political Thought, 1200–1600.* *American Historical Review,* January 1942, XLVII, 297–298.

Willey, Basil. *The Eighteenth Century Background. Studies on the Idea of Nature in the Thought of the Period*. Philosophical Review, May 1942, LI, 335–336.

Neumann, Franz. *Behemoth: The Structure and Practice of National Socialism*. Philosophical Review, July 1942, LI, 432–434.

Agard, Walter R. *What Democracy Meant to the Greeks*. American Political Science Review, August 1942, XXXVI, 752–754.

Marcuse, Herbert. *Reason and Revolution: Hegel and the Rise of Social Theory*. American Journal of Sociology, September 1942, XLVIII, 258–259.

Friedrich, Carl J. *The New Belief in the Common Man*. Harvard Law Review, October 1942, LVI, 318–321.

1943

Jordan, W. K. *Men of Substance. A Study of the Thought of Two English Revolutionaries, Henry Parker and Henry Robinson*. Journal of Economic History, May 1943, III, 90–93.

Ewing, A. C. *Reason and Intuition*. Philosophical Review, July 1943, LII, 421–423.

Adams, George P. (ed.). *Civilization*. Philosophical Review, September 1943, LII, 509–512.

Mossner, Ernest Campbell. *The Forgotten Hume: Le bon David*. Philosophical Review, November 1943, LII, 610–611.

1944

Cole, G. D. H. *Fabian Socialism*. American Political Science Review, April 1944, XXXVIII, 376–378.

Wright, Louis B. *Religion and Empire: The Alliance between Piety and Commerce in English Expansion, 1558–1625*. Philosophical Review, May 1944, LIII, 302–303.

Hallowell, John H. *The Decline of Liberalism as an Ideology, with Particular Reference to German Politico-legal Thought*. Philosophical Review, September 1944, LIII, 506–507.

1945

Haller, William, and Davies, Godfrey, *The Leveller Tracts, 1647–1653*, and Wolfe, Don M., *Leveller Manifestoes of the Puritan Revolution*. Cornell Law Quarterly, March 1945, XXX, 415–417.

Perry, Charner M. (ed.). *The Philosophy of American Democracy*. Philosophical Review, January 1945, LIV, 90–91.

Croce, Benedetto. *Politics and Morals*. American Political Science Review, August 1945, XXXIX, 816–817.

Harris, Frederick Philip. *The Neo-Idealist Political Theory: Its Continuity with the British Tradition*. Philosophical Review, September 1945, LIV, 520–521.

GEORGE H. SABINE: A BIBLIOGRAPHY

1946

Orton, William Aylott. *The Liberal Tradition: A Study of the Social and Spiritual Conditions of Freedom.* American Political Science Review, April 1946, XL, 352–353.

Russell, Bertrand. *A History of Western Philosophy and Its Connection with Political and Social Circumstances from the Earliest Times to the Present Day.* American Historical Review, April 1946, LI, 485–486.

Ortega y Gasset, José. *Mission of the University.* Philosophical Review, November 1946, LV, 698–699.

1947

Gerth, H. H., and Mills, C. Wright (eds. and trs.). *From Max Weber; Essays in Sociology.* Philosophical Review, January 1947, LVI, 100–104.

Cassirer, Ernst. *The Myth of the State.* Philosophical Review, May 1947, LVI, 315–318.

Weldon, T. D. *States and Morals; A Study in Political Conflicts.* American Political Science Review, June 1947, XLI, 556–557.

Sayre, Paul (ed.). *Interpretations of Modern Legal Philosophies. Essays in Honor of Roscoe Pound.* Philosophical Review, July 1947, LVI, 439–444.

Bryson, Lyman. *Science and Freedom.* Political Science Quarterly, September 1947, LXII, 431–432.